THE GUARDIAN
YEAR, 2002

THE GUARDIAN YEAR, 2002

Edited by David McKie

Introduction by Jon Snow

Atlantic Books
London

First published in 2002 by Atlantic Books, on behalf of Guardian Newspapers Ltd
Atlantic Books is an imprint of Grove Atlantic Ltd

10 9 8 7 6 5 4 3 2 1

A CIP record for this book is available from the British Library

ISBN 1 84354 015 0

Printed in Great Britain by CPD, Ebbw Vale, Wales
Design by Helen Ewing

Grove Atlantic Ltd
Ormond House
26–27 Boswell Street
London WC1N 3JZ

The chapter headings are taken from:

In the Year of Jubilee by George Gissing
War and Peace by Leo Tolstoy
The Power and the Glory by Graham Greene
He Knew He Was Right by Anthony Trollope
The Custom of the Country by Edith Wharton
Put Out More Flags by Evelyn Waugh
The Magic Toyshop by Angela Carter
Money by Martin Amis
The Naked and the Dead by Norman Mailer
The Way We Live Now by Anthony Trollope
North and South by Elizabeth Gaskell
Coming Up for Air by George Orwell
This Sporting Life by David Storey
Last Orders by Graham Swift

CONTENTS

This sporting life   219

Last orders   237

Postscript   249

INTRODUCTION

Jon Snow

Even though I was wearing thick-soled lumberjack boots, the bottoms of my feet were hot. Far beneath them, the heart of the compressed debris was still on fire. The water jets of the fire-tenders projected cribs of spray across the arc lights and everywhere there was a tangle of iron and steel. Stumbling across Ground Zero six weeks after 11 September 2001, it was as if it had just happened. It was Veterans Day and the rescue crews, some of whom had continued to burrow hopelessly with their bare hands, were stilled. This was to be the only interlude of silence in the helter-skelter eight-month clearance of the site in which one and a half million tonnes of wreckage were removed. I found myself trying to estimate the real consequence of the attack on the twin towers. For, even then, the immediate scar was curiously well defined. There came a moment quite quickly when, in downtown Manhattan, you simply stepped from hell into normality. Beyond a little dust, street life, office life, even home life, had resumed. Today Ground Zero is a squared zone of clean pre-construction. A year ago, the massive localised impacts in Washington, Pennsylvania and New York seemed containable: a short, sharp fight with al-Qaida, somewhere very far away, of which we knew little, and cared less, seemed survivable. But that optimism was to prove wrong.

The apparently fruitless heavy bombing of the mountains in eastern Afghanistan was challenging enough. But the rhetoric was worse. The vocal emissions from Bush's hawks conjured a year of living dangerously. Saddam and Osama became one. From Jerusalem to Kabul, from Kashmir to the Philippines, new enemies were defined together with new profiles of old conflicts. These were then shoe-horned into a new world disorder that 9/11 offered the prospect of resolving by force only. The rhetoric provided Israel's Ariel Sharon with the shroud behind which he could take apart the Oslo peace accord bomb by bomb, shell by shell. More destruction of the West Bank was achieved in this past year than by any Middle East war in history. More Israeli civilians died in the tit-for-tat suicide bombings than at any time since the birth of the Jewish state.

So 2002 has been a year during which we have found ourselves questioning America as never before and assessing the consequences of the collapse of the Berlin Wall in a new light. That questioning is at its most acute right here in this book, by some of the *Guardian*'s most seasoned America-philes. The provocation has been extreme: the unilateral abandonment of the Kyoto treaty on climate control and the equally unilateral tearing up of the Nuclear Test Ban Treaty. Then there was the International Criminal Court and the distasteful sight of America badgering Romania and Israel into leading the way to neuter the treaty where US service personnel were concerned. And finally there was the spectre of a solo US attack on Iraq, should the United Nations fail to take the actions the Bush administration deemed necessary. Many began to wonder whether living with a lone superpower was quite as much fun as we'd been led to expect.

Into all of this splashed a timely series of reminders of our own erstwhile superpower status: the Queen Mother's funeral, the Golden Jubilee, the World Cup and the Commonwealth Games. Escapology on the grand scale. Indeed, so impressive were the royal elements that, even for the most robust republican, the Guardian editorial reproduced here makes sombre reading. Somewhere here is the effect of that mass consumption of imagery and emotion first fully identified with the death of Diana. The crowds of people and flower-strewn tributes that disappeared almost as quickly as they had appeared were well and truly rekindled amid the colour and pageantry that accompanied the Queen Mother's funeral and the Jubilee. Yet, a few months on, the Jubilee already seems a distant and superficial memory, and I suspect many readers will only be reminded that it happened at all by finding it in these pages. In any case, by the autumn, the UK media was back to its old pre-Jubilee ways by rejoicing in the image of Prince Charles as a rustic eccentric, penning missives to all and sundry in support of traditional values.

There were no images of those who died in the Tora Bora mountains. We do not yet know what effect blow by blow pictures of our own boys in action would have. The Generals have a pretty good idea. Vietnam told them enough to ensure that when the going gets bloody, Diana-style emotion will be kept to a minimum along with access to the press. For the most part, televisually-induced hysteria is left to the relatively harmless arenas of sport. The World Cup ensured that the English were still left wondering who they were. White van man with a red cross tattooed on his forehead?

Before his untimely murder in northern Nigeria this year, I had the good fortune to meet the Yana of the Dagomba. He was a proud man whose receiving parlour, inside a complex of mud huts, sported both talking drums and CNN. The Yana was interested in only one man – David Beckham – and only one football team – Manchester United. It is therefore particularly uplifting that this anthology is able to bring us not only a thoroughgoing inspection of the state of the world, but also of Beckham's foot. For it was in 2002 that a survey revealed that more children could spell the word metatarsal than could spell sandwich.

The Guardian Year, 2002 is a graphic insight into a world in the most dangerous phase that anyone born after 1945 can remember. A world in which nuclear conflict is as near as at the time of the Cuban missile crisis, with fewer options for the international community to exert control. A world in which war and pestilence have a stranglehold on one continent – Africa – the scale of which mankind has never seen before. Yet it is also a collection of wonderfully contrasting writing about culture, sport and people: grateful tributes to intriguing men and women who shaped earlier periods of uncertainty. Perhaps, in the end, ours will prove not so uncertain a time. Either way, the pieces in this book provide wondrous stepping stones of immediate history. How was it in that year after the assault on America's east coast? The Guardian Year, 2002 goes a long way toward telling us.

EDITOR'S NOTE
David McKie

The good archbishop Odo passed away, *The Anglo-Saxon Chronicle* reported at the end of the year 961, and Dunstan was chosen archbishop. That was all; nothing else was thought worth recording. The previous year had no entry at all. They don't make years like that any more (which is just as well for newspapers). Nowadays, in our great global market place, we are buffeted day after day by noisy, imperious events. *The Guardian Year 2001* had to be taken to pieces and reconstituted after 11 September. *The Guardian Year 2002* has been put together amid expectations of a war on Iraq, perhaps under UN authority, perhaps conducted by the United States and Britain alone. This book is full of war and rumours of war – in Afghanistan, now possibly in Iraq, and throughout, most bloodily, in Israel and the homelands of Palestinians. It is also full of the United States, the one surviving superpower; forced by events to confront its vulnerability after 9/11, and exposed to uneasy reappraisal around the world. Which was it, people increasingly asked as the year progressed: world saviour (as much of America seemed to believe) or world bully?

These were dark days. Yet midsummer had been a time of celebrations in Britain, an occasion to put out more flags – first for the royal jubilee, then for an England World Cup campaign which promised much (especially when Beckham & Co mastered Argentina) but ended in the usual disappointment. The jubilee restored the quavering faith of monarchists that the institution they cherished would, after all, survive long enough to give us King William one day. Republicans (among whose ranks the *Guardian* is nowadays numbered) could enjoy it too, if sneakily, both as an excuse for a party and for the free entertainment. Inevitably, though, it became the occasion for a rigorous assessment of what kind of country this was, and what kind of country we wished it to be.

That is why this book starts not just with the political and constitutional implications of the year of jubilee, but with Polly Toynbee's assessment of a society still disfigured by inequalities. Inequalities, however, which seem trivial when compared to those across much of the world – as the Earth Summit helped teach us in August. As Charlotte Denny wrote in one of the many fine pieces for which I have failed to find room in this *Guardian Year*: 'For half the world's population the brutal reality is this: you'd be better off as a cow. The average European cow receives $2.20 (£1.40) a day from the taxpayer in subsidies and other aid. Meanwhile 2.8 billion people in developing countries around the world live on less than $2 a day.'

Though the concept of New Labour was now often soft-pedalled, Tony Blair continued to dominate politics as completely as Margaret Thatcher before him, not least when he took a line on Iraq which some of his cabinet, many of his MPs, most of his grassroots party and much of the country distrusted or denounced. The Conservatives (as Iain Duncan Smith completed his first year as leader) remained close to atrophy. Westminster, that magic toyshop, often seemed a place of slight consequence, though Simon Hoggart somehow contrived day after day to make it entertaining.

Newspapers, like political parties, must engineer change without losing continuity. The *Guardian* of 2002 was a bigger, brighter, brasher, more adventurous paper than it had been when Elizabeth II succeeded. In those days, politicians were on the whole treated with reverence, while the only horse race the paper deigned to report was the Grand National. Interviews appeared at the rate of roughly one a week: now, in a world which interests itself far more than it did in personalities and emotions, every part of the paper is full of them. Nowadays the *Guardian*, too, opens it doors to the kind of columnist whose purpose is to provoke, even to outrage.

Meanwhile, figures that *Guardian* readers have lived with for years move into retirement. One to reach full time this year was David Lacey, the paper's chief football writer for thirty years, of whom Frank Keating wrote as he departed: 'it remains a travesty that while manifestly lesser talents pose for preening pictures and demand double pay, Lacey has never won outright a single one of Fleet Street's plethora of annual awards. Somehow his ravishing daily consistency, week in, week out, has always been taken for granted.'

Keating himself, for many years one of our most loved columnists, was another to sign off during the year. That doesn't mean they will disappear from the paper or from subsequent *Guardian Years*. After all, Nancy Banks-Smith 'retired' about a decade ago, but it happily made little practical difference; her verve and inventiveness have never diminished over the years. The saddest event of the year was the death of Keith Harper, whose obituary by Geoffrey Goodman appears in this book – a reminder, this, that the essence of a newspaper lies less in the stars whose names are festooned every morning across the top of the front page than in the honest, faithful reporters like Keith – and also in those who toil in many departments without ever getting their names in the paper, let alone in this book. Mary Stott, a celebrated Women's Page editor of the *Guardian* also died, aged 95 years, as this book was going to press.

But there's proof here, I hope, that change has not swept the paper's core traditions away. The *Guardian*'s prime continuing purpose is to inform – and to do so in writing which seems to put the reader there, at the writer's side. This year, from the trouble spots especially, often in pieces by writers fairly new to it, the paper has been full of that kind of reporting. If this book does not reflect that, then – with so much to choose from, with so much of huge merit squeezed out in the final selection – it's unquestionably the fault of its editor.

My thanks to Helen Healy and the *Guardian* picture desk, to the *Guardian*'s Research and Information department, and to Gina Cross for help in assembling this book. And to Toby Mundy and Alice Hunt at Atlantic Books, who have been a joy to work with.

IN THE YEAR
OF JUBILEE

I support the Welsh football team. I am also a republican. This last week has been very difficult.

Letter from Steve Morris, Wokingham, Berkshire, 10 June 2002

TIMOTHY GARTON ASH

A confusion of flags

In England this has been the fortnight of two flags: a sea of Union Jacks for the Golden Jubilee, an ocean of the Cross of St George for England's football team. The Queen and Prince Philip gaze down from red, white and blue tea towels. But at a sandwich shop I see a page from the *Sun* taped to the window. It shows David Beckham's face superimposed on the flag of St George, with the inscription: *The King. We love 'im*. In the people's monarchy stakes it's Posh and Becks vs Lilibet and Phil. Englishness and Britishness dance a complex *pas de deux*. And the torrent continues of books trying to explain what it all means.

There is no doubt that there has been, in the last decade, a dramatic growth in the symbolic display and talk of Englishness. According to one report, thirty million flags of St George have been sold during this World Cup season – more than ever before. The many books about Englishness and Britishness are part of the phenomenon they purport to explain.

We have on offer one simple, seductive, speculative narrative about where it's all heading. Britain – the United Kingdom – this narrative says, was constructed with and for the purposes of empire. Empire gone, Britain will go. Scots and Welsh are fed up with the English equating themselves with Britain and dominating the union. Devolution won't stop at its present halfway house. One thing will lead to another, so we English had better start working out what state we want to be in.

This is all clear and seemingly rational – far too much so for our real, irrational, Burkean muddle of Englishness and Britishness. Of course, if Scotland voted for independence everything would change. Then the English question would be posed in a sharp and concrete form. Even now there will surely be some pushing and shoving about the rights of English regional assemblies, the number of Scottish MPs, reducing the higher level of per capita public expenditure in Scotland as opposed to England and so on. But if the Scots don't force the English question, my hunch is that the English certainly won't. Most of the English, it seems to me, are not unhappy with the strange muddle of Englishness and Britishness with which we have lived for so long. And maybe they are right.

For most people who see themselves as both English and British, being English is probably the stronger emotional identity. 'Do you feel more English or British?' Spontaneous answer: 'English!' This identity is not new. It is very old. There has been an England for more than a thousand years. It has not just been 'socially constructed' with 'invented tradition' – though there is that too, of course, bags of it – but also really existing, politically, legally, financially and in the language and symbols of a kingdom.

In the poetry of patriotism, England wins over Britain 10-1. 'That there's some corner of a foreign field / that is for ever Britain'? Come off it! When Neville Chamberlain seemed to want to continue appeasing Hitler even as the *Wehrmacht* rolled into Poland on 2 September 1939, the Conservative Leo Amery shouted across the floor of the House of Commons to the leader of the opposition: 'Speak for England, Arthur!' Not 'Speak for Britain!' If you go round second-hand bookshops they are full of wartime books, on that yellowing, slightly coarse paper (war economy standard), with titles like *For Ever England*.

Being English, we feel, is somehow a deeper identity. Britishness is more imperial, formal and remote; grander but colder. Unfortunately, English is also the more ethnic identity and hence more exclusive. In practice, of course, most of the English are mongrels – as Daniel Defoe famously pointed out in his poem 'The True-Born Englishman'. ('From this amphibious ill-born mob began / That vain, ill-natur'd thing, an Englishman.') So people say: 'Well, actually I'm a quarter Scottish and a quarter Irish, but I feel English.'

Yet this option of, so to speak, ethnic opting-in is not available to all. That's where Britishness comes to the rescue. For the post-imperial identity is also the more inclusive, civic one. I have heard two very senior members of the British establishment, both of continental Jewish origin, say privately: 'I feel British but not English.' It is, I suspect, easier to say and be 'black British' or 'Asian British' than 'black English' or 'Asian English – though I stand open to correction here by those who will know better than me.

If one spells out the English–British difference like this, however, it is unsettling – as if there is somehow a deeper identity which is unavailable to otherwise equal British citizens. Some are more equal than others. Yes, I know, as an Asian or black Briton (and what a strange, barely usable word 'Briton' is) you might not want that kind of depth. Or you might find emotional depth in other identities compatible with Britishness. But still, it seems unfair.

Fortunately, in a very English – or is it British? – way, we don't spell it out clearly. Instead, England football fans continue to sing 'Rule, Britannia' while waving the flag of St George. And all attempts to distinguish Britishness sharply from Englishness end in a higher confusion. 'The distinctiveness, even uniqueness, of the British as a people has long been taken for granted by foreign observers and native commentators alike,' writes the Welsh British historian Kenneth O. Morgan in his foreword to *The Oxford History of Britain*. The 'native' commentators he then refers to are Winston Churchill, who indeed generally spoke about the British people, or as often about the British empire, but whose polemic against appeasement is entitled 'While England Slept'; and George Orwell, who consistently and insistently wrote about the English people.

In his rich but tendentious new book, *Patriots*, Richard Weight quotes the lead singer of the Britpop group Blur explaining how their songs are 'about Englishness rather than being British'. Said Damon Albarn: 'There was a time when pop music wouldn't have been able to explain what being English was all about, but that's changed now. If you draw a line from The Kinks in the sixties, through the Jam and the Smiths, to Blur in the nineties, it would define this thing called Englishness as well as anything.'

Well, now, is that clear?

Some people think that if the Scots were to force the English question upon us, the resulting England would be a nasty, brutish, nationalist place. Turning even more against Europe, it would be 'England for the English', to quote the chilling title of a book by the former Conservative MP, Richard Body. I believe that, helped by the great cosmopolitan country that is London, we would surely find other voices in the rich polyphony of English history. However, I would rather not have to make the trial.

I say this not just out of concern for what might happen to England, but because the sort of complex, multi-layered identity that we have developed between Englishness and Britishness is the kind of thing we shall need more of in a century when people will be increasingly mixed up together. Ambiguity is a vice in thought, but not always in life. So let's keep muddling through. Long live the English-British blur.

5 June 2002

LEADER

A spectacular jubilee

We need to face up to the facts. The Queen's Golden Jubilee celebrations of 2002 have been in every respect more successful than either the organisers had feared or the critics had hoped. It is important to remind ourselves of this chiefly because it is true. Anyone seeing the bobbing sea of flags in The Mall yesterday following another exuberant day of celebrations was experiencing an unusual rapport between monarch and subjects. But it is important also because as memories of the long weekend become rose-tinted, this jackpot outcome will come to be seen as inevitable. In reality it was not as recently as the early spring the whole programme was still a considerable gamble. There had been a not especially successful royal visit to Australia. The set-piece parliamentary celebrations in Westminster Hall had passed almost without notice. When the Queen travelled to the south-west to begin her series of regional jubilee visits, the crowds were respectable and respectful, but not huge; the atmosphere was muted. Things got better as her travels around the country gathered momentum. Even so, only last month, the palace was said to be uncertain whether the jubilee holiday weekend would be a great occasion or a great embarrassment.

In the event it was much more the former than the latter. This has undoubtedly been a great weekend for the House of Windsor and for the Queen in particular. It would not be true to say that their popularity has never been greater, but it is undoubtedly true that this is one of the best mornings the monarchy has ever had. Nevertheless, the uncertainty, the sense of risk, the genuine fears that Britain might have become indifferent, or possibly even hostile, to the Queen were real. They did not come out of nowhere. They came out of a decade of roller-coaster rejection, some of it emotional, some of it rational, most of it tabloid-driven, of the kind of monarchy that had evolved under Elizabeth II's apparently indifferent rule. The court was right to worry. But in the end the crowds came and cheered. In the end, the mixed levels of irritation and anger against individual members of the royal family, against the House of Windsor in general, and against the irrelevance of modern monarchy in particular were not great enough to dislodge the nation's fundamental comfort and, yes, even its pride in its institutions.

Yet we again need to face up to the facts about why this was so. Three of them stand out. First, national respect for the Queen and for her long years in the job, crosses the boundaries of the monarchy/republicanism debate. She is not the divisive figure that both her husband and her eldest son are. That widespread respect was waiting to be tapped. Second, the jubilee calendar has been very cleverly choreographed, enabling yesterday's formal thanksgiving to proceed on the back of the wave of popular pleasure that was unleashed by the outstanding televised concerts and displays of the previous three days. It was, you might almost say, Diana's revenge, for this weekend was her sort of occasion rather than one that came naturally to the Windsors. This time, though, it was Ozzy what won it for the Queen. In that sense, too, the BBC, which paid for the Buckingham Palace concerts, has also been the indispensable catalyst of the jubilee's success. And finally, human beings simply enjoy ceremony and cele-bration. For most people in this country, the past four days have been a free party. It may have been a street or a village do, or the million-strong throng for the fireworks on Monday night, or it may have been something that most peo-ple only saw on television or simply chose to ignore. But it was a much more inclusive set of events than in the past, marked by great entertainment and visual splendours, both traditional and cutting-edge. In the past, it has been their show, not ours. This time, we were all invited.

But the need to face facts is not a one-way ticket. The Golden Jubilee may have given those of us who seek radical change in the way Britain is governed food for thought. But it should do just the same for those who think that every-thing is back in its place and all's well with the United Kingdom. The jubilee would have been impossible without the underpinning of national respect for the Queen. But that respect is not easily gained and is even less easily transfer-able. If we are going to have a monarch in this day and age, then a long period of rule by a decent, prosaic, uncontroversial, rule-bound and dutiful one like Elizabeth II is probably as good as it is likely to get. And even then, that is the best you can say about it. A good person, yes, but still a lousy system. The objec-tions – constitutional, legal, cultural and personal – all remain embedded, whether we respect the Queen for her achievements or not. When she goes, much of the respect will go with her. But the objections to the system will remain, now magnified by her absence. Unless proper and honest thought is given now to changing the British monarchy, this Golden Jubilee may in future come to be seen as a fool's paradise. For these are facts too, and they also need to be faced.

5 June 2002

POLLY TOYNBEE

After the jubilation, the reckoning

So there goes the jubilee. Whatever the uses or abuses of monarchy, it throws rare national parties and its odd anniversaries mark the passing of time. So in the past twenty-five years what progress has been made? What counts as progress? Standing back from the daily scramble of events, the recent past crystallises.

The more this government struggles to 'deliver', the more obvious is the full damage done to the social and public fabric since the last jubilee. Labour, afraid at first to herald too much change, dangerously underplayed and underestimated the effects of eighteen years of annual compound disinvestment – and even added in another two years of its own. Now they find the damage harder to reverse than was expected.

It would be absurd to suggest nothing improved in the last twenty-five years. A healthier nation is living longer. A richer country has more foreign holidays, laptops, mobiles, multi-channel TV; 73 per cent have cars. Above all, we have seen the most rapid change in social class in recorded history: the 1977 mass working class, with two-thirds of the people in blue-collar jobs, shrank to one-third, while the rest migrated upwards into a 70 per cent home-owning, white-collar middle class. The world turned upside down, a social pyramid inverted.

A revolution in social attitudes saw liberal values conquer: gays are out, marriage optional, bastardy obsolete. New freedoms bring new problems, but few would go back to lace-curtain hypocrisy, shotgun weddings and sexual oppression. Women are halfway to freedom, still straddled between home and work, underpaid with no childcare. Racists still stir strife in a Europe gripped by immigration phobia, but in the last twenty-five years second-generation black Britons talking Birmingham or Brixton have made Britishness unequivocally multicultural, a deep word that meant nothing then.

So the story since 1977 should be one of tolerance, pluralism, multiculturalism and meteoric upward mobility in a land of ever-growing plenty. But it did not feel that way. All this affluence and freedom was poisoned by the injustice of its distribution: it made people no happier because at the same time social cohesion and public collective goods were demolished by what looks, at this distance, like a strange cult that fetishised all things private.

By chance the 1977 Silver Jubilee marked the year that Britain was more equal in how income was shared than at any time in history. It also marked the end of that social progress. The trajectory since the twenties had marched towards fairer shares in income. But after 1977, it went backwards. All that extra national income was so unfairly shared that those left behind in the great upward-mobility push were thrown down into a deeper pit with steeper sides. The widening gap meant social mobility was all but over: those who did not make the jump then were now cemented to the floor. A recent Cabinet Office report on stalled social mobility spelled out its full gravity. Those 154 per cent increased university places since 1977, by making degrees essential, may have become a new barrier to keep down the poor.

It was not Mrs Thatcher or her council house sales that created the new middle class. The mass great leap forward from the working class sprang from the comprehensives and the plate-glass university boom of the sixties and seventies and an economic shift already well in progress. The embourgoisement that improved millions of lives belongs back then: a key recent study shows how children of manual workers born in 1970 entering Mrs Thatcher's society have had a weak chance of upward mobility compared with the children born in 1958.

At the time the mainly Tory-created widening income gap was clear for all to see, but the obvious corollary was less apparent: jumping across that gap became harder. In 1979, 9 per cent lived below the official poverty line, but by 2000 it had grown to 25 per cent. In a world of cars, not to have one (never to shop cheap at out-of-town Ikea for example) gives the word 'excluded' real force.

The wrecked railways are only the most glaring relic of the Tory era. The NHS now at last gets a large transfusion of the money denied it all those years when it fell ever further behind the rest of Europe, but it is too late? Education and council estates suffered the same dereliction. Neglect of public places, decline of public parks, ruination of civic space, decay of galleries and museums – add what you will to the list of social despoliation.

Atomising society at top and bottom, these ideological tax-cutters created a monstrous master race of the super-rich who exclude themselves from society as dangerously as the poor are forcibly excluded. A 34 per cent tax cut for the rich! Imagine if Labour had been a fraction as bold in the other direction. Their fear of the rich is a foolish mistake, for the emotional tide has turned against fat cats: trimming their whiskers would be a powerfully cohesive symbol.

Even Labour's most generous redistributive acts towards the poor have not yet returned benefits to where they were in 1977. For a single unemployed person the current rate is £53.05, but to keep relative pace with 1977 it should be £87 a week. Poor pensioners recently got their biggest increase ever with the minimum income guarantee at £98 a week but even that is less than the relative 1977 equivalent which would now be £107.40. This is only one sign of how hard Labour has to run just to catch up with twenty-five years ago.

In department after department the full scale of the tasks ahead looks daunting as they compete fiercely for the next spending round. A 'world-class' NHS and the abolition of child poverty look ever-tougher targets. The shock of a jubilee stocktaking is to realise how long repairing the damage of the past twenty-five years will take, how far we are still from the lost 1977 social trajectory. The Conservatives have never apologised: long may the voters continue to punish them.

We have all but wasted a quarter of a century. We have gained mobile phones but lost a social cohesion that was, at least financially, at its greatest in 1977. We can pick over the bones of others who were to blame – James Callaghan's name looms large, with unions and post oil-shock inflation out of control. But the successes of that decade have been too easily obliterated by the débâcle at its ending.

It is plain now that Labour should have started mighty rebuilding at once, but it feared that the ideological poison of those years meant 'no such thing as society' had entered the national soul. Only now, five years into power, has that fear finally proved groundless: Labour's first overt tax-raising Budget is the most popular since the last jubilee. 'Back to the future' may not be a good slogan, given the sorry ending to the seventies. But one way to celebrate this jubilee is by finally confronting the enormity of the social disaster of the past twenty-five years: it may be so obvious that it gets easily forgotten. Remembering it should lead to a little more patience with the government that is burdened with trying to reverse it.

3 July 2002

JOE KLEIN

The United Kingdom doesn't know where it belongs

Six weeks on the road and Heathrow looms. Funny how travel distorts time: I've been gone for ever and arrived only yesterday. Part of the problem is that I've done this jaunt the American way, as a mad dash rather than a leisurely stroll. Work, work, work. No time to visit a single museum, unless you count the city of Rome. No time to while away the hours in cafés. The apogee of my continental naughtiness: I was lured into smoking several cigarettes. I did get very drunk one night in Poland, with Adam Michnik, a catharsis I needed and enjoyed immensely. I should have loafed more, taken sick leave, filed a claim against the *Guardian* for exposing me to France, where existential anguish is contagious. It's a miracle I survived that hothouse of anomie. But no, I'm a tough American: my angst is limited to guilt over the size of my wife's sport utility vehicle.

And what have I learned? Let me tell you a story. Coffee one morning at an outdoor café in Rome, with two young people, one a student and the other a recent graduate. Both veterans of the past year's street protests in Genoa and Rome. As always, I began by asking, 'What's so bad about America?'

'It's not just America, it's the entire West,' said Pietro, the recent graduate, now a graphic designer. 'We've created a model the world can't support. If everyone in the world used toilet paper the way we do, there'd be no more trees.'

Maria Vittoria's problem with America was cultural. 'They've given us the model of the strong, victorious man, with an emphasis on professional success at any cost. The moral and spiritual penetration is insidious and it is everywhere. McDonald's, American movies . . .'

'I like American movies,' Pietro interrupted, with a guilty smile. 'I particularly like the violent fantasies, *Star Wars*.' And while he was at it, he admitted, 'I like my shoes, too,' displaying a rather battered pair of Nikes. 'I know this is probably juvenile, but I'm a child inside.'

Aren't we all! Inherent in that childishness is a need to be protected, a need for order – not just a sense of stability in everyday life, but a larger sense of order as well: something to believe in. The conversation took a very interesting turn when I asked them what they believed in.

'I believe this corporate system is wrong,' said Maria.

But what replaces it, I asked: socialism?

'No, no, no,' said Pietro. 'My parents were members of the communist church.'

And to which church did he belong?

'That's the problem. There are two churches now. Capitalism and Islam. Capitalism is crass and Islam is crazy. The anti-globalist movement is not quite a church, yet. There are different strands, things I believe and things I don't.'

About a hundred years ago, the American sociologist Thorstein Veblen wrote a book about the coming crassness called *The Theory of the Leisure Class*. It may be that the current anomie could be called the reverse: The Leisure of the Theory Class. Europeans, it seems to me, are unmoored in the midst of abundance. Pietro is right: they have no church. Their parents had communism and Catholicism (all right: they had Protestantism as well, even if it isn't alliterative). Both are pretty much gone now. Indeed, it is astonishing to an American how secular Europe has become. During a conversation with a woman here in England – I can't quite remember who she was – I casually uttered the words, 'Thank God for that.' The woman was shocked. 'Why do you say that? Do you actually believe in God?'

But there is a third church for Europeans, a rather powerful one: the church of national identity. It is a great source of pride and security and problems: a Frenchman knows exactly what being French means; the siesta sensibility still rules in Spain; and the tendency of Brits – even cool, young business Brits in the City – to need a pint and a gab at the end of the day seems encoded in the national DNA. There is an undercurrent of informed-élite concern about this: rampant ethnicity. It proved a European disaster in the twentieth century; it seems anachronistic, economically untenable and a bit crude now. That is why politics has become so brutish on the continent: demagogues are doing quite well selling the past. They exploit the threat to national sovereignty from above – from Brussels – and, most profoundly, from below: from the rush of immigrants, particularly those who do not share European values. As a Frenchwoman told me, 'We believe religion should be a private thing. Why must they take it into the street, the way they dress and all?' But immigrants are necessary to keep the national economies, and the social-services systems, afloat. And Brussels – which can create a market with 500 million players if Eastern Europe is included – is necessary as well if Europeans want to throw their weight in the world. Still, there is great anxiety about how Britain, how France – how Europe – will be defined twenty years down the road.

This, I suspect, is a prime source of the deeper resentments toward America – that is, those not related to the gratuitously ideological, blithely boorish behaviour of the current administration. America doesn't have an identity problem. It has a powerful national religion: Americanness. It has a national ideology, too: informality. It is threatened neither from above nor below; it is threatened for the moment from the outside, by terrorists, but that has only served to strengthen the national sense of community (and from the inside, by a nause-ating array of business scammers – although this is a less serious problem than some Europeanists would like to think). The true power of Americanness is that it beggars ethnicity: we luxuriate in the mongrelisation of our bloodlines – at least, a constant majority of us do; we believe that the things we have in com-mon are far more important than those which divide us. The rainbow cascade of immigrants, which began in 1965 after a forty-year closed-door policy threat-ened to bland us to death, has succeeded in making us even more American. The Latinos and Arabs and Africans and south Asians and east Asians have not only proved energetic entrepreneurs and spectacular citizens, they've also served to take the binary edge off the vicious old black-white racial confrontation.

The American identity can be summarised in a single polling question: we are the only country in the world where a majority has consistently believed – with the exception of a few years in the late seventies – that next year will be better. Such optimism must seem obnoxious to the rest of the world, especially when accompanied by overwhelming military and commercial power. The essential American credulousness – we believe in our nation, our system, our sensibility (those who demur usually do so on the grounds that we are not living up to our ideals), we even tend to believe in God – must seem pretty obnoxious, too.

I don't want to minimise Europe's 'America' problem. The anger seems to have grown during my six weeks here. I've heard about it constantly, and most credibly from sober sorts – such as Lord (Richard) Holme of Cheltenham, who has been deeply involved in British-American exchange programmes for years and says, with great regret, that 'America has never seemed quite so far away.' Of course, one hears it from less sober sorts as well. Each week seems to bring new outrages: most recently, George W. Bush's Middle East speech – in which he guaranteed the lifetime presidency of the corrupt terrorist Yasser Arafat – and the huge WorldCom fraud, and the mistaken bombing of an Afghan wedding. Each day seems to bring new evidence of an increasingly careless and thoughtless hyperpower – to use the French epithet *du jour* – evidence that causes pain to America's friends, and brings joy to the usual array of juvenile, leisure-addled leftist intellectuals. There are real problems, real differences, between Europe and America. But I suspect that the rift wouldn't seem quite so raw if Bush weren't president.

Last week, at a gathering of his diminished tribe in Memphis, Al Gore said that if he had the 2000 campaign to do over again, he would ignore his platoons of consultants, pollsters and marketers and 'let 'er rip'. Presumably this means he wouldn't have been so patently dishonest. It suggests that he might occa-sionally have told the American people something they didn't want to hear; at the very least, it implies that he would have dislodged the flagpole from the area just south of his lower spine. And what if he had won? There certainly would be less of the signature Bushian callousness towards our allies. Multilateralism – at least, the appearance of multilateralism – would rule. Petroleum wouldn't. Kyoto, or something like it, would be signed. There would be no American tar-iffs on steel; no pornographic corporate farm subsidies; regulators would actu-ally be attempting to control the excesses of enterprise, if not often succeeding. Officials of the United States government wouldn't be going around lecturing the world about the evils of abortion and the joys of gun ownership.

My guess is that Gore would have prosecuted the Afghanistan campaign much as Bush has – which means that civilians would, on occasion, have been mistakenly bombed. That is part of the price of war. I'd also guess that there would be great American reluctance about joining the international criminal court: we have very different notions about the proper use of force – this may be the greatest philosophical difference between Europeans and Americans. We would not want the American guards at Camp X-Ray called up on charges by foolish judges who believe that the use of masks and manacles while transporting the most dangerous of war criminals is a crime against humanity.

But those differences would be more tolerable in a general context of co-operation. Europeans wouldn't be so upset if the American assumption was partnership, interrupted by occasional disputes, rather than disdain interrupted by occasional spasms of condescension. But Bush is president, and may remain so for the next six years. The Atlantic does seem a bit wider these days. And there are questions now about the most basic political propositions: is there any alternative to the American way? Are we doomed to the mushy, technocratic, centrist politics that seems to be turning off so many people? Is there another European church waiting to be born? After my six-week wander through Europe, I sense a growing impatience among the Theory Class, a desire for some clear-cut resolutions. But there are some questions that just shouldn't be answered peremptorily; solutions evolve – messily, incoherently, stumbled upon by politicians. Or they don't evolve: the poor, for example, will always be with us, as a Jew from the West Bank once said.

For the past few weeks I've had a rather grumpy travelling companion: Will Hutton. Not Will himself, who is a charming and intelligent fellow. But I've been reading Will's new book, *The World We're In*, which is another story entirely: it is everything the author is not – simplistic, hasty and vituperative. It posits a stark alternative: there is the American way or the European way, and Britain must choose one or the other. The American way features rapacious capitalism and social insensitivity, undergirded by a radical intellectual conservatism that has swept all before it. The European way is far more mellow – a slower, more stable corporate culture; a far more generous welfare state; lots of museums and holidays; a political philosophy that draws the best from the two old churches, communism and Catholicism. Hutton has a point about the rapacious capitalism, the tendency to place short-term profits above long-term growth. He is also right to criticise the antisocial myopia of conservative thinkers such as Leo Strauss, who have had an influence on some of the more extreme sorts lurking in the shadows of the Bush administration. Hutton's right, too, that America's social safety net is deficient, especially when it comes to healthcare (but he totally misses the massive income transfer to the working poor that took place during the Clinton administration).

It is possible, though, to concede all these points and discard Hutton's general thrust as rubbish. He simply doesn't understand how America works, or why it is as vibrant as it is. He follows a long tradition of leftish pessimists who predict America's imminent demise. He sees 'an ominous echo of the 1920s' in the stock-market frenzy of the nineties and the recent frauds, without acknowledging the lessons learned and implemented during the Great Depression: the Keynesian manipulation of fiscal and monetary policy has had a very successful seventy-year run of blunting inflationary and deflationary cycles in the US. Worse, he links America's economic fate with that of the great corporations, such as Boeing, which seems, for the moment, to be losing its competitive battle against Airbus.

But the American economy isn't about Boeing; it's about the small businesses and new ideas constantly being born, most failing, some succeeding. It is about the freedom of employers to hire, fire, start, stop and change course. It's about the freedom of all comers to begin a business of their own, with a minimum of fuss or paperwork. In the early part of his administration, Bill Clinton had a wonderful statistic that he would trot out against the naysayers concerned by the 'massive' wave of layoffs besetting the Fortune 500 companies: in the past two years, he would say, there have been more new businesses started by women than there have been people laid off by the Fortune 500.

Actually, Hutton's analysis of America is somewhat more detailed than his account of western Europe. The latter seems a romantic fantasy at best. He apotheosises several large, well-run companies – Volkswagen, Nokia and Michelin – and extrapolates their practices to all European enterprises. There's a problem, though: these industrial giants represent a small and declining part of the advanced western economies. And Hutton's beloved Germany lags in most other economic sectors: the growth in information-age services and technology has averaged 8.9 per cent a year over the past decade in America versus 4.9 per cent in Germany.

There are, furthermore, powerful disincentives to start new businesses and hire new employees in most European countries. I spent a morning with Traugott Klose of the Free University of Berlin, where 20 per cent of liberal-arts students linger on campus for twelve semesters or more before getting a degree. Why? Because it is far easier for a company to give a temporary job to a student – only about one-third of social taxes need be paid and students have no right to protest if they are let go – than to hire a graduate permanently. There are now urban legends about German students – Grey Panthers, they are called – who go directly from school to pension: at the Free University, one 'student' is still drifting about after seventy-two semesters. (In Holland, the difficulty in firing employees has led to a rather remarkable statistic: one out of every sixteen Dutch workers is on permanent sick leave.)

There are other problems with Hutton's thesis. The first is the dog that doesn't bark: Will's World doesn't seem to include Asia. He doesn't mention China once. He mentions the other burgeoning Asian economies only as victims of American-led International Monetary Fund reform (though most seem to have recovered nicely). The truth is, Europe and the US are not just competing against each other, but also against Asia – and if Hutton thinks the American welfare state is sketchy, he should check out China's. There simply isn't any health insurance for most workers in non-state enterprises. There are practically no labour rules. America is a worker's paradise by contrast. This is The World We're Really In; it may be the Hobbesian future we're competing against.

In any case, why on earth must Britain choose one path or the other – the

European model or the American? Why not mix and match? Why not take the
freedom of the American labour market and combine it with an aggressive re-
employment programme for those who are sacked, for example? But Hutton and
a great many others are spoiling for a fight. In fact, there are competing intellectual street gangs on each side of the Atlantic these days, and both are filled
with a rather lunatic bloodlust. For all the salon talk in Europe about arrogant
super-duper-powers led by idiot cowboys, there is an equal amount of bleating
about anti-Semitic, Arab-loving, crypto-Trotskyite Euroweenies in America.

The caricatures are poison; they have consequences. They are too easily
digested, too easily passed through the public bloodstream; they provide a sugar
rush for the idle and foolish. We gave the last century over to the vehement ide-
alists: they gave us the Soviet Union, Nazi Germany and Britain's rail privatisation scheme. It's time for a new paradigm. And I have a modest proposal. Let
Hutton captain fifty Euroweenies; let Norman Podhoretz, the ancient neo-
conservative crustacean, captain fifty Amerigoths. Let us transport both squads
to a desert island and ask them to compete – not just in standard survivor games
such as worm-eating, but also in more erudite pursuits such as hieroglyph reading and grant-proposal writing. Let them box and wrestle and debate as well –
perhaps a new sport could be invented: debate boxing. We can televise all this,
although I'm not sure there would be many viewers. Then again, perhaps we
should avoid making intellectuals into celebrities. Perhaps we should leave them
on that desert island and go about the serious business of picking out what's best
on both sides of the Atlantic, and making a nice little society for ourselves.

I have several other modest proposals. The first is a basic principle: going it
together is better than going it alone – diversity trumps homogeneity. America's
diversity is its greatest economic and social asset; if the current president – who
has been quite courageous in confronting the xenophobes in his party on immigration – could extend himself just the slightest bit intellectually, he might see
that the diversity principle applies transnationally as well. On your side of the
Atlantic, it seems obvious that the European Union is Europe's only path toward
relevance, and the best chance to cleanse the continent's virulently ethnocen-
tric soul. This leads to the real world of policy: it is a moral imperative that the
EU expand to include the former communist countries to the east as quickly as
possible. It's probably also high time for Britain to adopt the euro. Indeed, let's
have some real fun: merge the dollar and the euro, since they've pretty much
achieved market parity, and the euro comes – at least, it appears to come –
equipped with fiscal disciplines that the budget-busting Bush administration
badly needs.

Finally, in order to return some much-needed religious pomp and circumstance to our public life, I have a few ceremonial suggestions. Silvio Berlusconi
should be put in charge of all social arrangements – all future celebrations, that
is, parties not policy – on both sides of the Atlantic. And Clinton should be hired
to deliver all major eulogies: if we have poets laureate, why not a mourner laureate? I have a few small changes I'd like to propose about soccer as well . . . but
we'll leave those until we meet again. For now, I board the plane and return
home – to search for a nice outdoor café that serves espresso and sweet cakes,
where I can sit and relax, and turn on my tape of the world's most ghastly accor-

dion music, and watch the pigeons chuttle about and the girls wheel by, and show all my American friends how truly continental I have now become.

26 August 2002

JOHN VIDAL

A glittering citadel next door to poverty

'Do the politicians care? Can they do anything? Will they find us work?' The speaker is Trace, an exuberant young Sowetan working for the next ten days as a hostess for the world's largest gathering of heads of state, grassroots groups, business, churches and charities at the Earth Summit 2000 in Johannesburg.

She greets the delegates with a wave as they file into the Sandton conference hall where governments today get down to the nitty-gritty of addressing ever-starker global inequalities.

She sings an impromptu verse of the South African national anthem to entertain another group of the 60,000 delegates who are still flooding into the city and are having to be parcelled out up to fifty miles away. They do not notice her, but she says she is proud that Johannesburg is hosting the Earth Summit, the Olympics of development.

But this conference centre feels about as close to the rest of Johannesburg as Mars. Sandton is a purpose-built business centre. Its hip restaurants, company HQs, international banks, silver BMWs, flash hotels, $300,000 flats and glass and brass architecture, all built in the decade since the Earth Summit in Rio de Janeiro, are surrounded by deep walls of police, electrified fences and miles of concrete barriers. To reach the conference hall by 9 a.m., Trace must get up at six, pass five cordons and four security checks.

Sandton is five-star Globoville, a corporate ghetto and the richest, brassiest, smartest suburb in a city that was built on the excesses of mining and retains the gold rush mentality. Its anonymous glass towers and imitation frescoes of the Sistine Chapel could place it in Docklands, Boston, or anywhere international financiers and corporations work and play.

For the legions of grassroots groups, farmers, indigenous peoples and others in Johannesburg to try to give a voice to the world's poor and concerned, Sandton is socially unconscious, unsustainable development at its worst. Its shops are from Paris, London and New York, its hotels trade only in dollars, and for most of Johannesburg it is unaffordable and elitist. Only the music of the townships and rural areas wafting from the shops and restaurants suggests this is Africa. The cost of staying one night in the Hilton or most of the other hotels here would keep Trace in university for a year and her family in food and shelter for three months.

Yet the billion-pound development built on the new globalisation of capital only exists because the business community has packed its bags and fled the terrible crime, impoverishment and physical degradation of the old city centre. Once the richest area in Africa's city of gold, the old business quarter has been taken over by the homeless and the street hawkers. It is a dangerous desert at night, and few people go out alone, even in a car.

A stone's throw from the conference hall – behind the barriers but in sight of Sandton's boardrooms and satellite dishes – is the old township of Alexandra. The global money found so easily to build Sandton in just a few years has not reached this sprawling slum with its rubble-strewn streets, and thousands of small businesses. The legacies of apartheid can be seen in the old watchtowers and single-sex hostels.

'Yes, things are better now than ten years ago, but here it is still survival. How can we think about tomorrow when we have nothing today?' says Tumi, a part-time driver who has lived in an Alexandra hostel for thirty years and can visit his family in the north only twice a year.

The government is trying to address the air pollution, the shocking state of rivers, the urban deserts in the poorer areas, the nightmares of the old mine dumps, and above all the deep poverty. South Africa has received more investment than any sub-Saharan country in the past ten years, and is bursting with positive initiatives, yet to turn round a century of unsustainable development, colonial rule and apartheid requires gargantuan investment.

Meanwhile, the rest of sub-Saharan Africa looks on in bewilderment as world leaders flock to Johannesburg. The region faces a poverty time bomb, says the World Bank, and has largely fallen off the economic map, with 500 million of the poorest people in the world scratching an ever-harder living. Neighbouring Botswana may be financially better off, but AIDS is crippling development. Angola and Mozambique are still recovering from civil war and are stymied by trade rules that bar them from exporting. Zimbabawe is imploding. And across the vast region, preventable illnesses are taking their toll, and hunger stalks the land. Yesterday the UN World Food Programme predicted a catastrophe could occur later this year as the region's food supplies dwindle. Ten million of the poorest are already suffering malnutrition, and the international effort to bring them food will have to be Herculean. More than a million tonnes of food must be imported, and the world community is reluctant to pledge the $500 million needed.

Six hundred miles north of Sandton, a million of the poorest Malawian farmers are growing more desperate by the day.

'The World Food Programme wants to target 30 per cent of the entire population from January to March,' says Al Smith, the USAID chief in charge of the relief operation. 'We are getting to 5 per cent of people, but it should already be 15 to 25 per cent.'

Not one sack of grain has come to Gumbi village, says Joffrey, a local health worker. He says twenty-five people have died of food-related causes so far in the emergency, and he expects many more to die in the next six months.

Nelson Kwenje, Gumbi's only shopkeeper, says: 'Tell the world leaders in Johannesburg from the people of Gumbi, that we are living in a crisis of poverty that never ends. Say that we want them to come and see for themselves. Tell them they are welcome, but we need work, we need food, and we need hope.'

WAR AND PEACE

Steve Bell, 21 June 2002

The London-based World Society for the Protection of Animals is sending thousands of pounds to help animals at Kabul Zoo, including Marjon, a one-eyed lion who has survived rocket attacks, stoning by the Taliban and a grenade thrown by the brother of a man whose arm he ate.

23 November 2001

5 November 2001

JAMES MEEK

Ragtag soldiers, Afghanistan

The anti-Taliban army facing its enemy on the critical front north of Kabul, known to the rest of the world as the Northern Alliance, likes to call itself the United Front. But it is becoming increasingly clear that there are, in fact, two anti-Taliban armies.

One, on show on a bare, dusty mountainside near the mouth of the Panjshir valley over the past few days, is a well-equipped, uniformed, regular fighting force, earnestly training for war and thirsting to launch an offensive on the Afghan capital. The other is an army of irregular, local part-timers, working by day and cycling to the frontline by night, with rubber galoshes on their bare feet instead of boots. Beneath their bravado they are deeply ambivalent about taking part in an attack on the Taliban, uneasy about killing – many on the Taliban side are their former friends – and desperately hoping the United States will finish the war for them. The question for Afghanistan, and for the less and less secret band of US military advisers here is: which is the real Northern Alliance army?

In exercises on the bleak slopes between the towns of Jabal os Saraj and Gulbahar, hundreds of Alliance *zarbati* or strike troops have been practising fire and movement tactics in small groups in the scree and scrub. Gleaming armoured personnel carriers, manned by soldiers in the bright green uniforms of Guards troops, have been lining up in parade-ground rows and bumping at speed across the lower slopes. Yesterday – watched by men believed to be US military advisers who were making desperate attempts to conceal their faces from journalists – tanks and batteries of artillery rockets joined the exercises, firing at targets up the hill. More men of American appearance, who declined to identify themselves when asked by journalists, arrived yesterday in a small plane, the first to land at the new airstrip being built in Gulbahar. The airstrip is expected to be used by Russian and US aircraft to ferry in munitions to the alliance.

All this could be interpreted as a sign that alliance forces north of Kabul – one of three fronts along with Mazar-i-Sharif and Taloqan in the north-east – are about to launch an offensive on the Taliban barring their way to the Afghan capital, only an hour's drive away. But the troops taking part in the exercise are pitifully few – no more than 500 men – and unrepresentative. There is only one Guards brigade. The main focus of the training seems to be less an imminent attack and more a military show scheduled for today to be witnessed by the alliance leader Burhanuddin and his senior military commander, defence minister Mohammed Fahim.

A different kind of army can be found at the disused Bagram air base, closer to Kabul, where for years alliance soldiers have faced off against the Taliban, their trenches and bunkers only a few hundred metres apart at the closest. From a wooden tower rising out of a cluster of old Soviet-built shelters for fighter bombers, the alliance commander, Nadir Khan, surveys the entire frontline running across the southern end of the Shomali plain, a green bowl in a rim of mountains. He has a single walkie-talkie to communicate with his soldiers in the trenches, and an ancient pair of Soviet binoculars. Around the tower is his eclectic arsenal – a single T54 tank, a rocket launcher cannibalised from a Soviet helicopter gunship, a heavy machine gun and a mortar. He wears a green *shalwar kameez*, the pyjama-like traditional dress of the Afghans, and flip-flops.

In the evening, Commander Khan's force is strengthened by men slowly bicycling up to the frontline, having spent the day working in the fields. Meanwhile, dozens of Taliban cars bring troops from Kabul to the front for the night. Despite the US bombing, the Taliban are confident enough to leave their headlights on. They twinkle clearly in the darkness, slow, easy targets, but Commander Khan's men do not shoot.

Yesterday afternoon, at the foot of the mountains to the Taliban's rear, dozens of jeeps and trucks could be seen, kicking up huge trails of dust. They lumbered along temptingly, taking half an hour to cross the horizon, yet still Commander Khan's men held their fire. It must have been a touchy subject, since when he was asked why, Commander Khan gave many different answers. 'If we hit and destroy ten trucks, they'll still have enough to supply their troops,' was his first, unconvincing suggestion. Then, with a laugh, he asked why he should risk the lives of his men when the Americans were going to win the war for the alliance anyway.

Commander Khan's third explanation as to why his men let the Taliban drive to and fro in full view, in range, with impunity, was that he could not risk drawing fire while a foreign journalist was present. His fourth sally: 'Our links with the artillery are not so good. If we ask them to fire at the trucks, it's a very imprecise business, and they often miss, so it's just a waste of ammunition.' Finally, he came up with an explanation which got to the nub of what is, after all, a civil war, where the lines between enemy and friend are more fluid than glib characterisations of Taliban versus alliance would suggest.

'These trucks, they don't just supply goods to the Taliban,' he said. 'They also supply us. During the day they supply the Taliban, and at night they smuggle goods to us across no man's land on donkeys and camels.'

Later, as if covering himself, he ordered Captain Merzagol to drive the tank up a ramp and fire three deafening rounds at two trucks scurrying back towards Kabul. The shells fell astride the vehicles, missing them by several hundred metres. Commander Khan seemed relieved. Captain Merzagol's tank has not been on exercise. He admitted he had no training in manoeuvring the ancient vehicle and that he had not seen the commander of his tank unit for almost three weeks. He also said he had exactly 900 litres of fuel – not much for a tank that uses ten litres for every kilometre it travels.

We eavesdropped on a radio conversation between a Taliban and an alliance commander. The Taliban side was thanking the alliance for returning to them a soldier they had captured, and for treating him so well.

'He's very grateful,' said the Talib. 'He'd like you to come and visit us.'

'No, you come and visit us,' said the alliance commander.

'What's the bazaar like there?'

'It's good. What's it like in Kabul?'

'Even better.'

'Aren't you afraid of the bombs?'

'We were afraid on the first day, but we're not any more.'

In a recent attempt to bring the two sides of the alliance forces together, military officials gathered several hundred irregulars like Commander Khan's men together, handed out new uniforms and announced that from now on, they were to behave like regular soldiers, staying in barracks and subject to military discipline. The irregulars crowded around the alliance officer responsible, Mohammed Aref, and bombarded him with questions.

'We can't be in the barracks every day. We have to work,' said one.

'Why aren't you giving us boots?' asked another.

'What about pay?' asked a third.

The officer was patient and anxious. 'We know we can't make regular troops out of them straight away, but we can give them uniforms,' he explained. 'This is just the first day.'

28 November 2001

LUKE HARDING

Mazar-i-Sharif

The spectacular revolt of Taliban prisoners in the fort in Mazar-i-Sharif finally ended last night when troops used a tank to kill the remaining hardliners who had improbably survived repeated American air strikes on their basement hideout.

Early yesterday, US planes blasted the mini-citadel inside the fort where the Taliban's foreign fighters had been holed up for the past two days. Incredibly, some survived. At 8 a.m. they even launched a counterattack, shooting dead several soldiers who had been sniping at them from ramparts.

Government troops blasted the Taliban with mortars, rockets and withering gunfire. By mid-afternoon, only three of the 400-odd foreign prisoners who had originally stormed the castle on Sunday were still alive. They refused all offers of surrender, shouting: 'You are American people! We won't surrender to you!'

Soldiers advised by British SAS and US Special Forces officers then poured oil into the thick-walled house where the Taliban were hiding. They set light to it. The last three fighters, by now armed only with a machine gun and a Kalashnikov, were forced upstairs. At 3.30 p.m. a tank roared into the citadel, crushing the bodies of several Pakistani and Arab Taliban volunteers lying in the way. It fired four rounds in quick succession at the Taliban's hideout from a distance of only twenty metres. The shells obliterated the building; then there was silence.

Last night a government commander, Kalaji, confirmed that the Taliban had been wiped out. 'We have checked all the rooms and there is no one left. We are checking again in case one or two people have survived, but this is unlikely.'

Witnesses who peered into the verdant compound filled with trees described scenes of carnage. They said hundreds of bodies were lying around the courtyard. The larger outer part of the fort was yesterday strewn with dust, empty rocket shells and bullet-raked remains of cars.

An errant American bomb had punched a vast gap in the castle's twenty-foot outer wall, flipping over a government tank. The bomb, dropped on Monday morning, completely missed its target – ploughing straight into the battlements where government soldiers were standing. At least six were killed. Several American officers were also badly injured.

Yesterday one soldier, Shafiq, said the Taliban's best foreign fighters were Chechen. 'The Chechens were fighting better than the Pakistanis,' he said. 'They can fight with every kind of weapon.'

Three Pakistani Taliban escaped from the nineteenth-century fort on Monday night by scrambling out of a water channel. Two were shot dead immediately, but a third got as far as the nearby mud-walled village of Sar-i-Pool. There, local people discovered him and killed him. He had some bread in his pocket, they said.

The British and American Special Forces who masterminded the operation had arrived at the castle, the Qala-i-Jhangi, soon after breakfast. The SAS, wearing jeans, jumpers and Afghan-style headscarves slipped into the compound in two white Land Rovers. The Americans were easier to spot and wore desert khaki uniforms and black woolly hats.

Sources last night said that the Special Forces had not joined in the attack against the Taliban's position, but had called in the air strikes. It was not clear whether the body of a CIA agent killed on Sunday by the prisoners had been retrieved from the compound. Witnesses said the riot broke out when the prisoners spotted the agent and another colleague, Dave, who apparently shot dead three Taliban before escaping.

The air strikes by a low-flying AC-130 gunship early yesterday played a decisive role in bringing the stand-off to an end by destroying the citadel's armoury. Flames billowed into the darkness as the depot full of mines, rocket launchers and explosives blew up. Once the Taliban ran out of mortars, it was possible to send in the tank that finished them off.

But the human price of what can only be described as an avoidable fiasco was measured yesterday in bodies carried out of the crumbling front gateway in blankets and on makeshift wooden pallets. The corpses of at least ten Uzbek troops belonging to the castle's occupant, the Northern Alliance warlord General Rashid Dostum, were carried out. Several died yesterday morning when the Taliban prisoners staged an attack.

'From our group, two are injured and two are missing,' Kabir, a 24-year-old Hazara soldier said. An elderly man added: 'One of my nephews is dead. I'm very sad. I would like to see his body.' Several wounded soldiers, dripping blood on to the dirt, were bundled into yellow taxis and driven away. As bullets twanged overhead, other troops nonchalantly munched on American ration packs of peanut butter and biscuits.

Gen Dostum, who negotiated Kunduz's surrender with the Taliban's other commander, Mullah Fahzel, returned to Mazar yesterday from his frontline position in the mountainous desert overlooking Kunduz. His troops disarmed hundreds more Taliban prisoners and bundled them into open trucks. The authorities are expected to re-open the Qala-i-Jhangi today after checking the bodies of the dead foreign fighters for booby traps. The bodies will then be handed over to the International Committee for the Red Cross. 'We need to make sure there is nobody pretending to be dead,' said one soldier, Shafiq.

25 January 2002

JULIAN BORGER

Guantanamo Bay

From one hundred yards – the closest civilians are allowed to venture – Camp X-Ray looks like a particularly densely packed zoo, its 2.5 metre cages arranged in tight metal blocks and its inmates all but invisible except for the occasional flash of orange through the wire. With the help of binoculars, some of the detainees could be seen slumped motionless in the corner of their pens. The only apparent sign of life was on the west side of the cell block where the prisoners were trying to fix their sheets to the chain link walls of their cages to take the edge off the intense evening sun, and were arguing with the guards, who wanted to keep them in sight, over how high they could hang these makeshift blinds.

In six plywood watchtowers positioned along the outer ring of two perimeter fences, snipers trained their rifles on these encounters, as if the detainees might break through the wire with their bare hands and mount a mutiny. It may not be torture, but the cramped metal cages baking in tropical heat in the US base in Guantanamo Bay seemed to belong to another more brutal era. This is a sort of Caribbean gulag, and without doubt the scene would raise concern if it were being run by any other country.

The man in charge of the camp, Brigadier General Michael Lehnert, has said that he will review procedures so as not to subject prisoners 'to more unnecessary handling than we absolutely have to'. The General made it clear, however, that 'security trumps everything'.

Security. The word upon which the entire US penal system is built. The word which in American penal thinking stands far, far ahead of that other word: rights. And so the General talked about security. Without blacked-out goggles, he argued, the prisoners would see the exposed hydraulics and electric cables in the military transport planes in which they are flown out of Afghanistan and possibly try to cut them.

Colonel Terry Carrico, the head of the camp's internal security force, said the blindfolds were necessary on the way from the plane to Camp X-Ray so that detainees are not given the opportunity to 'case' their surroundings. Asked what he would do if ordered to remove the goggles he said: 'If I thought it was going to jeopardise the security of my people, I'd speak out. But after that, I'd say "Yes Sir!" I'm a soldier.'

The guards at Camp X-Ray – who live in a corner of Cuba made American with a McDonald's and a bar-and-grill – are thinking constantly about security too. They have been informed that with this group of prisoners anything is possible. One inmate had already announced his intention, in accented but clear English, that he would kill an American before leaving Guantanamo Bay. A few days earlier a detainee being taken to the toilet in shackles had lunged head first at one of his guards and taken a bite out of his forearm.

'It makes you think what can happen,' said Fabian Rivas, part of the Texas-based military police unit guarding the camp. 'Walking through, I'm kind of scared. These people have trained at one point in their lives to give up their lives to take yours.'

About twenty guards had been lined up outside the camp for interviews. Most were young and shy, flown in suddenly from Fort Hood in Texas, and were wary of publicity, especially in the presence of journalists from Britain, a country whose press they had been told had labelled them as torturers. Almost all of them insisted that conditions for the 158 inmates were better than their own.

'Honestly, they have it better than we do. Their chow is hot,' said Staff Sergeant Monte Webster. 'And it's much cooler down here than up in our tents.'

Between two of the cell blocks is a strip of open ground where the notorious picture was taken showing inmates kneeling in blindfolds and masks, causing outrage and allegations of torture that swept through Britain and much of the rest of Europe.

The guards at Camp X-Ray are incredulous at the furore. Through their security-tinted glasses, they cannot see any cause for concern. The prisoners were being processed on arrival from Afghanistan, they said, and were only there for a few minutes. They had been told to kneel or sit.

'I think it's partially for their own safety. When I fly I get really disoriented, and I have to sit down for a while normally,' said Private Emily Monson. 'I believe that they are treated better here than they were where they came from.'

Camp X-Ray sits in a small valley scooped out from dusty brown hills in the dry south-eastern corner of Cuba. The sun beats down on the tin roofs of the cells and throws dazzling reflections off the bright razor wire on the twin perimeter fences. On one side of the main cell block is a cluster of olive-drab tents where the inmates are initially processed on arrival and where the Red Cross is now holding interviews with the prisoners. On the other side, a new block of sixty cells has been completed, and a few yards further on another is under construction. Beyond the western perimeter fence a group of five windowless plywood huts have just been built for the interrogation of prisoners. The 'interviews', as the camp authorities prefer to call them, have already begun. Inmates who have been questioned are separated from the others so that they cannot compare notes.

The others live cheek by jowl in their pens, and much of the day is spent, the guards said, in constant chatter and railing against their fate. According to the interpreters at the base some have cried and bewailed the fact that their fathers had no idea where they were.

'People are asking after their fathers,' said Colonel Carrico. 'If they want someone to know where they're at it's their father, not their mother.'

The guards say that a handful of the inmates speak fluent English and try to engage them in conversation.

'They'll say to us "How are you doing? What's going on?"' said Staff Sergeant Webster. 'We try not to respond. We don't want them to think there's going to be any complacency.'

He could not say whether any of the detainees had British accents: the guards have been instructed not to disclose details of nationality.

Every prisoner has been given his own Koran in Arabic and English, and there is a green-and-white painted sign nailed to a telegraph pole above the camp pointing the way to Mecca. General Lehnert has also agreed to paint green lines on the concrete floor showing the correct direction for prayer.

Yesterday, for the first time, a US military cleric, Lieutenant Abuhena Saiful-Islam, attended dawn prayers with the prisoners and claimed they 'were very appreciative of the efforts we are taking'.

Torture, no. But it was hard to picture the disconsolate orange overalls hunched up in their cages as anything approaching 'appreciative'.

14 December 2001

MARTIN WOOLLACOTT

What Afghanistan means for the Middle East

If there were such a thing as a radical Islamist headquarters intent on a strategic response to reverses in Afghanistan, we would have to conclude that it is enjoying a degree of success. Palestinians and Israelis are in an even worse confrontation than before, with the secular Palestinian nationalists caught in a tightening vice between the Sharon government and the Islamist movements. Western countries slip nervously from one terror alert to the next. And now it looks as if war has been carried to yet another capital with yesterday's suicide attack on the Indian parliament buildings. It only needs a bomb in Moscow or Beijing – perhaps planted by comrades of the Uighur al-Qaida men whose handover from Afghanistan China demanded this week – to round out a dark picture.

The tanks around Yasser Arafat's Ramallah office focus attention on the leader's plight, which is assumed to be that he is being forced to declare war on the Islamist movements. But the other old man, Ariel Sharon, may be hiding behind his reputation for unhinged belligerence his real plan of reducing the territories to a series of controllable slices ultimately supposed to be run, after cleaning up all the terrorists, by compliant local leaders.

Six months ago, sitting in his rooms overlooking the Arafat compound, the Palestinian analyst Khalil Shikaki identified this option as one which attracted Sharon, based on what he called the worst kind of 'Israeli orientalist thinking'. There may also be method to the madness of 'targeted interceptions'. The assassinations ensure, if that were needed, that Hamas and Islamic Jihad will mount operations which justify more and more Israeli incursions into Palestinian territory. And, even as they create new recruits for the extremist organisations, they are removing the limited cadre of experienced leaders. If this is the plan, then Yasser Arafat is indeed irrelevant to the Sharon government's purposes.

Whether Ariel Sharon has a plan or not, and even accepting that he is not solely to blame, the results are obscene. The suffering of Palestinians worsens by the day; hardly anyone escapes it, and it inevitably breeds a desire for vengeance. The suffering of Israelis, less universally experienced, is sharp enough. For them, violence is an interruption in what is still on the surface a more or less affluent, comfortable and normal life, while for most Palestinians such a life hardly exists at all. That, of course, is no comfort for those Israelis who lose their loved ones. Then there is the impact on attitudes throughout the Muslim world. How can anyone in Washington or anywhere else expect to win hearts and minds while a war of this kind goes on in the territories? Not the hearts and minds of those who are already committed but of those ready to listen?

What is happening can, some claim, be painted as a retreat punctuated by a few rearguard actions. Terrorists have been defeated in Afghanistan and are now being shown that they will not get their way in the territories, in Kashmir or anywhere else. The big cancers are being hacked out and the smaller growths will be identified and removed over the next few years. In Washington there are those who believe that the 'demonstration effect' of American victory in Afghanistan will be profound. Arabs and other Muslims have registered American power and determination and it will change the way they see the world. The trouble is that the attempt to create a shining tale of heroes and martyrs is a fundamental part of what is going on. Some of these enterprises do not need to be successful, in any ordinary military sense, to do what they are mainly intended to do. Israelis often saw themselves, or were accused by others, of 'creating facts on the ground'.

This kind of warfare, by contrast, while it aims eventually to undo those facts, is aimed for now at 'creating facts in the mind', at changing the way in which Muslims interpret events. For that purpose blows against the enemy – including the killing of civilians, heroic failures, martyrdoms and last stands – will serve very well. True, the speed with which the Taliban disintegrated under American bombs and with which the al-Qaida fighters are now disappearing into Pakistan does not quite fit that bill. But the past shows how easily the facts can be rearranged, particularly if the intended audience is inclined to disbelieve Western statements, the accounts of Western media and even, sometimes, the evidence of their own eyes and ears.

Establishing what degree, if any, there was of direction, common planning, or common purpose linking Kashmir with the West Bank, Somalia with Chechnya, or al-Qaida with a range of other radical groups, was recognised from the start as the most important of questions. To the extent that there were some connections, that had to be recognised. After all, the West looked the other way while an initially small extremist movement, basing itself in Afghanistan, radicalised three wars which had previously been mainly national conflicts, those in Afghanistan itself, in Kashmir and in Chechnya.

But the rub was that if the United States and others, including the European countries, Russia, India and China, made too much of any links they would be doing Osama bin Laden's work for him. They would be consolidating diverse Muslim movements of protest, religious purification and violent opposition to non-Muslim rulers into something like the single uprising which he wanted, or at least creating a single drama in the minds of millions of already disturbed onlookers.

Far better to concentrate on what was local and unique, including possible solutions, than to lump everything together under the single label of 'terrorism'. What was needed, according to Jonathan Randal, the distinguished American journalist who has thought a great deal about the interaction between American policy and Middle Eastern societies, was akin to needlepoint, taking painstaking account of every difference in each country and situation.

Some common planning or inspiration, it might be guessed, links the al-Qaida rump with Kashmir and thus with Delhi. None, or very little, links it with events in the territories. Even where there may be some connections, an independent dynamic drives the different conflicts. But that they are joined in the world of images and dreams is indisputable. The campaign against terrorism, supposed to be conducted with skill and sensitivity, is in danger of becoming a hostage to Ariel Sharon and his cruel and unworkable ideas about the relationship between Israelis and Palestinians.

It is true that there is no simple chain of blameworthy actions that led to this deterioration. But the United States will be making a mistake that goes beyond Israel and the territories and will affect its wider purposes for the worse if it allows itself to be pulled into Sharon's slipstream.

22 October 2001

DAVID GROSSMAN

An Israeli diary

Saturday, 13 October: Saturday is a great day to get your bomb shelter in order. As my wife and I try to evacuate all the junk that has piled up there since the last time we feared a war (it wasn't that long ago, just a year back, when the intifada broke out), my small daughter is busy making up the list of friends she wants to invite to her birthday party. A weighty question: should she invite Tali, who didn't invite her to her birthday? We discuss the problem, trying to mobilise all the gravity it deserves, just so that we can at least keep up an appearance of routine. The terrorist attacks in the United States robbed us of our illusion of routine, of the possibility of depending on some sort of logical continuity. A thought is always hovering in the air: who knows where we will be a month from now?

We already know that our lives will not be as they were before 11 September. When the World Trade Center towers collapsed a kind of deep, long crack appeared in the old reality. The muffled thunder of everything that might burst through it can be heard through the crack – violence, cruelty, fanaticism, madness. All is suddenly possible. The new situation has let loose the human temptation to destroy, to raze, to dismember every living thing, from the individual human body to society, law, state and culture. The wish that we might keep what we have, keep up a daily routine, suddenly seems exposed and vulnerable. The effort to maintain some sort of routine suddenly seems so touching, even heroic – to keep family, home, friends together (we decide to invite Tali).

Sunday: I'm lucky that the suggestion that I write this diary came as I was beginning a new story. If it weren't for that I'm afraid that my diary would have been quite melancholy. Several months have gone by since I finished my previous book, and I felt that not writing was having a bad effect on me. When I'm not writing, I have a feeling that I don't really understand a thing. That everything that happens to me, all events and statements and encounters, exist only one beside the other, without any full contact between them. But the minute I begin writing a new story, everything suddenly gets intertwined into a single cord; every event feeds into and charges all other events with vitality. Every sight I see, every person I meet is a hint that has been sent to me, waiting for me to decipher it.

I'm writing a story about a man and a woman. That is, it began as a short story about a man alone, but the woman he met, who was supposed to be just a chance passer-by who listens to his story, suddenly interests me no less than he does. I wonder if it is correct, from a literary point of view, to get so involved with her. She changes the centre of gravity of the story I had wanted. She disrupts the fragile balance that the story requires. Yesterday night I woke up thinking that I ought to take her out entirely and replace her with a different character, someone paler who wouldn't overshadow my story's protagonist. But in the morning, when I saw her in writing, I just couldn't part with her. At least not until I get to know her a little better. I wrote her all day.

It is now almost midnight. When I write a story, I try to go to sleep with one unfinished idea, an idea I haven't got to the bottom of. The hope is that at night, in my dreams, it will ripen. It is so exhilarating and rejuvenating to have a story help extricate me from the dispassion that life in this disaster area dooms me to. It is so good to feel alive again.

Monday: I keep reading hostile remarks about Israel in the European press, even accusations that Israel is responsible for the world's current state. It infuriates me to see how eagerly some elements use Israel as a scapegoat. As if Israel is the one simple, almost exclusive reason that 'justifies' the terrorism and hatred now targeted against the West. It is also astounding that Israel was not invited to participate in the anti-terrorism coalition, while Syria and Iran (!) were.

I feel that these and other events (the Durban Conference and its treatment of Israel; anti-Israeli Islamic incitement and racism) are causing a profound realignment in Israelis' perceptions of themselves. Most Israelis believed that they had somehow broken free of the tragedy of Jewish fate. Now they feel that that tragedy is once again encompassing them. They are suddenly aware of how far they still are from the Promised Land, how widespread stereotypical attitudes about Jews still are, and how common anti-Semitism is, hiding all too often behind a screen of (ostensibly legitimate) extremist anti-Israel sentiments.

I am highly critical of Israel's behaviour, but in recent weeks I have felt that the media's hostility to it has not been fed solely by the actions of the Sharon government. A person feels such things deeply, under the skin. I feel them with a kind of shiver that percolates down to the cells of my most primeval memories, to the times when 'the Jew' was not perceived as a human being of flesh and blood but was rather always a symbol of something other. A parable, or a metaphor that makes one's skin crawl. Last night I heard the host of a BBC programme end his interview with an Arab spokesman with the following remark (I'm quoting from memory): 'So you say that Israel is the cause of the troubles that are poisoning the world today. I would like to say good night to our studio audience.'

Tuesday: For two weeks already there has been a decline of sorts in the level of violence between Israel and the Palestinians. The heart, so accustomed to disappointments, still refuses to be tempted into optimism, but the calm allows me to get absorbed in writing without pangs of conscience.

The woman in my story is becoming more and more of a presence. I haven't the slightest idea where she is leading me. There is something bitter and unbounded about her that frightens and attracts me. There is always that great expectation at the beginning of every story – that the story will surprise me. More than that, I want it to actually betray me; to drag me by the hair and absolutely against my will into the places that are most dangerous and most frightening for me; to destabilise and dissolve all the comfortable protections of my life; to deconstruct me, my relations with my children, my wife and my parents; with my country, with the society I live in, with my language.

It is no wonder that it is so hard to get into a new story. The soul is alarmed. The soul – like every living thing – seeks to continue in its movement, in its routine. Why should it take part in this process of self-destruction? What is bad about the way it is? Maybe this is why it takes me such a long time to write a novel. As if in the first months I have to remove layer after layer of cataract from my recalcitrant soul.

Wednesday: 'The only one smiling is the one who hasn't heard the latest news.' So wrote Bertolt Brecht. At 7.30 in the morning the radio reports the attack on Israeli government minister Rehavam Zeevi. He was one of the most extreme Israeli politicians regarding the Palestinians. I never agreed with his opinions, but such an act of terrorism is horrible and has no justification. That is also my opinion when Israel murders a Palestinian political figure.

Of course, Israel and every other country has the right to defend itself when a terrorist bearing a 'ticking bomb' is on his way to attack. Rehavam Zeevi, despite his views, was not such a terrorist.

The heart fills with apprehension – who knows how the situation will deteriorate now? Over the last two days there was relative calm, and we were almost bold enough to resume breathing with both lungs. Now, all at once, it's as if the trap has closed in on us again. I am reminded how easily we can be overcome by the terrible lightness of death (as I write I have the feeling that I am documenting the last days before a great catastrophe).

Still, last night I had a small, private moment of comfort. As on every Tuesday,

I studied with my *hevruta*. It is two friends, a man and a woman, with whom I study Talmud, Bible and Kafka and Agnon. The *hevruta* is an ancient Jewish institution. It is a way of studying together and sharpening the intellect through debate and disputation. During our years of study together we have developed a kind of private language of associations and memories. I am the non-religious one of the three, but I have already had ten years of vibrant, exciting and stormy dialogue with these soul friends. When we study, I become intimately connected to the millennia-long chain of Jewish thinkers and creators. I reach down into the foundations of the Hebrew language and Jewish thought. I suddenly understand the code hidden in the deep structure of Israel's social and political behaviour today. Within the sense of confusion and loss that encompasses me, I suddenly feel I belong.

Thursday: It is all falling apart. Israeli forces are entering the Palestinian city of Ramallah. A day of combat. Six Palestinians are killed, a ten-year-old girl among them. Another of the victims was a senior official of Fatah, the majority Palestinian faction, who was responsible for the murder of several Israelis. An Israeli citizen was killed by Palestinian gunfire coming from the village of another, previously killed, Fatah operative. The fragile ceasefire is no more, and who knows how long it will take to reinstate it?

I call one of the people I can share my gloom with at such a moment: Ahmed Harb, a Palestinian writer from Ramallah, a friend. He tells me about the shooting he hears. He also tells me of the optimism that prevailed among the Palestinians until the day before yesterday, before Zeevi's murder. 'Look how the extremists on both sides are co-operating,' he says. 'And look how successful they are . . .' On Tuesday Israel lifted its siege of Ramallah for the first time in weeks. After Zeevi's assassination the roadblocks returned. I ask him if there is something I can do to help him, and he laughs: 'We just want to move. To be in motion. To leave the city and come back . . .'

Between the news bulletins, among the ambulance sirens and the helicopters that relentlessly circle above, I try to isolate myself, to battle to write my story. Not as a way of turning my back on reality – reality is here, no matter what; it is like an acid that eats away any protective coating – but rather out of a sense that, in the current situation, the very act of writing becomes an act of protest. An act of self-definition within a situation that literally threatens to obliterate me. When I write, or imagine, or create even one new phrase, it is as if I have succeeded in overcoming, for a brief time, the arbitrariness and tyranny of circumstance. For a moment, I am not a victim.

Friday: The week is coming to an end. Its events were so acute that I did not have time to write about many important things dear to me: about my son, who is writing a surrealist play for his high school drama club; about the soccer game we watched together on television, Manchester United vs Deportivo la Coruña (with Barthez's outrageous blunders); about my daughter, who is conducting a scientific study of her parakeet; about my eldest son, who is in the army and about whom I am anxious each and every moment. Also about our twenty-fifth wedding anniversary this week, celebrated this time with much concern – will we succeed in preserving this fragile and vulnerable family structure in the years to come?

So many cherished things and private moments get lost because of fear and violence. So much creative power, so much imagination and thought are today directed at destruction and death (or at guarding against destruction and death). Sometimes there is a sense that most of our energy gets invested in guarding the boundaries of our existence. I am afraid that if peace does not prevail here we will all gradually become like a suit of armour that has no knight inside.

9 April 2002

SUZANNE GOLDENBERG

Nablus

The stench of blood and rotting corpses carried far beyond the mosque where the bodies were laid out, tightly wedged together like firewood: young men, perhaps Palestinian fighters, and those with the sagging paunch of middle age.

At last, after five ferocious days of fighting in the vaulted stone alleyways of the old town, the Israeli army yesterday allowed Palestinian medical workers to take the sixty-two wounded to hospital and carry away the dead. Twenty-six corpses awaited them. Five had bled their lives away into the stained mattresses strewn beneath the chandeliers of the Jamal Bek mosque, which has been converted into a makeshift hospital and morgue.

Husam Juwahiri, the administrator of Rafidia hospital, the biggest in Nablus, said they had received thirty-five dead yesterday and thirty-four injured, thirteen of them in a critical condition. However, medical workers were prevented from reaching the dead and injured by Israeli snipers and tanks, and he believed many bodies were lying in the road.

'The first dead [man] was here on the first day, Wednesday,' said Nisar Smadi, a senior doctor. 'He was killed by a shortage of medicine. It was an abdomen wound.'

The frenzied evacuation began at sundown. Medics scrambled down a vast crater at the entrance to the old city or casbah, and stretcher-bearers collided in vaulted alleyways in a feverish effort to collect the dead before the Israeli army re-imposed its curfew. Most of the dead and wounded were men, cut down as the Israeli army blasted its way through the labyrinth of narrow lanes. The ground underfoot was littered with tank shells.

Water gushed from smashed pipelines; a child's lace-up black shoe lay abandoned. The corpses were stacked in a courtyard of the mosque. Some faces were blackened and pitted, apparently by an explosion. Blood curdled around mouths and seeped from gaping chest wounds. One wore the green bandana of Hamas around his neck, the face of another was masked with a black-and-white chequered *keffiyeh* or headdress, but it was impossible to say how many of the dead were Palestinian fighters and how many were civilians.

Yesterday was a turning point in the Israeli army's battle for Nablus. The city, the most populous in the West Bank, has a proud history of militancy and the lanes of its casbah, which are too narrow for some Israeli armoured vehicles, and three refugee camps are reckoned the toughest terrain the Israeli military will encounter on its offensive.

When the army entered Nablus last Wednesday and began the slow pincer movement towards the old casbah, Israeli military commentators said 'Now the real war has begun.' Yesterday it seemed as if the war may be ending as Israeli armour circled the casbah, and a soldier, reading in halting Arabic from a printed sheet, ordered the fighters holed up inside to surrender.

'The army of the Israeli occupation is surrounding the whole area,' the voice said. 'If anybody is harbouring any armed person, he should know the hand of the Israeli army can reach him anywhere.'

On Sunday, the hand of the Israeli army reached out for a five-day-old baby, Hala Amireh. The soldiers stormed the family's stone house in the afternoon, said her mother, Asma, perched on a cot in the mosque.

'The Israeli army came by and told us to get out of the house because they were going to blow it up.' The army later fired four rockets at the first floor of the home. 'All our rooms were destroyed.'

That was the threat hanging over all 30,000 residents of the casbah yesterday as the Israeli army tried to force a surrender. At first sight, it appeared the army was making headway. After a pounding from helicopter gunships and tanks, the fabled resistance of the old town appeared to be crumbling.

'The fighters are taking shelter in the old city,' said Walid Jardeh, a taxi driver who lives at the heart of the casbah, 'but when you are talking about tanks and bullets raining down in buckets, the only one that can help them is God.'

At sixty Mr Jardeh is too old to be of interest to the Israeli army; yesterday's surrender demand applied to men aged eighteen to forty. By mid-afternoon, about 150 men had trudged up the dusty road towards the Israeli armoured vehicles. They filed out two by two, a large group at first of about fifty men, hands behind their heads, followed by stragglers in groups of fifteen or twenty.

On a stairway leading up from the casbah another file of men formed – some young, some old. A few fluttered white handkerchiefs for safety. They said they came out because of Israeli army threats to blow up their houses. But while the surrender is beginning, few Palestinians believe the battle for the old city is over. They say most of the men who surrendered were ordinary civilians and that further desperate days of fighting lie ahead.

After dark, the Israeli army pursued its campaign of 'softening up' the casbah for its final fall, and several explosions ripped through the night.

'No, it is not finished,' said Futnah Masrujeh, a medic at the mosque. 'Tonight, they say they are going to destroy the whole area, and you know these houses are so old. If you touch even one house, you will destroy the whole area.'

9 April 2002

LEADER

Stand up to Sharon

Ignoring American, European and regional demands to desist, Israel continues to pursue a campaign of terror across the Palestinian territories. Some sensitive souls might prefer to describe Ariel Sharon's actions as a defensive security sweep, as a targeted military operation or, more fashionably, as a legitimate contribution to the wider 'war against terrorism'. But when civilians are killed or wounded in their hundreds, when a generation of children is traumatised, when the feeble structures of nascent Palestinian statehood are systematically destroyed, when a whole people is corralled, penned in, humiliated and denied basic human rights, when even the holiest of religious shrines is transformed into a battlefield, when hatred and revenge, individual and collective, replace reason and decency as the fount of government policy, and when hope is daily blindfolded, placed before a wall and coldly executed, what other word is there for this than 'terror'?

In fighting terrorists in this way, Israel has crossed a line no democratic government should cross. By its actions it weakens Palestinian rejectionist groups. But the suicide bombers, far from being defeated by such means, will likely become more numerous. By their rockets and tanks, they weaken and subvert Yasser Arafat's authority. Yet paradoxically, in theory at least, they want a stronger Palestinian leader to curb the extremists. By their ill-considered, indiscriminately brutal tactics they betray the duties and responsibilities of democratic leadership, they forfeit much of their claim to moral justification, and they weaken and undermine the legitimacy of Israel's historic case. No reasonable person any longer denies Israel's right to exist. Why, then, does Israel's prime minister seek to deny that same right to Palestine? Mr Sharon can huff and puff, as he did in the Knesset yesterday, vaguely proposing talks with Arab moderates and toying with Saudi Arabia's peace ideas. But for an appalled, watching world, Israel has a prior duty: to back off and get out – and forget all talk of 'buffer zones', too.

That Israel has been provoked, repeatedly and egregiously, is plain. That its own civilians have suffered terribly and horrifically is evident. That it has a right of self-defence, that it has a right to be angry, that for nearly two years the wounds of its long-held, well-founded sense of victimhood have re-opened and festered is not in dispute. Yet it is Mr Sharon's peculiar genius, in dire national circumstances otherwise fully deserving of sympathy, constantly to transform Israel from righteous victim into unlawful aggressor. Mr Sharon never loses an opportunity to lurch into importunity; he always goes too far. Now, like a terrorist set to catch a terrorist, he has finally completed that desperate, dismal circle.

Judging by recent opinion polls inside Israel, such destructive, almost anarchic behaviour at the top is highly contagious lower down – and must perforce be quickly isolated. That is the main challenge that awaits the US Secretary of State, Colin Powell, when he arrives in Jerusalem later this week. Mr Powell has plenty of other things on his 'to do' list: he must convince a sceptical Arab world that US mediation is sincere; he needs to show Israelis that George Bush is serious in demanding a rapid military pullback; he must try to create momentum beyond yet another, inevitably shaky ceasefire towards a resumption of talks on the substantive issues of lasting peace. But first of all, Mr Powell, chief envoy of a nation solemnly dedicated to eradicating terror wherever it lurks, must tell Mr Sharon himself to eschew the paths of terrorism and return to his senses – or stand aside.

16 April 2002

SUZANNE GOLDENBERG

Jenin

A fortnight ago, before Israeli forces invaded, this was a crowded, bustling place. The narrow alleys between the cinderblock homes – spanning barely the width of outstretched arms – were packed with children.

Yesterday the Hart al-Hawashin neighbourhood, the heart of the Jenin refugee camp, was a silent wasteland, permeated by the stench of rotting corpses and cordite. The evidence of lives interrupted was everywhere. Plates of food sat in refrigerators in houses sheared in half by Israeli bulldozers. Pages from children's exercise books fluttered in the breeze.

In a ruined house the charred corpse of a gunman wearing the green bandana of Hamas lay where it fell, beside his ammunition belt. Electric cables snaked through the ruins. Alleys leading off the square deepened the image of wanton destruction: entire sides of buildings gouged out, stripped to the kitchen tiles like discarded dolls' houses. The scale is almost beyond imagination: a vast expanse of rubble and mangled iron rods surrounded by the gaping carcasses of shattered homes.

Yesterday the first definitive accounts of the battle of Jenin began to emerge as journalists broke through the Israeli cordon and gained access to the heart of the refugee camp. Palestinians describe a systematic campaign of destruction, with the Israeli army ploughing through occupied homes to broaden the alleys of the camp and make them accessible to tanks and vehicles.

But they also say the demolition campaign increased dramatically in the last two days of the battle for Jenin, with Israeli bulldozers exacting harsh retribution for the killing of thirteen Israeli soldiers last Tuesday.

'When the soldiers were killed, the Israelis became more aggressive,' said Ali Damaj, who lives on the eastern edge of the camp. 'In one night, I counted seventy-one missiles from a helicopter.'

For the Palestinians the battle for the Jenin refugee camp has become a legend. Before the last of the militants surrendered last Wednesday, the camp saw the bloodiest fighting of Israel's offensive on West Bank towns. The brutal close-quarters combat claimed the lives of twenty-three Israeli soldiers and an unknown number of Palestinians, civilians as well as fighters.

Palestinians accuse Israel of a massacre, and there are convincing accounts from local people of the occasional summary execution. However, there are no reliable figures for Palestinian dead and injured. The Red Cross carried away seven bodies yesterday, but the smell of rotting corpses remained.

'The soldiers had a map with them of the houses they wanted bulldozed and outlined them with a blue marker,' said Aisha Salah, whose house overlooks the field of destruction. 'You could see the houses, you could see the trees. It was a very detailed map. I could even find my own home.'

Ms Salah's home was occupied by Israeli soldiers who entered her living room by punching a hole through the neighbour's wall. Before they withdrew, one of the soldiers wrote a message on the wall in neat blue ink: *I don't have another land.*

A week ago, one of the Israeli soldiers bedded down in Ms Salah's house was shot in the face by a Palestinian sniper as he stood at the window. Two days later, thirteen Israeli soldiers were lured to their deaths in a nearby alley by a series of booby-trap explosives, then picked off by Palestinian gunmen.

'When there was resistance, especially after the thirteen soldiers were killed, I could see a lot more squares on the map,' said Ms Salah.

The systematic bulldozing of Palestinian homes began four days after Israeli forces blasted their way into the camp on the night of 3 April, strafing houses from helicopter gunships and pounding them with tank shells. Several civilians were killed in the initial assault, including Afif al-Dasuki. An elderly woman who lived alone, she was evidently too slow when the Israeli soldiers pounded on her door and asked her to open up. Her neighbours discovered her body a week after her death by the smell of decomposition, huddled behind the yellow-painted steel door with the large hole in the middle.

Four days later the army razed six houses in the Damaj neighbourhood on its eastern edges. They began with the house of Fatima Abu Tak, flattening homes on both sides of the street.

'When I saw the house of Ahmed Goraj collapse, there was a tremendous amount of smoke and dust. I never expected that the bulldozers would continue moving. I was in a state of shock,' said Mr Damaj, who fled to a neighbour's when his own home became dangerously unstable.

A few hours later soldiers entered the camp on foot, shooting their way between the cinderblock homes in groups of fifteen or twenty. Israeli soldiers injured in Jenin describe this as the most nerve-wracking part of the battle.

'They booby trapped every centimetre. In one metre you would find twenty small booby traps or a big balloon attached with a wire. Every metre was very dangerous,' said Dori Scheuer, who was shot in the stomach by a Palestinian gunman a week ago on Monday. 'It was much more dangerous for us than it was for them because they knew the territory.'

People in the camp say the capability of their fighters did not run much beyond pipe bombs packed with homemade explosives. However, the fighters were organised. Palestinians admit the camp was liberally mined two or three days before the assault, but the strategy failed because Israel had no compunction about razing homes to make roads for its tanks.

'The thing we did not count on was the bulldozer,' said Mr Damaj. 'It was a catastrophe. If the Israelis had only gone one by one inside the camp, they would never have succeeded in entering.'

After the thirteen soldiers were killed, Israel appears to have abandoned foot patrols. Instead, the army knocked down houses indiscriminately, creating a vast plaza of rubble in the centre of the camp, a crossroads for the tanks.

'They just started demolishing with people inside,' said Hania al-Kabia, a mother of six whose flat is on the edge of the lunar landscape. 'I used to hear them on the loudspeaker saying "Come out! Come out!" Then they stopped doing that, but they went on bulldozing.'

13 September 2002

LEADER

Saddam in his sights

George Bush's warning that military action against Iraq will be 'unavoidable' unless Saddam Hussein complies with all relevant United Nations obligations and ends the 'silent captivity of the Iraqi people' has begun a countdown to war. At the same time, by agreeing to argue his case before the UN general assembly and to seek a new security council resolution, the US president ceded some ground, albeit possibly symbolic, to European and Arab critics of his unilateralist approach. He left a slim opening for diplomacy to head off the catastrophe.

Mr Bush's list of Saddam's crimes, both of omission and commission, contained little that was new, although much that was repugnant. There is no doubt that this is a vicious dictatorship. There is no doubt that its human rights abuses are legion; that it has at one time or another threatened and attacked its neighbours; and that it has sought in the past to acquire the full, grisly range of modern weapons. What was signally lacking from Mr Bush's speech was any information showing how or why these abuses have suddenly grown more egregious or less tolerable than before; or demonstrating that Saddam's quest for weapons of mass destruction has yielded results that now – unlike, say, a year and a day ago – mean that he represents an urgent, potent threat to regional or US security. In other words, Mr Bush had the chance to answer the much-asked question 'Why now?' – and he dodged it.

The president's professed concern for the United Nations as an institution also carried a hint of the self-serving. That the United States is to rejoin Unesco is a welcome step. That it has increased its foreign aid budget and that Mr Bush understands the challenge presented by global poverty and education is indeed good news. Likewise, his decision to take his worries about Iraq before the United Nations – rather than ignore or bypass it – is heartening. Tony Blair worked hard to persuade the president to observe the diplomatic proprieties and his efforts – in the teeth of opposition from Dick Cheney and the defence secretary, Donald Rumsfeld – were not all in vain. Kofi Annan, too, has argued powerfully against states taking international law into their own hands.

But while Mr Bush is right to say that the UN's credibility will be undermined if its resolutions are ignored and its weapons inspectors remain excluded, the damage may be even greater if, faced ultimately by a United Nations that will not do its bidding, the United States goes ahead and attacks Iraq anyway. The damage will be far-reaching if America does not now apply the same standards of compliance to other states such as Israel, China, Russia and Turkey that have often and repeatedly defied the international community's will. The damage may be incalculable if, in the future, the United States continues to veto or block UN actions it does not welcome simply because they do not serve the narrow US national interest. Support for the UN's integrity cannot be selective. For Mr Bush and the United States, à la carte multilateralism is not an option.

In any case, the rigour and sheer sweep of US demands reinforce the impression that, for all the show of consultation and debate, Mr Bush is going through the motions. If all the United States now insists upon is to occur peacefully, Saddam effectively has no choice but immediately to depose himself and fly to The Hague. In search of allies and votes, Mr Bush made some conciliatory gestures in New York. But there was no mistaking his tone or intentions, no doubt that he expects to fight. If the other nations of the world want to stop him, they now have their chance – but they will have to be quick.

13 September 2002

POLLY TOYNBEE

The last emperor

There he stood, this unlikely emperor of the world, telling the UN's 190 nations how it is going to be. The assembled nations may not be quite the toothless Roman senate of imperial times, but at the United Nations the hyperpower and its commander-in-chief are in control as never before: how could it be otherwise when the US army is the UN's only enforcer? This is, President Bush said, 'a difficult and defining moment' for the United Nations, a challenge that will show whether it has become 'irrelevant'. He pointed his silver-tongued gun with some delicacy and a certain *noblesse oblige*, but there was no doubt he was holding it to the UN's head: pass a resolution or be bypassed.

It was a fine and gracious speech that might have been borrowed from better presidents in better times. He spoke of a just and lasting peace for Palestine. He promised a surprise return by the United States to Unesco. He spoke of the tragedy of world poverty, disease and suffering, of offering US aid, trade and healthcare. Earnest and uplifting, it was very like the speech he made soon after the twin towers attack last year. But how long ago that suddenly seemed. Back then the world tried hard to believe him, full of sympathy and hope that this earthquake had indeed turned him internationalist. But this time belief was stretched beyond breaking. The skills of the best speechwriter could not blot out the gulf between last year's rhetoric and the reality that followed.

Maybe it was the cut-away to Hamid Karzai in his green striped coat of many colours sitting in the chamber. It came as a sharp reminder of America's failure to invest in serious nation-building in Afghanistan, failure to send in enough troops to stop the old warlords seizing power again, the paucity of aid and the brazen carelessness once the war was won. So Bush's conjured images of a post-war Iraq, peaceful and democratic, sounded like empty phantasms. War in Afghanistan to oust the Taliban was necessary – but so was investing in long-lasting security and prosperity if he wanted to prove how democracy wins over fundamentalist fury. From Kyoto and Johannesburg, to the International Chamber of Commerce, steel tariffs, National Missile Defence and nuclear testing, too much has happened (or not happened) since last year's speech to take this one at face value.

Even so, good words are still preferable to bad ones. It was, after all, remarkable that the president was there in that chamber at all. A month ago the strident voices coming out of the White House would have none of it. The Rumsfeld/Cheney axis of war was in the ascendant, the United Nations was for wimps. The hawks would never have let their emperor stand there soliciting UN support in dulcet tones.

It would be nice to believe that Tony Blair played some part in strengthening the arm of the Colin Powell internationalists who won the argument on the need for UN legitimacy. Sadly, the prime minister features hardly at all in US commentators' accounts of the internal Republican rows that finally brought Bush to the United Nations. For a very little influence, Blair has paid a frighteningly high price: the split with the rest of Europe, weakening his own influence by becoming Bush's tool, never again an independent honest broker. At home there is angry puzzlement among many more in his own party than the usual suspects. Was it worth such damage? Only if, in the end, this war is successfully averted.

Even now, the drafters are working at a UN resolution to square (or fudge) the needs of the US war party with French and Russian hesitation. Deals are brokered, poor countries' arms are twisted with aid and trade while Russia may be allowed to kill a few more Chechens. But a deal there must be. The only ones who hope the United Nations fumbles are the Rumsfeld/Cheney warriors who want no straitjacket, no option for Saddam to avoid the war now sharpening its knives on his borders. Moving command headquarters from Florida to Qatar could hardly send a louder message: America wants war, America means war.

The only hope of avoiding it is that Saddam takes fright at a security council resolution with a firm time limit for the weapons inspectors to return – any time, any place or else, no run-around or obstruction. The message that America means war has been conveyed to him forcefully by everyone who has his ear, including the former weapons inspector Scott Ritter. The US sabre is out of its scabbard: just let him look Cheney and Rumsfeld in the eye. The world will hold its breath and hope he blinks or, better still, that he is overthrown by others who see what's coming.

For those who supported the wars in Afghanistan, Kosovo and Sierra Leone, the enslaved peoples of Iraq are no less just a cause. Once legitimised by the United Nations and international law, there is no moral difference in the need

to liberate Iraqis and relieve the potential threat Saddam poses to his neighbours. None would mourn his passing from power. The difference is pragmatic,
not moral. There were very good reasons why Bush senior did not march on
Baghdad in 1991, reasons that remain unchanged. Saddam's elite troops around
Baghdad would inflict very heavy casualties. In his death throes, he would certainly use anthrax and nerve gases. Iraq might fall apart, with Shi'ite lands
defecting to Iran, strengthening another vile regime, destabilising others. If
Afghanistan cannot hold US attention for one short year, how would far more
complex Iraq be nurtured long term? Fermenting terror, recruiting generations
of terrorists to come, the cure looks worse than the disease.

Curiously, the louder Bush and Blair call for an end to this villain, the less
convincing it sounds. Why now? That remains the perplexing question.
Containment works well: few observers think Saddam can launch anything
under present no-fly, daily bombing pressure. What is Bush's obsession? It
remains a mystery. It is not a vote-winner in the States where the danger looks
not clear and present, but cloudy and distant. The risks are frightening and the
costs staggering. Petrol prices rise while stock exchanges fall at the prospect. Oil,
say some, but if US companies want Saddam's oil, an oil-driven cynical administration could make peace not war and help themselves to fat contracts.

No, it appears to spring from a new ideology, a neo-conservative dream which
Charles Krauthammer, guru of the Right, calls the US's 'uniquely benign
imperium'. Hyperpower is not enough unless it is exerted so forcefully that no
state ever again challenges benign US authority. One thing was made crystal
clear yesterday – there is no other source of authority but America, and that
means there is no other law but US law. What the US wants, the UN had better
solemnise with a suitable resolution – very like the Roman senate and one of its
lesser god-emperors. But this is not the real America. A small, cultish sect is battling for the 'imperium' within this bizarre administration, resisted by mainstream Republicans – so what is Tony Blair doing in there with them?

THE POWER AND
THE GLORY

Steve Bell, 24 May 2002

The abrasion sustained by President Bush in his pretzel-induced fall (page 1 yesterday) was near his left eye, as the picture clearly showed, and not as the text contrarily suggested, under his right eye.

Corrections and Clarifications, 16 January 2002

27 December 2001

HUGO YOUNG

I thought I knew the United States

I've been coming to the United States for many years, and thought I knew it. I studied here, reported here, and have kept the fruit of those connections. I married an American, which surely took me closer to this place, and even more affectionately into its heart. So I possessed most of the materials necessary to read America. Yet it turns out I did not know it. This may be for a simple reason. Until 9/11 and the Afghan war, perhaps America did not fully know itself.

What's most striking to a frequent visitor, holed up for a white Christmas in Vermont, is not that America has changed. Everything about the place may remain much as you suspected. But it is all more so. Each virtue and each vice, if vices they can be called, declares itself without the ambiguities of before. I dare to generalise from a small corner. But the shock of this war, I'm guessing, has forced America, all across the continent, to think about itself more urgently: to show itself, to say without complication what it is.

Americans always were considerate. They're now super-caring for friends and neighbours. Wherever they lived, they shared the attack for which history had left them totally unprepared. Three months later, not one iota of the memory has been stoically sloughed off. The shock reached the depths of the national psyche and continues to reverberate there. The people still blunder about, unsure why it happened. Their response is to care and share more tenderly, more generously even than they used to.

Americans always were self-confident. The events of 9/11 summon them to greater displays than ever of this singular faculty. There's no whining, no trace of self-pity. Self-sufficiency is second nature. American certainties (so maddening to Osama bin Laden) are redoubled. All that three months have done, after the due period of solemnity, is to liberate the humorous dimension, allowing Garrison Keillor, the great radio raconteur, to make innumerable funny jihad jokes, which show that Islam has been de-listed from the scope of political correctness.

Americans always were patriotic. Flags hung in many yards on the dirt roads throughout the ten peaceful years I've been coming here. But now patriotism is a far more intense experience. Vermont sends to Washington the only congressman who calls himself a socialist, and has more than the usual quota of plain-speaking residents who retain a low regard for President George W. Bush. But their patriotic response to 9/11 is unquestioning. This is a locality with no tourists, and very local local papers. Yet it has discovered the world. When Hamid Karzai was sworn in as head of the interim council to govern Afghanistan, it made the lead in the *Valley News*, White River Junction, which also had a down-page item on Yasser Arafat's pledge to pay a Christmas Eve visit to Bethlehem.

But I don't take this as evidence of a new internationalism reaching into the most obscure by-ways of America. It shows, though, that when the *patria* is under threat, Americans can shed their indifference to the world the threat is coming from. In another part of the polity, Washington as much as Vermont, they lose their angst about America's role. America's role is to protect America against all comers. That's what patriotism means, and it's nothing to be ashamed of. It is all remarkably simple, the more so for never having been made so forcibly clear before.

Americans, however, as well as being patriots, were also always constitution- alists. And here the change is marked. Even my liberal Vermont acquaintances have only modest dislike for the military tribunals and other weapons against due process that Bush has assembled. They're not rising up against them. Aware of their sensitivities, the government cites Abraham Lincoln and Franklin Roosevelt as precedents to show that great men are allowed to abolish habeas corpus and free speech when the Republic is threatened. It seems to be enough, in this hour of crisis when Americans see themselves facing a danger their ances- tors did not experience.

I don't say that politics has ceased in this new America. There are familiar arguments about the Budget. There is a left and a right, just as there is in Europe, and they argue about roughly similar things, namely the size of the State and the level of taxation and the finer ideological points concerning how best to stimulate a flagging economy. There are big elections in 2002, and each side is manoeuvring for position in the great game of modern politics, which is less about claiming credit for success than disclaiming the blame for damage wreaked by forces beyond politicians' control.

But in the great abroad, politics virtually has ceased. Over that terrain America has become easy to lead. Alarmingly so. Even Vermonters who detest Bush are prepared to put their trust in him because the situation seems to offer them no other course. He vows to get the job done, that archetypal American phrase, and it is clearer than it has ever been, at least since 1945, exactly what the job is.

They talk jestingly about seeing us next year, 'as long as we haven't been blown to pieces'. The implication is that Armageddon could come from either side. But fate, they seem to think, has taken over. America must do what America must do, which is to extinguish al-Qaida from the face of the earth. American idealism, that fickle jade of post-war diplomacy, at last has a purpose everyone can agree on: the saving of America itself.

It is not clear what this will mean for the world. But it's clearer than it has been since Jefferson what the world means for America: safety from sea to shining sea, and maybe not beyond.

14 February 2002

LEADER

Bush's dangerous new doctrine

Across Europe a chorus of alarmed but mostly constructive criticism of George Bush's 'axis of evil' State of the Union speech continues to grow. First, there was

Javier Solana, the European Union's foreign policy chief, warning against the global unilateralism of the American leader's conflation of Iran, North Korea and Iraq as his next targets. Then came Hubert Vedrine, foreign minister of France, soon echoed by his prime minister, Lionel Jospin, and then by the European foreign affairs commissioner Chris Patten. At the start of this week, Vladimir Putin chipped in, followed on Tuesday by the German foreign minister, Joschka Fischer. When such witnesses (all friends or would-be friends of America) make such points, they cannot be simply dismissed as the usual anti-American suspects. But, lest anyone still think that such views are confined to Europe, note that there are some very significant American voices of doubt too. Madeleine Albright, the former secretary of state, said last week that Mr Bush's 'axis of evil' notion made little sense. And the senate foreign relations committee chairman, Senator Joseph Biden, has cautioned that the three evil states are not allies, do not present equivalent threats, and have rightly been handled with very distinct foreign policy strategies by Washington in the past.

There is a significant empty chair in this increasingly large and harmonious chorus of concern. Almost alone among serious international leaders (a category from which the strident Italian leader Silvio Berlusconi naturally excludes himself), Tony Blair continues to believe that any public criticism of United States policy is self-indulgent and counter-productive. When the foreign secretary, Jack Straw, allowed himself to speculate – more in optimism than on any basis in fact – that Mr Bush's rhetoric might be a piece of mid-term electioneering, he was not just slapped down by the Bush administration itself but also by Downing Street, which regards all such apostasy as uniformly unhelpful and disloyal.

Mr Blair is in fact a friendly critic of American policy, but he believes that criticism of Washington can only take place in private between consenting adults, if at all. Whether Mr Bush really listens to Mr Blair is open to some doubt, not just in the light of speeches like the State of the Union, or of the continuing US neglect of the Middle East, but also of the *Washington Post*'s recent reconstructions of administration policy-making in the aftermath of 11 September, a process in which Mr Blair does not loom large and in which at one point Mr Bush reportedly said he did not want the allies making conditions.

'At some point we may be the only ones left,' says Mr Bush. 'That's OK with me. We are America.'

Well, we are not America. We are Britain. Our support for action against terrorism cannot be questioned, but our national interest is independent. It is not in our interest to reduce relations with Iran, North Korea, or even Iraq to the fight against terrorism. Still less is it in our interest to pretend that that these regimes can be dealt with only by overwhelming military means of the kind envisaged in Mr Bush's shocking new Pentagon Budget. These things need to be said from the position of credibility that this country possesses, and of which Rudolph Giuliani spoke in London yesterday. They need to be said for Britain's sake – and indeed for America's too. They need to be said by our government, and they need to be said, above all, by Mr Blair himself, who by his ill-judged silence risks more of his standing than he appears to recognise.

20 March 2002

JULIAN BORGER

Bin Laden slang

The attacks of 11 September have not led to the backlash of bigotry in US class-rooms that had been feared, but the national trauma has left at least one permanent mark in the playgrounds of America by reshaping teenage slang.

The putdown of choice these days is 'That's so September 10' – used on anyone obsessed with petty issues or behind the times. Another common insult is 'Osama Yo' Mama'. Unstylishly dressed girls may be asked 'Is that a burka?' Detention and other disciplinary measures are reported as 'total jihad'.

The new terror slang has surfaced in a survey by the Centre for the Study of Violence at Georgetown University, where Alan Lipman and his students have been interviewing teenagers to monitor the impact of 11 September.

'Kids are being scapegoated much less than had been expected,' said Dr Lipman. 'The degree of true hate-speech has been much lower than anyone had predicted.'

Many Muslim and Arab students have deflected attention by making jokes.

'They find a way of taking the experience of being in a negative spotlight, and take the power out of it,' Dr Lipman said.

Najwa Awad, a Palestinian-American pupil in Virginia, told the *Washington Post*: 'September 11 has been such a stressful thing that it's OK to joke a little bit.'

Among the other slang phrases reported are: 'firefighter cute' applied to boys; a touchy teacher is 'such a terrorist'; a messy bedroom is 'ground zero'; and very spicy food is 'weapons grade'.

13 March 2002

MATTHEW ENGEL

On the train to nowhere

The railways are a shambles. Decades of under-investment have come home to roost. The main company involved is effectively bankrupt. There is talk of breaking it up. The politicians have no idea what to do. Welcome to America.

Britain existed before the railways. The United States, as now constituted, did not and could not. If you stand in a small mid-western town of an evening – any evening, almost any town – when there is nothing to be heard on Main Street except the stray cats and the town drunk (a constitutional requirement), suddenly the silence will be severed by the most extraordinary set of noises. There will be roaring and clanking and a rush of wind as a freight train of almost infinite length comes through, accompanied by the unmistakable hoo-woo of the whistle. Half the history of the West is in the sound of the iron horse. And what a lonesome whistle it is these days.

For the role of the railroads (correct word in this context) is the reverse of Britain's railways. They move vast quantities of freight. But of the trillions of passenger miles undertaken by Americans every year, the train's proportion is so tiny, I dare not give you the figure for fear of mixing up the number of zeroes after the decimal point. Most Americans have never been on a passenger train. Millions will never have glimpsed one. I once asked a taxi driver in Maine if the town had a train station. 'How should I know?' he replied.

Anyone wishing to travel long-distance in a hurry goes by plane. Those with more time and less money go by Greyhound bus. The long-distance trains still cross the nation with names so evocative they can break your heart – the *Desert Wind*, the *Sunset Limited*, the *Southwest Chief*, the *Texas Eagle*, the *Empire Builder*, the *City of New Orleans* ('15 cars and 15 restless riders, 3 conductors and 25 sacks of mail'). But they are both expensive and slow, and are populated, in my experience, only by the leisured and the slightly cracked.

When the motor car was invented Americans fell in love and deserted the train like a middle-aged man leaving his first wife for a tart. But the infatuation is enduring, and the train is pensioned off and neglected. It's the pension that's now causing the problem. A nationalised corporation, Amtrak, runs all the trains on tracks owned by a hotchpotch of companies (again the effective reverse of the British situation). Amtrak gets $500 million a year at present but is meant to be subsidy-free by the end of this year. It has told the government that actually it needs to double the money just to keep going. That's gone down really well with the Bushies.

Only one major politician has ever shown much interest in the trains: Michael Dukakis, the beaten candidate for the presidency in 1988. The suspicion that Dukakis was the kind of person who liked trains helps explain why Americans refused to vote for him. He is currently Amtrak's chairman.

What Dukakis sensed was not that Americans ever could or would return to transcontinental rail travel, but that the major transport corridors of the country were actually made for the fast modern rail links that Europe has organised, and Britain plans and then screws up. It's 250 miles from New York to Washington via Philadelphia and Baltimore and a bit less to Boston.

Since 11 September fewer people have flown, and Amtrak has got extra passengers, especially on its north-eastern routes. It runs fast, regular trains with heaps of legroom and an electric socket by every seat: the ordinary seats are more comfortable than British first class. Unfortunately, the track is so clapped out that, though the trains can do 150 m.p.h., it still takes three hours plus from Washington to New York. Different set-up, same imbecilic lack of planning.

After the attacks, the aviation industry got a handout of $15 billion; Amtrak got $100 million, mostly for extra security in New York tunnels. The Americans are even missing the point about the British experience. The right wing is arguing that Amtrak should be privatised and broken up, supported by nonsense like a *New York Times* analysis last month claiming that British train 'ridership' had shot up because 'aggressive private operating companies have lowered fares and offered special promotions'.

People use British trains because the roads are so clogged; they are the least worst alternative. And for me, having left the country partly to avoid the possibility of one day strangling an employee of either Railtrack or Great Western, it is pretty galling to realise Britain is not the only country that is totally ludicrous on this subject.

7 March 2002

LARRY ELLIOTT

Trade war and the poor

Disastrous. Unacceptable. Deplorable. Regrettable. Wrong. George Bush was left in no doubt yesterday what the rest of the world thought of his decision to slap tariffs on imported steel into the United States. And with good reason. Mr Bush has risked a global trade war, embarrassed his political allies, poisoned attempts to launch a new round of trade talks and undermined the credibility of the multilateral trading system in order to pay off political debts to big business and perhaps win a couple of key states in the November mid-term elections. He may not even achieve that.

What Mr Bush has done is expose the hypocrisy that underpins the international trading system. Ever since 11 September the talk has been about making globalisation work for the poor. We now know – if we were ever in any doubt – that the reality is about how to make globalisation work for the rich.

The ramifications of Mr Bush's ill-judged move could be immense. For a start, the economics don't stack up. It will raise costs for the rest of US industry, it will not save a single job in Pennsylvania or Ohio and it will hold back recovery from the first synchronised global downturn in more than twenty-five years. It should be obvious to the White House that the rest of the world will only be able to buy American goods if they can sell into the US market.

Already there are signs of escalation. Europe's steelmakers were yesterday demanding instant retaliation and Moscow said the steel tariffs could affect relations between the two countries. Nor has it taken long for other sectors of US industry to wake up to the prospect that Mr Bush has taken the lid off the pork barrel. It was noteworthy that General Motors was talking yesterday of excess capacity in cars. If the US government can protect steel, then why not the auto sector? And if Detroit is to be protected, then why not the garment industry of South Carolina?

The impact on the multilateral trading system – still in intensive care as a result of the anti-globalisation backlash of the past three years – will also be profound. Washington and Brussels acted in concert last November to launch new trade liberalisation talks in Doha, cynically called a 'development' round. Many US industries – from Hollywood to the computer titans of Silicon Valley – want those talks to succeed, but the chances of an agreement any time soon have now receded drastically. Mr Bush has cut the ground from under Pascal Lamy, Europe's trade commissioner, who has done his best to be conciliatory and constructive in his dealings with the US. Washington's stock of goodwill in developing countries was already tiny. It is now non-existent.

If Mr Lamy has every reason to feel let down, then so too does Tony Blair, who has found that providing full-throated backing for the United States in its fight against terrorism counts for nothing when set against the interests of powerful vested interests in America. The prime minister is like the faithful family retainer who, after years of service, asks for a day off to see a sick relative and is greeted with utter disdain.

There are silver linings to this cloud. The first is that it has underlined the importance of a multilateral trading system. However flawed as an institution the World Trade Organisation might be, there is at least a body to which the rest of the world can appeal for legal redress following the US decision. The second is that Mr Bush has now illustrated that the real issue is not free trade but fair trade. Free trade is a myth.

20 March 2002

JONATHAN FREEDLAND

Love the United States, don't love Bush

On BBC TV's *Room 101* on Monday, Alexei Sayle made an unusual selection for the scrapheap. Along with Cirque de Soleil and the abuse of disabled drivers' permits, the comedian also consigned to fiery oblivion the general public – on the grounds that they were useless, carping and never came up with anything positive.

I beg to differ. When it comes to politics, the public often get it exactly right. On the current debate on Iraq and America, for example, the electorate is bang on. Look at yesterday's ICM/*Guardian* poll. A clear majority (51 per cent) oppose British backing for a US assault on Iraq, with only 35 per cent in favour. (Intriguingly, the most hawkish are Labour voters, with 43 per cent approving military action – a couple of points ahead of those hippy, peacenik pinkos who identify themselves as Conservatives.)

Glance next at one of those more general surveys that ask people to rank their favourite countries. Guess who comes top? The United States, by a country mile. When the *Observer* asked Britons last year where else they would most like to live, one in five named America – rising to one in four among the under-twenty-fours. For the public these two views are wholly compatible. They are against America's plans for Baghdad, but pro-America – all at the same time. No problem.

Yet, for some reason, this same feat of choreography seems to elude some of our finest thinkers and debaters. For them, you either support everything or you support nothing. If you oppose the policies of George W., then you are a vicious anti-American. Conversely, if you praise American values, then you're an apologist for every US excess – or inconsistent for failing to support every Washington action. Believe me, this either/or binary system really does apply: I have the e-mail avalanches to prove it.

So today I issue a plea, in defence of that little sliver of middle ground where I – and, apparently a good chunk of the public – want to stand. We want to be pro-America and anti-Bush. We want to applaud what the United States stands for, even as we express our dislike for this particular administration. This should not be brain surgery. No great intellectual agility is required to laud the founding ideals of the American republic while simultaneously lambasting Washington's current masters. You can admire the 1787 declaration that we, the people, should be sovereign – and still insist that bombing Iraq is not the best way to get at Saddam's weapons of mass destruction. No contradiction.

You can love the radical breakthrough represented by the US constitution, which codified and entrenched human rights in plain, accessible language – and still fear that the military pounding of Afghanistan was not the right way to disable the global network of al-Qaida, now active in an estimated fifty-nine other countries. No contradiction. Or you can marvel at the energy, can-do creativity and diversity of American society, much of it the fruit of the unique US constitutional set-up – and still lament the bellicose clumsiness of a phrase like 'axis of evil'. No contradiction.

Yet somehow this simple piece of footwork seems too tricky for some people. Condemn those three Bush actions and you will be branded a 'socialist European faggot' with a twisted hatred of the US (I'm quoting my e-mail pals).

That's at one end of the spectrum. But the other end appears similarly trapped.

Recent converts to the glories of the founding American idea seem to think they have to back the government because they admire the society. The group Tariq Ali brilliantly described on this page as the belligerati – Martin Amis, Salman Rushdie *et al* – have let their enthusiasm for the US culture of rights, democracy and innovation come over as a specific endorsement of current Bush strategy.

No such move is necessary. A neater stance is the one adopted by more than half of US voters in November 2000 (another case of the public getting it right). It is fair to say that all of those Americans were pro-America, but they preferred the Al Gore/Bill Clinton version to the George W. one. That's a legitimate position for outsiders, too: to admire the enduring US values of the eighteenth century, but to prefer a centre-left hue for today's republic.

But, as if to prove that no one is immune to the trap of either/or binary thinking, Tariq Ali refuses such a possibility. For him, as much as for President Bush, you are either with America or against it. It is 'a self-indulgence' he says, to want 'Clinton-as-Caesar' since it is support for the Empire itself that counts: who stands at the pinnacle is irrelevant.

That is flawed thinking on two counts. First, it plays to the worst kind of cynicism about democratic politics: that it doesn't matter who wins elections, they're all as bad as each other. In the case of recent US history such a view is badly at odds with the evidence. Bill Clinton's military interventions in Haiti and Kosovo, like his tireless efforts to broker peace in Northern Ireland and the Middle East, were political choices that it is hard to imagine the Bush-Cheney team ever making. There is no monolithic American policy, but a variety: some you support, some you don't.

Which brings us to the second flaw in the blanket anti-Americanism case. It only makes sense if somehow the current gung-ho, Bush line is written into the very logic of the American Revolution – so that support for the 1776 ideal commits you to support today's aggressive militarism.

But there is no such automatic, logical connection. There is nothing about the idea of a written constitution, or a system of checks and balances, or local democracy, or an abundance of elections that says anything about foreign policy. It is perfectly possible to imagine a US organised just the way the founders intended with a non-interventionist, pacific, stay-at-home view of the world.

More than just possible. Some of the founding fathers felt exactly that way: no less than Thomas Jefferson declared at his inauguration that the new United States sought 'peace, commerce and honest friendship with all nations, entangling alliances with none'. Later John Quincy Adams would say America 'goes not abroad in search of monsters to destroy'.

Indeed, there has been a wide streak of isolationism running through US history, not always commendable: the wariness to join arms against Nazism remains the most ignoble example. It is worth remembering that even as recently as the 1991 Gulf War, senate support for military action came by only the narrowest margin.

So if one dislikes the unilateralism of George Bush, then just remember the multilateralism of Woodrow Wilson and Franklin Roosevelt, which gave birth to the League of Nations and then the United Nations. There is no single US foreign policy creed, just competing traditions.

Today we ought to back the progressive legacy, combining it with praise for what Christopher Hitchens rightly calls the 'great idea' of the American Revolution. We may even want to see that revolution exported to those lands as yet unvisited by democracy. But the best method for the task remains a combination of peaceful persuasion, aid and example – not bombs. And it is hardly anti-American to say so.

4 May 2002

CLAIRE MESSUD

Do they mean us?

In Britain, people have strong opinions about America. Some of my husband's relatives, for example, went on a trip to Florida last year. They spent a fortnight zipping around Disney World and Sea World and the malls of Orlando, and when they went home they announced that Americans seemed nice enough, but awfully materialistic. Another of my in-laws, who won't set foot in the United States, believes that Americans don't (can't?) walk because they spend all their time in cars, and that the only restaurants in this vast nation are McDonald's and Burger King. At the moment, there seems to be a sense abroad that all Americans, when not scoffing burgers or buying Mickey Mouse sweatshirts, are busy rallying behind our unelected, sabre-rattling president and hoisting the stars and stripes on our front lawns. So I thought I ought to set the record straight.

My family lives in a picturesque town in western Massachusetts called Northampton (population 20,000). A hundred miles west of Boston, and 150 miles north of New York city, it is best known as the home of Smith College, an illustrious all-women establishment that has graduated, among others, Sylvia Plath, Janet Malcolm and Gloria Steinem. There's a single main drag, lined with shops and cafés and teeming with pedestrians. There are pretty clapboard houses on the shady streets, a fair number with picket fences; children ride bikes, dogs roam freely and citizens are neighbourly. It is, in many ways, a typical, even an ideal, American town.

If I were David Lynch, I'd now reveal Northampton's seamy underside, the lively heroin trade (which exists) and the hidden poverty (which also exists, in spades). Or I could tell you about the tobacco growing (an old local crop), or the gun-toting (there must be some: the Smith & Wesson factory is just down the highway). But, actually, this place is a *Guardian* reader's paradise. No chain stores; no corporations; no smoking (it is America, after all). There was some controversy last summer over the gang of leather-and-chain-clad bikers that loiters outside one of the cafés and makes a lot of noise, but it turns out they're all members of AA and they come to eat ice cream.

Scruffy youths amble aimlessly in droves, but they are oddly polite. The local beggars seem to be unionised and all have matching straw baskets in which to collect their cash. Almost every car is plastered with bumper stickers: *E-racism*; *Celebrate Diversity*; *Justice Not Vengeance*; *Love Animals, Don't Eat Them*; *Every Child Is An Honored Student at Jackson Elementary*. The hills outside of town are dotted with pottery studios and ashrams, and Buddhist monks in saffron robes join the crowds at the farmers' market at the weekend. And as we walked along Main Street last summer, my mother whispered to me: 'I've never seen so many girls holding hands.'

In the months after the outrageous presidential election of November 2000, people rallied at the main intersection with banners saying *Honk If You Support A Recount*, and everybody honked. On alternating weeks, others waved posters exhorting *Honk* to end sanctions against Iraq. Fewer people honked, but some did. The events of 9/11 baffled our townsfolk: patriotism doesn't come naturally in this self-declared nuclear-free zone. People held vigils, lit candles, were sombre. A few houses, it's true, raised flags. And then furled them up again, in time.

But in the past month, in light of events in the Middle East, Northamptonites have organised anew: a vast crimson sign was unveiled last weekend in front of the town hall, announcing a 'rolling fast' for the Palestinian cause. We wondered – particularly given the girth of the average American – what a 'rolling fast' might be. A swarm of concerned citizenry buzzed beneath the sign, signing petitions, donating money and, I imagine, not eating. Or at least, taking turns not eating. I could have sworn that I glimpsed a box of doughnuts.

Just down the road stands a church. In front of it, that day, perched a rickety card table, manned by a lone and surly fat boy of about fourteen. His scrawled sign implored *Support Our Youth Group Fast To End World Hunger*. Adults pushed past him without turning their heads. My impulse, upon seeing the lad, so plump and woebegone behind his table, was to snicker. His project was unutterably silly, doomed. My impulse, before the gathering at the town hall, was no different, just as it was when everyone was honking for Al Gore or against Iraqi sanctions – just as I snicker at the self-righteous bumper stickers (I prefer the one that says *I Love Animals – They're Delicious*; and another that reads *My Child Can Beat Up Your Honors Student*), and smile (I wouldn't dare to snicker) at the reformed bikers and their double scoops of chocolate chip. After all, Northampton is a speck of a town, far from the seats of power. Who cares how many horns honk here? Who cares how many chubby townsfolk shed a pound or two for a worthy cause? Doesn't it make you want to laugh?

But even though these gestures might seem silly, even though they are, to the wider world, invisible, they are heartfelt. What would you have the people of Northampton do, living as far from Washington DC as Aberdeen is from London? What would you do in their shoes? Because the people of Northampton – unlike Mickey Mouse or Ronald McDonald or George W. Bush – are just like you.

3 September 2002

OLIVER BURKEMAN

'I'm not sure what normal means any more . . .'

For the first few days back at work, Joe Moran Jr kept seeing after-images, phantom limbs on the New York skyline. But people get used to things, and there are some days now when the captain of the Statue of Liberty ferry barely even notices the gap.

'You know how it is – we do this every day,' says Moran, deeply tanned and peering through shades as he pilots the *Miss Circle Line* back across a sparkling Hudson Bay to Manhattan's southern tip, the huddled masses in their patriotic baseball caps snapping pictures from the decks below.

The statue is still padlocked, though – only the island where it stands has re-opened – and this is the kind of daily reminder that keeps Moran, stuck in his tiny wheelhouse all day, brooding about 11 September, and how he never did anything to help.

'We were there to take bodies – you know, injured or killed – but there were so few people injured that they really didn't need us. We just sat right where we were, at the dock, for probably seven hours. Just sat there. Seven hours, and we did absolutely nothing. And then they sent us home. It was the most frustrating thing you could ever imagine. You want some sort of purpose. I guess being there, that was our job, but . . . well, that's what we did that day. I wish it were more interesting.'

The ferry draws in to the shore, where the next boatload of visitors are removing their belts and shoes in a marquee beside the water. The security check is significantly more rigorous than at any of the city's airports.

Back on land the same weird mixture of humdrum routine and permanent scarring pervades the narrow, flag-strewn streets around Ground Zero. In Battery Park, flyers taped to lampposts (where the faces of the missing used to be) still refer to the attacks – *Curious about your exposure to dust and chemicals post-9/11? . . . Study participants needed!* – but now they mingle with the ordinary craziness of New York in late summer: *Photographer seeks 80s lookalikes: Richard Pryor, Simon LeBon . . .*

Tom Brady, a subway driver on the E Line, which passes under the corner of the site, still takes his coffee break at the corner of Church Street and Vesey (the station is still named after the World Trade Center) and only sometimes wishes he knew whether the people who used to wave to him from the platform are dead, or just got relocated.

'It's unsettling, the ones you used to see who you don't see any more, but how long can you go on thinking like that? It's exhausting, too,' he says, one of many New Yorkers still trying to figure out how everything and nothing could have changed.

Keep walking: turn on to Broadway, and try not to gasp at the doorway of David Cohen's narrow clothes store, Chelsea Jeans, where a rack of denims and sweatshirts still stands, thickly crusted with yellow dust, frozen in time within a glass cabinet. The tourists are mesmerised. More mesmerised, in fact, than they are by David's merchandise, which is why Chelsea Jeans is preparing to close later this month.

We hoped that things would get better, says a sign taped nearby, *but they didn't . . . About our memorial for September 11? We don't know what to do with it, but if you have any suggestions, I would love to hear from you.*

The tourists come to stare, but not to spend, says Stephanie Hryckowian, proprietor of the Beekman Deli on the corner of Nassau and Beekman. Her cramped coffee shop was directly in the path of falling debris – the floor tiles are still cracked from the shockwaves – and in the first weeks afterwards, exhausted firefighters took turns taking naps on the floor. Then she set about creating an elaborate window display of fire-department trinkets, miniature World Trade Centers and full-colour portraits of mayors Giuliani and Bloomberg. Business fell by half, but at least they were one of the few places Ground Zero workers could pick up a sandwich.

Now, though, everyone else is open again – and business is down by 70 per cent.

'Oh, we don't like the tourists,' Hryckowian says. 'I mean, I can't look at the pit, and they're coming just to gawk. I'm sure if I hadn't been here I'd have needed to look, but . . . well, that's not the kind of thing you want to combine with a shopping trip, and that's bad for people round here.'

The local residents aren't much better. 'These are people with other houses – many other houses. This is just where they sleep in Manhattan. So they just moved their families out to the Hamptons, out to New Jersey. Never see them.'

But things are a little different four blocks uptown, amid the luxury lofts and modish bars of Tribeca, where wealthy residents were rumoured to have received five-figure handouts from Red Cross volunteers desperate to dispense money in the months after the attacks. And business is booming for Drew Nieporent, bearded king of the downtown restaurant trade, who owns Nobu, Montrachet and, with Robert de Niro, the Tribeca Grill.

'I'm not sure I know what normal means any more,' says Nieporent, who spent the second half of September on the streets with his waiters and chefs, smuggling sandwiches past uncooperative police officers to the mouths of recovery workers, 'but it's not half as bad as I thought it would be. There's a concerted effort to feed round here. I guess people are less flamboyant about their spending these days – there's not the same "let the good times roll" atmosphere in the air. Maybe the celebrations are a little more humble. But we have to turn the page.'

Not everyone can, yet; not quite. At the intersection of Houston Street and Broadway, three pedestrians dressed for business, two women and a man, are waiting at a DON'T WALK sign. Something catches their eyes, and all three heads swivel: two black helium balloons, caught on the wind, are bobbing towards the upper floors of an office building over to the east. It's nothing, of course; obviously just a pair of balloons, tied together with string. And the perspectives are confusing: it's not even clear that they're headed for the building. Looking upwards in New York used to be a sure sign that you were a tourist. But several seconds pass before the people at the crossing realise that the signal ahead of them has changed to WALK.

Professor Charles Strozier has a haggard look about him. A year ago, the 58-year-old psychoanalyst and historian was happily at work in his homely office at New York University – Union Square ten floors below, the Chrysler Building glinting in the distance through his window. And he was only vaguely troubled by the apparent lack of fit between his two main research interests: extreme religious cults, and how people respond to cataclysmic disasters.

That, at least, has not been bothering him recently.

'I felt like I'd been preparing fifteen years for this. Fate dropped me into it,' says Strozier, who has spent the past eleven months running perhaps the biggest interviewing project in New York, cataloguing hundreds of accounts of survivors and witnesses. It isn't work that lends itself to academic detachment, and Strozier has heard things he can't shake from his mind. Like the woman he went to see on Long Island (she hasn't been able to leave her house since September, he says) who was so confused by the time she got out of the south tower that she thought a butcher's shop had exploded. ('All the blood,' he explains.)

'And the number of people jumping – this is a tremendously important part of the story, and it's been lost, because of self-censorship by journalists. I don't know, maybe that was ethically wise. But hundreds of people jumped. Those images of the Trade Center, they've leached death out. You have to imagine death. But I'd say 600, 700 people jumped. I'm calculating from the body parts they found: there were no body parts if you didn't jump. You were incinerated.'

Strozier has been mapping Manhattan according to 'zones of sadness'. South of Chambers Street, you could make out the people jumping, 'and the only question is how that transforms you. Not whether you're traumatised.' South of

Into a perilous future: Tony Blair – the first western leader to visit Afghanistan after the defeat of the Taliban – meets Afghan leader Hamid Karzai, January. (PA/Stefan Rousseau)

Monarch of all he surveys: President George Bush at a Republican fund-raising occasion, Wisconsin, February. (Reuters/Larry Downing)

One of the uncounted dead: the body of a Taliban soldier
on the road into Kabul, capital of Afghanistan, November.
(AP Photo/Marco di Lauro)

Right:
In the ruins of Jenin: a man shelters
from the rain while searching for his
possessions in the rubble, April.
(Guardian/Sean Smith)

Yet another bomb in Jerusalem: Israeli rescue workers at the scene of a suicide bombing in June. The victims included Jewish children on their way to school. (Getty Images)

Comrades of Israeli soldier Sergeant Erez Turjeman, killed with five others near Ramallah, weep during his funeral in Jerusalem, February. (AFPI/Thomas Coex)

14th, you could see everything – except individual human beings. And on the Upper West Side 'you probably saw it on TV. But you had to live with the smell. People are deeply confused about that, unless they're very psychologically alert to their feelings. But everybody knows what the smell was. Today, the victims are literally in the lungs of people in New York.'

Because of wind patterns, though, the smell never made it to the Upper East Side. 'The richest, most elitist area in New York, and it was never touched. And within a few weeks, the most important thing for them was whether they could get a reservation at a five-star restaurant.'

The Long Island woman, meanwhile, is making plans to leave the state. 'She said she's moving to Iowa,' Strozier says. 'I thought she meant it metaphorically or something, but she said both coasts are dangerous, Texas is out, because Bush is there, and Chicago's too big. The only safe place in America is Iowa.'

Walk, in the mid-morning heat, across Union Square, up past the Flatiron Building and on to Fifth Avenue. The flags are still everywhere here, on the smart apartment blocks and the Korean restaurants, and every firehouse is still a shrine of cards and flowers and thank-you banners. THESE COLOURS DON'T RUN! boasts the caption under one poster of the flag. It has been bleached almost white by the sunlight.

Near the top of the Empire State Building, at Fifth and 33rd, Jack Brod remembers how, a few weeks after the attacks, a woman drove into the city to buy a diamond from him. Then she got cold feet.

'She parked her car and she called us up and asked us to come down and show her the diamond,' Brod, who is 92, says today, sitting behind a broad wooden desk in his chaotic 76th-floor office. 'She said she was scared. I said, "Well, why don't you come in, and we'll meet in the coffee shop at the bottom?" But she said she was scared even to come in to the building. So my salesman went down, and he got into her car, showed her the $75,000 diamond. And he told her, "Lady, I'm taking more chances than you. I'm sitting in a stranger's car with a $75,000 diamond."'

Brod is the Empire State Building's longest-standing tenant – he took out the lease on his first office there while it was still being built in 1930. He says he can't understand why people are so scared of high buildings just because of 11 September, but, then again, he is a salesman. 'The main thing is, she bought the diamond. So it was worth it.'

In 1945, a stray bomber accidentally flew into the 79th floor – 'and it only did superficial damage. Damaged the Catholic Charities office. They just repaired the whole thing. Three floors above where my office is, and there's absolutely no trace'.

Back on the street, one block west, outside Macy's on 34th Street, David Garcia prowls the streets with Basie, an enormous German shepherd. Security is tight these days at the world's biggest department store. Garcia and Basie are part of a canine team on 24-hour duty. 'It's not like the police sniffer dogs,' Garcia says. 'These dogs are trained to attack. We have . . .' – he smiles slyly – 'special commands.'

The windows of the police station on Times Square are crowded with children's drawings and letters. *Dear policemen, I am very sorry about the tragic event,* one says. But in the window next to it is a cutting from a newspaper showing how New York police are paid far less than their colleagues in nearby jurisdictions. A couple of weeks ago, thousands of officers demonstrated in the square. The dispute is still unresolved.

Another sign of normality: Fifth Avenue is a cacophony of taxi horns. At 48th Street, seven people are queueing at a side door of Barnes & Noble to meet Lisa Beamer, wife of the Flight 93 hero Todd Beamer, who is in town to sign copies of her new book, *Let's Roll: Finding Hope in the Midst of Crisis.*

'Who is it?' an elderly woman with an unruly perm is saying, pressing her nose against the window. Someone tells her. 'Who?' she says. Then she remembers. 'Ohhh.'

And two blocks uptown, in the basement of the Rockefeller Center, Michael Tomasky, the seasoned political columnist of *New York* magazine, sips Starbucks Chai tea and wonders whether anything really changed at all.

'We did not come out of this as brothers under the gun with the residents of Hiroshima, Nagasaki, or London during the Blitz,' he says. 'Because there's this other narrative that's come in. There's still the narrative of the cataclysmic events we have suffered, but this other one, about rising from the ashes, is chiefly about political infighting and bureaucracy, the same old exasperating nonsense New Yorkers have been used to for years. Of course those six proposals [for rebuilding Lower Manhattan] were awful. It would be the greatest miracle since the parting of the Red Sea if something elegant, aesthetically innovative and economically useful were to rise down there.'

And anyway – 'although you feel like you're not supposed to say this . . . maybe it wasn't a great cataclysmic act of civic destruction. Maybe for each person it was their own cataclysm, but they all internalised it so differently. Everyone took it personally, in their own way. It's like some men don't mourn when their wife dies, but it doesn't mean they didn't love her. And other men will mourn for years.

'The metanarrative,' he says, 'is that there is no metanarrative.'

'Do you equate three months of being a nice guy with seven and a half years of being a prick?' Ed Koch is saying, thrusting himself back into a leather executive chair at his law offices, thirty floors above Sixth Avenue. The 77-year-old former Democratic mayor of New York, hyperactive and twinkling, clad in green braces and liberally peppering his conversation with quotations from Herodotus, is meditating on the legacy of his successor, Rudy Giuliani.

Koch once wrote a book about his successor. Its title was *Rudy Giuliani: Nasty Man.*

'It was magnificent behaviour,' Koch says of Giuliani's performance in the months after 11 September. 'But I thought the British were nuts when they invited him over and made him into a Sir Saint. He did what you're supposed to do. The reason that we New Yorkers admired him as we had berated him before was that he had clearly gone through an epiphany. He had come near death . . . and it changed his whole character. What he did for the balance of his term was to exhibit a sensitivity which, had he exhibited it for seven and a half years prior, he would have gone down as St Rudy even without 11 September. But he didn't.'

Outside, in the stagnant August heat, the ill-drained gutters of Sixth Avenue smell vinegary. At 60th Street, the smell begins to mingle with horse manure, where Robert Boyle, an Irishman in a top hat made of metal, is doing his best to lure tourists into his horse-drawn carriage for tours of Central Park. Christmas was supposed to be his big season, but what income he got came from well-meaning New Yorkers who came to show their support.

'I'd say, "So, where have you guys travelled from?" And they'd point and say, "We live just over there."'

Only now are the foreign visitors starting to pick up, and all they want to hear about is 11 September. 'In this job, though, you want people to be happy,' Boyle says. 'So when they say, "Were you there that day? What were you doing?" I say, "No, I wasn't here that day, and look, there's the Dakota building, where John Lennon used to live."

'There's nothing positive comes of talking about that day,' he says. Walking on into the Upper West Side, this turns out to be a not uncommon point of view: sipping coffee in the Olympic Flame diner, Melissa Williams announces her intention to go into temporary hibernation on the day of the first anniversary.

'I'm not going to read a newspaper, and I'm not going to watch television. I don't know what I'll do. I'll probably lie in the bath and read a book. I know what happened. Once is enough.'

But disconnecting is less easy for some. The telephone in Imam Feisal Abdul Rauf's smartly furnished Upper West Side apartment has been ringing off the hook in recent months. As the most prominent Muslim in New York, the Sufi leader – a soft-spoken 52-year-old academic with a salt-and-pepper beard and khaki slacks who lectures at Columbia University – has been telephoned by more television programmes and newspapers than he can remember.

'It's overwhelming. Overwhelming,' he smiles. 'Just massive media attention.' His university lectures have been similarly packed. 'You can feel the curiosity,' he says.

His mosque, metres from Ground Zero, was closed for two weeks after the attacks, but while Muslims around America started to feel the crackle of hostility, all he encountered were the good wishes of non-Muslim neighbours, taped on scraps of paper to the building's door.

Still, he adds, if he had been thirty years younger, from the way people stare at him now he might think he had suddenly become astonishingly good-looking. And no matter how many times he says 'Yes' to the phone calls, he's still criticised, he says, for being insufficiently condemnatory of Islamist fundamentalist violence.

'I'll give you a specific example. I was interviewed by CBS: *60 Minutes*. The presenter, Ed Bradley, he looked at me – they had four of us, lined up like sitting ducks – and he turned to me and asked me: "What have you done personally since 9/11?" So, I pointed out the various press conferences I'd participated in, condemning the attacks, explaining how it's outside the box of Islamic theology and law. And when I finished, the imam next to me said, "Yes, that's so, but we still need to do more."' He leans forward. 'And my comments were completely edited out. And so Ed Bradley asked the question – and the other imam's was the answer. The implication being that we're not doing what we're supposed to be doing.'

Still, he's pressing on with his plans for what he calls a 'huge new programme' of publications, media campaigns and events to promote his moderate brand of Islam. Did I know, he asks incredulously, that there are twenty-five centres for Jewish-Christian understanding in the United States, only two for Muslim-Christian understanding, and zero for Muslim-Jewish understanding? More are needed, he says: people have to talk to each other. 'This is what we call' – and he leans forward again, eyebrows furrowed, as if he is about to deploy a theological term that might not be familiar to me – 'a no-brainer.'

You have to shout to make yourself heard inside Nussbaum & Wu, a bagel shop crammed with Columbia University students at the corner of 113th Street and Broadway, but Ann Douglas, a professor of English at the university, says she and her colleagues more often find themselves whispering.

Columbia is a campus with a long tradition of dissent, she says, 'but in the months after [11 September], it just became regular that you called up your friends and said, "Do you believe what's in the papers?" It was always so nice for someone like me, on the Left during the Reagan years, that this was not a Reagan campus. We were always picketing against apartheid, picketing for African-American studies. There's been very, very little of that.' And as for Middle East politics: 'I just think, "When did I wake up in the Miami of Israel? When did I wake up and discover that it was treason to criticise?"'

But if dissent has been dimmed, Douglas has little time for the argument that there is, at least, a new warm-heartedness, a softness in the culture. 'New York is a hard city,' she says, and she likes it that way. Her most famous work, an award-winning history of New York's civic psyche, is called *Terrible Honesty*, and celebrates the hardness of the place: 'It's got sharp edges. It's abrasive. It doesn't streamline your way into assimilation. It is provocative, not consoling. A risk-taking city.' And a city that can accommodate even a cataclysm: 'The amazing thing, talking to my students, is not how much 11 September matters to them, but how little. But then the city is so much bigger than almost anything that life just goes on. Of course it does.'

In Harlem, north of 125th Street, the patriotism and the civic pride begin to take on a different tone. If there are fewer flags, it is mainly because there are still so many hundreds of boarded-up windows: the neighbourhood's much-celebrated regeneration is still confined to a few smart streets around 125th, and from five blocks further uptown, whole streets of tenements are abandoned or marked IN REDEVELOPMENT. But a poster in the window of a general store, advertising a celebration of lives lost on 11 September, makes another point that seems to be felt deeply: *A celebration of* ALL *our heroes*, it says, the 'ALL' in big blue capitals.

Patricia White, sheltering from an unexpected drizzle outside Survival Fish and Chips, on Adam Clayton Powell Boulevard and 133rd Street, raises her eyebrows at the mention of the word.

'Heroism? Oh, I think you'll find some people with some things to say about that around here,' she says.

One of them is Dabney Montgomery, a 79-year-old war veteran pottering quietly in the cavernous African Methodist Episcopalian Zion Church on 137th Street. 'The unity we saw was beautiful – for a few days,' he says. 'But it didn't last. And, you know, all this about America not having suffered domestic terrorism before: when the four girls were killed in Birmingham, Alabama, when the churches were bombed in the sixties – this is terror that we didn't call terror.

'And that was a black man, the mayor in Washington, and nobody played him up like they did Giuliani – who just did what every mayor would have done. It was [the emergency agency] Fema that did all the work. The mayor just went to all the funerals. For all that time, he had little or no contact with people of colour, and for him to go smiling as the mayor of America . . . no. We don't accept that.'

Alvin Durant, the church pastor, couldn't agree more. 'We were all hugging and crying at Ground Zero, but for the most part we went back to our segregated neighbourhoods,' he points out. 'And that's got to tell you something. All that togetherness didn't last – and I knew it wouldn't. I said it wouldn't. I told people, in my sermons, "A bigot's a bigot, and someday soon it's all going to be the way it was."'

There are still fewer flags up here, as Harlem blends into Washington Heights: only a few limp plastic specimens, strung up on lampposts by the local economic development council.

Walk west, the light begins to fade, as the storefronts give way to abandoned lots and buildings with glassless windows. Under the freeway bridges, huddles of young men have parked up their cars, set up garden chairs, and are picnicking to hip-hop from battered stereos.

A few blocks further on, though, something strange happens. The rumbling traffic abruptly gives way to silence, the cracked asphalt gives way to scrubby grassland, and suddenly you are standing at a neat wooden jetty, plunging out into the Hudson River. The shore has not been sanitised by concrete; there is mud and rock and swamp, and insects are buzzing in the long grass. Two men are sitting on the jetty, fixing bait to hooks and casting fishing-lines out into the water, chatting quietly in Spanish and sipping from bottles of Corona. The water at the bank beneath their feet laps in the wake of a distant barge.

Turn away from the lights of the George Washington Bridge, twinkling in the gathering dusk to the south, and watch the mist rising off the thickly-wooded coast of New Jersey on the other side of the river, and you could be forgiven for not thinking that everything in New York had changed for ever on 11 September last year. You would be forgiven for thinking that nothing had changed for centuries.

The aftermath of 11 September in numbers:

- Tonnes of debris removed from Ground Zero: 1,585,401
- Number of NY jobs lost in finance, insurance and real estate: 29,400

- Amount of office space lost in Manhattan: 10 per cent
- Amount given to every child of a New York firefighter who died on 11 September to spend on a Christmas party: $500
- Percentage of New Yorkers who say the city will be attacked again: 72 per cent
- Number of direct eye-witnesses to World Trade Center attack: 20,000
- Number who lost homes or livelihoods: 55,000

HE KNEW HE
WAS RIGHT

Austin, 22 February 2002

I have just seen a white van that is not flying the flag of St George. Is this legal?

Letter from Charlie Catchpole, Hampton Wick, Surrey, 6 June 2002

17 November 2001

CARYL PHILLIPS

Sangatte

He looks like a policeman. He wears a white shirt and tie, his shoes are well shined and his moustache is clipped and neat. As he leans against the bar he announces that he is from Runcorn in Cheshire and that he has been here, in Sangatte, for two and a half years. Through the window of the Off Road Café, I can see groups of Afghans and Iraqis drifting by. It is early evening and they are moving in the direction of the Channel Tunnel. He sips at his beer and eyes the refugees.

'They are stinking and disgusting. They shit on our beaches. I don't go anywhere without a can of Mace, which is legal here.' He offers a short, theatrical pause before he continues. 'I'm not a racist, but it has to be said. Stinky, smelly people. Sometimes they come into the bar and we have to move away because they make us want to retch.'

Again I look out of the window. The men continue to file by. They seem subdued and fatigued, marooned as they are on the north-east coast of France. Less than a mile away, in the Sangatte Red Cross centre, there are 1,600 men, women and children waiting for a chance to get into Britain. These few dozen are tonight's 'advance' party. Most will fail in their attempt, some will be injured, one or two might even be killed. Some time after midnight the French police will escort almost all of them back to the Red Cross centre.

Earlier in the day I had travelled from Paris to Calais-Frethun. The modernist Eurostar terminal is located outside the town of Calais and is entirely surrounded by green fields. There is an Avis rent-a-car desk and one taxi. I ask the cab driver to take me to Sangatte Central. He laughs. I ask 'Is there such a thing?' He shrugs his shoulders and turns up the music. 'Well,' he shouts, 'they've got a big hotel there.' He laughs loudly at his own joke and then tears along the narrow country lanes. In the distance, beyond a Eurostar freighter train, I can see two cross-channel ferries sitting high on the horizon, moving with a ponderous certainty towards the clearly visible white cliffs of Dover.

Sangatte is a collection of homes strung out on both sides of a half-mile stretch of the D940, a main road that connects Calais to Boulogne. Situated three miles to the south-west of Calais, it is a small, predominantly middle-class commuter suburb by the sea. The cab driver drops me at Le Week End bar, which is tobacconist, newspaper shop, bar, amusement arcade and restaurant. Once inside I edge past the table football. At the bar, a pair of local old boys are downing their beers, seemingly oblivious to the loud French rock music that emanates from the tinny radio.

The semi-shaven barman eyes me suspiciously as he makes me a coffee. Above the pool table I see a picture of him resplendent in a bright red jacket standing beside a woman I assume to be his wife. They were contestants on the French version of *Who Wants to Be a Millionaire?* Apparently they lost. The wife catches me looking at the photograph. She nods a silent greeting and then moves through into the restaurant.

The barman makes me a second cup of coffee, but it is clear he doesn't want to talk. I ask one of the old boys if it is always this quiet. He nods.

'What about the refugees?' I ask. 'Do they come in here?'

Again he nods. But he tells me that the barman will not serve them if they do not speak French or have French money. He tells me that they will be down later on. After lunch. They sleep until lunchtime, then come out at night, when they try to get through the tunnel.

He has been here since 1987, when he came to work on the tunnel, but he is retired now. He takes a sip of beer. They don't bother him, but he seems momentarily puzzled.

'They tell us they are qualified people. Doctors and lawyers. They are supposed to have skills, but I don't think so. Eighteen months ago, when they first came to Sangatte, some of them asked for jobs, but now they have stopped. They just stay up there.' He points in the direction of the camp. 'But I don't care.'

I begin to walk towards the camp. I notice small groups of refugees, mainly Pakistanis and Iraqis, walking slowly towards the town. We politely make room for each other on the narrow pavement. I also notice the French National Front posters that decorate the lampposts: *Dégage! Tu Niques La France* ('Clear off! You are fucking up France'). I enter the small Catholic church, which boasts beautiful stained-glass windows and is clearly an object of great village pride with its impeccably obedient rows of chairs. I look in the visitors' book. The last entry speaks in part to the village's 'problem': 'In Jesus Christ we fellow Christians pray for our brothers and sisters in Muslim lands who are being persecuted because they believe in the son of God who has been saved and cleansed for their sins. Elisabeth and Marie. Christian Pilgrims.'

The Red Cross centre sits on a small rise beyond a field in which cows graze. The huge steel warehouse was originally a storage shed for supplies used in the construction of the Channel Tunnel. Eighteen months ago it was requisitioned by the Red Cross to provide shelter for 400 refugees who were hoping to enter Britain illegally. That figure has now swelled to 1,600, with dozens of nationalities represented, although Afghans, Iraqis and Iranians still comprise the majority.

As I near the Red Cross centre I realise I am being followed, so I deliberately slow down until I hear the voice.

'Please, two francs.'

I turn and look at the tall, handsome man. He is shabbily dressed, but his thinning hair is brushed and swept back. He is making some effort to appear presentable.

I ask his name and he tells me that he is called Hassan and that he is an Eygptian. Hassan has lived in Europe for twenty-five years, mainly in Holland, Belgium, Luxembourg and Italy.

'Two francs please, for food in the supermarket.'

I give him two francs but, pointing to the Red Cross centre, tell him: 'I thought they fed you in the camp.'

He sneers. 'Camp no good. I live there one month, but now for one month I live in town in burned-out house. Every night I go seven kilometres to tunnel, but now it is very difficult. Two police cars, one on either side, and they bring me back.'

Hassan holds out his hand again, but I temporarily ignore it and ask him why he wants to go to Britain. Why not just stay in France? He is indignant.

'France no good. In England plenty people of my country. Friends. France no good.'

After a quarter of a century of migrant labour in Europe, this proud man in his late forties, in stained jeans and a thin, inadequate, jacket, seems both lost and angry.

As I pass through the gates of the camp and begin to walk up the long drive-way, I notice greater numbers of refugees now streaming out towards the village. For the first time I see women and children, all bundled up against the cold. At the entrance to the warehouse men squat idly in a scene that rekindles memories of prisoner-of-war films. Washing is hung out to dry along the fencing, and in the middle of this confusion there is a French riot police van. There seems little need for riot police, for a more somnambulant group of people I cannot imagine. And then I remember. Journalists are not permitted to enter the camp, so I try to affect the demeanour of a resident. I walk purposefully towards the open door and past the men queueing up outside the phone booth clutching precious phone cards. I can feel eyes upon me, but I look neither left nor right.

Once inside the warehouse I see the long lines to use the portaloos. Men are washing themselves at open sinks, while others stand bare-chested and wait their turn. The warehouse is a vast open space which contains both Portakabins and tents. They are all numbered, and I peek through open doors and see that there is not a single inch of space between the camp beds. Some Portakabins are marked with a sign that simply reads FAMILY. There are large numbers of families in each one. Privacy is a luxury that has no place here.

In an empty corner of the washroom I notice two dozen Muslims praying together, and then I realise that I am freezing. I look around and feel as though I have entered a vast exhibition hall where the tents and Portakabins are the exhibits and the refugees have been assigned the part of extras adopting poses of extreme boredom, misery and anxiety. And then two Red Cross men, who look like security officers, shout at me. The game is up. As they approach me, I explain that I am looking for a West African friend, but they insist that they will have to escort me back to the door and check my identity.

They place me in a chair and three Red Cross officials-cum-guards keep an eye on me while somebody goes to enquire about my 'friend'. While I wait, I read the signs in four languages warning people of the 'mortal danger' (and 'squash-ing risk') of trying to board trains going through the tunnel. I notice a man who looks Iranian in a Bob Marley hooded sweat-top. He scrutinises me as he walks by. The Red Cross man reappears and says that he cannot find my friend.

I stand and thank them all, and then I notice that an African man has sud-denly materialised.

'Excuse me, sir. Are you the one asking about West Africa?'

I nod. 'Where are you from?' I ask.

'Cameroon, sir.'

'I think this man may know something about my friend,' I say. 'He will come with me for a walk.'

The Red Cross officials seem displeased, but they say nothing, so my new friend follows me out of the warehouse.

We walk back towards the village, treading the worn path littered with crushed Coke cans and empty cigarette packets. Along the way, Manuel from Cameroon introduces me to Jacob from Benin. Once we reach the village I offer to buy them both lunch and a beer, and the three of us enter the Off Road Café. The blonde Frenchwoman behind the bar insists that the kitchen is closed. She makes no attempt to offer the three strangers a drink and so, for a moment, we stand there. I suggest to Jacob and Manuel that there might be another place and we leave and walk further up the street to Le Week End bar.

My retired friend is no longer there, but the disgruntled barman studies us as we walk in. I usher the two men to a seat in the corner and then order three beers and some crisps. The barman says he will bring them over. As I take my seat, Jacob and Manuel visibly relax. When the beer arrives, they drink with enthusiasm and I wonder how long it has been since they last had a beer.

Manuel is the more articulate of the two. An English-speaking Cameroonian, he tells me he has been in the camp for three weeks. He fled his country after three of his colleagues were killed by hard-line secessionists who want English-speaking Cameroon to become independent of French-speaking Cameroon. A gradualist, Manuel's politics embrace compromise, so he knew that he would be the next to be killed. A lecturer in history in his home town of Bamenda, he arrived in Paris knowing nobody. He spent what money he had on a ticket to London, but was pulled off the train at the cross-channel border and sent to the camp.

'Why Britain?' I ask him. 'Why not claim asylum in France?'

He smiles. 'Everybody says Britain is better. Sometimes I hear the BBC news and they say they need 300,000 workers. And English is my language. But I will not risk my life jumping on a train like the Muslims. They have no fear. They are crazy.' He pauses. 'It looks like I will have to claim asylum here in France.'

Jacob listens carefully. I ask him if he is also a political migrant. He laughs.

'I am hoping to be.'

It transpires that Jacob is a classic economic migrant. A car mechanic, he is proud that back home he passed his City and Guilds and is therefore 'qualified'. Like Manuel, this is his first time out of his country. He paid a 'fixer' to get him into Europe via Istanbul and Greece, and then took a train from Italy to Paris. He was sleeping rough in the station until somebody told him that if he could get to Calais there was a place where he could eat and sleep and maybe eventually reach Britain.

But now Jacob is disillusioned. 'It is difficult to go to Britain. It is just there,' he points, 'but so far. Maybe Holland,' he muses. 'They speak English. To get asylum here in France can take eighteen months, and I cannot stay in that camp for eighteen months. I have no money and nowhere to go. I know nobody.' He pauses. 'And it is cold. We have a Slovenian in our tent, and the rest are all Muslims. They talk all night, but there is no trouble between us.' Manuel nods in agreement, and Jacob continues. 'The only racism is between us and the Red Cross people. At present there are only three of us from Africa, but I know they don't want us there.'

I look beyond Jacob and Manuel to the roadside where, in the gloom, an Afghan squats on his haunches and contorts his body into a twisted sculpture that describes misery. Cars, many with British plates, flash by, but the man does not move a muscle or blink his eyes.

I pay the solemn barman and shake hands with Jacob and Manuel. They have already made it clear that they prefer to return to the camp by themselves.

Manuel apologises. 'The Red Cross people can ask you to leave if they think you are a trouble-maker.'

I understand. I also understand that Jacob will most likely take advantage of the fact that free repatriation is available to any who wish to go 'home'. Manuel, on the other hand, will claim political asylum in France and eventually begin a new life. He seems far too resourceful to end up in Hassan's predicament.

As the daylight begins to fade I decide to walk back to the Off Road Café. The moustached man from Cheshire is propping up the bar. I order a beer from the same barmaid who seemed reluctant to serve me in the company of Jacob and Manuel. Recognising my accent, Cheshire-man begins to offer his trenchant views on the refugees now filing past the window in the direction of the tunnel. Having offloaded his opinions on their hygiene, and insisted that they really have money, he begins to advocate applying lethal electric shocks to them, or simply shooting them.

'After all, there's no gun laws here, you know. You can shoot rabbits on another man's property, if you see what I mean.'

I ask him if he would ever consider moving back to Britain.

He snorts. 'What for? I came here with fifteen words of French and they helped me.'

He gestures to the three people in the bar. As he does so a Frenchman enters. '*Ça va?*' says Cheshire-man, shaking hands. The Frenchman shakes hands with me too. 'You see,' says Cheshire-man. 'And the standard of living is cheaper too. But we've got to get rid of the scum. House prices have fallen nearly 20 per cent.'

House prices? The refugees continue to file past the window. I want to tell this man that whether economic or political migrants, these people's lives are broken and they are simply looking for a chance to begin anew. A chance to work, to contribute, to make something of themselves. To begin again at the bottom of the pile. There will always be those who will abuse the system; one needs to just look around any social security office in Britain. But I say nothing and I simply finish my beer.

'What do you do?' I ask.

He stares and then smiles, in a manner that he considers to be enigmatic.

'I work for the tunnel.' I look at him. 'I could tell you what I do for Eurotunnel, but then I'd have to shoot you.'

I now understood why he looks like a policeman.

He continues. 'Let's just say I'm in pursuit of illegals.' He smiles.

Again I look beyond him to the stream of hunch-shouldered refugees walking with grim determination in the direction of the mouth of the tunnel. And I silently wish them all good luck.

24 April 2002

JEAN-MICHEL HELVIG

Shame of the French Left

The people who ran for cover when the thunderbolt struck that Lionel Jospin had been knocked out of the second round of the presidential election – these people were leftists. People who stayed at home, people who voted for 'protest' candidates, their faces bore mixed expressions of staggered stupidity and belated remorse. 'We didn't want this,' they pathetically repeated to their friends and, of course, to themselves. But it was they who caused Jospin's downfall; it was they who mathematically lowered his percentage to the benefit of the far-right candidate who outpolled him.

Today these people march the streets shouting 'No to Le Pen!' with a determination equalled only by the casual, offhand manner with which they approached the polling booth. Of course we are only talking about a minority but then, the difference between Lionel Jospin and Jean-Marie Le Pen was a mere 194,558 votes out of 41,196,339 registered voters. So this minority of useless idiots – or rather useful idiots for Le Pen – thoroughly deserve to be pilloried, because although there are structural factors that explain the prime minister's defeat (he was betrayed by his populist electorate, paralysed by crime, and ran a mediocre campaign), such factors could not be overcome in a space of mere weeks. In the space of a single day, however, those who fought the wrong fight in the polling booths could have changed their mind and put the presidential election on the right track by voting usefully.

So who are these leftist cretins, many of them our friends with whom we will, inevitably, make things up eventually? First, there are those who simpered 'We thought Chirac and Jospin would get to the second round anyway', and who preferred, rather than voting, to go away for the weekend, or not to interrupt their precious holidays. They decided, with a clear conscience, not to budge until 5 May, for the second round. Like children caught red-handed, they now plead 'But the polls and the media told us there would be no surprises.' They are right, of course, about the polls. But the polls have been wrong many times, and as for the media, they have often described a French society in which fear of crime, feelings of xenophobia, and doubts about France's national identity are all on the rise.

But a journalist is not an electoral soothsayer. Besides, if these people are so cultured and well informed, do they really need to look to anyone apart from themselves merely in order to fulfil their civic duty?

There were other deserters too: those who chose the cunning option of voting for one of the three Trotskyist candidates in order to send a social 'message' to the mainstream Left. In doing so, they brought triumph to two candidates, Arlette Laguiller and Olivier Besancenot, who spent their entire campaign attacking the 'reformists', never mentioned Le Pen let alone Chirac, and pursued the sole objective of boosting their own organisations. Very few of their voters actually backed their strategic vision, which remains inspired, in a pretty dogmatic way, by Russia's 1917 revolution. At the very least you can say that their 'message' was destined to get somewhat lost en route. And how can we forget the extraordinary scattering of mainstream leftist candidates? There were four of them, and their essential preoccupation was to distinguish themselves from the outgoing prime minister to justify their own existence.

Of course, everyone has the right to run in the presidential election, democracy demands it, and every man has the right to cast his personal vote. But what characterises French leftists these days is a genetic incapacity to overcome self-interest in the name of collective efficiency. And whatever Jospin's mistakes may be, or those of the Socialists during the presidential campaign, it is first and foremost the leftists who have indirectly scored victory for Le Pen. Thank God there are now some serious anti-Le Pen demonstrations for us to redeem ourselves.

Jean-Michel Helvig is deputy editor of Libération.

24 April 2002

ROD LIDDLE

Le Pen: it proves what we always said

Who shall we blame for Jean-Marie Le Pen and the British National party? Pretty much anyone or anything you like, to judge from the pages of analysis in the newspapers. Luckily, most of the eminent commentators and politicians have discovered that the reasons for the ascendancy of the far-right just so happen to be the very things they have been banging on about for years. Here's a rundown of who blames what for Le Pen and the BNP:

Richard Littlejohn (the *Sun*): The *Guardian*, the BBC and the commission for racial equality.
Trevor Kavanagh (the *Sun*): Faceless accountants in the European Union.
Peter Mandelson: French socialists soft on crime and, presumably, the causes of crime.
Bronwen Maddox (*The Times*): 11 September.
Libby Purves (*The Times*): Smug, platitudinous, centrist politicians.
Tony Benn: New Labour.
Tony Blair: The European Union being too remote from ordinary people; therefore we should have a European Convention.
Daniel Johnson (the *Daily Telegraph*): The French character: the revenge of Vichy!
Hugo Young (and others): Proportional representation.

Stephen Byers: South American killer bees.

Yes, you are right. I have deliberately misrepresented Byers. He has not, so far as I am aware, offered his particular analysis. He may be one of the very last people in the country to do so. I bet somebody has already asked Sven-Goran for an opinion, in between equally interesting stuff about Ulrika. I notice the *Daily Mirror* solicited the opinions of Pierre-Yves Gerbeau the man from the Dome. He thinks Le Pen is ghastly and that people should vote for somebody else on 5 May.

Still, all this at least enables us to be simultaneously smug and sanctimonious, which is always an important viewpoint from which to discuss France and the French.

9 May 2002

ALAN TRAVIS

Today, Lancashire . . .

It would be wrong to dismiss the success of the British National party (BNP) in Burnley and Oldham last week as a local difficulty confined to two Lancashire towns. According to a *Guardian* analysis of the sixty-six council wards contested by the far-right party, there are a further sixteen wards around the country where it made real progress last week. Among them are Sunderland, Sandwell, Wigan and Kirklees – some of which have no history of an organised fascist presence in their local politics. Overall, it was the best result for the party since its founder, John Tyndall, split from the National Front (NF) in 1982 and ranks with the NF's seventies heyday.

But it would be a mistake to portray the election of the three BNP councillors as a 'breakthrough' on to the national stage for the party. In places such as Bexley and in Tower Hamlets, both in south-east London, the party's candidates turned in performances which were a mere shadow of their former polling. The BNP got an average of 12 per cent in the sixty-six seats they contested. On the face of it, that sounds worrying – but presumably these were the sixty-six seats in which the BNP had the greatest hopes for being elected among the 6,000 seats in England and Wales being contested. The BNP leader, Nick Griffin, has made no secret of the fact that he is more interested in trying to win council seats where turnout is low and voters more willing to cast a protest vote.

Apart from Burnley and Oldham, the party averaged 10 per cent of the vote in the contested seats. This is not a national share of the vote and so cannot be compared to the 34 per cent the Conservatives secured last Thursday (or Labour's 33 per cent). In national terms, the fascist share of the vote would be negligible. Yet it is more than the 5.8 per cent the United Kingdom Independence party polled in its 160 seats, or the 6.5 per cent for the Socialist Alliance across 200.

The election of the three BNP councillors in Burnley actually had more to do with the party exploiting split voting and the way the elections work in wards in which three councillors are elected in the same ballot. In the three cases the pattern of voting in each ward appears to be the single BNP candidate polling just ahead of two independent candidates. In one of the wards where a BNP councillor was elected, the Conservatives failed to put up a candidate. The clever tactic of targeting three-member wards with a single BNP candidate meant that the party was able to make the maximum political and media impact, despite only polling 12 per cent of the votes cast in Burnley. In two wards they were elected alongside Labour councillors and with Conservatives in the other. Even in their most successful ward, Gannow, they won the seat on only 15 per cent of the vote.

The more disturbing achievement in Burnley comes when you look at the raw voting figures. In the 2001 general election some 4,151 people voted for the BNP candidate. Last Thursday the number of BNP voters in Burnley had doubled to 9,984 votes in the thirteen out of fifteen wards contested by the party. It shows that the BNP has built on its general election success, and the three council seats could provide them with the platform they need to keep a longstanding presence in the town.

In Oldham the BNP result was in some ways more alarming. It stood candidates in only five wards and took an average of 28 per cent share of the vote in each, almost beating the Liberal Democrats to a council seat in St James ward where the Lib Dems only won by a margin of 3 per cent.

Outside Burnley and Oldham, the *Guardian* analysis shows that sixteen of the remaining forty-eight BNP candidates broke through the 10 per cent barrier. In Sunderland the party stood in six wards and gained more than 14 per cent of the vote in four of them. In one, Town End Farm, it took 28 per cent of the vote, pushing the Conservative candidate into a poor third place. The Sunderland contests took place in single-councillor wards, and although there is little danger of the BNP getting elected to the council, they have established a firm base in a part of the country which has no history of a fascist presence. It could prove a fertile area for future BNP activity. They also established a presence in Gateshead. It was the same story in Wigan where the BNP took 23 per cent of the vote in Abram, which they had never fought before.

The BNP's results in the Black Country reflected something of its Powellite history. The party's third best result outside Oldham came in the Princes End ward of Sandwell, West Midlands, where they took 24 per cent of the vote. But they could not repeat the performance in neighbouring Tipton – once the scene of a BNP by-election surge – where they could only manage 7 per cent, or 334 votes. Their ground was undercut by a local Freedom party candidate who received 1,070 votes.

The failure of the BNP in London was the untold half of the story on Thursday night. Even in Bexley Northend – once the site of the national party headquarters and where they had polled 27 per cent of the vote in the past – they could manage only 7 per cent this time. In Tower Hamlets' Millwall ward the BNP candidate scraped together only 3.7 per cent of the votes. The collapse in the London vote was the price the BNP paid for its strategy of pushing all its resources into exploiting the growing racial tensions in northern cities.

14 May 2002

IAN BURUMA

Pim Fortuyn

All fanatics are dangerous, and vegan fanatics especially so. That is about the only lesson to be drawn from the murder of Pim Fortuyn by an animal rights promoter. Talk about the lost innocence of Dutch democracy (much aired in the Dutch press) is surely nonsense. When was Dutch democracy ever innocent anyway? When troops were shipped off to the Dutch East Indies after the war, to crush Indonesian independence? Nor does the assassination herald the end of tolerance in Holland if, as seems likely, Fortuyn's killer was a lonely wacko.

No, what needs an explanation is not Fortuyn's death, but the extraordinary success of his aborted life. How did this gay sociologist with a taste for rococo furnishings, Muslim lovers, and pet dogs manage to gather such a following, and provoke such gushing emotions after his death? (Dutch phlegmatism, by the way, should go the same way as other clichés, such as the bicycle-riding queens: straight into the nearest dustbin. I can't remember the last time a Dutch monarch rode a bike in public.)

Mourners at the largest public funeral since Queen Wilhelmina died forty years ago have compared their hero to Martin Luther King, President Kennedy, and Princess Diana. The first two are absurd. The last perhaps less so. Fortuyn was, in a way, to Dutch politics what Diana was to the British monarchy: a spoiler, a populist jester who managed, with consummate public relations skill, to poke a stuffy, complacent, out-of-touch establishment in the eye. And, as with Diana, the press which first excoriated him, canonised him after his death. Of course Fortuyn, with his camp Woosterism, was no more a man of the people than Diana was a 'people's princess'. But he managed to convince 'the people' that he was on their side, that he spoke for them, and understood their concerns.

The Dutch political establishment, with its cosy 'consensus' model of politics, is perhaps especially stuffy and easy to lampoon. The Netherlands has one of the oldest, possibly even *the* oldest democratic tradition in Europe. But it is a tradition without much democratic rough and tumble. The governing élite of the eighteenth-century Dutch republic was a patriciate, known as *regenten*. These worthies, who emerged from the Amsterdam merchant class, were, on the whole, liberal-minded and decent men. They governed in a civilised, paternalistic manner. They knew best what was good for the people, and they did not expect their judgment to be questioned.

Their natural heirs are the social democrats who defined the vaunted Dutch consensus, which Fortuyn tried to bust wide open. What has happened over the past two decades, particularly since the end of the cold war, is that *regenten* now govern in most democracies, from Britain to Japan. More or less decent technocrats, who feel deeply uncomfortable with ideologies, or even ideas, men and women who know how to tinker and spin, political managers who actually dislike the necessary human contact of campaigning, these are the people who preside over our fortunes.

When there was still a Right and a Left, and class interests were plain to see, politicians were forced to take sides. Now, as politicians so often tell us, there is no more Left or Right. There is only business. The problem is not only that people feel deprived of political choices – hence, presumably, the low voter turnouts in countries such as Britain, France, and the United States – but also that our present-day *regenten* often appear to have a tenuous grip on the business at hand.

And I am not only talking about railways and other public transport débâcles. Multinational corporations, often but by no means exclusively based in the United States, seem to have more power to affect our lives than the men and women we elect to represent our interests. Labour mobility, that is to say legal and illegal migrations, cannot be separated from the world economy. European governments have no idea how to cope with the problems that result from this, and prefer not to discuss them.

In international affairs European nations count for little these days. And the European Union doesn't count for very much more. The United States is the only superpower, and even it often looks like an impotent Gulliver in a world of many, sometimes murderous, Lilliputians. One of the arguments advanced for strengthening the European Union is that only a pan-national web of institutions will be able to cope with all these bewildering global phenomena. This might be true. But the effect has been to make elected governments look even more hapless. And what is the European Commission if not a bunch of typical *regenten*: well-meaning, highly educated patricians who know best and are not open to criticism?

This, then, is why Fortuyn and other telegenic populists – of whom we will probably see many more – score. They have no answers to our most pressing problems either, but at least they raise them in a way people can understand. Like Princess Diana, they manage to embody a multitude of often conflicting discontents. Others, such as Tokyo's governor, Ishihara Shintaro (a man whose racial views make Fortuyn's look positively enlightened), are waiting their turn. Dutch voters, barmy with sentimental grief, might well remember their late hero by electing a string of second-raters, ranters, and has-beens into the government this week.

It probably won't make very much difference. The country will continue to be managed by domestic bureaucrats in Brussels. But that is precisely the problem. For we live in a world were politics don't seem to matter any more. To show us the folly of this was Fortuyn's most valuable lesson.

THE CUSTOM OF
THE COUNTRY

Austin, 11 March 2002

The building identified as the Imperial Hotel, Vienna, page 14 yesterday, is in fact the Karlskirche, one of the city's great baroque churches.

Corrections and Clarifications, 22 May 2002

JON HENLEY

Mind the doors

Mrs Fereira is retiring next month. After thirty-four years scrubbing the stairs, waxing the parquet, watering the plants, dishing out the post, looking after the spare keys and helping the increasingly antiquated residents of our apartment building into the lift, she's calling it a day and going to live with her sister in Burgundy.

This poses something of a problem, because good concierges are getting hard to find. Few people are prepared to live in a dark and cramped ground-floor lodge, at the beck and call of every resident nine hours a day plus four hours on Saturdays, for the equivalent of £600 a month.

'I've tried to find someone,' says the ever-cheerful Mrs Fereira, who is universally acknowledged in our street as *une perle rare* and has been the object of more or less aggressive transfer bids from neighbouring apartment buildings more times than anyone can remember.

'But it's not easy. Young people don't want this kind of work any more. When I came to France you were happy to have somewhere to live and enough francs to feed the baby while your husband looked for a job. Nowadays, it's seen as demeaning.'

Mrs Fereira was part of the mass wave of immigrants who arrived in France from the impoverished Portugal of Salazar's dictatorship in the fifties and early sixties. The unsung success story of French integration, they made no fuss, learned French, sent their kids to school, found themselves jobs as concierges, childminders, seamstresses, odd-job men, builders and electricians.

Today, many of their children – including Mrs Fereira's youngest son, Antonio, who runs a booming computer business in Faro – are heading back to a country their parents barely recognise, transformed by tourism and EU money. These days, Portugal is no longer exporting its labour but importing it: the labourers are Ukrainian, the cleaning ladies come from Belarus.

The house where Mrs Fereira was born, a whitewashed two-room cottage, looks down on the high-rise hotels of Albufeira. In 1962, when she left it with her brother and two cousins to join her husband in France, it had no running water.

'When we first got here we slept on a sofa in my aunt's lodge in the fifteenth arrondissement for the whole winter,' she says. 'My mother in Portugal looked after our first two children until they were four or five, because we were living in a maid's room on the sixth floor and couldn't afford to look after them and keep working.'

So when, thirty-four years ago, Mr Dufayet (the now-deceased but apparently much-feared former chairman of our block's residents' committee) asked the Fereiras to move into the relative comfort of the one-bedroom lodge, they jumped. They raised four children there, in 420 square feet (40 square metres), Mrs Fereira sweeping and scrubbing and polishing, and Mr Fereira working in the shoe-repair and key-cutting franchise at the République métro station.

'Oh, I have some stories to tell,' said Mrs Fereira. 'Mr Dufayet and Mrs Bellanger, now there was one. They thought no one knew, but everyone did. And the time the de Mazeres boy ate four rum babas and fell down the stairs, he was only six. Lots of stories.'

We had a note from Mr de Mazeres last week, the current residents' committee president. Mrs Fereira's lodge and salary represented 20 per cent of our annual outgoings, it said. She was proving hard to replace. Should we not investigate the cost of a contract cleaning company instead?

6 March 2002

CHRIS McGREAL

Mugabe's hard men

Comrade Zhou is old enough to imagine that he fought in the war. At thirty-five he is too young to have borne arms. But the black liberation fighters who ended Ian Smith's deluded vision of perpetual white rule in Rhodesia were a regular part of the landscape of his Mashonaland village during the seventies.

The teenage Zhou, who insists on giving only his recently adopted *nom de guerre*, was caught up in the great struggle as white soldiers periodically swept past his door in pursuit of his heroes of the day. Which makes him a 'war veteran' of sorts.

Now, though, he is looking forward to fighting for real in the war he feels certain will come if Robert Mugabe loses the presidential election this weekend, or, as Comrade Zhou puts it, the 'colonialists try and rule us again'.

The line is pure propaganda, lifted from the perpetual rants on state radio claiming that the opposition Movement for Democratic Change (MDC) is a front for whites and funded by Britain. But Comrade Zhou's scepticism about the election is all his own thinking.

'I do not understand why Comrade Mugabe has to have an election. He is our leader and he won the war. He should stay our leader until he dies and then our chiefs will choose a new leader,' he said. 'Who said we had to have elections? The colonialists. It is a colonial invention and Comrade Mugabe says we are getting rid of these colonial things.'

Comrade Zhou, a short, quietly spoken man who looks older than his years, is the leading 'war veteran' on one of more than 300 farms in the Chinhoyi area, about eighty miles north of Harare. The region has been the scene of much violence, with farmers driven from many properties and thousands of workers either forced to flee or corralled under the control of the 'war veterans' and ruling party militia.

It is also an area Mr Mugabe must win in the presidential ballot on Saturday and Sunday if he is to remain in power. Mashonaland West is traditionally a key

Zanu-PF stronghold and if he cannot take a sizeable chunk of the vote in the province, Mr Mugabe stands little hope across the rest of the country.

Comrade Zhou, an unemployed former bicycle messenger with a wife and five children, is dedicated to ensuring the president's victory on his patch, whatever his doubts about the need for an election. The twenty or so other war veterans and their families under his command and a similar number of farm labourers who profess loyalty to Comrade Zhou – perhaps out of fear, perhaps out of a genuine desire for their own land – know there is no debate about how they will vote.

'We will know if there is a single vote for the colonialists and that person will regret,' he said.

The opposition says it will turn to the courts if Mr Mugabe does not relinquish power. To Comrade Zhou, the law is as much a foreign import as elections.

'There is no law in a war,' he said. 'You try to kill your enemy, and he tries to kill you. You do not say he is breaking the law for trying to kill you. You say, he is your enemy and you must kill him, not put him on trial.'

Still, that has not discouraged either the war veterans or Zanu-PF's militia (now dressed up as the National Youth Service Brigade and given uniforms) from running their own kangaroo courts. Most of those hauled before them are accused of political crimes.

'We had to beat one man because people heard him say it was the president's fault there is no food,' said Comrade Zhou.

Zanu-PF's adverts make clear whom it blames for the fact that millions now go hungry in Zimbabwe: white farmers who are 'hoarding grain' or burning their crops to starve black people.

The ruling party's Youth Brigade was summoned to a nearby property, Nyamgomba farm, after a poster of Mr Mugabe was defaced. The militia threatened to send the entire workforce for 're-education and interrogation' if the culprit did not confess. A mechanic and a foreman were beaten in an attempt to get information.

Eventually one of the workers confessed that he and another man were responsible and they were dispatched to the base camp where they remain. Yet there are growing tensions between Zanu-PF's militia and the war veterans. The new settlers on the farms frequently do want to make the land work for them, but they often need the white farmers' help in ploughing and irrigating the soil.

That is won mostly through intimidation or strikes on those farms still functioning, but sometimes a working relationship is forged. Farmers help out the settlers in return for being allowed to remain in their homes and maintain the rest of their property unmolested.

That accommodation often draws the ire of the ruling party militia which sees it as collaboration with the whites, and it has led to clashes between the war vets and the Zanu-PF Youth Brigade. The militia was created only last year, perhaps because Mr Mugabe no longer entirely controlled or trusted the war veterans, despite Comrade Zhou's loyalty.

These days the veterans and settlers are often preoccupied with food. But the Youth Brigade is dedicated to one thing – political intimidation and terror aimed at pressuring voters to cast their ballots for Mr Mugabe, or at least discouraging those who would vote against him from going to the polls.

The opposition claims there are twenty-three Zanu-PF militia bases in Mashonaland West from which violent political attacks are regularly launched to assault opposition sympathisers, and to which the politically suspect are dragged for indoctrination and beatings. The MDC has organised occasional raids on some of the base camps – some on the farms, some at the back of beer halls – to free its abducted members, although it does not like to boast about them for fear of drawing accusations of provoking violence.

The militia has set up roadblocks at which drivers and bus passengers are forced to show ruling party membership cards or risk a beating. Almost every-one carries one these days. And the Youth Brigade organises 'political meetings' at which MDC supporters are pointed out and carted off. Last month, Zanu-PF thugs rampaged through Chinhoyi town, beating up passers-by and assaulting foreign election observers to the embarrassment of the government.

Behind the militia in the area is the local Zanu-PF member of parliament and party chairman, Phillip Chiyangwa. A member of Mr Mugabe's Gushungo clan, he is described by the pro-government press as a businessman and by the opposition press as a gangster. He drives a Bentley he bought last year after wrecking his Mercedes-Benz.

Mr Chiyangwa claims that the militia is there merely to keep the peace and that it only responds with violence when it is attacked by the MDC. Yet last October, Mr Chiyangwa was caught on camera urging his supporters to kill opposition supporters and burn white-owned farms.

'If you get hold of MDC supporters, beat them until they are dead,' said Mr Chiyangwa. 'Burn their farms and their workers' houses, then run away fast and we will then blame the burning of the workers' houses on the whites. Report to the police, because they are ours.'

Mr Chiyangwa was a soldier in Ian Smith's Rhodesian army but that has done him no harm with Comrade Zhou, who is a big fan. Comrade Zhou is more concerned about what he says is the coming war.

'The colonialists have a lot of power but if they try and rule us we will fight them,' he said. 'Comrade Mugabe has said it, we will never accept to be ruled by Britain again. We know who our enemies are. It does not matter if they are white or black.

'If they do not support Comrade Mugabe, then they are working with the colonialists. We will have to fight them just as we fought Ian Smith and won.'

11 March 2002

CHRIS McGREAL

Ducking democracy

The diehards stuck it out as a matter of principle, but the optimism that their vote might spell Robert Mugabe's doom had gone. Last night, some voters in Zimbabwe's largest township, Chitungwiza, were casting their ballots by candlelight. But many more had finally given up in the face of the obstacles thrown up by the government to prevent its opponents voting.

'I stayed but others went,' said McLaren Hove. 'People thought we were going to get rid of Mugabe, but now they're not so sure. He stopped the people voting because he does not want to leave power. If we cannot vote him out, how do we get rid of him?'

Some people – women with small children and those with jobs – simply could not afford the time to stand in a queue for two days in order to exercise their basic democratic right. Others lost heart and left the seemingly endless lines of people spiralling from the 'voting stations' designed to discourage people from doing just that.

In the parliamentary elections two years ago the ruling Zanu-PF party barely pulled in a quarter of the vote in Chitungwiza. Mr Mugabe was likely to have fared a lot worse in the presidential election, because food shortages, rampant inflation and bitterness at an increasingly abusive government have done considerable damage to his already limited support. And the president knew it.

So the government made the voting process in opposition areas as protracted as possible. At Zengeza 2 voting station, several hundred people were already in line well before it opened on Saturday morning, and the queue kept growing. People who finally emerged from voting accused electoral officials of deliberately 'going slow'.

Respect Sinaro said it had taken him more than half an hour just to have his name checked on the electoral register and receive his ballot papers. One complaint repeated at a number of polling stations was that election officials began at the very beginning of the list and worked their way through the entire voters' roll in search of a name.

'My name is Sinaro,' he said. 'She began looking under "A". I told them: It begins with an "S". She told me she knew how to do her job. It took her twenty minutes just to find my name!'

Zanu-PF slowed the vote further by, for the first time, combining the presidential ballot with local elections, despite a court order that they should be held on separate dates.

As the day got hotter, tensions grew. Zimbabweans are a courteous people and in any other circumstances old ladies being ushered to the front of the queue would receive general approval. But the mood of suspicion outside the voting stations yesterday was such that some saw it as further evidence of conspiracy.

'See those old ladies?' muttered one potential voter. 'They all support Mugabe. They are Zanu-PF. That's why they get to vote first. It's wrong.'

On Saturday morning, the notorious war veterans' leader, Joseph Chinotimba, arrived to 'consult' election officials. In breach of electoral law, he marched into the voting tent and held up the ballot for ten minutes while he harangued nervous officials. The crowd booed Mr Chinotimba and gave the open palm MDC salute.

Late last night, about 1,900 people had managed to vote at Zengeza 2 polling station. There were more than that in the queue when it opened on Saturday.

16 July 2002

ANDREW MELDRUM

Four-minute milestone

Press freedom doesn't last long in Zimbabwe these days. It lasted precisely four minutes for me yesterday. Four euphoric minutes between the moment the magistrate bravely found me not guilty and the heart-sinking instant when immigration officials told me that, courts be damned, I had to leave the country.

Let's start with that first moment of elation: 'The government finds the defendant not guilty,' he said.

As those magical words filled the courtroom, I stepped out of the stinking dock into a flurry of hugs, kisses, handshakes, congratulations. Euphoria.

Over the weekend I had prepared for this moment, deciding to make the same statement to other journalists covering my trial whether the verdict went for or against me: 'This case has succeeded in exposing the Mugabe government in perverting the rule of law, in order to stamp out a free press. I have not committed any crime or broken any law. I have only done what any responsible journalist would do, which is to report on gross human rights abuses and rampant corruption in order to hold this government accountable for the good of the Zimbabwean people.'

My unhappy distinction has been to be the first of more than a dozen journalists to stand trial on charges under the government's Access to Information Protection of Privacy Act. The new law carries a benign-sounding name, but that disguises its draconian intent to hobble the country's critical press. The charge against me was that I had published a 'falsehood' that a woman was beheaded by President Robert Mugabe's supporters in front of her children because she supported the opposition Movement for Democratic Change (MDC). The horrific story purportedly came from the husband, but it turned out that he had lied.

The magistrate, Godfrey Macheyo, found that I had tried to verify the story by calling the police. I had also made inquiries with the MDC and with human rights organisations, who said they were investigating the report, adding that it was consistent with a pattern of state-sponsored violence since the presidential election in March. I had verified reports of eighteen deaths due to political violence since the elections and a total of fifty-seven deaths since the beginning of the year.

It is worth sparing a thought for the magistrate at this point. These are bleak times for Zimbabwe and any act of courage stands out. Mr Macheyo found me not guilty despite all the pressure that he must have been under. That has deep personal significance for me in that my name has been cleared. More importantly, it will give hope to the thirteen other journalists facing trial under similar charges, who can refer to the ruling as a precedent. The bad news is that the government seems determined to ignore the will of the courts. Hence its action to expel me against all legal rights.

I know I committed no crime. Even so, the relief was overwhelming when the magistrate ruled I had acted as a responsible journalist.

'This is vindication not only for me but for all journalists in Zimbabwe and the freedom of the press,' I told journalists. 'We have won the first round but the battle for genuine press freedom in this country is far from over.'

How right I was.

Four minutes after Mr Macheyo's verdict, an immigration official handed me papers that removed my permanent resident status and ordered me to leave Zimbabwe within twenty-four hours. Back swept the sober, sombre determination which has been my lot since I was arrested and jailed on 1 May. Courthouse flurry turned into a frenzy of loved ones, friends, supporters, snapping cameras, microphones.

'This action by the government to expel me from the country,' I told them, 'highlights the same thing as my trial, that the Mugabe government wants to silence me and other journalists. This shows just how far they will go.'

As I write, we are waiting for the high court to hear an appeal against what is clearly an illegal deportation. But even if that appeal is successful, a cloud now hangs over me. Just over a year ago, the BBC correspondent Joseph Winter was ordered out of the country. He appealed, and won a court order allowing him to stay for two further weeks. It did not end there. At 2 a.m. on the night of the appeal, Winter's home was attacked by a gang of thugs, later identified as agents of the notorious Central Intelligence Organisation. Winter and his wife and young daughter quickly left their home with British high commission officials. Shortly afterwards, the gang ransacked their home.

This is a far cry from the law-abiding Zimbabwe, the land of liberty, equality and reconciliation that greeted me twenty-two years ago. In the eighties it was thrilling to report on a newly independent Zimbabwe and its success in building a new, just society on the wreckage of the violent repression of Ian Smith's Rhodesia. Gradually, the stories turned more gloomy as the Mugabe government committed ever more glaring misdeeds, including the Matabeleland massacres in which Mr Mugabe's élite fifth brigade is blamed for the deaths of an estimated 20,000 civilians.

For the past two years of Zimbabwe's unrelenting political and economic crisis, my dispatches, along with those of my colleagues in the local and international press, have focused on the Mugabe government's human rights abuses, rampant corruption and erosion of the rule of law. Such reporting is what any responsible journalist would produce. It must not be stopped.

Andrew Meldrum, an American citizen, has lived in Zimbabwe since 1980 and has been a Guardian *correspondent there since 1983. He was still in Zimbabwe when this book went to press.*

21 January 2002

PETER PRESTON

Spanish practices

I suppose you could say that my current inquiries into the state of European healthcare went rather deeper than anything managed by Dr Liam Fox or Alan Milburn. I didn't just go and look at hospitals. I became the involuntary English patient.

Too easily done. A dark night in a pretty deserted Catalan village. A trip and a heavy fall, cannoning sideways into a giant flowerpot. When I got back to home base, the ribs were shrieking and I was bleeding internally. Kidney damage? Not (even by my battered lights) a good scene.

The ambulance came – from the local town, six miles away – in fifteen minutes. On to that town's little all-night clinic; then, at the double, to the hospital in Palamos (population 15,000). Ninety-two minutes after the fall, I'd been x-rayed, assessed, put on a drip and given a bed in the emergency ward, blood pressure monitored on the hour. By eight in the morning, I'd had an ultrasound scan of the kidneys.

NORMAL said the scanner lugubriously. NORMAL. But the bleeding hadn't stopped. Getting better (on solemn doctor's orders) involved four more days and nights lying immobile in a bed upstairs. Plenty of time to think and observe, as well as ache.

What was different about this place? How was it different from, say, the south London hospital of rather grim repute where my mother-in-law once took her 89-year-old broken hip? Here are a few of the differences – some physical, some social, some organisational.

Physically, there weren't any wards in the old British manner – and certainly not the mixed-sex agglomeration my mother-in-law found so humiliating. Palamos gives you a large room to share (suitably curtained) between two, a phone at your right hand, a light switch and buzzer at your left. The room comes with a loo, shower and basin and coin-in-the-slot TV. In no sense lush; indeed, rather bare. But fresh and clean. The first person in each morning, before it was light, was the cleaner.

Socially, you might as well have been on another planet. There are no defined visiting hours. My wife slept with me the first night upstairs on an aeroplane-type chair by the bed. Standard practice in Spain: all relatives welcome. My roomshare beyond the curtain had an operation at six one evening, was wheeled back from theatre at 9.30 and seemed then to stage a bustle of comings and goings till twenty-five minutes to midnight. You don't feel – from the noise – as though you're in hospital. It's more like a good party where the drinks have run out. Revitalisation? Si. Recuperation? Maybe.

Organisationally, they believe in clockwork. You could set your watch by the appearance of meals, temperature-takers, linen-changers (new linen every day at 10.30), bed-bathers. Everybody – except one glum night nurse – smiled. I made the average bell response time fifty-one seconds. No demarcation lines. Nurses or radiographers turn porters in an instant if that's sensible. No queueing. On discharge morning, they fetched me for a second x-ray and scan exactly when they'd said they would. The doctor arrived on cue. I was checked and on my way out in three meticulous hours. Efficiency – even in the middle of a Catalan flu epidemic – lives. As you arrive, they give you a report card to tick on the way out about your treatment.

I've no way of knowing whether Palamos hospital – founded 1761 – is in any way exceptional. The boys in my village bar say it's fine, better than Girona. 'Though you should try France. That's perfecto.' And, of course, there are surely many better hospitals around than the decrepit, rigidly dour place my mother-in-law encountered a few days before she died. Even so, Palamos came up trumps. It was cheery, carefully organised and care-filled. I'd have done brilliantly to have found its like in Britain at the first time of asking (and I might have found the Portland).

Now for the nitty-gritty. Five nights, drips, drugs, ambulances, food and two complete sets of tests cost £980 on travel insurance – because I hadn't got an EU form E111 with me. That, stacked against £300 for an annual forty-five minutes of Harley Street check-up, is amazing value. It also points to the door where Messrs Fox and Milburn might like to knock.

The way Spain finances its health (at around the European average that Mr Blair would aspire to immediately, if only his defence spending wasn't far above the European average) is calculated to invite a British frown. The State, via taxation, buys you what Ally Campbell would probably call 'bog-standard care'. In time of emergency need, nobody worries. (I'd have been treated the same in Palamos whatever scheme or non-scheme operated.) But that isn't the whole of the story. Beyond the bog standard, there's also private insurance and super-private insurance.

We don't need to worry about the super club. That's just big bucks as usual. But the modest insurance route (a mix and match with state provision) is much more interesting. For one thing, it's relatively cheap. My daughter pays just under £1 a day – a cup of coffee – for coverage which allows her access to a chosen doctor, chosen hospitals to give birth in, and stay for four days, annual dental checks – the lot. For another thing, millions of people – a huge majority – take out the policy. It is the norm rather than the exception.

It echoes a mix of means and methods (where the State sometimes finances private hospitals). It sanctions choice and convenience. It separates the good from the slack, because quality follows the funds flow. Being a customer matters. It buys the equipment. It puts extra cash directly into the central system.

Is that what Nye Bevan would hail as his dream made flesh? Perhaps not. Egalitarianism gags at the public/private divide. So, in British terms, does the political necessity of paying something extra for a supposedly 'free' service. New Labour has seen this future – and dived for cover. For all his Swedish foreplay, Iain Duncan Smith will probably do likewise.

'But why shouldn't people who can afford to pay be asked to pay something?' enquires a Spanish doctor. It is what makes their health service viable – for the price of a grotty package holiday. It can, as a matter of priority, be afforded. It is pitched low because it needs to keep costs down for the many – not set them high for exclusiveness. It trains the extra doctors and nurses Mr Milburn would like to recruit. And all for the price of a cup of coffee. There's the principle (paradise lost) and the practicality. And the question – as the bleeding man said when he cannoned into an amphora – is: what's so wrong, if those who were ill get better?

16 May 2002

MAGGIE O'KANE

In pursuit of Karadzic

Our spy's flat has large rooms with grey, speckled marble floors. Below his balcony is the mark left behind by an exploding mortar that missed his bedroom. He survived for forty-two months of Sarajevo's siege without a scratch.

He is the kind of man who had electricity when nobody else did; knew how to get his telephone working during the war when nobody else could; and managed to keep his drinks cabinet stocked with a rare, lavender-scented herbal brandy from the beautiful Croatian island of Kortula. He had contacts. He watched Dr Radovan Karadzic in his early days working with the Yugoslav secret service. He knows how the inside works – who's watching whom.

We are in his flat scrutinising a list of locations where Karadzic has been hiding over the past two years – locations provided to the *Guardian* by Bosnian intelligence sources. There are nineteen of them, including Orthodox monasteries, private houses, military barracks and hunting lodges – some known to the international forces, some not.

'It looks a pretty reasonable list to me,' he says, reading down through the locations. 'He's got huge support in those mountains in eastern Bosnia, and the Orthodox Church is hiding him. There is intelligence coming in, but they can't move fast enough and Karadzic has his own people tipping him off if anything strange moves on the roads. The border is like Swiss cheese and he can move in and out.'

I first interviewed Karadzic on the seventh floor of the Holiday Inn in Sarajevo just four days before the Bosnian war broke out in April 1992. Back then he surrounded himself with the trimmings of the power he loved, such as bodyguards in black leather and sunglasses ushering journalists in to meet him. But Karadzic, who turns fifty-seven next month, had a friendly, almost puppy-like demeanour in those days. Eager to please, he had the air of the friendly local GP he once had been. Then, like an enthusiastic weekend hiker, he laid out a map of Bosnia on the glass table in what was know as the Holiday Inn's Olympic suite.

Looking at the patchwork quilt of mixed races and creeds that made up the map, he began: 'The Croats will have this bit. The Muslims will have to be moved to here. We will control this area.'

I remember thinking and writing at the time: 'Is this man mad?'

Now, 170,000 deaths later, Karadzic has twice been indicted for genocide in Bosnia, but he is still free.

'I will have the three of them [Slobodan Milosevic, Karadzic and Ratko Mladic] here shortly,' The Hague's chief prosecutor, Carla del Ponte, told the *Guardian* last year. Now she has grown tired of waiting and last month said she didn't believe NATO forces in Bosnia (19,000 troops) were capable of picking them up.

The subtext is that it is the United States that will now finish the Karadzic business. It is the only country with a technological and intelligence network capable of picking him up. America is also applying huge financial pressure on Belgrade and Karadzic's runt state of Republika Srpska to hand him over. Last Friday, for the first time since the indictments were first handed down seven years ago, the Republika Srpska handed over five indictees to The Hague.

At 8.35 a.m. on 28 February, Goran Nogovic, a 42-year-old teacher of Russian at the Branko Gagovic school, looked out of the window of his grubby, white-washed secondary-school building on the brow of the hill in the muddy mountain village of Celebici. At the bottom of the slope four US military transport helicopters were landing simultaneously on the football pitch. About half of the eighty men on board wore masks. All wore German and US military badges.

They began by kicking in the doors of the municipal offices next door to the potato store. Watching them from a peeling whitewash wall was a poster of Draza Mihailovic, the nationalist hero of the second world war hanged by Tito for war crimes. Mihailovic only managed to hide out in these same Durmitor mountains for a year before the partisans caught up with him.

Karadzic has survived for seven, mainly because, until now, nobody has really been looking for him. Since his indictment for genocide in 1995, Karadzic's time as a fugitive has gone through various phases. First, he claimed he was assured by the United States envoy, Richard Holbrooke, that as long as he kept out of sight he would be out of mind. For a number of years he was regularly seen by NATO troops who were reluctant to risk destabilising the peace and left him alone.

Over the past two years, as Britain has led the way in picking up war criminals, his days have looked numbered. Then, after 11 September, the mood changed. The United States wanted a massive scaling-down of their forces in Bosnia. Colin Powell has called Karadzic their 'exit strategy' from Bosnia.

Serb President Vojislav Kostunica says the pressure from the United States to hand over the indicted men is 'unrelenting'. The ransom on offer is US$120 million in aid. It seems that these are the last days of Karadzic. It's also becoming clear that it is the United States who run the Radovan show. When the first major swoop to lift him took place in Celebici on 28 February, key figures in NATO did not even know of the US action.

'There was a bit of a time-lag before we were informed,' says a NATO spokesman.

This is Radovan country. In the mountains of eastern Bosnia he has become a folk hero. Songs are composed about him: 'He's been hiding in the mountains of fir trees – so the Americans can't reach him. Romano mountains spread your fir trees, brother Radovan keep safe.' But with the US now offering $5 million for information leading to his arrest, the pressure is building. Hundreds of thousands of ransom leaflets are being dropped on the mountains of eastern Bosnia. A slick US-funded advertisement offering the ransom is being touted to Bosnia Serb TV – rates of around $1,000 per second are being offered to get the ad on air.

So far there have been no takers, but the mood is changing as more and more indictees including Milosevic are ending up in The Hague without an outbreak of civil war.

'I'd sell my father to The Hague for that kind of money,' says a shop owner in Celebici. Even heroes have their price.

Few will now admit to being a Karadzic friend; even fewer will go public. Marko Vesovic, a poet and professor of philosophy at Sarajevo University, was a friend when they both arrived as teenagers in the city.

'If it hadn't been for the circumstances,' he says, 'Karadzic would have died a respectable and esteemed doctor in Sarajevo. He was created by the situation. His weakness was money. But when he first started out as a politician he was communicative, hearty and people liked him. Even the Muslims were stopping me on the street and saying "That friend of yours, he's a pretty decent guy."'

'I'd say he's got a couple of months at the most,' says a British intelligence source in the Bosnian Serb capital of Banja Luka. 'They didn't get him, but kicking down doors in Celebici was a way of letting the locals know that it is coming soon.'

Tracking and intelligence used for watching Karadzic is limited to either paid spies or unmanned drones that scan the mountains – although the war in Afghanistan has led to a shortage of drones.

High in the mountain is the now abandoned national park of Sutjeska, where families once came to spend their summers. Now the lack of business has left it in a dilapidated state. The park keeper knows the lodge we are looking for at Gacka. German troops last visited it two months ago, checking for arms and Karadzic. They had to wade waist-deep in snow, and found it empty. According to Bosnian intelligence, Karadzic now rarely spends more than forty-eight hours in one location before moving on, sometimes by foot, sometimes on unmarked roads. The problem for the US Special Forces is how to mount an operation when the locations are constantly shifting and they are relying mostly on spies to provide the information.

'Kick them out,' Bishop Radovic Amfilohije of Cetinje monastery tells his aides when we attempt to ask him why he's on our intelligence list as one of three bishops offering support and shelter to Karadzic.

When we visit he is conducting a three-hour service around the town of Cetinje to mark the first day of Orthodox Lent. He says he is too tired to be interviewed about his monastery being listed as a refuge for Karadzic.

'This is a place of God and God offers refuge to any man who needs it,' he says, describing Karadzic as a poet and politician.

In the church's shrine they still keep the pickled head of Mahmut Pana, the Turkish commander who dared to defy the might of the Serb army.

Brother Luka, one of the monks based in Cetinje monastery, is more upfront. 'Of course we would give him shelter,' he says, 'but he is not here. He is with his own people in eastern Bosnia. Radovan Karadzic has found refuge.'

The village graveyard is filled with black marble headstones with the name 'Karadzic' marked in gold lettering. In a place where the mountain snows close them in for months, the only solace is the brandy brewed from rosehips and the salted ham and mutton hanging in the smoking shed ready for another winter.

In Karadzic's home village of Petnijica he is a local hero. They are wary of outsiders. His cousin, Vusko, is one of the few members of the family who have stayed in the village in the Durmitor mountains.

'What did he do that is different from his ancestors? His ancestors were warriors and they fought against and killed the Turks. Today the Muslims are the new Turks, so why should we be ashamed of him?'

Radovan, one of four children, grew up in a single-room stone cottage. The family left for the city after Karadzic's father was convicted of the rape and murder of a young cousin – something his cousin Vusko admits openly to us but that Karadzic has never mentioned in public.

Last Friday, Mirko Sarevic's government took the step The Hague has been waiting for since Republika Srpska's foundation. It handed over five indicted men – former police officers charged with rounding up Muslims for torture, murder and deportation in the summer of 1992. Although blackmailed into the handover by a block on international aid – instigated by the United States – Republika Srpska's move marks another bad omen for Karadzic.

It's a big change from February, when Carla del Ponte demanded that the president hand over the sixteen indicted war criminals on his territory. Sarevic told her he couldn't find any of them.

Republika Srpska, like Serbia, is feeling the unrelenting pressure from the United States. Without aid, they will become the subsistence farmers that they were in the nineteenth century. The population is just over one million – the same as that of Birmingham. There is no industry, no tourism. Men with nothing to do play giant chess outside the president's office. The local hotel in the kingdom's second city, Foca, has no guests, except for a couple of journalists wearily following the list of Karadzic locations. A waitress trips across the icy dining room to a single occupied table.

'Any toast?'

'No, just eggs.'

'Any butter?'

'No butter.'

'Maybe jam?'

'No jam. Just eggs,' she blazes.

Trapped in a land mass the size of Wales, Serbs make bad victims. They see themselves as the targets of an international conspiracy and are unable to look their past in the face. As far as many Serbs are concerned, Karadzic has never made it to The Hague because he has committed no crime.

In Belgrade, the Committee to Defend Radovan Karadzic inhabits a strange Orwellian world where there was no genocide. The Committee has published the latest volume of his poetry, *From the Crazy Spear to the Black Fairytale*, and its publication was marked by a reading to a select gathering at an élite literary salon in Belgrade. Here, they paint a picture of a mild-mannered poet who only did what he could to save his people.

In the literary drawing room of committee member Momo Kapor, artist, raconteur and poet, there was never a genocide; the 10,000 who died in Sarajevo were mostly targeted by their own side to gain international sympathy. On Kapor's sideboard is a picture of him with Karadzic's General Ratko Mladic – also indicted for genocide. The same General Mladic who patted the head of a boy in the UN safe haven of Srebrenica, assuring him: 'Nobody is going to hurt you.' In the three days that followed, 8,000 Muslim men and boys were massacred. The general and Kapor are smiling in the picture. General Mladic has his arm around the slight waist of Kapor's beautiful wife.

Does he have no concerns about being photographed with General Mladic, the man wanted for genocide in Srebrenica?

'No,' says Kapor, passing around the brandy again. He then explains to the group around the table: 'What you don't see in the picture is that it is taken with us standing on the bodies of dead Muslims.' He laughs.

There is a barely discernible intake of breath around the table from the other members of the Committee to Defend Radovan Karadazic – still mostly sober. Then the breath is released. It is a joke. He is drunk. Poetic licence. Kapor keeps laughing. The other members of the committee laugh.

'Oh Momo,' says his beautiful wife adoringly.

7 June 2002

JONATHAN STEELE

Milosevic in court

Fixing him with a supercilious smile, Slobodan Milosevic asks the witness: 'If there is armed combat between two groups, on what part of the body will you see wounds?'

'There are too many variables,' says Dr Eric Baccard, the chief forensic pathologist of the International Criminal Tribunal for former Yugoslavia. He sounds defensive.

'Isn't it routine training to aim for the head and trunk?' Mr Milosevic sneers

After four months of the former Yugoslav president's trial for crimes against humanity in Kosovo, Bosnia and Croatia, Mr Milosevic is on the attack. Far from embarrassed by the sixty-six counts, he enjoys cross-examining the witnesses.

The press and public galleries are barely a quarter full for the most momentous trial in Europe since Nazi leaders were convicted at Nuremberg. Yet Mr Milosevic does not care about the meagre attendance. He is playing to the audience in Serbia, which was sceptical of the tribunal before its former leader took the stand. This is his chance to prove them right.

Today the subject is the January 1999 Racak massacre, often seen as the trigger for NATO bombing of Yugoslavia two months later. Forty-five ethnic Albanians were found dead in a gulley. The Albanians say they were villagers, executed in cold blood by Yugoslav forces and Serb police. The authorities counter that some were Kosovo Liberation Army (KLA) fighters, while others were civilians who died in crossfire – the KLA, they say, moved the bodies to fake a massacre.

Mr Milosevic is focusing on the head wounds received by twenty-three of the dead, suggesting that the police and soldiers were well-trained marksmen who shot them from a distance rather than executed them. He queries whether autopsies can determine the distance from which weapons were fired, implying that it is not clear that the men were killed at close range, and ignores evidence in which the pathologist states that more than half of the dead were shot in the back of the head or trunk.

Silence is not part of his armoury. Although he declined to make a plea when the trial began in February, refuses to accept the court's jurisdiction (he calls the judge 'Mr May', never 'Your honour') and rejects defence lawyers, Mr Milosevic is conducting a ferociously energetic defence on his own. He uses all of his available time and regularly demands more.

Whether witnesses are professional experts, Kosovo Albanian politicians, British army officers or ordinary peasants, Mr Milosevic treats them all as though they are evading the truth. No witness is too humble. He tries to catch all out in minor contradictions or memory lapses which he builds as major flaws.

At the Nuremberg trials, death camp survivors were able to speak freely before the Nazi leaders who ordered mass killings. In The Hague, ethnic Albanian villagers find themselves cross-examined by the very man whose forces killed their loved ones.

Some victims hope for catharsis from their confrontation. Few get it. Shukri Gexhaliu – a doctor who was on a convoy of civilians that Serb police stopped before executing most of the men – thanked Judge Richard May profusely at the end of his evidence for the chance to testify. But most are not so composed by the time Mr Milosevic finishes with them.

Visibly distressed by the fierce questioning, Agim Zeqiri told Judge May that he had had a sleepless night and asked to be let off testifying for a second day. Sadik Januzi, an eighty-year-old peasant, was the only man to emerge alive from a massacre in Izbica after hiding under the bodies which fell around him.

'You haven't asked about what I went through at the massacre,' he said in despair when Mr Milosevic said he had no more questions.

Boredom and depression are every prisoner's worst enemies. For Mr Milosevic, held in detention for over a year, the trial is a psychological escape. He arrives every day with great energy for the fray and is well prepared by a team of legal advisers in the public gallery and in Belgrade.

Showing a surprising lack of sensitivity about the special nature of this case, the prosecution has never invited psychologists to warn witnesses about Mr Milosevic's bullying and prepare them for the strain. Many witnesses call for doctors and suffer severe anxiety after their testimony.

Mr Milosevic aims to show that ethnic Albanians lived well in Kosovo, and that independence demands were not motivated by Serb discrimination, but by the KLA and the West. Similarly, it was the NATO bombing, and not Serb repression, which caused ethnic Albanians to flee.

The main charge – that regardless of the existence of KLA fighters Mr Milosevic ordered the use of excessive force against civilians – gets lost. He constantly complains that the court is biased. In fact, procedures are stacked in his favour. By rejecting the court's jurisdiction he won several advantages.

For one thing, he looks more dignified. Officials of the chief prosecutor, Carla del Ponte, were afraid he would take no part in the trial and switch off the headphones that give translations. So they rigged up a small loudspeaker just out of his reach. As a result, he is the only person who never has to don clumsy headphones. He lolls back in his swivel chair, often with his left arm draped round the back in a pose of relaxed contempt.

At one point, when the judge told him not to argue with witnesses, Mr Milosevic snapped: 'Mr May, I only insist on getting an answer. I am not aware of having quarrelled with any witnesses. These false witnesses do not merit my arguing with them.'

By refusing to plead, he also escapes the necessity of having to take the witness stand and be cross-examined. Although Judge May regularly cuts his questions short for straying into political irrelevancies, Mr Milosevic is given more time because he is not using lawyers.

Like a filibustering US senator, he insists on cross-examining every prosecution witness. Under pressure of time, the prosecution has had to curtail the list. Because their evidence is 'cumulative', each one telling a similar story, they were permitted to give it in written form. While Mr Milosevic uses his right to question them for an hour, prosecutors get five minutes.

Florence Hartmann, the chief prosecutor's spokeswoman, accepts that her side seems poorly organised, with witnesses appearing seemingly at random. This is largely due to tight schedules, she says.

Another reason for the slow progress is that this is the first case covering Kosovo. As there is no defence team, the two sides cannot produce an agreed statement of facts. Evidence has to be led just to show that killings and an exodus of refugees took place, even though the historical record leaves no doubt.

Ms Hartmann complains about lack of time. The three judges have ruled that the prosecution's evidence on Kosovo must finish in July. The prosecutor will then have until next April to bring evidence against Mr Milosevic for Croatia and Bosnia. Mr Milosevic will have an equivalent fourteen months to mount a defence.

The prosecution is trying to prove Mr Milosevic ordered systematic and widespread attacks on civilians, but in Belgrade the media has made much of its failure to get a significant Serb 'insider' to testify. To win a conviction the prosecution only needs to show that Mr Milosevic was aware that his subordinates were committing crimes and that he failed to stop them or punish them.

There is a banality about justice, and if you dip into court for only a day or two Mr Milosevic's energetic and confident style can give the impression that he is doing well. But the mounting weight of evidence against him appears overwhelming.

PUT OUT MORE FLAGS

Steve Bell, 1 May 2002

Two hundred and fifty thousand people lining the streets. Stuff that, you chippy republican nitwits.

Letter from Sean Thomas, London, 6 April 2002

20 June 2002

JONATHAN GLANCEY

St George's cross

Every country has its cross to bear and England's is St George's. Never in the field of English history, or at least not since the Crusades or Agincourt, have so many red-cross flags been waved by so many for so many. Today's crusaders are not mythically chivalrous knights but, among other emanations of this patriotic breed, white-van drivers hurtling their unstoppable, gear-crunching mounts through city centres, horns blaring. Or teenage girls, beer bottles in hand, yelling the technically witless yet emotionally resonant cries of modern, foot-ball-mad England. You can easily imagine them charging down from East Anglia to Londinium with Boudicca to tackle the Romans 2,000 years ago. 'We're gonna beat the Italians . . . yeah.' Like the Iceni, these contemporary warriors paint their faces before going into action – and drink and shout a lot.

I talk to a white-van driver in London's Smithfield. Seven in the morning. Rap music pounding from the cab. Thumpa-whoompa. Two huge red-cross flags fluttering from his mechanical steed, a Ford. He sports a Nike baseball cap, Gap sweatshirt, trainers and jeans. He chews gum.

'Call myself English?' He attempts a James Dean sneer. 'Course I'm fuckin' English.'

England has changed since 1966, when its football team trounced the old Hun and brought the World Cup home. Telly was black and white, steam expresses still ran from Waterloo, Leeds and Liverpool Lime Street. Old Labour sat in Westminster. Decimal currency was five years off. The class war, despite the Beatles and the future Sir Michael Jagger, Twiggy, satire and David Bailey, waged on. Footballers were working-class heroes with saggy shorts, terrible hair-cuts and, in the case of Nobby Stiles, no front teeth. Beer was warmly and frothily English, the baseball cap 100 per cent all-American. And football fans waved the union flag.

That year, 1966, the union flag was all the rage, the begetter of minidresses and underpants, paint jobs for Minis and jackets for shampooed pop stars. In the intervening years, the poor old union flag has become increasingly associated with football hooliganism and rightwing extremists, the kernel of an ever-growing debate about what it means to be British – or, closer to the bone and blood, English, Scottish, Welsh, or Irish. For immigrants coming into the country in the sixties what the union flag spelt was Empire.

The revival of the avowedly English cross of St George might have something to do with devolution, the English taking a leaf from the book of patriotism as practised by an increasingly proud and defiant Celtic fringe. It might simply be a striking and memorable pattern or logo that, unlike the union flag, even an idiot can paint across their face. It does look good. Which hugely paid advertising agency or design consultancy could come up with a more powerful logo?

This red-cross flag of In-ger-land has, by happy accident, been saved from being tarred with a blunt nationalist brush this summer because, almost unimaginably, it has become an emblem that embraces football fans of every class, creed and colour. It flaps from the nation's Indian takeaways, from the fly-blown, fluorescent-lit offices of minicab firms staffed by the latest waves of what spiteful, Little England newspapers insist on calling 'bogus asylum seekers', when what they mean is low-paid workers from even lower-paid countries willing to do our dirty work, and yet choosing to fly the flag of old England's whiter-than-white patron saint.

Such has been the demand for St George crosses that Aggy Akhtar, a businessman in London's East End, has sold £6 million worth of them since going into business two months ago. Even four years ago, at the last World Cup, the flag had yobbish baggage; now it has been embraced by everyone. A flag that, in recent decades, had been kept flying mostly over old parish churches in preened and polished villages has become an unlikely partner in the creation of an In-ger-land where Pakistanis and Afghans, Ghanaians, Ukrainians and the descendants of the Iceni can live cheek by painted jowl. Perhaps.

A peek into any of the Lives of the Saints, however, shows that St George is not such an unlikely patron of multiculturalism after all. He is, in fact, a perfect saint for our times and for a national team managed by a quietly spoken Swede and made up of black and white players with names like Émile rather than Nobby.

Not that the story starts out this way. We know virtually nothing about the life of the real St George. Eusebius of Caesarea, writing in around AD322, tells of a soldier of noble birth who was put to death under Diocletian at Nicomedia on 23 April (St George's Day) AD303. Eusebius had no name for this gallant, much less a place of birth, or even the site of his burial. The Crusaders believed this to be near what is now Tel Aviv.

In the fifth-century Acts of St George, our hero was said not only to have defended Christians against Roman persecution, but to have visited Caerleon and Glastonbury while on active service in the imperial army. Before the Norman invasion, churches had been dedicated to St George. Adopted as the patron saint of soldiers, he was said to have appeared to the Crusader army at the Battle of Antioch in 1098. Richard the Lionheart put his armies under the protection of St George when campaigning in Palestine in 1191–92.

The red-cross flag made its debut in 1284, and in the fourteenth century English soldiers donned their legendary red-cross battle dresses. When Richard II invaded Scotland in 1385, every man was ordered to wear 'a sign of the arms of St George', both before and behind, with death promised to enemy soldiers who dared to 'bear the same cross or token of St George'.

St George had become the acknowledged patron saint of England, and in 1415, the year of Agincourt, Archbishop Chichele declared St George's Day a feast to be observed like Christmas Day. One of St George's arms was delivered to Canterbury cathedral where it became a huge pilgrim attraction. In 1940, during the Blitz, King George VI instituted the George Cross for acts of heroism; on one side of the medal St George is depicted slaying the dragon – at the time, of course, Adolf Hitler.

Despite this English devotion to St George, he was fêted elsewhere. And here, perhaps, lies his strength and even his relevance today. For George is venerated not just by the Church of England, but by the Orthodox and Coptic churches. He is the patron saint of Aragon, Bavaria, Catalonia, Georgia, Lithuania, Palestine, Portugal, Germany and Greece, and of Moscow, Istanbul, Genoa and Venice (second to St Mark). He is the patron saint of soldiers, cavalry and chivalry; of farmers and field workers, boy scouts and butchers; of horses, riders and saddlers; and of sufferers from leprosy, plague and syphilis. He is – remember Agincourt – the patron saint of archers.

Of course, George is a Christian saint, as Spenser reminds us in *The Faerie Queene*:

> But on his breast a bloody Cross he bore
> The dear remembrance of his dying Lord,
> For whose sweet sake that glorious badge we wore,
> And dead (as living) ever he adored.

His bloody cross and the bloodier crusades it signalled were rightly feared and justly despised by Muslims. Today, though, World Cup football might just have redeemed this ancient symbol. Although many of us were brought up to believe that the English had no need to shout their identity and that patriotism was the last refuge of a scoundrel, and many more of us, whatever we feel about England, or In-ger-land, have never waved a red-cross flag (nor even a union flag) in our lives, the fact that so many people from so many different backgrounds can wrap themselves in this antique emblem shows that there might – might – just be a little chivalry behind the effing, blinding, beery bravado after all.

10 April 2002

JONATHAN FREEDLAND

Farewell to an age that has gone

'Stop all the clocks,' demands the poem. Halt time in its tracks; let the world stand still. That, W. H. Auden knew, is what every mourner wants and can never have. But for the Queen yesterday, for two transforming hours, the impossible seemed to come true.

She came to bury her mother in a building nearly a thousand years old in a ceremony that could have taken place a century ago. Surrounded by kings and queens and dukes and duchesses from faraway lands, guarded by soldiers in uniforms of an antique past, they recited prayers and verses as old as England.

The very space around them seemed to shed years. The cars around Westminster Abbey were banished, only horses remained. The clatter of traffic was gone, replaced by the music of marching feet, pipes and drums. For one morning only, the twenty-first century was held at bay. 'Let the traffic police-men wear black cotton gloves,' wrote Auden. The gloves were white yesterday, but they worked the same magic.

Everything went perfectly, without a hint of crass modernity to break the spell. There was an announcement to switch off mobile phones and the occa-sional photographer's shutter, like the flutter of a bird's wings overhead. But nothing more.

At the Great West Door of the abbey stood Douglas Hurd in a costume that might have come direct from the court of the first Queen Elizabeth. In orange cape and white ruff he looked like a medieval plotter, a Norfolk or Walsingham, rather than a former cabinet minister. But Hurd is High Steward of Westminster and, since that is what the High Steward has always worn, that is what he wore yesterday.

Inside, the redcoats and white-plumed helmets of the Gentlemen-at-Arms appeared, only their headgear visible to most of the 2,311 guests who had by now taken their seats. It was a sight that might have come from a storybook of old England published when the Queen Mother was a little girl. Or a century earlier, for that matter.

The politicians were in their pews, too, but they arrived with no ceremony: this was not their show, after all. Tony Blair looked a solitary figure, bereft of jewels and garbed in a plain dark suit.

By 11 a.m. everything was ready, waiting only for the royal party to arrive. They were in two groups. The first led by the Duke of Edinburgh and his four children: Charles and Andrew heavy with medals and ceremonial garb, Anne making more protocol history as a woman in a man's ritual, and Edward, luck-lessly looking like a head waiter in a morning suit that denoted his non-record of military service.

They walked behind the coffin as it made its journey from Westminster Hall, where it had rested since Friday. It was borne atop the Gun Carriage of the King's Troop, Royal Artillery. In 2002 there is no king but there is still a King's Troop: the Queen maintained it, in deference to her late father. In that, as in so much else, it could have been 1950.

Meanwhile the Queen was setting off by car, in a limousine so grand it would not have looked out of place at her own coronation. At her side was the Duchess of Grafton, not because she is a friend or relative but because she carries the time-honoured title of Mistress of the Robes.

When the Queen finally entered the abbey, she was greeted with a Mexican wave of bowing and curtseying, a domino effect as one noble head after another dipped to note her passing. All the while, the abbey seemed to tremble with the bass notes of the Bach fugue sounded by the organ.

And when it stopped there was a distant sound, hard to make out at first. It was the massed pipes of the thirteen regiments of the funeral procession, out-side but coming closer. Through the stone walls of the abbey you could hear them, and a regular, if muted bass beat. They had followed Auden's imperative once more: 'With muffled drum / Bring out the coffin, let the mourners come.' Finally, at 11.30, exactly as planned, a perfect hush fell. The choir began to sing 'I am the resurrection and the life . . .' to a melody written on this same spot 300 years ago. The voices were clear and beautiful: if heaven has a sound, it must be like this.

And then the coffin began to move inside. With everyone on their feet, it was impossible to see the red-tunic'd pallbearers straining underneath. Instead the 33-stone casket, draped in the Queen Mother's own standard, seemed almost a living thing, gliding on its own. With her crown gleaming in the gilt light of the abbey, the choir outbidding the angels, their voices rising to the vaulted ceiling, the moment was full of ancient power.

What followed was a funeral that deviated not once from tradition. The readings were set texts of English Christianity: Ecclesiastes and Revelation, John Bunyan and John Donne. There was no impassioned eulogy from Earl Spencer, no Elton John, no applause inside the abbey.

The result was a ceremony of grandeur and elegance, but with few moments of personal warmth. Indeed, not much of it was really about the Queen Mother at all – except that in its style and content, entirely traditional and correct, it was her all over.

The only direct talk of her life came from the Archbishop of Canterbury. He spoke of the almost primeval resonances of a title that anointed one woman as both Queen and Mother to the national tribe. But the favourite moment came when he said: 'Like the sun, she bathed us in her warm glow. Now that the sun has set and the cool of the evening has come, some of the warmth we absorbed is flowing back towards her.' At that the TV cameras caught Prince Charles's lip wobbling, holding back a grandson's tears.

Later the congregation stood as two buglers sounded the last post, making explicit what had been an unstated motif of the ceremony: its military quality, its tacit elevation of the late royal into a warrior queen. And, maybe for those who remember her role in the last war, she was.

Finally came a rite which could have been performed half a millennium ago. A man called Garter King of Arms stepped forward, in another resplendent uniform, and declared: 'Thus it hath pleased almighty God to take out of this transitory life unto his divine mercy the late Most High, Most Mighty and Most Excellent Princess Elizabeth, Queen Dowager and Queen Mother, Lady of the Most Noble Order of the Garter, Lady of the Most Ancient and Most Noble Order of the Thistle, Lady of the Imperial Order of the Crown of India, Grand Master and Dame Grand Cross of the Royal Victorian Order upon whom had been conferred the Royal Victorian Chain, Dame Grand Cross of the Most Excellent Order of the British Empire, Dame Grand Cross of the Most Venerable Order of the Hospital of St John of Jerusalem, Relict of His Majesty King George the Sixth and Mother of Her Most Excellent Majesty Elizabeth the Second . . .'

It went on like that – not so much a farewell to the past as an attempt to clasp it once more, for a few splendid hours.

1 May 2002

SIMON HOGGART

The pomp, the pageantry, the posh suits

The Queen, shimmering in electric blue, came to Westminster Hall yesterday to address both houses of parliament. It was the first important event of her jubilee celebrations, though you might think they had been going on for several years already. Don't worry, there's lots more to come!

She is one of the few reigning monarchs to have left the hall without receiving a death sentence. The old place, 905 years old and still standing, looked superb. So did the Tory MPs, most of whom were in morning dress in order to show up the slovenly slatterns and slobs of the Labour party. Thousands of furry sponge bags must have been slaughtered to make their trousers alone. Some of the women wore hats the size of cartwheels.

It was a wise political move. In tomorrow's local elections, voters will no doubt say: 'Well, the economy's doing well, and they're putting more money into the NHS. On the other hand, the Tories know how to dress properly.'

It was the Queen's fifth appearance at a similar event. I spotted Shaun Woodward. He comes to parliament less often. There should have been a fanfare of trumpets just to welcome him back. And Keith Vaz, the Great Vaz of Vaz, was making an equally rare appearance. Truly we were privileged!

The Speaker arrived on the dot with his eight followers. It was a moving moment. How many people raised in the Gorbals have their own procession, or 'posse' as the rock stars call it?

Then the Lord Chancellor, Derry Irvine, with, among others, his trainbearer, Mrs Nora Dobinson. Say what you like, but New Labour makes the trainbearers run on time. Next came the honourable corps of gentlemen, wearing enough egret feathers to stuff an executive sofa at World of Leather. And, even more magnificent, the Yeomen of the Guard. They marched up towards Lord Irvine, a riot of scarlet and gold. You could almost see him thinking: 'Hmmm, Beefeaters. Soon be time for a gin and tonic.'

The band of the Grenadier Guards at last stopped playing elderly, mimsy, wispy British tunes, elevator music before we even had elevators, and switched to Handel. Our blood began to course at last.

The state trumpeters, all in embroidered primrose tabards, filed in along a balcony and stood under the great stained-glass window. For them it works as camouflage. The scene was perfect: rich, grandiose, deeply dyed, sodden with history, ceremony and flummery. It only needed Charles I to appear with his neck bare to make it look complete.

The moment had come. She was a minute late, then two, then three. Surely Byers wasn't in charge of this? Finally, she appeared and processed, looking frightfully happy, down towards the dais at the end, where there were two big armchairs, thrones by Ikea, perhaps.

Then we heard from two Scots. The Lord Chancellor, his voice plummy, orotund and essentially English, heaped praises on her. She hadn't actually conquered Everest, or run the first four-minute mile, though you sensed that it was thanks to her that other people had.

Lord Irvine even praised 'the Royal website, royal.gov.uk' which raised a chuckle. It could have been worse; mentioning hotbabes.com would have been a terrible solecism!

Next, another less privileged Scot, Michael Martin, talking about diversity of races, cultures and faith which make this country a vibrant place to live, sharing power with our European partners – much of it straight out of the New Labour manifesto.

Then he solemnly handed his speech over to her – no, not so she could work out what he'd said! He had spoken gently and carefully. We understood almost every word he said. And at this moment some wretch's mobile phone rang out across the pageantry.

Finally we heard Her Majesty, tinged too with Blairspeak: 'Change has become a constant; managing it has become an expanding discipline,' all perhaps off tonytalk.com.

And at the end an echo of Mrs Thatcher, with her promise to carry on, and on, and on. Prince Charles was not present. But could we hear a groan carry on the winds from Highgrove?

5 June 2002

MARTIN WAINWRIGHT

Majesty and Mitchell Terrace

If the lion and the unicorn support the crown, the garden shed and chopped-egg bap do much the same for streets like Mitchell Terrace, Bingley, which spent all day yesterday partying in the Yorkshire sun.

As the golden coach trundled back from St Paul's to the palace, Shirley Dixon and her team were spooning out sandwich mayonnaise and debating which question – what breed of dog is usually associated with the royal family? or name the TV soap the Queen visited in 2001? – should be tiebreaker for the street party quiz.

It was the fifth time in twenty-five years that the 200 people of the terrace, and neighbouring Unity Street South and Oak Avenue, had carted out the trestles for a royal celebration. Under the honeysuckle arch which nicely hides her parents' wheelie-bins, Nicola Hudson was showing her fiancé, Andrew Brown, album photos of the last time round.

'I'm not appearing like that this time,' said the 22-year-old, who courted Andrew at the Bradford and Bingley building society where both worked until last year. 'That' was two-year-old Nicola without a stitch on, about to jump into the terrace's Charles and Diana wedding street party paddling pool.

Triggered by the long row of fancy buns and melting chocolate teacakes, other memories went further back. Mary Woodcock, ninety this month and fifty-six years in the terrace, remembered Elsie Rhodes dressing up in her husband's baggy Eighth Army shorts – plus medals – for the street party commemorating VE Day.

'We've got into the street party habit here, it seems,' said Mrs Dixon, who cleans at Bingley Grammar School and couldn't help keeping an eye out for bits of clingfilm or cake wrapper dropped by pupils sitting at the trestles. 'It's like an injection of community spirit every so often, to keep us all topped up.

'There's something special about these streets, and the parties are part of it. When one of my children died, I got proof of what I already knew: I've the best neighbours in the world.'

Part of a severe grid on the Aire valley bottom, all right angles and stone-flagged backyards, the terraces got a pasting in the fifties from John Braine, former unhappy municipal librarian at Bingley, in his novel *Room at the Top*. But his characters' longing to get away from small-town Yorkshire seems to have been genuinely the stuff of fiction. Mrs Woodcock's long stay in Mitchell Terrace is a distant second to several others, including her neighbour Herbert Waterhouse.

'I came here when I was three months old,' said the retired engineer, before proposing the loyal toast and getting ready to tease the Lord Mayor of Bradford, who called in for a bap. 'I'm seventy-seven now and I'm still here. I'd like to have invited my whole family today, but we'd have needed another street.' He's got seven sons, one daughter, eight granddaughters and nine grandsons.

Herbert's shed – 'Seven foot by five foot; I wanted a bigger one but Betty wouldn't let me take any more of her garden' – is the terrace's main flagpole, with a union jack and a St George's cross flapping overhead. Bunting links it to a safe storage area for street party treasures like The Firework.

Still dazed by the Buckingham Palace display the night before, Shirley Dixon said: 'We've just the one, but apparently it goes on in red, white and blue for four-and-a-half minutes. At any rate, it cost £55.'

In an area where budgets can be tight, the party was given a kickstart by a £250 grant from Bradford council, part of which has got the sixty Mitchell Terrace children a Golden Jubilee mug each. The smallest guest, blinking inscrutably at her souvenir, is meanwhile evidence of how traditional values are mixing with changing times. Ten-week-old Annie Brown wouldn't have been at any of Mitchell Terrace's previous street parties. Her father died of cancer two and a half years ago. But modern medicine has allowed his wife Yolande, a local charity worker, to give birth in March to their daughter, who is now the toast of Bingley's neighbourly streets.

22 June 2002

EMMA BROCKES

A dream dies in Trafalgar Square

In the moments before kick-off, England fans asked themselves the question: 'Who are ya? Who are ya? Who are ya?'

The chant, sung by 8,000 people in Trafalgar Square, was easy to answer: 'We're England 'til we die!' It remained easy to answer throughout the ninety minutes, although the nature of the reply became progressively less palatable. At the final whistle, those who still had the heart to sing responded to a feeble chorus of 'Who are ya?' with 'We're shit and we know we are.' England had lost. But it was a feeling that, through force of habit, they knew how to deal with.

If the mood was more resigned than despondent yesterday, it was because even the most committed England fan had to allow for the possibility that the usual consolations of defeat – bad refereeing, unlucky injuries, dirty opponents – would not stand up this time.

Exercising his talent for understatement, Sven-Goran Eriksson said, 'They were better than us, which is the difference,' an interpretation that, to the surprise of those expecting trouble, was quickly and widely accepted. There were too many damaging images being replayed for the fantasy that England were cheated to persist: loose defending, panicky passes and most powerfully of all, the sight of David Seaman sinking despondently into the net after misjudging a free kick and letting in a goal from so far away that the 'was it a fluke/was it intentional?' debate rages still.

That it was scored by Ronaldinho, a Brazilian whose sexual exploits with a lap dancer called Lisa were that morning splashed on the front page of the *Sun*, compounded the sense that England were being outclassed on all fronts. The Brazilian number 11, sent off for a tackle on Danny Mills, became suddenly harder to laugh at.

'They were the better team,' said Richard Taylor, a 29-year-old accountant, emerging from the pub, blinking back tears and looking for a Brazilian to unburden himself to. 'I just want to find one so I can say well done. It would make me feel better.'

In London, fans expressed their frustration for the most part mildly. A hardcore of flag-wavers in Trafalgar Square jumped in the fountains and splashed ineffectually about, while American tourists filmed them and asked, 'Are they the soccer hooligans?'

In Charing Cross Road, location of a popular salsa bar, police barricades were erected to separate England and Brazil fans, although there was not much appetite for violence. Brazil fans blew whistles and bopped around while, across the police line, England fans in St George's flag boxer shorts lolled sulkily about, hurled the occasional insult and turned pink in the sun.

'Look fellas,' said a young policeman to a group of moody fans, 'why can't you just be happy for them?' The dumbfounded silence was broken, eventually, as an England fan summoned his most deadly insult.

'What are you,' he spat, 'German?'

Perhaps losing was easier this time – easier than on the three previous occasions when England have been knocked out at the quarter-final stage of the World Cup – because of the serene example set by Eriksson, with his suit and tie and impeccable sportsmanship. Dr Simon Szreter, lecturer in history at Cambridge University, calls him 'the magic Swede'.

'England fans must recognise that the match was a moral encounter and that, in the sense of moral justice, they have nothing to complain about,' Dr Szreter said. 'They were beaten by a side that played better than them.'

Brazil even had the injustice of having a player sent off for a foul nobody thought was valid. 'The overall feeling among the English is that we were not robbed. It is just frustration that a very good side couldn't break down an even more cunning side.'

Perhaps, too, the combination of an early morning start, the eating of a McDonald's before 9 a.m. and the draining effect of the muggy weather ensured that by midday, many spectators were too tired to summon much outrage and those wandering around in Brazil shirts went largely unmolested.

The match was watched by an estimated 25 million people at home and a further 5 million in specially licensed pubs. At 7 a.m., the flat anticipation of the night before had given way to dread and a suppressed sort of hysteria. At stations and bus stops people jittered nervously, making tentative breaks from Englishness to share with each other the fear that if transport didn't arrive soon, they might miss kick-off.

The tension did not last. After the excitement of the first goal, fans watching on the giant screen in Trafalgar Square were so easily distracted that the distribution of free packets of Twiglets held their attention for a large portion of the game.

The loss of a game in which the majority of the country had an emotional stake will inevitably be blamed for every social and economic downturn of the coming months. The impact, if there is one beyond the immediate lurch of defeat, will be registered in the nation's self-image, although an England win would, perhaps, have required greater adjustment.

Television commentators on the BBC and ITV, shown with their heads in their hands after Ronaldinho's goal, were soon restored to equilibrium and saved their most heartfelt expressions of regret not for England's exit from the tournament, but for the sorry figure of Seaman, crying inconsolably, before running endless, masochistic replays of his blunder at the goalmouth.

'A game like this exaggerates underlying anxieties,' said Dr Szreter. 'There are only very few countries – the Italians, Brazilians, Argentinians and the Germans – who experience winning as a repetitive phenomenon in their history. Those countries regard winning as a regular tonic and get very depressed when they lose.'

After Italy lost to South Korea, the South Korean striker who scored against Italy was fired by his Italian club team Perugia, an act that Dr Szreter called 'extraordinarily infantile'. The English, with their lower expectations, have so far been graceful in defeat, consoling themselves with the thought 'we didn't do badly' and, with such a young side, hoping that in four years' time, England will be as mature and formidable a team as Brazil is now.

As they trailed out of Trafalgar Square, England fans slung arms round each other and – albeit sniffing a bit – said: 'Back to work.'

THE MAGIC TOYSHOP

Austin, 11 April 2002

In our television review yesterday (page 18, G2), we suggested that Cecil Parkinson was portrayed as a slug by *Spitting Image*. In fact, that was Kenneth Baker.

Corrections and Clarifications, 12 January 2002

SIMON HOGGART

The frog in Duncan Smith's throat

In a weird prime minister's question time, Iain Duncan Smith raised the topic of the NHS.

It may have been a mistake. For the Tory leader sounds as if he has his own armchair in death's waiting room. He wheezes and hawks. He grunts and rattles. His voice sounds as if someone had gone over it with an emery board, then put it through a mangle, and finally sprinkled it with broken glass. For an old Eurosceptic like him, it must be a great embarrassment to have a permanent frog in his throat.

'What urgggh areas of the NHS have gone burrrrrkwards, as, wug, his chairman said?' he somehow managed to ask Mr Blair. 'In 1997, the prime minister said he had twenty-four hours – vwuk! – to save the NHS. Yesterday the – currghh – chancellor needed twenty more years . . . The prime minister hasn't a gwug – and he hasn't a kwark!'

It didn't go away – in fact, as question time continued it became slightly worse. Fans of *The Fast Show* would be reminded of Bob Fleming, who couldn't utter a sentence without a coughing fit.

The prime minister was too polite to ask if he wouldn't like an ambulance. And who wants to spend forty-eight hours on a hospital trolley? But it left us all wondering about the state of the opposition leader's throat. One theory is nerves. He's scared of the big occasion. The same thing happened to John Moore, Mrs Thatcher's health minister.

Others suggest that he has 'nodules' on his vocal cords. Possibly he has one of those terrible colds that just won't go away. Or maybe he is suffering from a ghastly, fathomless grief, something so terrible that whenever he talks about health spending or military cuts the sheer desperation overwhelms him. Then the misery bubbles up inside him, like a traction engine with a faulty valve.

What could have caused this tremendous unhappiness? Perhaps it was the fate of the imprisoned plane-spotters, which was raised by the Tamworth MP Brian Jenkins. Unfortunately, in reading out his question, Mr Jenkins said that the tourists had been held in Spain. The entire House hissed 'Greece!' at the top of their voices, so they sounded like a crowd of opera-goers booing an experimental production of *La Bohème*, set in a medieval sewage farm.

Luckily Mr Jenkins hadn't been given another planted question; he might have wanted the prime minister to insist that the people of Gibraltar would have a vote before being handed over to the Greeks.

Or maybe it was the danger faced by the animals in Kabul Zoo, whose case was raised by Tony Banks. He wants a special airlift to rescue the lion that lost an eye in a grenade explosion, and a black bear, whose nose was sliced off by a hooligan.

Well, it would sort out the question of what British troops should do there. We could send in the SAS, the Special Animal Squad. With their fabled daring they would parachute into the zoo, put the animals into canvas cradles, and medevac them by helicopter to the safety of Rolf Harris.

Of course, at the other end, they'd find the regimental goat had been eaten, and that would set Iain Duncan Smith off all over again.

23 January 2002

TONY BENN

Privatising the C of E

The announcement that the Church of England is to be privatised has been welcomed by the Confederation of British Industry, the World Trade Organisation and the Central Bank in Frankfurt as a bold new initiative to bring religion closer to the consumers, which is how congregations are described in the White Paper, *New Christians*, launched in Westminster Abbey yesterday.

Speaking at a press conference, the prime minister explained that the success of the policy would have to be judged mainly in terms of the new resources that a public-private partnership would make available for the renewal of the church, which had suffered from falling attendance for many years. Christos, one of the biggest multinational corporations in the world – based in Los Angeles and already well-known for its success in the arms trade – has offered to invest billions in this 'exciting project' and provide a new management able to make fuller use of the assets now owned by the Church.

Graveyards are to be cleared and re-turfed for sporting events and pop concerts, but the headstones will be carefully preserved and sold to bereaved families to keep at home, instead of having to go out to see them at the weekends. Consultants are already at work assessing ways in which Church property could be developed and have begun discussions with the new minister appointed to conduct the negotiations on behalf of the Archbishop.

The new Department for Excellence in Anglican Development (DEAD) has modernised the Ten Commandments. Two redrafts of existing commandments have aroused a great deal of interest: 'Thou shalt not kill' has had these words added by the Ministry of Defence: 'unless ordered to do so'; and 'Thou shalt honour thy mother and father' has been amended by the Treasury to add: 'by seeing that the cost of their care in old age does not fall upon the State'.

Prayer books are to be reprinted with advertisements and both Pret A Manger and McDonald's have commissioned leading designers to provide suitable copy to accompany the Holy Communion. Churches are to be opened for commercial performances and Madonna is to be asked to sing next Christmas, with tickets priced in euros to help familiarise the audience with the new currency before it is introduced in Britain.

Confession is now to be made much more widely available by putting it on TV, after the success of the *Jerry Springer* and *Kilroy* shows, where people have opened up about their private lives – and the high ratings have proved how popular sin can be with a national audience. When a vacancy for a bishop or archbishop occurs, any individual will be free to put in a bid, and it is hoped that many people in the City of London who may never have thought of a career as a New Christian might be tempted to test their entrepreneurial skills in a completely new field, while continuing to enjoy comparable financial rewards.

The synod will be replaced by a focus group which specialises in the needs of the market to test public reactions to sermons before they are delivered; to maintain the non-political nature of the Church, none will deal with controversial issues such as peace or social justice.

In a clear statement of the need for responsibility and accountability, the prime minister has decided to set up a new regulatory body, Ofgod, to name and shame ministers who have failed to live up to the high standards expected. Chris Woodhead is to be asked to take it on, following his success at Ofsted.

Lord Birt, whose experience at the BBC in privatising its services won the respect of broadcasters, is to be appointed to Number 10 as the prime minister's spiritual adviser, with the task of seeing that standards of management are maintained at the same level we have seen in Railtrack and other public services moved into the private sector.

Critics have been dismissed as dinosaurs who are living in the past and reminded on many occasions that we must live in the real world and try to forget the Old Christians who are always harping on about Bethlehem and Jerusalem, which simply do not interest the younger generation and are responsible for the decline of religion in modern Britain.

One New Labour minister, speaking on *Newsnight*, summed it all up by saying: 'Jesus drove the money changers out of the Temple, but as a business-friendly government, we are trying to get them back in there.'

Here again Britain is now in the lead and the prime minister's decision to visit the Vatican to persuade the Pope to follow suit has been hailed as a new example of his global leadership and determination to put Britain at the heart of Europe.

28 February 2002

HUGO YOUNG

The Blairites and the civil service

When Labour came into office in 1997, it had no experience of running anything. A handful of ministers could point to their time in city or local government, but the leader hadn't had to balance the books of a whelk-stall, and the collective record of New Labour included not a single hour of management or delivery at the coalface of national government. They were abject innocents, the product of eighteen years' opposition, as Tony Blair acknowledged. Asked, towards the end of his first term, how the second would be different, he said the answer was easy. He wouldn't have to spend the first two years finding out how government worked.

Greeting him was a civil service that was for the most part overjoyed to see him. Most senior civil servants are sort-of social democrats. But as an institution also, the service had reasons to be pleased. Officials now in their prime had lived through the Thatcher years of turmoil and reproach, and then the Major years of a government's declining ability to achieve anything at all. They were frustrated. The rise of Blair promised to restore the seriousness of public business, and lever public servants up the social hierarchy. So when the prime minister entered Downing Street he had a receptive machine at his disposal.

He and his colleagues, however, didn't see it that way. Their lack of experience, rather than drawing them towards these natural allies, seemed to redouble both their suspicion and their arrogance. They assumed they were confronted with a bunch of Thatcherites and strode into Whitehall convinced that their own theoretical preparations for government were vastly preferable to anything the civil service might offer. At the Treasury, the topmost permanent official, mandarin of mandarins, was excluded from the chancellor's operations room. The latest episode in the life of Stephen Byers, serial destroyer of departmental functionality, is another climax in the pattern that began at the beginning.

To make good the civil service's defects, Labour enhanced the cadre of so-called special, or political, advisers. Their number has more than doubled since Major's time. Some of them matched the practice of decades by bringing genuine expertise in particular policy issues, though few had any more experience of delivering anything than their ministers. In Number 10 itself, the advisers prodigiously multiplied to form, in effect, a para-government, second-guessing departmental civil servants at every turn. In most departments, the expertise of the specials was and is as information peddlers whose cardinal faculty, denied to regular civil servants, is an understanding of the definition of truth: that it consists exclusively of what is politically convenient.

The latest Byers episode shows this more luridly than ever. Disputes about the nature and presentation of truth brought the system to its knees. In this case, the civil servant, Martin Sixsmith – who contested the truth-manipulations of the special adviser, Jo Moore – has been expelled from the system, for no good cause except to save the face of Stephen Byers. The minister is permitted to lie to the public at his own convenience, and is then carried in triumph over the threshold of Downing Street, his conniving permanent secretary at his side, once Labour MPs, at their most nauseatingly cynical, have given their blessing to his performance. It's a moment to note, in the evolving pathology of New Labour as a party that respects no values except those that sanctify, come what may, its own ineffable rectitude.

But it's also a moment to mark for the civil service, which New Labour is not, of course, the first party to challenge. Political impatience with Whitehall has a history. The Fulton Report, commissioned by the Wilson government, strove to modernise the civil service in the name of better management. Mrs Thatcher notoriously asked whether there was anything they could deliver better than well-crafted policy advice. She raged – with far more reason than Blair – against a service reluctant to join her in dismantling the current orthodoxy, in her case the post-war welfare consensus. Her impatience with officials who did not match her own activist zeal left scars on the careers of many whose promotion was denied at her personal whim.

In retrospect the Thatcher period looks like a model of decorum. There were limits to the disrespect she was prepared to show the system. The Foreign Office may have been beyond redemption in her eyes, but Whitehall continued to operate by well-understood rules about who was political and who was not. With occasional diversions, such as the Spycatcher affair, the cabinet secretary's independence was respected, and he remained the arbiter of what it was proper for special advisers to do. As the definer of propriety, he never had his writ challenged.

The Blair period has deconstructed most of this. Both the ethic and the structure of the civil service have been gravely damaged. The organisation of power around special advisers, headed by the prime minister's chief of staff, is paralleled by the submission of policymaking to the verdicts of focus groups. For politicians who are supposed to believe in the public good and the enabling State, Blairite ministers have been staggeringly dismissive of the talents of civil servants as against the presumed superiority of the private sector.

Blair's occasional gushing interludes of praise for teachers and nurses and policemen are not enough to efface the visible presumption that the public sector is to blame for its own inadequacies. The morale of the senior civil service, I have been told by many closely informed judges, has never been lower.

There are two ways to go from here. One is to set about reinventing a service whose reputation for impartiality is unquestioned. Impartiality, after all, was the hallmark of the British civil service. What the Thatcherites began to question, the Blairites have now, at least when it comes to the definition of truth, abolished. Restoring the civil service's status probably requires a Civil Service Act, enshrining the terms and conditions that formally separate administrators from politics. It also requires an honest understanding of the difference between the official whose job is to serve his minister, and the official whose duty is to abandon the authority and self-respect that comes from the right to exercise impartial judgment. Until Thatcher, this subtle distinction was recognised and understood. Under Blair it is ridiculed as sophistry in the service of disloyalty to the great governing project.

The other way is to decide that the civil service, in the power positions at the top, should no longer be impartial but become an arm of the party. This is where Blairism has stealthily begun to take it. The Civil Service Commission, with its role in appointments, tries to hold the line. But the argument should become more open. Is it the role of Whitehall to keep its distance from the politics of politics, and uphold values that modern politicians are driven constantly to violate? Or should it become the pledged accomplice of a minister like Stephen Byers, who lies through his teeth?

29 May 2002

MICHAEL WHITE

Bye bye Byers

Stephen Byers last night blamed a lethal combination of mishandled spin doctors and vengeful Railtrack shareholders in the City for the campaign that finally pushed him out of Tony Blair's cabinet. In an exclusive interview with the *Guardian*, the fallen transport secretary admitted that 'with hindsight' he might not have become such a media target if he had persuaded his spin doctor, Jo Moore, to resign after her notorious 'good time to bury bad news' e-mail on 11 September.

'That was an issue which led the media to scrutinise in far more detail my conduct. Also there was a major political decision in relation to Railtrack [it went into administration on 6 October], which meant you had a group of vested interests, including the Tory party but also some of their friends in the City, who launched the most hostile attack.'

As his many critics at Westminster and among the travelling public celebrated the first major political scalp since Labour's second election victory, Mr Byers admitted that his accident-prone record since taking over from John Prescott – almost exactly a year ago – had made him too much of a damaging 'distraction' for the government.

Cabinet colleagues, led by David Blunkett, loyally rallied behind his decision – saying that he had been blamed for offences he had not committed. The home secretary called it 'a personal tragedy' for the arch-Blairite whom opposition MPs and the Tory media have repeatedly dubbed an incorrigible liar. But after months in which he had been involved in a relentless series of scrapes, few ministers tried to persuade him to stay.

One Labour loyalist called it 'death with honour by a big man'. Less flatteringly, Iain Duncan Smith, the Tory leader, complained of a lack of remorse, symptomatic of a culture of 'half-truths, secrecy and spin over substance'. The Liberal Democrats' Charles Kennedy called it 'the honourable thing – and not before time'.

On top of the running battle over the dismissal of Ms Moore's departmental rival, Martin Sixsmith, this month's trouble over a euro briefing that went wrong and Sunday's damning attack by MPs on his transport plan were the last straw. Last week Mr Byers' credibility was even attacked by Pam Warren, the Paddington rail disaster survivor.

Mr Blair did not demur when Mr Byers told him of his weekend decision at Number 10 on Monday morning after consulting close friends, including his partner, Jan, and the health secretary, Alan Milburn. Mr Blair's thinking is understood to have been influenced by last week's *Guardian* ICM poll, which showed that Mr Byers had a popularity rating of minus 49 points. The prime minister was understood to have been shocked at how far his minister's stock had fallen.

In his solitary statement for the TV cameras – made inside Number 10 with the prime minister away at a NATO summit and MPs in recess – Mr Byers offered no apology for controversies which have dogged him, from the Rover sale to the decision to put Railtrack into administration.

'I know that I have made mistakes but I have tried at all times to behave honourably and with the interests of the British people at heart,' he said. In his interview with the *Guardian* less than an hour after his resignation he explained: 'Personally I could have stuck the personal criticism for the greater good if that was necessary. But we arrived at a political situation where I felt, because of the attention I was getting, I was damaging the government. That was my political judgement.'

Even the decision to announce the resignation on a day when the Commons – bitterly critical of Mr Byers over the past six months – is in recess will be cited as another example of unrepentant stage management. Mr Blair wants to bring new, young faces into the junior ministerial ranks. But the pointers last night were that it would be an experienced cabinet member who would move into Mr Byers' old job.

'Ideally we want a safe pair of hands who is slightly boring – in whom the media has no interest,' said one Whitehall official.

The job went to Alistair Darling.

27 March 2002

JACKIE ASHLEY

The lady vanishes

'Rejoice, rejoice'? Oh yes. The poor, the trade unions and the Left are rejoicing as Margaret Thatcher is forcibly retired. Yes, undoubtedly Iain Duncan Smith and his band are privately rejoicing too. No more will their carefully crafted veneer of moderation be shattered by those hectoring tones. But what of Britain's women? Surely they regret the silencing of Britain's first and only female prime minister? As Mary-Anne Stephenson of the Fawcett Society remarked: 'A lot of younger Labour women have said they were inspired to get into politics because of Margaret Thatcher – she made them think a woman could do it.' She was indeed a dominant, room-dividing, row-provoking politician. She was modern Britain's greatest alpha female; and yet, I believe, she ultimately had a destructive effect on all other women wanting a public role.

Lady Thatcher herself was always ambiguous about her gender, from her early, often wryly quoted remark that she'd never become prime minister because Britain wouldn't have a woman, to her later poses between the tank turrets, declaring she was 'more of a man than the rest of them'. Then there was her private sexual flirtatiousness. Mitterrand's famous description of her – 'the eyes of Caligula, but the mouth of Marilyn Monroe' – was vivid shorthand for the enigma. In her final public years she became, let's face it, a terrible drama queen.

The problem for other women was that she was such a dominant, challenging role model that there seemed no alternative for female politicians. Who'd want to become another Thatcher? Who'd be prepared to have another Thatcher? She smashed through the glass ceiling OK, but then patched it up and danced around on it, bossing the rest of us about.

Before her there was a range of successful female politicians, not many, but a variety: the dishevelled, academic-sounding Shirley Williams; the fiery fighters such as Barbara Castle and Bessie Braddock; the upcoming seventies feminists Harriet Harman, Helene Hayman and Patricia Hewitt. Abroad there was no shortage of women leaders either: Indira Gandhi in India; Golda Meir in Israel; Sirimavo Bandaranaike in Sri Lanka; and Gro Harlem Brundtland in Norway. There was a sense, at least, that women in power could be different.

Thatcher changed all that. The first time she broke upon the world was with that disturbingly unfemale playground tag 'Maggie Thatcher, milk snatcher', an early version of the later 'iron lady'. Here was a woman who had succeeded by discarding most of what we had thought of as female, who turned the homely handbag into a weapon of war, whose shoulder pads seemed steel-edged, whose hairdo increasingly resembled a *Star Wars* helmet. Nor was it symbolism only; she pursued strategies of confrontation and aggression, from the Falklands to the miners' strike to those famous Euro-battles at home and over there.

And this all happened at a time when women were breaking through publicly, thanks to the post-war education revolution, the feminist revolution, the pill and abortion and changes in the workforce. This was our moment, our dawn. Then she came, mocking us, from the wrong side of the political tracks, a triumphant creature who had never fought for women's rights at all. We didn't know whether to cheer or jeer.

Men have never experienced this kind of problem. There has never been only one acceptable male role model. No one ever said the problem with Jim Callaghan was that too many young Labour men would take to pig farming and kipper ties, or that John Major created a negative role model. There was always a broad variety of male behaviour. But there was at the time only one top-table, dominant-female place available in this small country and Thatcher had it. It is no coincidence that during her heyday there were no other senior female politicians in any of the main parties.

Since her exit from office we have returned to something a little more traditional, a modest number of female power types, each of them questioned and mocked, but more or less accepted. There is the earthy, direct, battling model, usually coming with the tag 'indomitable': Ann Widdecombe, Gwyneth Dunwoody, Mo Mowlam. Here the female politician is valued for her connection to commonsense, day-to-day experience.

Then there's the brisk, business-suited female type, a style partly copied from the City and the law, where a few driven women have succeeded by being more organised, more focused, and sometimes more ruthless than the men around them. Watch out for Patricia Hewitt, Ruth Kelly and, from benches behind them, Helen Jones and Fiona Mactaggart. These women, overwhelmingly New Labour, are brisk, tough, efficient and popping up more and more.

There are undoubtedly a few babe-politicians, but only a very few. Politics is not only a famously rough old trade, but a jealous one where you rely on your friends; in general, it seems that women who hope to get on by being flirty are pulled down early by other women, in the constituencies or at Westminster.

During the Thatcher era these trends were either hidden or simply suppressed – as far as public comment was concerned the 'women in politics' debate seemed to begin and end with the Lady herself. She'd broken through, so what was the problem? If she could do it, so could everyone else. The fact that she was financially supported and prided herself on being more male than most Tory men – more confrontational, harder, even more of a whisky-drinker – hardly came into it.

But what is starting to happen now, just starting, and is the real cause of the springlike feeling I have at the proper end of the Thatcher era, is that the 'women in politics' debate itself is beginning to dissolve. We are still grossly under-represented in the Commons and in local government. Women politicians are still patronised by male sketch-writers and underrated by male columnists, but we have now got enough of a range of them – from Margaret Beckett to Julie Kirkbride, from Clare Short to Yvette Cooper – that the very idea of a female role model is starting to seem redundant. If you are a woman and you want to go into politics, you can be this, or that, or the other – but most of all you can start to be yourself.

And that is new since Thatcher went. It wasn't the case when that singular and extraordinary woman dominated public life in this country. She did cramp female political styles, just as she cramped the politics of the Right. At a personal level, I hope she has a tranquil, secure – and, above all, private – old age; but as a woman and an observer of politics I am just so very glad to wave her goodbye. Her final gift to political women is that now she's gone, we can start to be normal again.

22 May 2002

SIMON HOGGART

We are a statue

To the Guildhall in London to watch Lady Thatcher unveil a statue of – Lady Thatcher. Iron Lady meets Marble Woman! The effigy is made of stone, it is around seven feet high, and it is so alabaster white you yearn to spray it with slogans: it could not be more perfect for the time or the place.

The sculptor is Neil Simmonds. Michelangelo said that he didn't create statues; what he did was chip away the surplus stone to find the image within. Imagine cutting away all those tons of rock and finding – Margaret Thatcher! What a terrifying surprise! (Apparently the sculptor's studio in Dartford, Kent, is next door to a depot that provides clothes for Bosnian refugees. I am told she kept breaking off from her sittings to give them lectures on The British Way of Life.)

The Guildhall was full of chaps wearing those neck ruffs that look like the antimacassars in a very posh boarding house. The statue itself was covered in a black velvet shroud, so that she looked a little like an Afghan woman shortly before the fall of the Taliban.

She and Denis arrived. She was wearing a purple outfit, like a housecoat, as if she were about to do the vacuuming with a gold-plated Dyson. She had that famous swept-back, wind-tunnel hair.

Tony Banks, the plebby Labour MP who happens to be Chairman of the Commons Art Committee, introduced the statue to us. 'She is almost as famous, dare I say it, for her handbag, which you will see when it is unveiled.' There were dark mutterings of 'but it's on the wrong arm'. Would she have to hit her handbag with her own handbag?

He explained how there were rules which forbade the statue from appearing in the Commons lobby, though these might be changed. It may appear there in 2004. At the moment there is nowhere to put it. But, as Mr Banks didn't quite say, some day her plinth would come.

The cost of the statue (thought to be between £40,000 and £50,000) had been met by an anonymous donor. 'I don't know who he is, and I think it's better that I do not know.' (At this point, Norman Tebbit, I gather, went round the party saying that it was probably Richard Desmond, Labour donor and publisher of *Monetarist Babes*.)

'You are as controversial in marble as you are in life.' Controversial in marble! She looked thrilled. She would like to be controversial in marble, in bronze, in granite, stainless steel, or pink blancmange. She was adoring every moment.

And Mr Banks, desperately trying to find things to say that would meet the occasion without enraging the Labour party, wasn't done: 'When policies are forgotten, if I may say so, the fact that you were the first woman prime minister will not be forgotten!'

She looked even happier. How could she be forgotten? Was he mad? Were we mad? Finally she got to whisk the shroud off the statue.

'It's marvellous,' she said. 'But it's a little larger than I expected. Though as the first woman prime minister, I am a little larger than life!' (Murmurings of approval at this piece of – literal – self-aggrandisement.)

'I was fortunate to be there rather longer than some of my colleagues, and so that is the way to portray me!' (I would like to have heard some quiet retching at this point, but heard yet louder grunts of approval.)

'I am very grateful to the sculptor for portraying me in a way that pleases me very much. Do remember! We had staunch Conservative principles!'

I looked up at the oeuvre. It has no eye sockets. I don't quite know why.

30 July 2002

MICHAEL WHITE

Alan Duncan soars through the ceiling

A few yards from where Alan Duncan was buying lunch for his office staff in Westminster's Portcullis House cafeteria yesterday, another Conservative MP,

Old Etonian David Cameron, could be seen bottle-feeding his infant son, Ivan. Times are changing, even in the social culture of the Tory party.

But times are changing even faster outside the party laager. So, does it matter that Mr Duncan, a 45-year-old oil trader turned frontbench spokesman on foreign affairs, used an interview in *The Times* to declare what most colleagues and acquaintances already knew: that he is gay? The answer is yes and no, judging by the steady flow of e-mails received yesterday by Mr Duncan, MP for Rutland and Melton in Leicestershire – and the first Tory MP to come out. The overwhelming tone was supportive: 'Good on you' and 'Extremely impressed by your courage'.

Several wrote that they were not supporters of the Conservative party but 'it's nice to see an honest politician'. One said: 'It's good to see the beginning of something like modernity in the party.' A number of people offered to buy him a drink. That response – if confirmed by wider public comment – underlines what Princess Diana and Mo Mowlam grasped instinctively: that in touchy-feely times voters who are alienated from conventional party politics respond to what they see as emotional candour, even from MPs.

In his interview, Mr Duncan said of being gay: 'It's how you're born, and it's no different from being born Jewish, Catholic, short, tall or anything else. Why on earth should the self-esteem of perfectly decent people be so permanently derided?' He said the State had no business to be bossy about bedroom morality and that he was tired of colleagues 'muttering behind their hands' about his sexuality and a 'glass ceiling' which he believes has held back his career. 'If I were married with two kids I might be in a different position,' he said. 'The only realistic way to behave these days, particularly if you're a politician, is to be absolutely honest and upfront, however inconvenient that may be at first. Living in disguise for your whole life simply isn't an option.'

He added: 'The Conservative party has taken a long time to catch up with the world as it is. Nobody under thirty-five gives a damn about being gay these days, but they feel repelled by people who sneer or condemn.'

Iain Duncan Smith was quick to offer support. *I understand how difficult it must have been for you to have made such an open statement about your private life*, the Tory leader wrote in a pre-arranged letter. *What you have done is honest and will not affect you in any way politically in the future.*

Your talents as a politician have put you on the frontbench and I know our colleagues will join me in saying that you are a valued and valuable member of the parliamentary party and the frontbench.

Other frontbenchers also offered support. Only Ann Widdecombe, the former shadow home secretary, sounded a public note of disapproval. The party should spend less time worrying about its own 'ideological purity' and concentrate more on attacking Labour, she told the *Today* programme. 'Unless we as a party wake up to the fact that the government is in severe difficulty . . . instead of forever going on about ideological purity within our own party, then we will not make the gains that we could.'

But conspiracy theorists were quick to smell a rat. Surely Mr Duncan's move was part of a modernisers' plot to see off David Davis and the old guard and rebrand the party as one of 'caring Conservatives'? Mr Duncan is adamant that it was not. He had agreed to an interview, knowing there 'was a risk, a 50-50 chance' his sexuality would be raised.

'I did the interview on Wednesday, and told the chief whip and Michael Ancram [his boss], "This has happened, it will be news, we need a strategy." Iain was fabulous. He said, "I'll write a letter of support."'

If it was not a plot it was certainly convenient, reinforcing the Duncan Smith message about inclusivity and pushing the row over Mr Davis off the front pages.

'I didn't vote for Duncan Smith, but he's been making welcome changes and deserves some support,' one gay Tory activist, long blocked as a potential candidate, said last night.

The mood is a far cry from the 1940s when Labour's Tom Driberg, a recklessly promiscuous gay MP, felt the pressure to marry, or the fifties when Tory Ian Harvey's career was ruined in a park with a guardsman. Labour's Chris Smith outed himself at a gay rights rally in Rugby in 1984. He went on to higher things. More recently gay Tory MPs, including Michael Brown and Matthew Parris, have been advised to shut up about their sexuality, though the magnificently camp Norman St John Stevas, while a reforming cabinet member, did not mind when the *Guardian* called him 'the thinking man's Larry Grayson'.

Many older gays and lesbians in public life, politics included, take a more reticent view. Mr Duncan supports their right to do so. Nick Brown was outed, so was Peter Mandelson, several times. But the trend is to candour. Angela Eagle, Gordon Marsden, Ben Bradshaw, Michael Portillo retrospectively – as the list of volunteers grows longer, the public grows less interested. Alan Duncan believes he has done public life a favour.

MONEY

Steve Bell, 6 November 2001

It's perfectly reasonable for train fares to go up 17 per cent – the journeys are taking at least 20 per cent longer, so we're getting more for our money ('Train fares rise', 22 December).

Letter from Tom Freeman, London, 24 December 2001

WOLE SOYINKA

After the Deluge

Once, for a dare,
He filled his heart-shaped swimming pool
With bank notes, high denomination
And fed a pound of caviar to his dog.
The dog was sick; a chartered plane
Flew in replacement for the Persian rug.

He made a billion yen
Leap from Tokyo to Buenos Aires,
Turn somersaults through Brussels,
New York, Sofia and Johannesburg.
It cracked the bullion market open wide.
Governments fell, coalitions cracked
Insurrection raised its bloody flag
From north to south.

He knew his native land through iron gates,
His sight was radar bowls, his hearing
Electronic beams. For flesh and blood,
Kept company with a brace of Dobermanns.
But – yes – the worthy causes never lacked
His widow's mite, discreetly publicised.

He escaped the lynch days. He survives.
I dreamt I saw him on a village
Water line, a parched land where
Water is a god
That doles its favours by the drop,
And waiting is a way of life.
Rebellion gleamed yet faintly in his eye
Traversing chrome-and-platinum retreats. There,
Hubs of commerce smoothly turn without
His bidding, and cities where he lately roosted
Have forgotten him, the preying bird
Of passage.

They let him live, but not from pity
Or human sufferance. He scratches life
From earth, no worse a mortal man than the rest.

The Queen Mother lies
in state in Westminster
Hall, April.
(Guardian/Graham
Turner)

Muslim Britain celebrates
the jubilee: a street party
in Stepney, East London,
June. (Guardian/Martin
Godwin)

Disaster! Supporters of left presidential candidate Lionel Jospin learn that he's trailing Le Pen and won't make the final round, Paris, April. (AP Photo/Remy de la Mauvinière)

Flowers for the dead Fortuyn: the funeral procession of the assassinated Dutch politician Pim Fortuyn, Rotterdam, May. (EDA Photo ANP/Vincent Jannink)

The long, vain, wait for democracy: a queue of frustrated would-be voters outside a polling station in Harare, Zimbabwe, March. (AP Photo/Jerome Delay)

In the year of the earth summit: one of thousands of child victims of famine across southern Africa, Malawi, June. (EPA/Debbie Yazbek)

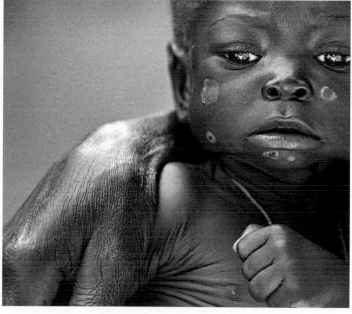

Another railway horror: 7 people died when a WAGN trail came off the rails at Potters Bar, May. (David Levene)

Putting his foot down: an official picket in action during a one-day strike of council workers, Brighton, July. (Guardian/Frank Baron)

Far, far away in dreamland splendour,
Creepers twine his gates of bronze relief.
The jade-lined pool is home
To snakes and lizards; they hunt and mate
On crusted algae.

from Selected Poems *by Wole Soyinka (Methuen)*

27 December 2001

JON HENLEY

Death of the franc

A long time ago, in 1350, Jean II, aka Jean le Bon, was crowned king of France. His timing wasn't what you'd call terrific, the Hundred Years War against the English having been under way for the better part of two decades and the country being pretty much *dans la merde*. But John the Good did his best, as it were, until the day the dastardly Black Prince walloped him and his army at the Battle of Poitiers in September 1356.

The King was taken prisoner and packed off to London, where his captors demanded a right royal ransom of three million gold crowns. Four years later, with the first slice of the ransom paid and a truce declared, a new coin was minted to mark Jean's liberation. It showed the King in full armour on horseback, holding his sword in his left hand, surrounded by the words *Ioannes Dei Gratia Francorum Rex*. This, as every French schoolchild will tell you, was the first franc, so called because Jean was at last free – or *franc* – of perfidious Albion (though sadly he only stayed that way until 1364, when he made the bad mistake of failing to keep up with the ransom payments).

As every French schoolchild will also tell you, this means the notion of liberty has been enshrined in the nation's currency for exactly 641 years. So when the yoke of the euro descends, albeit invited, on New Year's Day, France will be kissing goodbye not just to a big chunk of its history but to a potent symbol of Frenchness as well.

In all its multiple incarnations, the franc has reflected – in a fashion more or less unique among the world's currencies – a major event in the country's history: not just new kings or presidents, but big and bloody foreign and civil wars, revolutions, occupations and depressions. In a few days' time, all that will be gone.

Perhaps oddly, this does not seem to excessively worry the French, who, in a scientific *Guardian* survey conducted in assorted shops, restaurants and cafés over the past few weeks, have shown themselves brutally unsentimental about the demise of one of the world's great coinages.

'The things that really matter will still be here,' says Renaud Girard, a waiter on the rue Montorgueil. 'The Eiffel tower, "La Marseillaise", Marianne, cheese, wine, baguettes – those are the real French symbols. Beaujolais Nouveau will still arrive every year, and paying for it in euros isn't going to change France.'

Marine Salin, my astute seventeen-year-old neighbour, can't wait for the euro to arrive. 'I wish we'd stop talking about it and just do it,' she says. 'Plus which, the 150 francs you give me for an evening's babysitting is 22.87 euros. You'll never pay me that, it's too complicated. You'll make it 25 euros.'

There are a few jilted franc-lovers around, of course. An Association for the Memorial to the French Franc has been set up to mark the currency's end with a suitable monument. But according to its president, Olivier Bidou, it hasn't really met with overwhelming support and is still arguing over where the memorial should be.

'It could be Compiègne, where Jean le Bon decreed the first franc,' he says. 'But some people want it in Chamalières, where the Bank of France prints its notes. And others want a place with a name that begins with franc, like Franconville. There's rather a row, I'm afraid.'

Even the intellectuals aren't particularly exercised. 'To abandon the franc is to destroy one of the key instruments French society uses to identify itself,' thunders a lone voice of protest, the arch-conservative writer Paul-Marie Couteaux. 'What's left now? The language is shot to pieces, the army going to the dogs, the social security system is in a pitiful state. History, essentially, is over. The end of the franc is part of all that.'

But in a country where highbrow opinion still counts for something, Couteaux is one of surprisingly few to mourn the passing of the franc. The anthropologist Emmanuel Todd reckons the link between currency and nationhood has been 'altogether exaggerated. There are so many more important things – language, customs, manners, food. We shouldn't take mere money too seriously.'

And the economist and academician Eric Orsenna points out, entirely reasonably, that in these days of direct debits, internet shopping and electronic wallets, minting one's own money no longer means very much. The franc, he says, has become 'an illusory, nostalgic identity, a fake symbol of glory that in fact has undergone multiple erosions and devaluations'.

It did, it has to be said, endure a rather chequered early history. The franc's first appearance can only be described as feeble, lasting just a quarter of a century. In its second major incarnation, beginning in 1575 during one of France's many wars of religion, it survived a mere eleven years before giving way to the trusty *testoon*. Third time around, however, the silver franc was here to stay. On 7 April 1795 – or 18 Germinal, l'an III de la République in Gallic revolution-speak – the National Convention decreed a decimal coinage system (it also decreed a 100-minute hour, a 10-hour day and a 10-day week, but somehow they never caught on).

Four months later, the franc became France's official and unchallenged monetary unit and rapidly embarked on an expansionist march across Europe. Switzerland and parts of Italy, given little choice in the matter by Napoleon, succumbed to it during the early 1800s. In 1864, the Latin Monetary Union saw a standard coinage based on the franc introduced in Belgium, Greece, Spain, Austria and Hungary. Then came the colonies: most of west and much of central Africa, Algeria, Morocco, Tunisia, Martinique, Guadeloupe, Cambodia, New

Caledonia, the New Hebrides. Many former French dominions, members of the African financial community (CFA), still use it.

The doughty franc allowed France to weather the recession of the twenties and thirties better than most. It went through a sticky patch during the second world war, struck in shoddy aluminium and zinc, and forced to sport the wholly un-French motto of Travail, Famille, Patrie (Work, Family, Fatherland), rather than the resounding revolutionary principles of Liberté, Égalité and Fraternité.

The currency stayed in bad shape during the later forties and fifties, plumbing its lowest-ever depths during the unstable Fourth Republic before rebounding under Charles de Gaulle's Fifth Republic with the launch in 1960 of the new 'heavy' franc. This replaced 100 old francs with one new one and mystified an entire generation of Frenchmen. In fact, more than forty years on, an estimated 20 per cent of the French population, particularly those in la France profonde, when dealing with large sums, still count in old francs, prompting some official concern about the speed at which the nation will adapt to the euro.

False alarm, says 76-year-old Jean Raynaud, a former top-ranking civil servant who was one of the fathers of the new franc: 'They'll give up the new franc far more easily than they've given up the old. The conversion rate is so impossible they'll start thinking in euros straight away. In ten years' time, nobody will even refer to the franc.'

French concern at the passing of the franc is in fact practical, not sentimental: the cost of bread, olive oil, sugar and indeed babysitters has inevitably inched up to allow for a nice round figure in euros, despite a five-month moratorium on price rises, decreed by the Finance Ministry, that started in November.

The Catholic Church is most perturbed at the prospect of the ten-franc coin, by far the most common in end-of-mass collection plates, being replaced by the €1 piece, a move that would instantly deprive it of 40 per cent of its charitable income. It has come up with its own catchy slogan for 1 January: 'Ten francs plus a bit of generosity equals two euros.'

Casino owners face something of a similar problem: will gamblers who traditionally favour the ten-franc slot machine be put off by one that takes the €2 piece? But criminals will do well out of the deal: fines are to be converted and rounded down to the nearest full figure in euros. And contestants on French telly's equivalent of *Who Wants to be a Millionaire?* will henceforth win one million euros, a happy 6.55957 times more than before.

Just about the only serious franc-related lament to be heard on the lips of the French, in fact, is for all those words they use to denote the doomed currency. For no one here calls a franc a franc. You never pay 100 francs for a haircut, you pay *cent balles* or *cent boules*. You don't fork out 50,000 francs for a car, you offer *cinq briques* or *cinq patates* or *cinq plaques* or *cinq batons*.

'A whole chunk of the language will forcibly disappear,' says Josette Rey-Debove of Le Robert dictionary, an expert in the matter. 'A *patate* of euros is 65,597 francs, that's a whole lot more than the old *patate*. New words will come in, of course, maybe from the financial sector or the rap scene, but it'll take quite some time. I won't particularly miss francs, but I will miss my *balles*.'

4 February 2002

JOHN TILLEY

A railwayman's tale

You say 'privatisation', people accuse you of being political. But as a signalman, I can't make decisions I used to be able to make. An example: when it was one railway, if I could see a local train and an InterCity train were going to miss their connection, I'd hold one for a minute or two, just keep the signal on, allow the passengers to cross the platform and get on their train – because you're running a service for the public! Or passengers as they used to be called: I still call them that.

If I held that train now I'd be on a disciplinary charge and Railtrack would be facing a penalty for the delay. That one instance tells you all about what's gone wrong.

They're all making money off each other: the train companies, Railtrack and the infrastructure companies: there's a pot of money – most of it taxpayers' money by the way, even though the system's 'private' – and they're all like piranhas fighting over it, all billing each other for delays to this and delays to that. It's like pass the parcel.

I've always been a signalman. We're the people the public never sees, the people in the background who actually run the trains – we set the routes for them. If we make a mistake, people die.

Used to be, the highest grades of signallers were on a par with train drivers when it came to pay – in fact the highest grade was just above. Today those with the biggest snouts are getting most from the trough.

Come April, our new basic will be [grades of] £16,000 to £25,000 for a thirty-six-hour week. On top, there's time and a half for Sunday working, time and a quarter for working rest days [days off] and 10 per cent for night working. A top-grade signaller on £25,500, if he worked a lot of overtime, could make another £5,000 to £7,000. But those signallers in top grades, the pressures, you just want to get home, get out of the box. It tends to be the lads at the lower end or the middle.

A common form of overtime is: someone on the average eight-hour shift is asked to work an extra four hours. But you can also have twelve-hour rostered shifts – which in a thirty-six-hour week could give you a three-day week. Both Railtrack and ourselves are a bit wary: we don't want to find people work a three-day week and then take that as an excuse to work another three days at twelve hours, on overtime.

The training's changed a bit from my day. They do psychometric testing. I got in before all that mumbo jumbo. The old-school signal inspectors, they knew whether you could make it. These days, quite often you find the person testing and training has been at it about five minutes.

For the psychometric testing, you sit at a computer. They tell you to practise on your kids' Gameboys. I've never used a Gameboy in me life, but I've been a signalman since I was eighteen and I've not derailed one yet.

In some parts of the country, particularly the south, there is a skills and labour shortage, so people can work their first job in quite a complex box. The most common sort of big signal boxes now are what they call PSBs: power signalling boxes. They have an operating room and between three and six operating panels, and you'll see the signaller standing at the panel pressing the buttons, setting all the route lights.

Once the signaller sets the route for the train, that sends signals electronically out to the ground, and the equipment sets all the points. The average signaller handles between 6,000 and 10,000 people's lives every day he goes to work. Until last year, Railtrack was spending most of its money on big glamour projects. I think they forgot we were still there. But we're the people who delivered the trains for them.

The first few years, you'd get these Railtrack newsletters about somebody's birthday, handing round cakes in the office, a very office sort of culture. Totally alien to over half the staff who were signallers working out in signal boxes or production supervisors out on the track.

I wouldn't say signalmen are loyal to the company, but they're loyal to the railway. Quite frankly, I and most of my colleagues don't care what the name of the company is that runs it; what they want to see is a railway they can be proud to say they work on. You go in your local pub or shop and people start making jokes. The type of job we do, I think we should be respected like a civil servant would be, like in Germany. We're a laughing stock.

Yes, there are strikes, and there's likely to be a few more. There's issues bubbling in a number of companies.

What the railways need is a post-war Marshall Plan. Anybody thinks it's an overnight fix they're kidding themselves. Take twenty years. I'm a railway signalman. I just wish we could go back to one railway.

from the Guardian*'s Public Voices series*

8 March 2002

LARRY ELLIOTT

Fat cats

The City is threatening to go on strike. Angry with the government over its decision to pull the plug on Railtrack, a score or more of the square mile's finest fired off a letter to Gordon Brown this week effectively telling him that they want more compensation for their worthless shares in the company. Unless the chancellor agrees, he will have to pay more for City participation in Labour's cherished public-private schemes.

Uniquely, this is one strike that has been widely praised by the rightwing press. Strikes by unions are always bad, since they involve unreasonable 'demands' for extra money. A strike by the City, on the other hand, is not 'holding the country to ransom' but a reasonable response to a government that has betrayed a trust.

The government's response to this attempt at blackmail has so far been commendably robust, but the inescapable conclusion of this spat is that the relationship between the government and business is coming under severe strain. And not before time. It's neither healthy nor desirable for business to wield the political influence it has increasingly enjoyed over the past two decades. It is bad for government and – ultimately – bad for business as well.

Politicians once understood this. In his inaugural address in 1933, President Roosevelt didn't waste time trying to cuddle up to Wall Street: he blamed the excesses of big finance for the Depression and said so: 'Practices of the unscrupulous money changers stand indicted in the court of public opinion, rejected by the hearts and minds of men.' Nor was FDR content with mere words. The Glass-Stegall Act, for example, ruled that banks should act like banks and stockbrokers should act like stockbrokers and that each should stick to its own speciality.

Bankers, in Roosevelt's eyes, were supposed to be sober and cautious, lending money against collateral rather than extending unlimited credit for speculation in the markets. Naturally enough, Wall Street hated Roosevelt. Legend has it that the flunkies of the financier J. P. Morgan Jnr had to cut out the picture of the president from the papers every morning before showing them to their boss.

Despite what Wall Street might have thought, Roosevelt was neither anti-market nor anti-business. He believed that the market had the power to deliver a remarkable array of goods, but that it was inherently unstable. Governments had the responsibility for regulating the economic environment to ensure that the market could operate to its full potential. This was a sensible position. The most cursory glance at what has happened to living standards, life expectancy and levels of nutrition in the past 200 years suggests that business has delivered, but it has been most effective when it has been treated as a dangerous beast that needs to be caged.

Times change. In the post-war years, business in both the US and the UK chipped away at the rules and regulations set up by the New Dealers. Markets were deregulated and restrictions on capital abandoned. Bill Clinton (who else?) repealed Glass-Stegall. All this added to the power of the business interest, and was reinforced by the sense of overdone pessimism that governments were powerless in the face of globalisation.

But there was more to it than that. Ceding power to business was seen as an ethically correct thing to do. Business, it was said, exemplified the new virtue. The myriad transactions in markets every day reflected public wants and needs in a way that government never could. Markets were honest, markets were safe, markets were democratic.

This was all tosh, as Adam Smith – the supposed grand-pappy of the whole gleaming New World Order – foretold back in 1776. Smith knew that, left to its own devices, business had a tendency towards collusion and corruption rather than integrity: 'People of the same trade seldom meet together, even for merriment and diversion, but the conversation ends in a conspiracy against the public, or in some contrivance to raise prices . . .'

And so it has proved. Enron is but one example, with the biggest bankruptcy in corporate history; the result of systematic dishonesty on a colossal scale. All the elements of the New Business Order – a light regulatory touch, a suborning of government, speculation in new 'exciting' financial instruments – combined in a conspiracy against the public.

Enron is not a one-off; it is symbolic of a deeper corruption. What's more the public is gradually waking up to the way in which it has been gulled. The losses made by small shareholders following the collapse of the internet bubble were partly their own fault; they were greedy and stupid. But it was also the case that they were being advised to buy stock in 'exciting' new dotcoms by analysts working for firms advising the very same companies. Legal action is looming, and rightly so.

In the UK, the public now knows that it was fleeced by the pensions industry. Markets only work effectively if both buyers and sellers are in full possession of the same information. This was not the case either when those in sound company schemes were mis-sold much less attractive portable pensions or when the usurious commissions on new plans wiped out any gains from rising share prices in the long bull market of the nineties.

The government's response to this has been right. It has insisted that charges of no more than 1 per cent should be levied by firms selling the new stakeholder pensions, and that has had a knock-on impact on non-stakeholder policies. Regulation is working.

In other areas too there have been signs that the government is reappraising its stance. The role of supine non-executive directors is coming under scrutiny following the Enron collapse; the banking industry is in a panic over the possibility that the government will impose a windfall tax on the excessive profits made from small businesses.

The extent of this change of heart should not be exaggerated. The government is still wedded to big-tent politics, and sees an injection of private-sector 'values' as the key to reform of the public services. Trade unions were understandably spitting blood yesterday over reports that the prime minister is planning to veto proposals to protect the rights of employees when they transfer from the public to the private sector.

Moreover, Labour's own relationship with business is deeply suspect. Tony Blair's critics have tried to establish that he was either a fool or a knave to take a £125,000 donation from Lakshmi Mittal and then write a letter in support of the Indian multi-millionaire to the Romanian government over a steel company takeover.

They might be better off accusing him of being a pimp, for the prime minister and some of his colleagues make no secret of the fact that they – like previous administrations – see it as their job to go around the world procuring for British business. It isn't, and the sooner the government cuts the apron strings the better for all concerned. There is nothing wrong with business. But it needs to know its place.

31 July 2002

KEVIN MAGUIRE

King Arthur hangs up his crown

As strikers return to disrupt public services, union leaders once again trot in and out of Downing Street and editors of rightwing tabloids dust down headlines denouncing leftwingers, Arthur Scargill prepares to retire. The irony of his timing – he steps down tomorrow as president of the National Union of Mineworkers (NUM) after twenty-one years – underlines his marginalisation, and that of the once-mighty NUM.

Tony Blair's government is at a crossroads, vulnerable to pressure from an increasingly confident union movement which is flexing its muscles, yet Scargill is not so much sidelined as not even in the game. True, he has survived his archenemies: while he is retiring voluntarily several months short of his sixty-fifth birthday, Margaret Thatcher was forcibly retired a dozen years ago by her party, and Ian MacGregor, the Coal Board chairman, and Robert Maxwell, the *Mirror* baron, succumbed to the grim reaper. But as Old King Coal lost his kingdom, the labour movement's mightiest regiment was reduced to a bedraggled platoon. The Yorkshireman inherited a 250,000-strong union when he won a pithead ballot to succeed Joe Gormley in 1981. He bequeaths an organisation affiliating 5,001 miners to the Trades Union Congress (TUC), a pitiful figure – though many suspect even that is inflated. TUC bodies representing magistrates' clerks, airline pilots, probation officers and chiropodists can boast bigger memberships.

No other union leader since the war has been simultaneously so demonised and lionised as Scargill, who helped Gormley defeat the Tories of Ted Heath in 1972 and 1974 before losing to the Conservatives of Margaret Thatcher in the epic struggle of 1984–5.

Enemies, inside as well as outside the Labour party, vilified him as a Marxist demagogue plotting to overthrow elected governments to impose his own brand of pro-Soviet socialism on Britain. Supporters, admittedly a dwindling band in recent years, hailed him as the hero who, wedded to his principles, stood up for the ordinary people against the bosses and politicians.

Two decades on from his election, it can be difficult to recall the sense of excitement and expectancy generated by Scargill when he first shook up the ranks of grey, elderly men who dominated the NUM high command. That gloss faded in the tragedy of a defeat that cleared the way for a closure programme that reduced the United Kingdom coal industry – privatised along the way – from 170 pits to just sixteen, five of which face the axe.

Thatcher deployed the full force of the State to defeat a man she regarded as the enemy within, using the police and intelligence services to halt and, at times, attack pickets. Perhaps no union leader could have avoided defeat, but if one could, it was not Scargill, who made a series of fundamental errors. The confrontation – and thus the future of coal – might have turned out differently if Gormley had not stayed on at the NUM to prevent Mick McGahey (a communist who recognised that pragmatism was needed to put principles into action) taking over as president. Gormley's tactics opened the door for the Yorkshire miners' leader who tried to use his position to bring down Thatcher, instead of winning an industrial dispute.

He went into battle without calling a ballot, splitting the union as the Nottinghamshire miners worked on, and weakened support by refusing to condemn picket-line violence. When a compromise was put on the table in September 1984, he missed an opportunity to achieve a victory of sorts, instead leading his troops to defeat in March 1985.

Scargill claimed that the struggle was a triumph in itself, though that was exposed for the posturing it was as pits closed, miners lost their jobs and his voice in the Labour party and TUC waned. When Blair and his modernisers seized the leadership in the mid-nineties, instead of staying and fighting – as he had urged the Notts miners to do – Scargill set up his own party.

The Socialist Labour party joined a mature market in struggling leftwing factions, failed to make any impact and further marginalised its founder. Scargill's control freakery is in the New Labour league and disagreements saw Mick Rix and Bob Crow, the heads of the two main rail unions, quit what became known as Scargill's Leaving Party.

In a sense, the obituaries will be premature, because Scargill has no intention of spending his retirement gardening at his Barnsley home opposite Wentworth Castle and its fine rhododendron collection. The outgoing NUM president, who is entitled to a pension worth two-thirds of his £67,000 salary, used branch block votes to be elected NUM honorary president for ten years on a £1,000 a month 'consultancy' fee.

Scargill, who has taken to comparing himself to Nelson Mandela, is preparing his memoirs and may yet find a new platform. But, given his record, will anybody listen?

25 July 2002

RICHARD ADAMS

Figures of fun (City Diary)

Good morning. In the event that the courts decide to sequester the *Guardian*'s assets next week as part of the legal action with Interbrew, the City Diary has been handed over to a team of accountants in preparation for their possible takeover of the newspaper as a whole. As a result, any or all of the jokes in this column are now regulated by the financial services authority, will be ISO-9000 compliant, carry corporate membership of the UK accounting standards board and come under the 1997 financial reporting standard for smaller entities. Further, all jokes within the City Diary will use transitional FRS17 disclosure, based on the most recent valuation by independent qualified actuaries. Each item will be amortised using the straight line method over the estimated average lives of the material. This column is not authorised to give advice under the financial services and markets act 2000. Past performance is no guarantee of anything. By reading this far, you will be deemed to accept these terms in full.

Now we've got all the technical stuff out of the way, let's make it clear that accountants are not as humourless as they are often portrayed. It's actually a profession with a colourful collection of characters – just take Arthur Andersen for example. In fact the whole Enron collapse was probably just one of their jokes which got out of hand. Seriously, though, the profession has come in for some bad publicity recently. But members of the public shouldn't let a few incidents such as Enron and WorldCom stop them from remembering the 60 per cent of accountants who are honest and ethical.

Beer drinkers in the Romanian town of Mizil are angry because their local beer has been banned by government officials. The beer is cheaper and tastes better than rival brews, according to the locals. But the bureaucrats feel the brand is in poor taste – the beer is called Bin Laden. While this story is amusing as far as it goes, what are the accounting implications for the loss of goodwill by the brewery in this case? Generally, goodwill is amortised through the profit and loss account over its estimated useful economic life. But on the termination of a brand such as this Bin Laden beer, the loss on termination should be calculated by including any remaining capitalised goodwill or the gross amount of any related goodwill previously written off directly to reserves, as appropriate. You see, it's really that simple.

In preparation for possible sequestration, a list of the City Diary's fixed assets has been audited by a team of accountants. They comprise, in total: One (1) used copy of *Pocket Oxford Dictionary of Current English*, seventh edition. Three (3) white plastic beverage stirrers. One (1) photograph of BBC economics editor Evan Davis, inscribed *Keep up the great work! Love, Evan XXX*. One (1) copy of Merrill Lynch booklet Y2K: *Implications for Investors*, published June 1998. Eighteen (18) notebooks, various states of use. Total resale value: nil (pounds 0.00).

Time, surely, for some good accounting jokes.

Q: What do accountants suffer from when they get sad?

A: Depreciation!

Of course that answer isn't correct: depreciation wouldn't make anyone sad, as it's the amount that an asset has decreased over time. And that's good news, since the total amount that assets have depreciated by during a reporting period is shown on the cash flow statement, and also makes up part of the expenses shown on the income statement. So that's not funny at all.

For obvious reasons, the Consignia/Royal Mail special that was to have been delivered today has fallen behind its delivery target. This failure will be accounted for by writing it off against derivative financial instruments.

THE NAKED AND
THE DEAD

Austin, 28 March 2002

In a column – 'My five tests for the euro', page 15, 15 July – the
president of the European Central Bank, Wim Duisenberg, was
inadvertently transposed into Dim Wuisenberg.

Corrections and Clarifications, 17 July 2002

SIMON HATTENSTONE

Wiesenthal, Nazi-hunter

Vienna is shrouded in fog, and Simon Wiesenthal's offices are barely visible. The nonagenarian Nazi-hunter has lived here for forty years. A tiny plate, one of a dozen or so, says *Dokumentazionszentrum*. I ring, and Rosemary, one of his secretaries, lets me in. To the left of his office, sitting on the stairs and again barely visible, is a guard. It seems both perverse and logical that Wiesenthal chose to live out his post-Holocaust life in Austria – a country he claimed was responsible for half the six million Jewish dead.

The door is open. 'You're late,' says Rosemary, who has worked for Wiesenthal for twenty-six years.

I apologise. She glares. The three small rooms are claustrophobic, crammed with terrible reminders of the Holocaust and tributes to Wiesenthal. Numerous doctorates, a bronze bust, a poster of Ben Kingsley playing him in a film, take their place alongside photographs of Nazi victims and a huge map of Hitler's Germany.

'You are late,' Wiesenthal says. 'You should have come at 10.30 a.m.' He doesn't smile. I apologise and say that it was beyond my control the plane was late. He says he will be leaving for home in half an hour. I remind him that I have come over from England, ask him if he please could see his way to giving me a little extra time.

'No,' he says.

Wiesenthal looks much as he did thirty years ago. His belly is bigger, his trousers are hoicked that little bit higher up his chest, but he still presents a dapper image – grey suit, grey pullover, grey handkerchief, grey socks, all beautifully coordinated with his grey 'tache and hair. His rheumy eyes weep a little as he talks. Outside his office there is the constant clicking of heels as his two secretaries strut back and forth depositing their files. Stern and rigorous, they have an air of the dominatrix about them.

A few weeks ago, a newspaper ran a story saying that Wiesenthal was finally hanging up his boots. I ask him why he's retiring.

'Ach,' he says. 'I have not decided to retire. It was a false interpretation of what I have said. I said that I have survived the majority of all the people I have searched for in fifty years. And now I am not searching for more people.'

That sounds pretty much like retirement to me. No, he says, there is still so much to do in the way of documentation. It will take three years to computerise the records, and he is determined to see it out.

Anyway, he says, he may not be searching for more Nazis, but that doesn't mean that no more will come his way.

'From time to time we may wish to find someone.'

He says another part of the work is of increasing importance – documenting the rise of the neo-Nazis and historical revisionists. 'There are now small groups in Germany and Austria who say not everything about Nazism was bad. And one day when the situation is good for them, these small groups could grow into a bigger group of neo-Nazis.'

Wiesenthal's huge family came from the Austro-Hungarian town of Buchach. He was a mature man, in his early thirties, when his mother was carted off to Belzec. He ran after the railway truck to no avail. By 1941, both he and his wife Cyla were in concentration camps. He was moved from death camp to death camp – thirteen in all – but somehow managed not to die. He tried to kill himself twice, and failed. He was lined up to be shot three times, but each time the gunmen failed to reach him. Once the executions were halted when a church bell tolled. As the Germans retreated at the end of the war, he was shot at point-blank range by an SS officer. Somehow the bullet missed him.

In 1944, an SS corporal asked Wiensenthal how, in the unlikely event of escaping, he would describe the camps. Wiesenthal replied that he would tell the truth. The corporal told him that no one would believe anyone was capable of such brutality. That was when Simon Wiesenthal decided it was his responsibility to document the Holocaust, to root out the architects of Nazism, to make sure we never forget.

When he was liberated from Mauthausen, the strong young man who had entered the camps was a skeletal 100 pounds. But he was still proud and tough. More than eighty members of his family, including his mother, had been wiped out. He was told Cyla had been killed. She was told he had killed himself.

Wiesenthal was born with a photographic memory. After liberation, he provided a list of war criminals that ought to be brought to trial, and of the ninety-one names he tracked down seventy-five. Since then, Wiesenthal has caught, or helped catch, more than a thousand Nazis. He used a motley crew of former concentration-camp victims, his 'agents', to track them down. They often spent years looking for evidence in the form of photos and first-hand accounts, but it was never going to be easy – most of the witnesses were dead.

His most famous find was Karl Adolf Eichmann. During the search, he asked one of his agents, a concentration camp survivor, to seduce Eichmann's former girlfriends as a means of getting hold of a photograph of him. The agent delivered, and the photograph was used as evidence in convicting Eichmann.

I ask him what he regards as his greatest achievement.

'Ach. Look. I had many cases. One case I was working on for nine years, and I finished it. Hermine Braunsteiner was responsible for the death of many hundreds of children in a concentration camp.' Eventually, he tracked her down to America, and she was tried and given a life sentence. 'Six or seven months ago, the judge informed me that she had become so sick that he must relieve her from prison, and do you know what had happened?' He smiles for the first time. 'She had lost both legs. Her American husband bought an apartment in Dusseldorf so he could see her in prison twice every week, and now he has the apartment and the wife that could not walk. So!'

Did he feel there was a form of justice in her having her legs amputated? He doesn't answer. Often, I ask Wiesenthal one question and he answers another. The one that he wants to answer. It's not age, just obduracy.

'Look. We have only small cases because the bigger ones were all made by the Americans, and we didn't have enough money to send people to Argentina and Brazil.'

The most common criticism thrown at Wiesenthal is that he exaggerated his role in capturing war criminals and that for many years the likes of Mengele roamed around Sao Paulo, known and unchallenged.

'When I had the money, I sent people to Argentina and Brazil,' he says. 'We had a few cases from there, but we needed a hundred, maybe two hundred officers at my office. What can be done by one person alone with two secretaries?'

The heels continue to click up and down the corridor outside. It's funny, I say, I presumed the Wiesenthal Centre, with its offices in Vienna and California, was huge.

'Nah, nah.' He shakes his head with disappointment. The US centre, a museum of tolerance, uses his name, but doesn't do his work.

Has he never been tempted to put the horror of the Holocaust behind him? Did he not feel he had suffered enough?

'Yes, I understand. This is absolutely the reality. Look. For twelve years before the war I worked as an architect. When I started doing this a few weeks after my liberation, I was so naive, thinking, I will not build houses now, I will build justice. In two or three years we will have justice.'

He says there were other Nazi-hunters who also thought the same, but realised that the search for justice was endless and gave up. He is dismissive of them.

'They left. They emigrated to the United States, one to Israel, one to Australia. And now I feel my office is the last office in the world. Could you close the last office?'

Eight months after he was liberated, he found his wife in Poland. Cyla, who was in the same class at school with him, is, like Wiesenthal, ninety-three years old. Did she not want them to live a normal life?

'Look. When I found my wife, she said to me: "You have studied architecture seven years, you were working twelve years, why not go back to it? You are not the only one who has suffered through the Nazis."' She was desperate for him to stop hunting Nazis and earn a decent, calm living? 'Yes. She says: "Why can't we live a normal life, let us go to Israel, let us go to another place and be normal people." And I couldn't.'

His obsession is total. He finds it impossible to turn his attention to anything else. He has said that to talk of the slaughter in Bosnia or Rwanda or Iraq in the same breath is to undermine the unique suffering of the Jews in the Holocaust. I ask him how he would go about capturing Osama bin Laden, and whether he should have to face a tribunal. I expect him to light up at the thought of tracking down Bin Laden. But he simply bypasses the question and returns to the Holocaust.

'Look. Today, we have one person that we know killed 130,000 Jews and he lives in Syria, in Damascus: Alois Brunner.'

He tells me of Anton Gecas, an alleged Nazi who died a few months ago in Edinburgh, just before he was due to be extradited to Lithuania. Did he feel anger, a sense of failure, or simply relief that the man was dead?

'A trial is very important,' he says. 'We need the trial of the man. We need this in newspapers, this is the best way against repetition.'

I ask him whether he thinks there is a pattern to abuse – so many abused people end up being abusers. Does he think the same could be said of the people of Israel? Again, he ignores the question.

'I hope that Israel will survive. When I was a young man it was my hope to live in what was then Palestine, so I feel this is a part of my heart.'

His daughter and three grandchildren live there now.

What has given him most happiness in life? 'My son-in-law: he's a lawyer,' he answers instantly.

Wiesenthal wags a finger at his watch. 'My dear friend, I told you at 11.45 I must leave, and now it's 11.55.' But there is nothing friendly in the voice. He doesn't seem tired, or in a hurry, just impatient. I ask him whether the Holocaust made him lose his faith in God.

'I will not answer that. That is a personal question.' Did it make him lose his faith in humanity? 'For humanity we must work.'

Does he feel his experience has made him less humane? 'That is not relevant; it is about justice.' The trouble is, he says, so many people allow their judgment to be warped by sentimentality. 'You should write this down. I myself am ninety-three. When you bring for a trial a person over eighty, the whole sympathy of the public is for him. Young people come to me and say "Let this old man die in peace."' Does that upset him? 'Yes, and I tell the young people how many old people he killed. Because the Nazis did not care whether it was a baby or an old man.

'Look,' he suddenly whispers with savage intensity. 'A few years ago groups in different countries decided that we need help, so they collect money for us. Because without money you can do nothing. And now the situation, the tragic situation, is I have enough money, but we have not enough cases.'

Wiesenthal has been telling me that I must leave for fifteen minutes. Now he gets up to leave. Rosemary wraps him up in a coat and his black beret. For a second, I see the ghost of a tough, young resistance fighter. As they get into the lift, I join them. They look annoyed. We reach the ground floor.

'OK,' Rosemary says. 'We go this way.' She points to the car park. 'And you go that way.' She points to the front entrance. They disappear without another word.

16 April 2002

DIANE TAYLOR

And then there were two

On a bleak Yorkshire moor overlooking a stretch of turquoise sea stands one of the most isolated communities in Britain. 'Blink and you miss this place,' says my taxi driver, Val Hutchinson, as she abruptly swerves off the main road out of Whitby and on to a long bumpy track. We drive past a stern sign: MONASTERY

ENCLOSURE, DO NOT ENTER. Another decidedly unwelcoming sign follows: THE MONASTERY DOES NOT RECEIVE VISITORS. THERE IS NO GUESTHOUSE. And another: THE MONASTERY, CHURCHYARD AND CHURCH SERVICES ARE CLOSED TO VISITORS.

At the end of the track, there is a long, neat building and a garden full of spring flowers and industriously cultivated rows of vegetables. On the moor beyond, newborn lambs stagger about. Inside, all is white and wood and ordered calm. The air smells of incense and creosote. Small, delicate vases of flowers from the garden decorate the window sills.

This is a Greek Orthodox monastery – apparently the only one in the country to adhere to a strict Orthodox tradition. It is home to just two nuns: Mother Thekla, the Abbess, and Mother Hilda. They have agreed to talk to the *Guardian* – which means a visitor – because they would like to attract new nuns to their community of two. In a letter to me, arranging the visit, Mother Hilda wrote: *All we can do is let people know that we exist and something of our way of life.*

It was twenty-seven years ago that Mother Thekla and another nun, Mother Maria, moved here from a monastery they had founded in Buckinghamshire some thirteen years before. In Buckinghamshire, they were prey to casual, curious visitors: here there is none of that. Today Mother Maria lies buried in the monastery's cemetery, along with another nun, Mother Katherine. Since then women have come to join, but Mother Hilda was the only one to stay.

And so there are just the two of them in residence. When I meet them, both are dressed in black, close-fitting veils and long, loose black robes. They say they wear black as a symbol of their own deaths to the world: 'Our work is the work of corpses in the face of the world.'

Dead to the world or not, these nuns practically explode with exuberance. Mother Thekla is eighty-three, with sharp brown eyes. Every so often she giggles. Mother Hilda is perhaps thirty years younger, although she politely declines to reveal her age, explaining that she cannot discuss details of her pre-monastic life. She does reveal, however, that she joined Mother Thekla nine years ago.

As we talk, some details do emerge about the women's lives. Mother Thekla was born in Russia during the Revolution. She had to be baptised in a vase, she says, because there was too much shooting going on in the streets for her parents to get to church. Soon afterwards they moved to England and she grew up in Richmond.

'I climbed every tree in Richmond Park and could recognise them all,' she says.

She took English at Cambridge and worked for British intelligence during the war, partly in India, although she will not elaborate. She later became an English teacher.

Mother Hilda is a specialist in Byzantine studies, but is reticent about her academic background. She is from Philadelphia, and the odd Americanism pops into her speech as she talks – once she refers to cleaning up 'dust bunnies'.

'She has a PhD, she's quite erudite,' confides Mother Thekla.

'Oh Mother, come on – I'm an amateur,' says Mother Hilda.

Neither nun leaves the monastery unless it is strictly necessary – an appointment with the doctor, for example. Their daily life at the monastery – the official name for it is Hesychasterion (prayerhouse) of the Koimisis (Assumption) –

follows a regular cycle. Prayers they refer to as 'offices' begin at 6 a.m. and are repeated at regular intervals until 'midnight office'. In all there are six prayer sessions each day: eight hours in all. Some of the prayers date back to the fourth century and are said in a beautiful church with icons on the walls. On Sundays and feast days an all-night vigil is added to the eight hours of prayer completed on ordinary days.

'This used to be the cowshed,' says Mother Thekla as we enter the church. 'It's why we bought this place. We saw it and knew this would be our church.'

In between prayers, the nuns are engaged separately in creative and practical work, coming together for simple meals in the refectory.

'Spreading manure on the vegetables is one of my tasks for today,' says Mother Hilda.

The monastery differs from a traditional convent in that the nuns live in what they describe as self-contained hermitages, or hermit cells, where they work and sleep, meeting only for food and prayer. It is not a life of abject poverty.

'We have the things we need but not the things we don't need,' says Mother Hilda. There are no curtains or easy chairs but the furnishings are simple rather than spartan, as is the delicious lunch of rice, beans and salad that Mother Hilda prepares for us.

There is a microwave, a washing machine and a computer, but no fripperies. They grow much of their own food and freeze their produce to see them through the winter. Shopping for essential supplies is done a handful of times a year by Mother Hilda. Mother Thekla bakes bread, and eggs are supplied by the local farm. They do not eat meat and dairy products are forbidden during Lent.

'It is the monotony of our lives which frees the spirit – all the imminent things drop away,' says Mother Thekla. 'It's quite painful being faced with your real self without the trimmings. There's time here to pray for the world. That's our work: it's not something we do on our Sunday off.'

Nationally, the number of women signing up for a life of poverty, chastity and obedience is falling by 8 per cent a year. Mother Hilda believes there are a number of reasons.

'Some blame the "vocation problem" on luxury and self-indulgence, but we will never manage to be as decadent as Rome or Byzantium,' she says. She believes that one of the reasons fewer women choose to enrol is a growing inability to sustain an 'inner life'. 'We have been robbed of our inner resources – elevator music is all around,' she says. 'All the silences are covered. These days it is considered cruel to have a quiet classroom for children.'

Is there too much instant gratification? She nods vigorously. She says that the women who came to the monastery but did not stay, did not 'know what to do sitting in a room by themselves'.

For Mother Thekla the decision to become a nun was sudden. 'I went on a retreat and met Mother Maria and that was it. I was called to it. It's a bit like a thunderbolt. You can't deny it when it hits you. I used to love things like visiting second-hand bookshops but you can't compare life now with life before. It's like walking through a mirror backwards.'

At one time choosing a life as a nun was an obvious career option. Poverty propelled many women into convents and although the lifestyle involved various degrees of separation from the world, nuns were a much more visible presence in mainstream society than they are today.

'In the past strong, independent women with views of their own were attracted to this life but now because there are so many more opportunities for women to lead independent lives, fewer from this group are choosing to be nuns,' says Mother Hilda. She says that people still want spirituality. 'But they are looking for a magic key to unlock this spirituality and shift the responsibility for finding that on to someone else.'

So why should anyone consider joining their monastery? 'For a woman who is self-reliant and independent there is space here for her spiritual growth,' says Mother Hilda.

'We have the knowledge that nothing worldly matters,' says Mother Thekla. 'We don't need success and achievement in the worldly sense. The soul is free and there's no competition and no jealousy.'

'And it's great not to think about what clothes you're going to put on in the mornings,' adds Mother Hilda.

Does feminism play a part in their lives? Mother Thekla isn't sure what it is, but favours a traditional family set up with a husband and children for women, while Mother Hilda believes that neither men nor women should be held back by artificial barriers and gender expectations.

'In the eastern monastic tradition we are considered neither monks nor nuns,' she says. 'Our garb is the same as that of male monks and our offices are the same. Here we are beyond gender.'

7 November 2001

EMMA BROCKES

Mr Sharon at home

Between Tel Aviv and the small town of Sderot there is a turn-off for Shikmim Farm. You can't miss it. A white gazebo has been pitched at the gate and a mass of pink bougainvillea trained up the wall on either side. It looks like the kind of place you might go to experience deep-pore facials with mud from the Dead Sea. Two men with sub-machine guns stand in the shade, not an uncommon sight in Israel, particularly this close to Gaza, but unlike most out-of-the-way security details they are rigid with vigilance. Ariel Sharon, the Israeli prime minister, lives half a kilometre down the drive. For some reason, he has invited us to spend the afternoon with him.

The prospect of meeting the 73-year-old former general is complicated by his vast, almost cartoon-like reputation. Sharon has fought in every Israeli war since 1948. His autobiography is called *Warrior*; his nickname is Bulldozer. He is variously held up as the single biggest obstacle to peace in the Middle East and the saviour of Israel. ('Even the sheep are afraid of me,' he has said.) In 1983 he was forced to resign as defence minister under Menachem Begin after an inquiry found him responsible for the slaughter of more than 800 Arab refugees in southern Lebanon. 'Sharon Rotzeach' ('Sharon the Murderer') read the placards of protesters who regularly gathered outside his Jerusalem home.

Now he is prime minister. 'He is a doer,' one Israeli Jew told me in Tel Aviv. 'Doing', in this context, can be taken as a euphemism for violence. And since 11 September Sharon has been 'doing' more than usual. While the world's eyes were on the smouldering ruins of downtown Manhattan, his soldiers and agents were carrying out a string of brutal attacks on targets in Gaza and the West Bank. After the assassination of his friend, the rightwing tourism minister, Rehavam Zeevi, the tanks were rolling again, this time into the heart of four West Bank towns, in the biggest occupation of Palestinian territory since the post-Oslo withdrawal of the early 1990s. At least forty-five Palestinians have been killed since the Zeevi assassination.

With this in mind, we are deposited by a bemused taxi driver outside the gate and checked-in by security. Israel is too small to keep the location of Shikmim (Hebrew for 'Sycamore') Farm secret. Everybody knows where it is: 1,500 acres in the dry, Negev region of southern Israel. It is even signposted from the road. Any visitors quickly have a sense that the two entry guards are only the tip of a huge, invisible security system monitoring every approach. After a cursory check, we pass through the gates and a Jeep runs us up to the house.

Even by the standards of the past month it has been a furiously paced week for Sharon. Last Thursday, Tony Blair flew to meet him in Israel on the last leg of his Middle Eastern tour. The day after our meeting, three people were killed in a terrorist attack by a Palestinian gunman on a bus in Jerusalem. So busy has Sharon been these past few weeks that he has even cancelled a long-planned trip to Washington and London. All of which makes the scene that greets us on entry to his farmhouse absurdly discordant. We enter to the sound of a Mozart piano concerto. A female assistant leads us through a corridor to a whitewashed lounge with terracotta floor tiles, furnished with Mediterranean chic. Mr Sharon, we are informed, has a little business to finish and will be with us shortly. A different assistant enters, says, 'I am here to spoil you,' and brings us a plate of Jammy Dodgers. We are left alone with Sharon's Alsatian dog, Schwartz, for twenty minutes.

If the afternoon has been carefully stage managed – and it is hard to perceive it as anything but – then this time alone in the lounge is clearly intended as an opportunity for us to get to know Sharon through his soft furnishings. On the beige sofas are scatter cushions painstakingly embroidered in needlepoint. *What a Mensch!* reads the stitching on one (*mensch* is the Yiddish word for a man of integrity). On the coffee table stands a brass sculpture of a woman in some sort of ballet pose. Above the piano are sepia photos from the Sharon family tree.

The books are big, neutral tomes with titles such as *World of Ceramics*, *Rembrandt After 300 Years* and *Big Cats*. On the walls hang paintings with a farm-yard theme: a Francis Bacon-like interpretation of two hens, a pencil drawing of a cow's head and a pastoral scene of peasant women tilling a field. The only ref-erence to Sharon's public image is a small drawing of soldiers marching in line and a sketch of orthodox Jews studying the Talmud. Out in the hall, there are saddles thrown over the balustrades of the staircase.

The prime minister enters the room heavily. Sharon is a big man who heaves from side to side like a metronome. He is dressed in turned-up jeans hiked high above his waist and a blue-checked shirt. After shaking hands, he settles himself in an over-stuffed mustard armchair and, without preamble, starts talking.

'Through irrigation the colours in this part of the world are changing,' he says, waving a hand at the window. 'I was born on a farm. My strength has nothing to do with political apparatus. I get my strength from nature, from flowers.'

His parents were Russian immigrants who in 1922 moved to a rural outpost fifteen miles north-east of Tel Aviv. His father, Samuil, was an agronomist; his mother, Vera, a frustrated medic who reluctantly aborted her studies to commit herself to the Jewish settlement. She was never a Zionist, but, says Sharon, she eventually learned to love the land.

'Traditionally, commanders and pilots and special units came from farm country. Danger was a part of life there. You know? In the evenings – this was during the British mandate, so weapons were illegal – we used to dig in the stable and take out the gun from under horse manure. I remember that from a very early age. I did it many times.'

Sharon does not make much eye contact. He talks either to the window or to the middle distance. I begin to ask if he felt unnatural as a child bearing arms. He reads the question as critical – a suggestion that he has been brutalised from infancy – and interrupts to defend himself. 'It's a struggle. Over a hundred and twenty years. Very recently of course it has became local terror, regional terror and you have international terror. Maybe the world understands better now that one should not get into any compromise with terror. You cannot surrender to terror – you have to fight terror.'

No matter the subject, it is a mantra Sharon always returns to.

At this point, a peculiar snuffling sound issues from the far side of the room. Schwartz, the Alsatian, has deftly lifted a piece of cake from a china plate on the coffee table and thrown it down his throat. Sharon stiffens. He speaks sharply to his assistant in Hebrew.

'It's a terrible thing,' he says. 'He never did that before.'

The dog is dragged off by the scruff of its neck.

'Bad manners,' mutters Sharon furiously.

The big question hanging over Sharon at the moment is the extent to which his relationship with Bush and Blair has been damaged by the pressure put on him by them to satisfy Washington's Arab coalition partners. When talking about Blair's recent visit, he chooses his words with the care of a man walking a minefield.

'First of all,' he says, 'Prime Minister Blair is a friend of Israel. Second, I think, he's got very good intentions. That he finds time with all the problems to come here to try to solve and help is admirable. I believe that he understands. It doesn't mean he is supporting everything. I never ask any of those leaders to be fully on our side. I don't expect that and I don't want it. There could have been better support from the rest of Europe, but if you ask "Is Prime Minister Blair trying to help us?" there is no doubt about it.'

Through a combination of selective hearing, political bluster and tactical convolution, Sharon explains that there is no rift with Bush, no angry exchange of phone calls with Colin Powell, that he never likened American foreign policy to appeasement and that there will be no negotiation with Arafat until he rounds up the men who assassinated Rehavam Zeevi.

'We are together with the British and Americans because one should fight terror,' he says. 'But we are not going to pay the price for it by endangering Israel and its citizens. That is what I told him.'

The risk this policy entails is deadlock. Critics of Sharon want to know what practical proposals he has to bring about the peace he professes to want. As things currently stand, they say, any maniac with a bomb can throw Israel into impasse.

'I heard that,' says Sharon. 'But the problem is I cannot use this term that you use now.' He smirks; his assistants on the sofa smirk. 'This is a word for the one who is fully responsible for our situation: Yasser Arafat. You said "something done by a maniac" – I don't want to refer to him in these terms, because the readers of the *Guardian* might be shocked.' He chuckles. 'He could have avoided the steps that we are taking – he's got the names, he knows them, he could have arrested them.'

In the absence of action from Arafat – who Sharon has tried energetically since 11 September to depict as a regional Osama bin Laden – Sharon's special forces have sought out Zeevi's killers themselves, even if it meant occupying the Palestinian cities of Ramallah, Bethlehem, Nablus and Jenin in the process.

'We have managed to arrest quite a number of dominant terrorists. Some of them we managed to arrest, some of them' – he gives me another conspiratorial smirk – 'are not any more with us. People don't like the word to kill. They were removed from our society.'

The phone rings. After a brief conversation, Sharon picks up where he left off: 'So I decided to postpone [my trip to London and Washington], which means that I'll miss the beautiful breakfasts in England.'

The glide between subjects isn't marked by a change of register. British breakfasts and the 'eradication' of the 'terrorist threat' are both delivered in the same placid drone.

I wonder how Sharon would go about capturing Bin Laden if he was commanding Britain's special forces? (As a 25-year-old he commanded Special Unit 101, which undertook just this sort of operation.) He says he has the utmost respect for the SAS.

'We've had strategic relations for many years. I trust that Britain and the United States will find him.' Is he offering them advice? 'It is better not to elaborate. I'm fully convinced that Israel will win its struggle against terror . . .'

Ten minutes later he surfaces from the script and looks at his watch. 'We must go. The light for the photographs is fading.'

And so we enter the second, still more surreal, phase of the visit. Sharon leads us into the courtyard, where we climb into a fortified Land Rover with bulletproof glass. Sharon, the photographer and I squeeze into the back seat. Two men with Uzi machine guns get in the front. We drive onto the main road flanked by two further Land Rovers packed with armed guards. Sharon is utterly distracted, leaning forwards in his seat, eyes flitting, talking urgently in Hebrew to the men in front. More armed guards can be seen behind the tree-line. Once off the road on to farmland, he relaxes a little. In formation with the other trucks, we climb the hill.

'I like animals,' he says abstractly. We stop at the top of the hill. The guards get out, Sharon gets out, we get out and all stand for a moment in silence, admiring the expanse of brown earth before us. It is the golden hour, the sun is like honey. Squinting, Sharon turns and leads us to a small, fenced area at the very summit of the hill. In it is planted a willow tree, a bench and a single grave with a headstone inscribed in Hebrew: *Lily Sharon*.

'In spring this place is all covered in bee-yoo-tiful flowers,' he says. 'One day, I will be buried here too, next to my wife.' There are tears in his eyes. He turns his back and takes several steps towards the willow tree, before bowing his head. Then he lifts it and looks across the land, like Nelson at the prow of a ship. 'What will happen to the Jews in 30 years, 300 years, 3,000 years? I feel all the ties and roots of the Jewish people in this place. There has been non-stop Jewish life here for thousands of years. That is what I stand for. This is not a campaign. It's a war for our survival. The Jews have one, tiny, small country. A country with many talents, but a tiny small country. We demand only one thing: to live peacefully. We have the right and the ability to defend ourselves and we will never give up. It is our duty. That is what I feel.'

How can he live like that? How can anyone live when living is just a matter of survival? Sharon snaps out of his reverie and looks annoyed.

'What do you mean, to live?' he says. 'You don't have to be a scared person. I've had so many tragedies. I've managed to withstand things that you may think you cannot tolerate. But I have the strength. First of all I am a Jew. That is my duty.'

It is tempting to speculate that the personal risk that Sharon has lived under for practically all of his life has influenced his political decision-making. He says not.

'Look. I have worries, but in difficult times, that is when I am quiet. You cannot allow yourself to do things thinking that, otherwise you're dead. It's dangerous. Would you like to see the cows?'

We troop back to the convoy. We are not allowed to enter through the same car door as Sharon, but are instructed to go around and slide along the back seat. On the way down, he instructs the driver to stop beside some cattle.

'Do you want me to pose in front of the bull?' he asks. He approaches the bull; the bull walks off; Sharon pursues it across the field. The armed guards exchange glances. Eventually, the bull and the prime minister reach accord some way in the distance. When we return to the car, Sharon looks thoroughly dreamy. I try to engage him on the subject of animal husbandry. He tells me that his brown cows 'don't give the same quantities of meat as the black-and-white ones' and that George Bush knows more about cattle than Tony Blair. His love of the land is plain to see but, I ask him, don't the Palestinians love the land too?

'Yes,' he says, 'they love the land.'

Does he respect that? 'I respect it. In point of fact, they are wonderful farmers.' He says he had Arab friends as a child and that until recently, Arab employees at the farm. That had to stop because of the security risk.

'We've been living with Arabs all our life. But one cannot live together with terror. Look – that is our heliport over there.'

The question of racism is not one he likes to discuss. When I ask if people were right to call Zeevi a racist (he referred to Palestinians as 'lice' and a 'cancer') Sharon becomes inarticulate with annoyance.

'I don't see any place for that. I will stop there. There is no time to refer to all those kind of things.' Those 'kind of things' are international opinions he finds objectionable and so-called 'gossip'. But his own views on the subject are controversial. He answers a question about whether there are essential differences between Arabs and Jews – the cornerstone of any racist doctrine – by expounding the inability of Arabs to live democratically.

'Oh, they are different,' he says of the two races. 'Israel is a democracy. The only democracy in this part of the world. From Iran across Africa to the Atlantic there is one tiny, small democracy and that is Israel.'

I suggest that the Palestinians in the occupied territories don't see much democracy. 'They suffer heavy casualties, we suffer heavy casualties and there is one man, only one, to blame and that's Arafat, because he could have avoided it. Look, they committed the most terrible murders. In wars, civilians are killed. We know that. It's a tragedy, but to take civilians as a target is something that one cannot forgive.'

This will strike some as rich coming from a man famous around the world for the quantity of blood on his hands. In 1953 Sharon led a raid on the Palestinian village of Qibya, during which his men massacred sixty-nine civilians. Later, as many as 20,000 people died in Israel's invasion of Lebanon, which the then prime minister, Begin, claimed he ran like a personal project. And most notoriously, he was held partially to blame for the massacre at the Shatilla and Sabra refugee camps in southern Lebanon. In 1982, Sharon was defence minister when Christian militias were allowed to enter the camps to root out 'terrorist factions'. They wound up killing at least 800 innocent people. Some accounts put the death toll as high as 2,000. How is that not an unforgivable targeting of civilians? Sharon tuts dismissively.

'They can accuse us as much as they want to.' The car stops. 'You want to see some sheep?'

After standing with the sheep for a while ('these sheep are a special breed that go back to our forefathers. All the ones you see were born here') we pile back into the car and head for the citrus grove. Some discussion ensues as to whether the orange fruit are tangerines or clementines. Whichever, Sharon is confident they are 'easy-peelers'.

'We were talking about Arafat,' I venture. Sharon is so vexed he actually swivels round in his seat to look at me.

'I'll tell you something. We are here with the citrus trees and the cattle, how can you speak about Arafat?' He corrects himself instantly. 'Oh, but you have to, you have to. What was the question?'

'Does Israel have anything to apologise for in relation to its treatment of the Palestinians?'

'Apologise? For what? What do I have to apologise for?'

'For the conditions under which the refugees live . . .'

'They could have solved the problem. The one who is responsible for their suffering is Arafat. The Palestinian refugees are there not because of us. They are there because when they invaded Israel in 1948 they were urged by the Arab countries that invaded to leave their homes. You want to pick some fruit?'

We pick fruit. Sharon says there are rabbits on his land which he defends from hunters. I suggest that he is a man of war, singularly ill-equipped to see Israel through peaceful negotiations. He looks weary for a moment.

'You have to understand one thing. I am seventy-three years old. I've seen everything. I've met the kings, the queens, the presidents, I've been around the world. I have one thing that I would like to do: to try to reach peace. It's a complicated thing. But I believe that I'm one of the only ones who can do it and I'll tell you why. Look, I've participated in all the wars of Israel and I went through the ranks from a corporal to a general. I saw the horrors of war; I know the fears of war. I saw my best friend being killed. I was badly injured twice in battle, once as a platoon commander when we were fighting in the siege of Jerusalem. Then several years later I was badly wounded against the Jordanians. And I had to take decisions of life and death for others and for myself. And believe me, I understand the importance of peace much better than many of the politicians that speak about it but never had the experience. I saw it myself. Peace should provide security. It should be durable. I'm ready to go far in making painful concessions. But there is one thing I will never make any concessions on and that's the security of the Israeli citizens and the very existence of the state of Israel. The Palestinians are losing time.'

Sharon has yet to detail these 'painful concessions'. He says he will never make the mistakes made by his predecessor, Ehud Barak, at the doomed Camp David talks last year. Barak offered Arafat withdrawal from Gaza, most of the West Bank and a share of Jerusalem, greater concessions than had ever been offered. Arguing that they did not amount to the basis for a viable Palestinian state, Arafat rejected them.

'May I tell you something?' asks Sharon. 'My predecessor, Barak, came to them and told them from the beginning what he would like to do for them. But they will never get what he promised them. I'm ready to negotiate in order to get a ceasefire. But it will be a major mistake to say now what we are going to offer them, because that will then become the start line of the negotiations.'

We return to the farmhouse. Sharon leads us back through the house and shows us his family photos, including one of his son Gur, who died in Sharon's arms at the age of eleven after a shooting accident.

'That's my grandfather and my grandmother on my mother's side,' he says. 'That's Lily's father. That's my father. They came from a town, the family of my mother came from a village. One Jewish family for four generations in that village in Russia. That's my mother. That's myself as a corporal.'

What made him such a good soldier? Sharon laughs.

'Need. And curiosity for what was on the other side of the hill.'

Does Sharon have any vision of a future for Israel in which his people are not simply standing guard, steeled for the next attack? He looks tired.

'Listen. My grandfather, my parents, myself, my sons all faced this terror for five or six generations now. So it is not the case that we are just sitting and waiting with the sword in our hand. But we are not waiting until Arafat decides to take steps against terror.'

Sharon has another strategy – as ambitious as it is improbable – to guarantee Israel's security: 'We are planning now to bring in another one million Jews to Israel.'

It is a bizarre alternative to peace talks, but as things currently stand Arafat 'is not a partner for negotiation'. And so things threaten to go on as before.

'It is up to him,' says Sharon. 'There is no chance that I will change my mind.'

24 May 2002

IAN TRAYNOR

The Jesus of Siberia

Four thousand feet up a mountain deep in the Siberian taiga, the middle-aged man appears in a velvet crimson robe, long brown hair framing a beatific smile. He sits down in a log cabin perched on the brow of the hill. It is a room with a stunning view. The snowy Sayan mountains sparkle in the distance. The silver and pink of the birch forests shimmer in the clear sunlight. Down to the right, the pure blue water of Lake Tiberkul mesmerises.

Behind the cabin, for much further than the eye can see – a thousand kilometres – the Siberian wilderness stretches, bereft of human habitation.

'It's all very complicated,' he starts quietly. 'But to keep things simple, yes, I am Jesus Christ. That which was promised must come to pass. And it was promised in Israel 2,000 years ago that I would return, that I would come back to finish what was started. I am not God. And it is a mistake to see Jesus as God. But I am the living word of God the Father. Everything that God wants to say, he says through me.'

Meet the Messiah of Siberia, Vissarion Christ – the Teacher, as he is known to his thousands of disciples, who are convinced that he is the reincarnation of Jesus of Nazareth, come back to earth to save the world.

'He radiates incredible love,' sighs Hermann, fifty-seven, a Bavarian engineer who is now selling his home in Germany to join the self-proclaimed Messiah of the taiga. 'I met Vissarion last August. He told me we had to follow two laws. It was like an electric shock, like bells ringing.'

To find Vissarion, you fly 3,700 kilometres east from Moscow to the southern Siberian town of Abakan, north of the Mongolian border, then drive for six hours along rutted roads through a string of villages. Where the road ends in a roller-coaster of craters, the bog begins and you trudge knee-deep in mud and ice for three hours before the final ascent to the 'saviour', a steep hour's climb up a mountain path.

To witness the lives of these New Age dropouts in the hamlets of Kuragino, Imisskoye, Petropavlovka and Cheremshanka is to get an inkling of how things must have been in seventeenth-century New England for the pilgrim fathers toiling away at their new Jerusalem.

'Life is so hard here,' says Denis, a 21-year-old Russian émigré who arrived last week from Brisbane to see if Vissarion really was the answer to his questions. 'No doubt about it, mate,' he affirms. 'Definitely the Son of God.'

To his critics in the established churches who accuse him of brainwashing and embezzling his followers, Vissarion is a charlatan deluding the devotees of 'a destructive, totalitarian sect'. More prosaically, he is Sergei Torop, a 41-year-old former traffic cop and factory worker from Krasnodar in southern Russia, who moved to Siberia as a youth, experienced his awakening a decade ago, and now leads one of the biggest and most remote religious communes on the planet.

Combining New Age eclecticism with medieval monasticism, the 'Vissarionites', clustered in around thirty rural settlements in southern Siberia, now number around 4,000. They are unquestioningly dedicated to their guru. They utter his name in hushed tones. They decorate their homes, temples and workplaces with his image. They reverentially swap tales of the Teacher's every act or word. They pore over his four fat volumes of musings. His aphorisms are learned by rote and regurgitated daily.

Vissarion – like all the followers of his 'Church of the Last Testament', he goes by his adopted first name only – is untroubled by this cult of personality and its sinister resonance in Russian history.

'It depends how a person uses my image,' he explains. 'Man has to bow down to the Father. But it is a mystery and the image enables a person to connect with me. The image can help in that sense, strengthen his efforts.'

Vissarion's commune is governed by arcane rituals, laws, symbols, prayers, hymns and a new calendar. A strict code of conduct is enforced: no vices are permitted. Veganism is compulsory for all, though exceptions can be made for infants and lactating mothers, who are allowed sour milk products (if they can find them). There is no animal husbandry. Monetary exchange is banned within the commune, and only reluctantly allowed with the outside world.

'We're not allowed to smoke, or swear, or drink,' laughs Larissa, a glowing 28-year-old mother of three who arrived here from Moscow with her mother as an eighteen-year-old. 'Everything is banned here. We're not allowed to do anything except fall in love.'

The devotees include Russian musicians, actresses, teachers, doctors, former Red Army colonels, an ex-deputy railways minister of Belarus, as well as a growing band of adherents from western Europe. They drink the sap of the birch trees that they fell for housing, tools and furniture. They live off berries, nuts and mushrooms gathered in the forest. They scratch potatoes, cabbage and Jerusalem artichokes from the unyielding soil. They barter handicrafts and vegetables for buckwheat and barley from nearby villages.

'Man can live in any extreme conditions,' Vissarion pronounces, a permanent Mona Lisa smile playing on his lips. 'Of course it is hard, especially for intellectuals and those used to working in the towns. But it is important for people to see themselves and to see one another. That is easier when the toil is hard. There is salvation in hardship.'

On an adjacent peak, a large bell has been mounted by the believers. It tolls across the valley three times a day. On hearing it, the faithful drop to their knees to pray. The bell weighs 270 kilograms. The followers carried it on foot for fifty kilometres in torrential rain from the village where the metal was cast, and then hauled it up to the summit. Vissarion himself is spared much of the physical toil. While teams of young men dig irrigation trenches beside his chalet, he whiles away the long days on the mountaintop painting oil canvases.

At the age of eighteen Sergei Torop enlisted, starting his compulsory two-year stint in the Red Army and finishing as a sergeant on construction sites in Mongolia before working for three years as a metal worker in a factory in the Siberian town of Minusinsk. From there, the self-proclaimed saviour embarked on a career as a traffic policeman, also in Minusinsk, winning nine commendations during five years' service. Job cuts in 1989 left him unemployed just as the Soviet Union was descending into chaos. Millions of Russians were bewildered and craving answers. The advent of the new era also coincided with Sergei's rebirth as Vissarion.

Thousands of people, the majority of them educated professionals from cities in European Russia, abandoned wives, husbands and children to flock to the Church of the Last Testament, replicating the flight of the schismatics to Siberia from European Russia 350 years ago to escape persecution by the Orthodox Church. The schismatics' descendants now share some of the same villages with the Vissarionites, who have assimilated many elements of Orthodox ritual but whose belief system also embraces an eclectic, some say incoherent, mish-mash of Buddhist, Taoist and green values.

For centuries, the wide-open spaces of Siberia have drawn the sectarian, the wacky and the nonconformist. The post-Soviet decade has revived that tradition, bringing a boom in evangelism and New Age cults. Of 140 religious organisations registered in the republic of Khakassia, says Nikolai Volkov, the chief local government official dealing with religious affairs, twenty-eight are 'new religious movements', as New Age sects are dubbed.

For the Church of the Last Testament, it is now year 42 of the new era, which the believers date from Vissarion's birth in 1961. Christmas has been abolished and replaced by a feast day on 14 January, the Teacher's birthday. The biggest holiday of the year falls on 18 August, the anniversary of Vissarion's first sermon in 1991, when the 'saviour' descends from the mountain on horseback to join thousands of revellers cavorting in the river running by the hamlet of Petropavlovka.

To the east lies Sun City. It is here, at the foot of the mountain where their saviour lives with his wife and six children (including a little girl adopted from a single mother in the commune), that the hardcore faithful, the most committed of the Vissarionites, congregate. On a patch of taiga peat bog that they have cleared of birch and cedar, forty-one families live in timber cabins and felt yurts. The men sport ponytails and beards, the women long hair and long skirts. Most of them are in their mid-thirties. The giggling of children is all around. There is a school and a kindergarten. The birth rate here is much higher than in the average Russian village.

The mood is cheerfully apocalyptic. 'Have you not heard?' laughs Igor as he guides us through the swamp. 'A comet is going to smash into the earth next year.'

With his beard, birch stick, tunic and pointy Uzbek felt hat, the 48-year-old recovered alcoholic from St Petersburg looks like he has walked off the set of *Lord of the Rings*.

If the looming comet imperils most of humanity, Sun City is Noah's Ark. Russia's mission, in the best Orthodox tradition of 'Third Rome' messianism, is to redeem the rest of us.

'This central part of Siberia is the part of the world that can survive best,' explains Vissarion. 'And this is a society that can endure big changes and be more receptive to a better understanding of the truth.'

For now, though, the apocalypse can wait. There's work to do and word to spread. In recent years Vissarion has been to New York, to Germany, the Netherlands, France and Italy seeking converts. For the first time he has just been 'invited' to Britain, where he hopes to preach 'soon'. Such international jet-setting feeds suspicions that he is living at the expense of his disciples. He insists that neither he nor his church has any 'regular income', that his foreign travels are 'sponsored' by his hosts. His chalet, powered by solar batteries and a small windmill, is modest, if more comfortable than the homes of his followers. It is also more remote, a steep hour's climb up a path from Sun City.

'I've been with him ten years, I know him,' says Vadim, a former drummer in a Russian rock band and Vissarion's right-hand man. 'He's the only person I know who lives what he preaches. They say he's a liar and a cheat, taking the money. They're only describing the way they behave themselves.'

At 7 a.m., the menfolk and a few women emerge from their cabins to stream towards the 'city' centre, marked by a mud circle ringed by stones, at the centre of which stands a carved wooden angel, wings outstretched and capped by the Vissarionites' symbol – a cross inside a circle. This is a daily ritual. The faithful kneel on short wooden planks, murmur prayers and sing hymns, led by a man with a rich baritone. Then they join hands in a circle around the stones, raise their heads to the mountain, from where they believe Vissarion is watching, and sing paeans to 'our tender father'.

'Immortality is the unique quality of the human soul, but mankind has to learn how to achieve it, how to live eternally,' Vissarion says quietly before shrouding his head in a white shawl and shuffling away. 'There's a place in the New Testament where Jesus says the time will come when I will no longer speak in parables. That time has come: the time for people to see the aim of life.'

1 December 2001

RICHARD WILLIAMS

George Harrison

George Harrison was the youngest and prettiest of the Beatles and, although it may sound improbable now – thinking of latter-day images of a crusty, grey-haired chap supervising an army of gardeners behind the electrified fence guarding a vast estate near Henley-on-Thames – in the beginning he was the one the girls fancied and the boys instinctively wanted to become.

At first sight, Paul McCartney displayed a hint of puppy fat and an ingratiating air, while John Lennon seemed curiously and inappropriately grown-up:

there was no innocence in that thin, sarcastic grin. Ringo Starr alone presented himself as exactly the man he would turn out to be. George was only nineteen but he was born with the kind of lost-angel looks – hooded eyes, good cheek-bones – that all rock stars should have. And he had the best hair, which was supremely important just then: he had the first perfect Beatle cut.

So for a while – between, say, 'Love Me Do' in late 1962 and 'From Me To You' the following spring – he gave the impression of being the face of the Beatles, possibly even the leader. And he was, after all, the lead guitarist, a role with its own glamour.

It took a while to work out that what made the Beatles different from every-thing that had preceded them was coming from the puppyish one and the sar-castic one. After all, beat groups had not contained their own songwriters before. As that recognition sharpened the outlines of their characters, so the young guitarist receded into a supporting role, greatly to his frustration.

It would be some years before the true George Harrison emerged – if, indeed, he ever did, at least in public. He was, it turned out, the shy one. And then, after a further interval, the prickly one. No doubt these characteristics were con-nected to each other, the product of the eternal resentment of the youngest child. For so long he had been overshadowed by the enormous public acclaim for Lennon and McCartney, whose first group, the Quarry Men, had been going for almost a year when he joined them in March 1958 as a skiffle-crazed fifteen-year-old.

And now he has become the second member of the group to die. With John, the world lost the Beatle who engineered the death of deference, taking a cer-tain tendency within English humour and turning it into a weapons-grade wit that was sometimes delicately sardonic – 'the rest of you can rattle your jew-ellery' – and at others cruelly sarcastic.

George's demise removes the impressionable enthusiast whose inquisitive nature guided the Beatles beyond the frontiers which had hitherto constrained the attitudes and behaviour of four-piece beat groups from the industrial cities of the north. He may not have written the songs for which they will be remem-bered, but without his gift for discovery the group might have taken quite a dif-ferent course and possibly a much less interesting and productive one.

It was George who, in Paris in the early weeks of 1964, during a nineteen-night season at the Olympia music hall, bought the copy of Bob Dylan's *Freewheelin'* that was to change the way the Beatles thought about songwriting. Brought up on the work of Chuck Berry and professional songwriters such as Carole King and Gerry Goffin, their horizons limited by pop song conven-tions inherited from Tin Pan Alley, they seized on Dylan's example to help them make the giant leap, in both content and form, from 'She Loves You' and 'I Want To Hold Your Hand' to 'Norwegian Wood' and 'Strawberry Fields Forever'.

If Harrison's enthusiasm had generated the breakthrough, his colleagues were the immediate beneficiaries. The lead guitarist's contribution as a songwriter had begun with 'Don't Bother Me' on their second album, *With the Beatles*, in 1963, but his output was restricted and overshadowed by the blossoming genius of Lennon and McCartney. By the time of *Rubber Soul* two years later he was demonstrating, in 'If I Needed Someone' and 'Think For Yourself', his ability to write a good mainstream rock song, but not until the appearance of *Abbey Road* in 1969, when the Beatles were already in the throes of divorce, did he produce a song, the glowing ballad 'Something', worth much more than a footnote in their discography. And then, as if to make up in hyperbole for what he had lost in time, no less an authority than Frank Sinatra was to describe it as 'the greatest love song of the last fifty years'.

In some respects Harrison resembled a conventional pop star. As the Beatles accumulated fame and fortune, he developed a taste for fast cars, married blonde model Pattie Boyd, whom he met on the set of *A Hard Day's Night*, became a backer of Sibylla's, a West End nightclub, and lived in a bungalow on National Trust land near Esher, Surrey.

On his twenty-first birthday he received sixty sacks of mail containing an estimated 30,000 cards and presents. After he told an interviewer of his liking for jelly babies, he found himself subjected to showers of the sweets during concerts. A sign of affection from the girls in the front stalls, it interfered with his playing and, like the incessant screaming which obliterated the sound of the music, soon became tiresome.

So did life on his stockbroker belt estate, and on 1 June 1966, four nights after joining Lennon in a box at the Albert Hall for a concert by Dylan, Harrison returned alone to the same venue to see Ravi Shankar, the Indian classical sitar virtuoso. A few days later Harrison met Shankar, who turned out to be barely aware of his existence.

'He told me how impressed he was with the sitar and my playing,' Shankar recalled. 'I asked him if he would show me what he had learned on the sitar, and he very humbly told me it was "not very much". I was struck both by his sincerity and his deep humility.'

There was one sitar lesson from the master at the Esher bungalow, followed by an invitation to India. Shankar, now fully apprised of Harrison's celebrity, told his pupil it might be advisable to grow a moustache to help preserve his anonymity during the journey. And so in mid-September, a fortnight after the Beatles had played their final concert, George and Pattie Harrison flew to Bombay, where they checked into the Taj Mahal Hotel under assumed names. When their presence was discovered midway through their five-week stay, they attempted to lift the siege of their hotel by giving a press conference at which they announced they were in India to study yoga and the sitar, and to get some peace and quiet. When they returned to Heathrow airport on 22 October, George was seen to be wearing a moustache. When he returned to the airport to meet Shankar four days later, he was wearing Indian clothes.

If the Harrisons were not the first westerners to fall in love with the culture of the East, they were certainly the most famous and influential. Their Indian adventure became a significant catalyst in a mass shift of thought and taste that ranged from the adoption of non-violent resistance in the counter-culture to the desire for a purer, simpler, more natural way of life symbolised by the popularity of organic food and loose-fitting clothes.

Within a year, indeed, the Harrisons were leading John, Paul and Ringo – all with moustaches, soon to be emulated by most western males under thirty – and their kaftan-clad partners on a trip back to India, to learn meditation techniques from the Maharishi Mahesh Yogi, a journey that kickstarted the personal-growth industry.

Of the four, Harrison was probably the most enthusiastic about the prospects for Apple, the co-operative company they set up in 1968 to manage their affairs and develop their interests after the death of Brian Epstein. His utopianism produced mixed results when he invited the Hare Krishna people and a party of Hell's Angels from California to stay in Apple's headquarters, an elegant town house at No 3 Savile Row, where good intentions were gradually soured by competing egos.

But the occasional disillusionment never removed his capacity for turning those utopian impulses into constructive action. In 1971, with the wreckage of the Beatles still smoking, he corralled Dylan, Eric Clapton, Leon Russell and Billy Preston into playing the Concert for Bangladesh at Madison Square Garden in New York, a charity event which established the template for Live Aid and all the many similar star-studded charity concerts up to the televised benefit for the families of the World Trade Center victims at the same venue in October.

For, curiously enough, the shy, suspicious one had also turned out to be the most successfully gregarious. Where McCartney gathered the surrogate family of Wings around him, and Lennon flitted from the street musician David Peel to the superstar David Bowie, Harrison's friendships with fellow musicians were built to last, probably to compensate for the feeling of being excluded from the creative centre of the Beatles.

He and fellow guitarist Eric Clapton played on each other's records, their bond even surviving the upheaval when Pattie Harrison completed rock's most celebrated eternal triangle by leaving George, who had written 'Something' for her, to move in with Clapton, who had wooed her with 'Layla' and was to serenade her with 'Wonderful Tonight'. He and Clapton toured with Delaney and Bonnie, a US duo, and in 1988 George co-founded the Travelling Wilburys, a sort of half-joking anti-supergroup, with Dylan, Tom Petty, Jeff Lynne and Roy Orbison.

He was, in short, a 'muso' – a term derisively applied in the post-punk era to a musician who was proud of his craft and strove to improve his instrumental technique in order to broaden his expressive range.

Harrison was thirteen when he discovered rock and roll and the study of the guitar as an alternative to academic education. He had used the instrument as a channel into which he could pour every ounce of the single-minded intensity that characterised his nature. He grew to love the company of other musicians, but he loathed the demands of the sort of immoderate fame that was the Beatles' reward for their gift.

He despised the music business, too, and no wonder. The Beatles were surrounded by sycophants, incompetents and thieves. Even Epstein could not protect them, lacking the experience to stay away from the elephant traps set by those who wished to market Beatle wigs, Beatle guitars, Beatle boots, Beatle mugs and a thousand other gewgaws.

He continued to act on his beliefs, taking part in demonstrations against nuclear energy and against the demolition of the old Regal cinema in his home town, Henley. He maintained his long-standing interest in motor racing, frequently turning up in the paddock at grand prix meetings, and used his company, Handmade Films, to back a series of British films, including Monty Python's *Life of Brian*, *Time Bandits* and *The Long Good Friday*. A mellowing of his attitude to his own history could be detected when he released a single called 'When We Was Fab', an amusing, poignant pastiche of *Revolver*-era Beatles, complete with layered sitars and tape-reversed drums.

Of the four, he was always the least comfortable with the demands of fame. 'I am not really Beatle George,' he said in 1995. 'Beatle George is like a suit or a shirt that I once wore on occasion, and until the end of my life people may see that shirt and mistake it for me.'

Sometimes he had harsher things to say about life as a Beatle and about the people who expected him to be fab forever. From 'Don't Bother Me' to 'Taxman' and 'Piggies', his songs sometimes seemed to be the product of irritation. It would be fairer to conclude that what occasionally sounded like ingratitude and sanctimoniousness was simply the reaction of a sensitive but uneducated boy confronted by unimaginable fame and wealth, and trying to find a satisfactory response.

George Harrison, guitarist, singer, songwriter, born 25 February 1943, died 30 November 2001.

5 March 2002

W. F. BYNUM

Roy Porter

A man of prodigious energy – needing only a few hours' sleep a night – the eminent historian and broadcaster Roy Porter, who has died aged fifty-five, seemed to write faster than many people read, and the steady stream of books became an avalanche once he had mastered the computer.

Roy took his historical scholarship seriously – from 1993 until last year, he was professor of the social history of medicine at the Wellcome Institute for the History of Medicine – but he became something of a populist as he grew older. His style became more dazzling and bemusing as his brilliant command of language and playfulness led to distinctly Porterian turns of phrase. He moved easily between social, medical and psychiatric history, and was never better than when describing eccentricity and extremes of temperament.

Within medical history, he pioneered the now fashionable concern with patients (instead of doctors), and his books on eighteenth-century medical history (two of them written with his third wife, Dorothy Porter) rescued this century from the clutches of historians blind to its medical richness. He also wrote widely on the history of psychiatry and its patients, and on sex and the history of the body. *The Greatest Benefit To Mankind: A Medical History Of Humanity* (1997) was a blockbuster history from Plato to NATO.

In many ways, Roy's best book was *London: A Social History* (1994). He poured

'After agonising consideration…' Disgraced former Enron chairman Ken Lay pleads the fifth amendment and declines to testify to a congressional committee, Washington, February. (Reuters/Win McNamee)

Derailed: transport secretary Stephen Byers at Downing Street after offering his resignation, May. (Guardian/David Sillitoe)

Barbara Castle, former Labour firebrand and cabinet minister, who died in May. (Gavin Smith)

George Harrison, who died in December, photographed by Jane Bown in 1964.

Keith Harper, the *Guardian*'s long-serving labour editor and transport editor, who died in May.

Roy Porter, historian and polymath, who died in March.

Margaret Thatcher admires a bust of herself, Guildhall Art Gallery, London, May...

... but others are less admiring, July. (Corporation of London/Clive Totman and *above* Guardian/Graham Turner)

his heart into it, and his deep love and understanding of the city of his birth is reflected on almost every page. For several years, he spent his weekends tramping about Greater London, getting a feel for the subject of this biography of a city. His introductory invocation of his south London childhood makes me regret that he wrote so much about other people, and so little about himself.

Roy was the only child of a Bermondsey jeweller. Although the home was without books, his early intellectual precocity led to a family myth that he was a changeling. A teacher at Wilson's Grammar School, Camberwell, opened his eyes to the world of culture; he never forgot how much he owed to the school, returning each year to talk to its students.

His starred double first in history at Cambridge University (1968) led to a junior research fellowship at his college, Christ's, where his fascination with the eighteenth century had been awakened by Sir Jack Plumb. In 1972, I attended Roy's lectures on the English enlightenment; they were the beginnings of one of his last books, *Enlightenment: Britain and the Creation of the Modern World* (2000). He had also acquired an abiding interest in the history of science, and his PhD thesis, published as *The Making of Geology* (1977), became the first of more than a hundred books that he wrote or edited. He moved to Churchill College, Cambridge, as director of studies in history in 1972. When he was appointed dean of the college in 1977, many were amused that this secular man should hold such a title. In fact, he would have made an excellent eighteenth-century parson, as long as his beliefs were not too closely scrutinised.

He found Cambridge too cosy, however, and, in 1979, we lured him back to London, to the academic unit of the Wellcome Institute for the History of Medicine, where, fourteen years later, he became professor. He was a natural in the classroom – a fluent speaker, able to explain complicated things in simple ways, and to infect his audience, no matter what the medium, with his enthusiasms. What also developed was an exhausting schedule of public lectures, and frequent broadcasting on both radio and television. He wrote effortlessly, although the final version would often bear little resemblance to the first draft. He became a shrewd but generous reviewer, and a stickler for deadlines, which made him an editor's dream.

Roy maintained this hectic pace for years. As he became busier and busier, he came increasingly to value efficiency. He once announced one of his divorces (there were four) by sticking a Post-It on the notice board in the mailroom. In his eyes, this was not brutal, merely an efficient way of letting everyone know his news. His communications were often scribbled notes at the bottom of letters, faxed back by return. He came to e-mails only in the last year or so.

Roy was larger than life in all that he did. He was forever bursting out of his clothes, mostly denims, with two or three buttons on his shirt undone. Rings and earrings came and went, with no discernible relationship to his moods, so far as I could tell. He was, in fact, also a very private person. Although he had great sympathy with the underdog, he kept his own political beliefs hidden.

Although unconventional in so many ways, Roy was embraced by the establishment. Elected a fellow of the British Academy in 1994, he was also made an honorary fellow by both the Royal College of Physicians and the Royal College of Psychiatrists. He gave practically every lecture in established series for which he was eligible, and was delighted to go, last year, to Peru on behalf of the British Council.

When he took early retirement last year from the Wellcome Trust Centre for the History of Medicine at University College London, as the unit had become, he wanted to take up a musical instrument, learn some foreign languages and cultivate his garden. Alas, he had time to make only a beginning of that last ambition. His sudden death is a shock for everyone who knew him, so full of life was he.

Roy's preferred transport was the bicycle he was found beside at his death, en route to his allotment. He was at the height of his powers, relaxed and happy with his partner, Natsu Hattori. The Greeks would have called it a good death, but it came much too soon.

Roy Sydney Porter, historian and writer, born 31 December 1946, died 4 March 2002.

6 May 2002

ANNE PERKINS

Barbara Castle

Barbara, when I saw her last week, was at home, a small but not insignificant figure propped up in a double bed opposite the window. Outside, spring was blazing brilliantly blue and green.

'I can see the red kites wheeling and diving,' she said.

Barbara had been more or less blind for several years. Watching her cross a room could be heartstopping. In the House of Lords she once got tangled up with the bishops and only found out hours later. But if Barbara told you she could see, you didn't argue.

Courage in adversity was Barbara's stock in trade. We, the audience, expected it of her. Last week, though, the grey was showing in her hair, which was one sign that things weren't quite right. Barbara's hair had been red, a vivid, glorious, uncompromising red, for ninety-one years.

I wanted to cheer her up by reading to her one of the great journalistic recantations of all time, Andrew Alexander of the *Daily Mail* admitting that the cold war had been a colossal misjudgment. But she said she couldn't concentrate. And then I knew things were badly wrong. Barbara could always concentrate, formidably. She called it keeping her eye on the ball, and her eye was like a gimlet, drilling into an argument with unforgiving focus.

'Think, think, think,' she said she had been told once. 'It will hurt like hell at first, but you'll get used to it.'

Politicians in the sunlit uplands of retirement tend to become pompous, chatty, avuncular, clubbable. They admit mistakes, embrace their enemies, even manage to smile over defeats. Barbara didn't retire. She was an evangelist, a crusader, and she merely allowed time to hone her convictions to a finer edge and carried on campaigning.

We have spent a lot of time together, Barbara and I, in the past three years. I am writing her biography and she has given me access to all of her papers. Because there are some she doesn't want out of the house, I have sat at Hell Corner Farm (did she buy it for the name, I always wonder?) amid boxes of files, and boxes of documents, and boxes of letters and souvenirs and postcards and government White Papers and newspaper cuttings and minutes of meetings. She has a diarist's mentality: she has lived a life of record.

We spent a lot of time together, but she gave nothing away. There was no atmosphere of the confessional about our conversations. What I learned about her came from observation, from the roller-coaster mood swings from peremptory to charm school, from watching her metamorphose on the ring of a doorbell from a cross old lady using an inhaler in her dressing gown, into Labour's Gloriana.

Like Elizabeth I, Barbara didn't do jokes. But she was unfailingly sharp. Once (we were discussing the impending wedding between Gordon Brown and Sarah Macaulay) Barbara said the first question she always asked was: what's the motive?

I'm not sure I was ever confident of Barbara's motive for authorising a biography on top of her published diaries and her own autobiography. After all, she more than most has left a real memorial in legislation. Remember her each time you collect your child benefit or decide to take a taxi home from the pub. In 1997 Patricia Hollis's brilliant life of Jennie Lee, Barbara's old comrade (a loaded term in Labour history) was published. Once again the columns of newspapers were full of the beautiful, fiery Mrs Bevan and her role in the history of the Labour movement. Why not a book too about the other beautiful, fiery Labour MP, Mrs Castle? Another factor was that an unofficial biography was being written. Barbara didn't like people messing with her image. She knew about symbolism. Researching this book is a kind of game of human archaeology, deconstructing her own account of history.

Her most famous recollection of her early years is her manifesto (written when she was eight) for the first post-war elections (the first world war, that is): 'Citizens! Vote for me and I will give you houses . . .' The tale, with its undertone of precocious commitment, first appeared in a newspaper profile in the early fifties when she was a young MP in the Attlee era. It was rarely absent from them thereafter. It's true – I've seen the notebook and the girlish handwriting – but how much of the truth is it? What does motivate an eight-year-old to produce political manifestos?

Barbara was a tireless diarist and observer, especially of the Wilson governments in which, in her own subtly reworked account, she played a starring role, seducing (metaphorically, I think) the prime minister with her passion and cudgelling her enemies with her arguments. So her authorised biography was to be 'Barbara – the final cut', a summing up, not substantially different from what had gone before.

I think there was more to it. Unexpectedly, for a twentieth-century political titan (only a very recent accolade) she wanted some independent, or at least outside assessment of what she had achieved, how she had made a difference. She wanted recognition that it had been done by force of will, not by some serendipitous chain of events. She wanted it recognised and respected. She wanted, she told me often and sternly, a 'political' biography, not what she dismissed as 'kiss-and-tell' biography, a steamy saga of sex and scandal by the Thames.

Barbara lived at the centre of a compelling drama – her own. I was a willing audience to the closing scenes, to the reprises of the greatest moments, an admiring prompt. That was my role, and I could not escape it, nor, frustratingly, move her from hers. I couldn't even pick a fight with her, not even about hunting. I never made her say: 'Now, that's an interesting idea.'

Listening to Barbara was always a privilege, if not always a rewarding one for the biographer. Reading her papers was quite different. Focused and ordered in the final phase of her life, she had sorted her vast collection of letters and diary scraps and souvenirs, the scribbled notes on old cigarette packets, the cables and newspaper cuttings, all the dog-eared manky jetsam of a long and passionate life.

Yet there remains, in letters to her and from her, in her published and unpublished diaries, the real Barbara, leaping off the page, passionate, coherent, self-absorbed, demanding, vile-tempered, coquettish. For example, in 1934 she wrote to her lover, William Mellor (a leading socialist who was much older than her, and married): 'I'm afraid of men's greed and ruthlessness. I'm afraid of the crushing of beauty and life. I've been brought up among the perils of debt and I shall never lose the sense of the danger. I feel kinship with those who always live on the borderline. I hate the greed and the selfishness – I want to break the combination! Oh William, if the workers would only dare to fight.'

For three years I've been finding and rearranging these fragments to try to reveal Barbara's humanity, the woman beneath the driven, impassioned, sometimes doctrinaire, sometimes shrewish politician, and to answer the question: why? Politics is a human activity, driven by human emotions of ambition, sympathy and tribal identity. It was also a route to love. Barbara, the actress, passionately wanted to be loved. She was – you can see it every image on thousands of feet of grainy film and early videotape – a raging flirt. She believed she could make people love her and she saw it as an important and legitimate part of her political persona. I was merely the last to be seduced by her starriness, her style, her courage, her intellect and her sense of purpose.

Barbara Castle, socialist, born 6 October 1910, died 3 May 2001.

14 May 2002

GEOFFREY GOODMAN

Keith Harper

Labour correspondents (aka industrial reporters) are no longer state of the art in journalism. But they were a generation ago, and Keith Harper, who has died from cancer aged sixty-five, was an outstanding talent among them. He had vision, a sympathetic understanding of his subject, and a perceptive analytical eye: he was present in all those moments when the warfare that was British industrial relations in the sixties and seventies provided front-page news every day. His talent was not just for chronicling the drama of that social and political conflict as it spread through national life. He also added a special journalistic quality: he genuinely understood the problems without being drawn into the quagmires of bias and prejudice. That was the Keith Harper I worked with.

The ink of his trade had flowed in him from birth, as both his father and grandfather were newspaper printers. Keith was born in Manchester, where his father, Jack, was a linotype operator with the *Daily Mail*. Jack wanted to switch to the *Mail* in London, but was refused a transfer by his union; he never did get to London despite repeated attempts to fight his union's ruling. That might have influenced Keith's views on unionism. But he never allowed it to deflect his reporting of, or sympathies with, union affairs.

When his father joined the army during the second world war, Keith's mother, Olive, did move to London (the family joke was that they meant to dodge *Luftwaffe* bombs); he went to school there, winning a place to Marylebone Grammar School. Instead of going to university, he decided that he wanted to be a journalist. His first job was as an editorial assistant with the magazine *National Builder*; his first reporting stint was on the *Bucks Free Press* in 1959. In 1960, he had six months on the *Express* and *Echo* in Exeter, and then went to the *Bristol Evening World* as a reporter and feature writer. There he met another young reporter, Tom Stoppard, and established a friendship which remained close and firm.

In September 1961 Keith began his long association with the *Guardian*. First he did four years in Bristol as its west of England and Wales correspondent, and then he moved to London in 1965 as a reporter. Three years later his byline began to appear over industrial stories: he had arrived in that zone from which he reported for twenty-seven years, writing on the nation's labour and industrial problems.

In the summer of 1972, he took over from John Torode as leading labour correspondent, which was then one of the most prestigious assignments. John Torode remembers that 'He was wonderful about being my Number Two when I became labour correspondent. Although older than me and with longer experience on the *Guardian*, he was so loyal, and a delight to work with.'

I remember especially one Friday morning in August 1973 I was sitting quietly in my office at the *Daily Mirror* when the prime minister's press secretary called: 'Would you be free to join the prime minister [Edward Heath] at Chequers this afternoon for a private chat? I have also invited Keith Harper of the *Guardian* and John Elliott of the *Financial Times*.'

We had been chosen because our newspapers were regarded as critical platforms for the forming of opinions, and went off to Chequers together. Heath wanted to discuss industrial and labour problems with us, off-record. At that time the words industrial or labour correspondent mattered as much, if not more, than political lobby bylines. There was spin, although it was not as crude then as now. The visit was remarkable; Heath played the piano and discussed music with us all, but mostly with Keith, who matched Heath's expertise.

There were less auspicious moments. At the famous Labour party conference in Bournemouth in 1985, when Neil Kinnock faced up to the militants and Arthur Scargill, a playful, or perhaps malicious, photographer caught Keith snoozing in mid-Kinnock speech. Keith was not always popular with the union establishment with whom he spent many hours and years. He detected early that the TUC general secretary Norman Willis was not a star performer, especially in a crisis, and began to run stories about Willis's imminent departure, one of them on the eve of a TUC Congress.

Keith was severely rebuked by Len Murray, Willis's predecessor, a painful experience for both since they admired each other. But Keith's permanent motto was 'this story has got to be written': contacts and friendships were all very well, but there was a moment when journalists had to decide to write what they believed to be the truth, regardless.

He did that at the outbreak of the miners' strike; his opening sentence began: 'Arthur Scargill's determination to bring about his revolutionary change in society is threatening to produce an important casualty in the NUM.' You cannot get it more right than that.

Keith's consuming passion outside journalism and family was cricket. He followed the vagaries of his county Lancashire, and played the game with a talent that might easily have made him a top-class player. He toured India with a *Guardian* team; he toured Australia with the Fleet Street Strollers; he played in the US and Austria. Most of all he developed the annual match between industrial correspondents and the TUC on the eve of the TUC Congress – continuing a tradition that Keith McDowall and I started in the sixties.

When Keith became *Guardian* transport editor in 1995 he turned the subject into one of the best elements in the paper, a precedent other papers had to follow. His remarkable success, with many scoops, should have won him a press award. In fact, Virgin Trains decided to give him something even better, despite his frank and critical views of Sir Richard Branson: it planned to name one of its new locomotives *Keith Harper*.

He married Eileen Ripley in 1965; they had two daughters, Katie and Amelia. His second marriage to a television publicist, Janine Thomason, was in January 1980. They had two children, Tom and Alice.

Keith Rex Harper, journalist, born 8 April 1937, died 13 May 2002.

Virgin went ahead with the naming of the locomotive, which pulled its first train – to the TUC conference in Blackpool – in September 2002.

11 June 2002

MICHAEL ELLISON

John Gotti, gangster

John Gotti, who has died of cancer at the age of sixty-one, was the best-known American gangster since Al Capone, and one willingly assimilated by popular culture. But if the Dapper Don perceived himself to be at the pinnacle of a milieu epitomised by the operatic grandeur of Francis Ford Coppola's *The Godfather*, in the end the more appropriate analogy was *The Sopranos* television series.

Tapes of Gotti's prison conversations produced observations more suited to the on-screen lexicon of James Gandolfini than that of Marlon Brando. Prison food: 'Give me some prosciutto with some fucking mozzarella.' Improving literature: 'How many times I tell you I don't read murder mysteries?' The Clinton sex scandal: 'If he had an Italian last name, they would have electrocuted him.' The head of the Gambinos, once the most powerful of New York's five great organised-crime families, spent the last ten years of his life in jail. Before that he had constructed a camera-friendly fame, an image in suits costing thousands of dollars, a diamond ring on one little finger, and topped off with his perfectly groomed silver mane. This put him on the cover of *Time* magazine, between the covers of several biographies and on silkscreens by Andy Warhol.

Gotti acquired a celebrity commensurate with those who drew on his legend for their art, winking at the law enforcement authorities and, if not exactly endearing himself to the public, earning its respect as an operator who knew how to beat the system. Finally, though, the FBI's relentless pursuit put him on trial in 1992 for murder, conspiracy to murder, illegal gambling, loan-sharking, obstruction of justice, bribery and tax evasion.

But whether in solitary confinement or in hospital – he was moved to a secure medical centre in 1998 when throat cancer was diagnosed – he continued to receive fan mail, some from couples who said they were naming their newborn after him. The actors Mickey Rourke and the late Anthony Quinn attended his last court appearance, and there were complaints on websites that his conditions were unreasonably harsh and that his trial had been unfair.

Gotti was the fifth of eleven children, brought up poor in New York's south Bronx. In time, the family moved to East New York, in Brooklyn. By the age of twelve he was doing small jobs for hoodlums on street corners and, four years later, he finally left the school he had never bothered with much in the first place. Stealing cars and robbing drunks were the stock in trade of his Fulton-Rockaway Boys, and, by the age of twenty-one, he had been arrested five times.

Gotti even tried his hand at legitimate jobs – as a presser in a coat factory, then as a truck driver's assistant – after he married Victoria DiGiorgio in 1962. But work did not stick, and by the time he joined a Gambino hijacking crew in 1966, he had been jailed twice for theft. The gang had a particular liking for the traffic in goods at John F. Kennedy airport, and in 1969 Gotti was on his way back to prison, from which he emerged in 1971.

'I don't know what he does,' said his wife. 'All I know is he provides.'

Jarry Capeci and Gene Mustain, writing in *Gotti: Rise and Fall*, were more specific: 'He was fierce, violent, foul-mouthed and clever.' These qualities were sufficient to put him at the head of his Gambino crew, though not enough to earn him the rapid promotion he craved from the boss, Carlo Gambino, who liked to quote from Machiavelli's *The Prince*.

Two events secured the early Gotti legend. The first was the killing of Jimmy McBratney at the Snoope bar and grill on Staten Island in 1973. McBratney was in a gang that, improbably, made a good living kidnapping crime family members and demanding ransoms for their return. Gotti was among the three men who shot McBratney dead and, at his trial three years later, he cut an advantageous deal: in return for a plea to attempted manslaughter, he served less than two years.

Free again, he was obliged under the terms of his parole to take a proper job, and this time he chose a plumbing and heating firm. Later, his boss was to testify about the nature of his duties: 'What John does is point out locations.' Later, Gotti's twelve-year-old son was killed in a traffic accident. John Favora, the driver of the car – and a neighbour of the Gottis in Howard Beach, Queens – endured four months of death threats until the day he was shot, abducted, and never seen again.

By this time, the Gambino boss was Paul 'Big Paulie' Castellano, a more remote figure who fancied himself as a businessman – and who did not hold in high regard streetwise individuals such as Gotti, whom he considered uncouth and unreliable. Nor did Gotti's gambling habit – around $30,000 a night in the late seventies and early eighties – help his case for promotion.

Big Paulie was a considerable problem. He had got the top job over Gotti's mentor, Aneillo 'Mr Neil' Dellacroce, and he was an adherent to the old rule against narcotics: 'You deal, you die.' Or, at the very least, don't get caught. When Mr Neil died, the buffer between Gotti and the boss went too. Big Paulie, who was said to have had a penile implant after becoming impotent through diabetes, was scorned by some underlings, though not in his hearing. True or not, they believed it. One thing they knew for sure was that Big Paulie was nowhere at Mr Neil's wake, sacrificing Mafia propriety to fear of surveillance.

Many believed also that Big Paulie, holed up for much of the time in his replica of the White House on Staten Island, was about to do a deal with the FBI. On top of that, he wanted to close the Ravenite social club on Mulberry Street in Little Italy, where the Gotti crew liked to gamble and carouse (much of it caught on tape by FBI bugs).

On a street crowded with Christmas shoppers in December 1985, Big Paulie's driver-bodyguard pulled up outside Spark's steak house in Manhattan. Four gunmen in trenchcoats and fur hats approached the car with a back-up man close behind and others positioned to help with the getaway. Castellano died instantly from six bullets in the head, while Gotti and Sammy 'The Bull' Gravano, the architect of the hit, looked on from a Lincoln limousine. Soon Gotti was the Gambino boss.

His was not an easy reign, but it provided some sport for those who were not personally involved. A year after taking control, he was in court accused of assault. The victim failed to appear to give evidence, having repaired to a hospital instead. When he did make it to the stand, he said that he was unable to identify Gotti. Case dismissed. I FORGOTTI said the *New York Daily News* headline the next day.

The first four days of jury selection in his next trial were marked by a bomb scare, absent defendants, allegations of witness intimidation and the murder of an associate, whose car was blown up. 'The only family John Gotti knows is his wife and children and grandchildren,' said Bruce Cutler, his attorney.

Cocksure throughout, the Dapper Don had reason for his comportment. When the jury went out to consider the case, George Pape, one of their number, told the rest of the panel: 'This man Gotti is innocent. They are all innocent as far as I'm concerned; there is nothing left to discuss.' Pape had been paid $60,000 in advance for his evaluation of the evidence. Not guilty. Gotti applauded the jury.

Arrested again, this time for assaulting a union official and conspiracy, Gotti told the arresting officer: 'I'll lay you three to one I beat it.' He did, helped in no small part when the victim, who had been shot four times, gave evidence for the defence.

Five years after Big Paulie's death, Gotti was picked up for the last time. 'They arrested John Gotti the other night the same way they arrested him before, flamboyantly and theatrically,' said the *New York Times*. 'Why all the melodrama, including handcuffs and a platoon of fifteen FBI agents? The only obvious purpose is for the prosecution to preen for the cameras.'

But this time there was to be no escape. The prosecution persuaded the judge that members of his legal team – including Cutler, who had worked on the previous three cases – should be disqualified because they might be called as witnesses; Gotti was rumoured to be behind six more killings; the jury was out of reach, anonymous and kept in isolation; there was the FBI tape from the Ravenite club; five of the six defence witnesses were ruled ineligible; and, crucially, Sammy 'The Bull' Gravano, irked at his old friend because of disparaging remarks on the tape, joined the other side.

Gravano, who conceded that, yes, he had been involved in nineteen murders, told all, and Gotti was sentenced to life without parole for the murder of Big Paulie and his bodyguard and other charges. 'The Don is covered with Velcro and every charge stuck,' said James Fox, assistant director of the FBI's New York office.

Outside the Brooklyn court a riot, organised, it is said, by his son John 'Junior' Gotti, ensued, in which up to a thousand people, brought there in chartered buses, attacked cars and cried 'Free John Gotti!' Two jurors signed affidavits saying the conviction was unfair; four requests for a new trial were denied.

Gotti leaves his wife Victoria, two daughters and their two surviving sons. Of these, Junior, who became the acting boss in the absence of his father, is serving seventy-seven months for extortion, loan-sharking, illegal gambling, fraud and tax evasion. 'I wish every mother in America had a son like mine,' said Mrs Gotti.

Their daughter Victoria, a bestselling writer of romantic novels, with a weekly column in the *New York Post*, is estranged from her husband Carmine Agnello, who is awaiting trial for coercion, conspiracy, grand larceny and arson. He claims that his actions were conditioned by bipolar dysfunction. The Ravenite social club on Mulberry Street is now a boutique called Amy Chan.

John Gotti, gangster, born 27 October 1940, died 10 June 2002.

THE WAY WE
LIVE NOW

The former heroine addict, page 4, 'Office Hours', 14 January, was a former heroin addict.

Corrections and Clarifications, 16 January 2002

31 December 2001

MADELEINE BUNTING

Living with danger

It's hard to remember a year that has so tested parents' ingenuity in interpreting the world to their children. You could go the honest route and tell all. Yes, millions of sheep are being killed; no, they're not sick, they threaten our meat exports. Yes, those are people jumping out of a New York skyscraper; no, they haven't done anything wrong. You could take the blank-out option – with censorship even of *Newsround*. Or you could muddle along in the middle, trying to think of ways to explain to your children what you didn't understand yourself; all the time conscious that a parent's primary role is to convey exactly what was in short supply in 2001 – the reassurance that the world is a predictable, trustworthy, safe place.

After 11 September it's hard to recollect just how huge the emotional impact of foot and mouth was. Last Easter, we were marooned in our cities, and if we ventured out, we were cooped up in car parks and lay-bys, banned from any hilltop or green field. It was claustrophobic – and it profoundly shook that deep nostalgia for the English landscape that has been so bound up with English national identity throughout the twentieth century, the idea that our landscape represents a timeless detachment from commercialism (Rupert Brooke's honey still for tea). Furthermore, the death on funeral pyres of four million animals horrified a nation in which most people care far more for their pets than they do for their neighbours.

Six months later, such anxieties seemed impossibly parochial and petty in comparison with the global impact of more flames – this time in a city on the other side of the Atlantic, but the danger felt a hundred times closer: our lives, not just our fantasies and dreams, were at risk. Again, we felt trapped in our cities – only this time it was under the flight paths of aircraft, whose every sound one listened out for with a catch in the breath in the days immediately after 11 September.

It was a year that painfully highlighted two of the biggest dilemmas of modernity. The first is trust: who and what do we trust? What can we safely rely on? We thought hi-tech agriculture had mastered the vagaries of nature – but no, it had made it, by its dizzying movement of animals, unprecedentedly vulnerable to the oldest catastrophe in the book: disease. And this realisation came only a few months after a petrol blockade punched home the fragility of the whole system, timed to supply 56 million people so that it is only ever a few days away from total breakdown. We thought planes pretty safe, but the West's fondness for quick and easy mobility proved a deathly weapon; we thought skyscrapers safe, but the World Trade Center was felled by the simplest trick in the book, the game every two-year-old boy plays with a Lego tower and a toy plane.

The second dilemma is our fantasy of omnipotence – human beings can do anything – and the intense frustration and anger generated by evidence of the opposite, our impotence. The conflict between the two fuels many debates, making impossible demands on politicians 'to do something' – whether it is to stop a highly infectious disease or ensure 100 per cent airline security and wipe out al-Qaida – and childlike rage when the 'something' proves inadequate or vulnerable to human error.

When we are surrounded by the extraordinary achievements of human ingenuity (fiddling with our genes, reaching Mars) it seems absurd that we can't crack any problem in the book. What we seem to find infinitely difficult, both politically and personally, is to recognise where we have power, and where we do not, and act accordingly.

It is hard to remember in the recent past a year that has left such an emotionally disturbing, bitter legacy. We have to reconfigure our understanding of human nature to incorporate a form of ruthless violence and, even more painfully, a degree of insecurity in western cities, neither of which we had imagined possible a year ago.

So in many ways it's not surprising that there is a collective will to drown our sorrows in a shopping spree: £18 billion in the run-up to Christmas and another £15 billion in the sales. That's 20 per cent up on last year and it's all on the tick – household debt is now at an all-time peak of 107 per cent of the average household's disposable income. It's a grim solution; but at least it staves off anxieties that cannot be assuaged and questions that have no answer: shop, shop and be merry, for tomorrow we die.

12 November 2002

GARY YOUNGE

British Muslims on trial

What have you done to assert your British identity recently? Have you declared yourself a moderate, explained the peaceful nature of your faith or condemned members of your own community to justify your existence here? Have you been asked to choose between the flag and your faith, or the colour of your skin and the crest on your passport? Have you been called upon to cheer a war you do not believe in or renounce beliefs you never had?

In short, have your rights in this country been called into question not because of what you have done, but simply because of who you are? As Britain continues to support America in bombing Afghanistan back into the Dark Ages, so our racial discourse in this country is reverting to its own prehistoric era. We are moving towards a resurrected, revamped version of the Tebbit test.

Back in 1990, the defining issue was which side black and Asian people supported in cricket. Now the stakes are far higher. The right of Muslims to live in this country now hinges on which side of the B-52s they are on – the bombers or the bombed.

While the test targets a religious group, it is racial in essence and nationalist in motivation. Racial, because it lays out a set of criteria for national allegiance for Muslims – who are overwhelmingly of Asian and African origin – that would never be considered for whites. When football hooligans go abroad giving Nazi salutes and clashing violently with police and foreigners, they are roundly condemned for bringing disgrace on the country, but nobody questions their right to be British.

Making no distinction, even, for those who are born here, it suggests our understanding of cultural hybridity goes no further than Robin Cook's chicken tikka masala. What those who make it or serve it might think about world events is deemed at best of little interest and at worst an act of treachery.

Moreover, it assumes a British identity that is both static and established. The word from Whitehall is that they want to move 'beyond multiculturalism' to a debate about 'core British values', as though those values are agreed rather than contested and fixed rather than fluid. Given the debates over Europe, devolution and the Lawrence Report, this is less true now than ever.

But if the roots lie in racism then they have been fertilised by the surge of nationalism following 11 September. Since then, to be a Muslim is to be under suspicion, under threat and, given the huge increase in racial violence, under attack. The fourth estate believes it has found a fifth column among British Muslims and is desperate to seek out the traitors.

There is no empirical evidence for these assumptions. The closest they have come is a *Sunday Times* 'poll' last week which claimed four out of every ten Muslims believe Osama bin Laden was right to mount a war against America. This was not conducted by Mori or Gallup using established methods of questioning and weighting. It was carried out by the *Sunday Times* itself, which interviewed people as they came out of mosques. It was not a poll but a huge vox pop. It has about as much validity as the *Guardian* sending its staff to stand outside Catholic churches on Sunday mornings to ask them what they think of the peace process or the monarchy and then presenting it as 'Catholic opinion'.

Nonetheless its 'findings' have informed many an ill-informed column. In the absence of any factual evidence we are left with the anecdotal. Calls to those who work in or alongside Britain's Muslim communities suggest the overwhelming majority of Muslims both abhorred the attacks on 11 September and oppose the bombing of Afghanistan. This simply puts them ahead of a growing trend in Europe at large, where the war is proving increasingly unpopular. Then there are a handful of British Muslims who are thought to have volunteered for the Taliban and a larger, but no less unrepresentative, number who have voiced support for Bin Laden here. Organisers of a pro-Taliban march in Blackburn yesterday promised 7,000 but delivered only 150.

An attack on a church in Bradford by youths last week was troubling, but it should also be put in perspective. In June, 14,000 voters in Oldham and Burnley supported the far-right British National party. Pakistanis and Bangladeshis (who make up the vast majority of Muslims in Britain) are by far the groups most likely to suffer from racially motivated attacks. Islam is not alone in attracting extremists and, arguably, poses far less of a threat to mainstream British society than white society poses to it.

Nonetheless, the number of fundamentalists will certainly grow as the war continues, for the same reason that Bush's approval ratings have grown and Ian Paisley is always more popular when the peace process in Ireland is faltering. War polarises. That indeed is the problem with this particular military campaign. It is creating more terrorists, globally, than it could ever hope to extinguish.

This does not mean that the liberal left should stand by while Islamic fundamentalism installs itself unchallenged. Fundamentalism, of any religious hue, is a thoroughly reactionary political and social current. It brooks no dissent, tolerates no debate and can rarely engage with other political forces because it is based on devotion to eternal truths. But while individuals may be attracted by its moral certainty, social movements are born from it thanks to a mixture of political, economic and social alienation. That is as true in West Yorkshire as it is on the West Bank.

In 1998 the employment rate among Bangladeshis and Pakistanis was 35 per cent and 41 per cent respectively – compared with 75 per cent for whites. Women fared even worse. The average hourly wage of a Bangladeshi/Pakistani woman was around a third less than for white men. Such figures expose the hypocrisy of those western 'feminists' who wish to cluster bomb Afghani women out of their burkas. They have displayed more interest in Muslim women thousands of miles away in the past two months than they have shown to those in their own country in the past two decades.

Meanwhile, there has never been an MP of Bangladeshi extraction. The Muslim MP Mohammed Sarwar was suspended from the Labour party within weeks of being elected on trumped-up charges of bribery of which he was completely cleared in court. In the list of ills preventing Muslims from becoming full and valued citizens in British society, fundamentalism must take its place at the back of the queue, behind racism and exclusion.

Blair's conversion to the redeeming qualities of Islam is itself emblematic. He embraced it only days before he was about to drop bombs on Afghanistan, but several months after organised racists lobbed bricks and threw punches at young Muslims in the north. He did not venture to the depressed northern towns to tell white working-class people about tolerance then. Today, there is no finer photo opportunity than for him to stand alongside an imam, so long as the latter is explaining the inherently peaceful nature of the faith. He loves Islam. It's the Muslims he has a problem with.

30 May 2002

ERWIN JAMES

My new freedoms

These are the days that, years ago, I wondered if I would ever see. When I first arrived in open conditions it was so difficult to accept the difference in people's attitudes. From the first warm welcome by the prison probation officer, which I found so upsetting, to the common courtesy of my fellow prisoners – holding doors open, respecting the order of meal queues or just taking the time to assist when a new chap needed directions to some area of activity or other – it was all so alien. For weeks after I landed I found myself constantly thinking back to the dark places, the landings of the closed prisons, and asking nobody in particular: 'What the hell was that all about?'

Now it feels like the new beginning I always hoped it would be. For some months I have been going out in the prison van with the community work party – repairing public buildings, painting and decorating old folks' homes, youth clubs, Scout huts and the like. Apart from the relatively short six-hour day (and the prison officer in civvies discreetly working alongside us while monitoring our conduct and assessing our risk potential) the experience is not so far removed from a normal working day in real life.

The community work party has two main functions, both equally important. Spare money in the community is often so scarce that many small repair and refurbishment projects might never get done if it wasn't for the cheap prisoner labour. To this end the initiative fosters good relations between the prison and the outside community. It also reintroduces prisoners to the reality of life outside.

Don't get me wrong. Breaking into a sweat is a phenomenon regularly experienced by people inside, though rarely as a result of a hard day's work. It's not because prisoners are any more averse to hard graft than people on the outside. But opportunities to do real work – the kind that makes your back ache and ensures a good night's sleep – are just so hard to come by in jail. Through the work party, prisoners on the verge of release can get used to the work routine again, which is probably the single most important factor in a successful resettlement programme. But then there is another, bigger step to be taken, and last week it was my turn.

The Celtic Poet was waiting when I returned to the house block.

'Well?' he said. It was hard to keep a straight face.

The risk assessment board had sat to consider my case. I fitted all the criteria. No concerns had been raised. The presiding governor stamped the paperwork: Actioned.

'I got it,' I said. 'I've been passed for unsupervised voluntary work in the community!'

This stage of the sentence has been such a long time coming. But it also seems to have arrived all of a sudden. Where have all those years gone? Not much time to spend on contemplation now though. There's work to be done, and the Poet has already got me a job.

He told me about it the next morning after breakfast. 'Potholes,' he said, 'they need filling.'

He could have told me that our task was to fill a disused quarry by hand and my smile would have been no less enthusiastic. The Poet took me through the procedures to get my licence (the piece of paper that would get me out of the gate unescorted). He introduced me to the activities officer and took me to meet the head gardener and pick up some tools. My voluntary work placement had still to be decided. In the meantime I was allowed to work on the roads outside the prison.

'That's it,' he said. 'Let's go.'

The Poet pushed the wheelbarrow, I carried the shovels. A female officer held the gate open for us. 'Mornin',' she said, adding: 'Have a nice day.'

Have a nice day? Was she kidding? The sun was shining, the birds were singing – it was all I could do to stop myself from bursting into a chorus of 'Heigh Ho, Heigh Ho . . .'

We worked on the track by the copse at the back of the jail. Rolling green acres stretched out for miles. Nearby rabbits played, occasionally startled more by the sound of a woodpecker than by our manic shovelling and spreading.

'How does it feel then?' said the Poet when we stopped for a breather.

At that moment a pair of Canada geese strolled by, shepherding a brood of young as they tumbled through the bluebells. It was one of the most beautiful sights I had ever seen. I never gave the Poet an answer. If I had I would have said: 'Undeserving.'

Erwin James is serving a life sentence. The fee for this article was paid to charity.

27 February 2002

PETER MATTHEWS

A fourteen-year-old on phonejacking

The story of the twelve-year-old girl in Croydon who was stabbed by teenage phone thieves will have confirmed many parents' worst fears. It's a familiar situation to me. I'm fourteen and I go to a state school in north London. Over the past year or so, I've had two phones stolen, or 'jacked' and I've been threatened with a knife countless times. Someone tries to jack me probably every week.

Most parents, including mine, would like their kids to come straight home. I prefer to hang around in the street with my friends. Although this makes me a natural target, I've found some ways to deal with the situation. The most important rule is to give up your phone rather than get hurt. It's also best to avoid a confrontation in the first place. I would never walk down the road playing with my phone. It shows you have something worth stealing.

It helps to spot trouble before it happens. My friends and I are 'trendies'. We wear American-type skateboarders' clothes: hoodies and baggy trousers. The kids who jack mobile phones we call 'rudes' – rude boys. They're working class, mainly black, though not always, and at the moment they wear these funny woolly hats with two bobbles, and big jackets with fur-lined hoods. (Obviously, only a minority of kids who dress like this go jacking phones.)

Kids from all backgrounds get robbed; it's unusual for rudes to jack girls, though this is what seems to have happened in Croydon. Mostly, they get girls to jack girls. On the whole, rudes don't cross the road to jack you – they try to get you to walk over to them. So avoid eye contact and develop bad hearing. Don't respond to 'Oi mate, got a cigarette?' or 'Do you want to buy a draw?' If you look like the sort of kid who wouldn't be interested in this kind of offer, they'll ask you the time, hoping you'll be naive enough to pull out your phone.

Should you run away? Yes, if you're fast on your feet. But it's a very bad idea to run and then get caught, as it will (a) tell them you've got something worth taking and (b) annoy them. If you stand your ground, the conversation is likely to start like this.

RUDE: Oi blud, wanna buy a draw?

ME: I don't have any money, sorry.

Always say you don't have any money and always be polite. It's bad manners to say you don't smoke pot – you risk a punch in the face. This way you haven't ruled out buying weed at a future date.

RUDE: Cool, cool, take down my number.

ME: Yeah, safe *(pulling out pen and paper)*.

RUDE: No, no, take it in your phone, I don't want you to lose it.

ME: Sorry mate, I don't have a phone. It got jacked.

Strangely enough, he's likely to sympathise and offer to track down the culprit. But if he doesn't buy this sad story you're into the unfriendly jacking scenario. He'll mention that he's got a 'borer' – a folding knife. Nine times out of ten they don't, but you don't want to find out.

Bad luck: a rude has just discovered your hidden phone. This is how I lost my first phone. It was a tall kid who was able to look straight down into my side pocket.

RUDE: Why did you lie to me? *(Silly question)*

ME: *(Incoherent mumble)*

RUDE'S FRIEND: Allow him, man. *(In other words, let him off lightly)*

There is a code of honour – as in the rule that only girls jack girls – plus usually there's quite a bit of ego involved. Though when I recently tried to use this to my advantage, the kid said: 'I'm jacking you. I'm not your friend. I'll bruk you up.' (Luckily, he didn't.)

But when I lost my first phone, the rudes were pretty chivalrous. In fact, they seemed to be familiar with the fashionable idea that criminals should apologise to their victims. When they offered compensation, though, it was probably to discourage me from reporting them to the police.

RUDE'S FRIEND: Do you want a bike for it? But it's got a flat tyre.

ME: Nah man, I'm cool.

A stolen bike with a flat tyre wasn't that tempting. And I was already late for my English tutor.

30 January 2002

VICKI WRIGHT

A fifteen-year-old on her baby

Just before my fifteenth birthday I felt sick, dizzy and more tired than I have ever felt in my life. So, like any normal person, I decided to go to the doctor. The waiting room was like institutional rooms everywhere, the walls a pale off-yellow which, to my mind, must make the patients feel even worse, and it was full of patients, quietly coughing to themselves and not looking at each other.

Doctors always try to make themselves look friendly, but only one I have ever met has made it work. This one had the overall appearance of a fairy that had spent too much time at the top of the Christmas tree. Her dyed blonde hair stuck out at all angles, her bright red lips were bent into a permanent smile, pinned on like a badge, and just as unshakeable. We ran through the routine – eating, sleeping, urinating, questions, and she took a sample to see if I was pregnant, which I thought was possible but not likely. After all, it'll never happen to me – will it?

I was called back in to the doctor's room. I sat down and she told me, with that fake smile of hers, that I was pregnant. There was a moment of immeasurable time where I could only think: Yes! No! Not now, not with him. What is going to happen to me, us?

'Perhaps you will have to talk about it,' she grinned, and in that second I knew that no amount of procrastinating (the usual defence of a teenager under siege) could get me out of this one. I would have to make my first major decision.

The ride home was a silent one. I looked from the window as Janet, my foster mum, drove us home, and saw pregnant woman after pregnant woman, baby after baby – were they always there and I hadn't noticed, or had they come out of hiding especially for me? We arrived home and Stuart, my foster dad, asked how it had gone.

'She's pregnant,' was Janet's reply.

Just when I thought the day could get no worse, Stuart suggested, in a firm manner, that we go to my boyfriend Martin's house and tell him. I was filled with dread but I knew I had to do it. While speeding up the M1, I called Martin's mobile and asked where he was. He was at school and I told him to stay there and that I was going to meet him. I always wondered why he didn't like me to meet him from school – it was always completely out of bounds to me – and now, as we pulled up, I could see why. He looked small, hunched up and grumpy in his school uniform. I had been dating a school geek.

'Well,' I told him, 'the good news is I'm not ill.' He looked at me, swore, and said: 'You're pregnant.' It was not a question. He swore again: 'What am I going to do? I wanna blow stuff up on the computer!' It was then that I knew the relationship was not going to work.

We drove to his house in silence. I don't know to this day what Martin was thinking, but I was praying that Stuart wouldn't leave me alone with him. My fears were confirmed a couple of days later when he started to hit me to gain control. Thank God for my foster parents – they gave me strength to leave him (I'm ashamed to admit I dumped him by letter).

His mother, Helen, had the best reaction to my pregnancy so far. She really should be an actress; her response certainly gave a new meaning to the word melodrama. She screamed, cursed, cried and beat the poor bin up so badly that I was ready to call the Society for the Protection of Household Appliances. Ashleigh, my foster parents' daughter, was the funniest. When I told her I was pregnant, the six-year-old asked me why I didn't 'put a balloon on Martin's willy'. I endeavoured to explain that I hadn't taken my pill properly and made a hasty exit.

I protected my precious, invisible bump as I trekked round the over-crowded corridors of school, already paranoid that people could tell I was pregnant. I had resigned myself to the fact that I was 'expecting', or maybe I was still numb; I'm not sure which. Rumours, embellished by the teenage grapevine, started to fly, so for that reason, and the safety of my baby, my teacher decided to tell the class my news. She told them straight out, and warned that any unpleasantness would result in trouble. Possibly the world's friendliest girl squeaked 'Congratulations!' to break the silence. The usual hubbub of chatter once again filled the room, and I heard someone say 'Did you see *EastEnders*?' I was safe.

Soon word was all round school that I was pregnant and I had swarms of people pinning me against the fence, all feeling my bump and the kicks that weren't yet happening. I am a personal-space person at the best of times, so I felt this was a gross invasion of my privacy. I burst into tears when I got home and said that I was never going back, but I have now started my A-level courses there. My mother didn't seem to have much of a reaction at first (I think her response was, 'Did you get the birthday present I sent you?'). But then she told me: 'Kill it at once.' I chose to ignore her, and my grandfather who was very disappointed in me. (For the record, he and my son are now inseparable when I visit.)

Despite these minor difficulties, I kept to my decision. I started at a 'mum and baby' school, where the head had breath that could kill at twenty paces. The most surreal moment was when the caretaker told us that we couldn't bring buggies or prams through the front door in case we got the carpet muddy. Also, I know that a lot of teenage mums go on to have a second baby PDQ, but when you are pregnant or have a small child isn't it a little late for a contraception talk?

Have you ever got ready for a party far too early? That's what the rest of my pregnancy was like. I was ready, prepared, had all my information and equipment sorted; I was just waiting for the main event. I even had one of Ashleigh's baby dolls in my Moses basket. After what seemed like a million years of pregnancy and (literally) at least two months of false labour, I had a show (disgusting) and started to feel my first twinges of labour.

Assuming it was false labour (although I was nearly three days late), I went upstairs to lie in bed, stuff my face and watch *Frasier*. By the end of it, I was doubled up in pain so much that I didn't know if Daphne and Niles kissed. After a 28-hour labour, my beautiful son, Ryan, was born in Bedford Hospital at 6.10 p.m. (how civilised is that?).

After Janet left, I spent a couple of hours stroking him, talking to him, exploring him (he has the cutest dimples on his knees). Now I didn't know what life was like without him. I thought of my childless friends and, instead of envying them as I thought I would, I pitied them.

I successfully breast-fed my son up to the age of eight months. It was strange feeding in public, women generally smile and men generally don't know where to look. My son is now just over a year old. His father is a continuing saga, but still hasn't seen our son. I'm studying government and politics, philosophy and ethics and communication studies at AS-level. My son goes to a day nursery, which he loves, and he took his first few wobbly steps yesterday. He is usually such a dynamic lad, he charges about, bashing people, objects and animals out of the way in his frenzy to get to places and see new things, but after those first steps he hugged his mummy for a whole five minutes. Miracles do happen.

23 November 2001

IAN KATZ

I can't spell

There are, very occasionally, moments that shatter the invisible wall that separates politicians from the rest of us: Tony Blair's sweat-drenched shirt at the end of his repentant 2000 conference speech; John Prescott's left jab; half the shadow cabinet admitting they had smoked dope. Yesterday, another joined the list: the time the prime minister misspelled the word 'tomorrow' three times in a single letter.

I confess that I may be more delighted by this display of cringe-making fallibility than most. Until yesterday morning, few would have challenged my claim to be Britain's Worst Speller, or at least Worst Speller Currently Employed in the Media Political Complex. After all, how many people can imagine what it was like to watch colleagues guffawing at Dan Quayle's infamous 'potatoe' gaffe without being at all sure whether he was right or wrong to add the 'e'.

My first reaction on hearing of Blair's undoing was sympathy. 'Tomorrow' is always a tricky one for those of us who are challenged in the letter-ordering department. How many 'm's? One 'r' or two? (Three even?) But not even I could have managed a howler of the scale and novelty of the prime minister's. This was a truly Archeresque performance: an extra 'o' to make 'toomorrow'. Now, where on earth did he get that from?

Downing Street had an instant explanation: it was just Blair's idiosyncratic handwriting. Anyone who studied the letter closely would see that the surplus 'o' was really a bit of 'm'. Or something. To which the only fitting answer is: pull the other one. I know all about spelling and confusing handwriting, having long ago developed an ambiguous squiggle (for cases just like this) that could conceivably be one 'm' or two. There's no ambiguity here; this is a bust.

While political opponents and leader writers have dwelled on the PM's spelling, those of us who share his frailty are surprised by his more basic mistake: writing anything by hand in the first place. If you can't sing, you don't do karaoke. If there really is no way of avoiding putting pen to paper, those of us who missed out on the spelling gene know how to take precautions: a smudge here, a strategic fold there.

The truth is that we are privileged (privilaged?) to live in an age where even the most catastrophic speller need not face regular humiliation. E-mail is a godsend. So error strewn is the average electronic missive that a properly spelled (spelt?) one is generally taken as a sign that its sender has too much time on his or her hands.

What makes people like Tony and me – beneficiaries of first-rate education and without any recognised learning disability – disastrous spellers? My wife has an uncharitable theory that I cultivated the weakness as a sort of rakish eccentricity. This is grossly unfair because, at least since leaving university, I have tried really hard to spell. Somehow, though, a (longish) list of words defies mastery: 'persuade', 'background', 'acknowledge', to name a few. They're like a bar of wet soap on the edge of the bath – you place it there ever so carefully but next time you look it's always gone. The testimony of Blair's former English teacher, Ian Roberts, suggests to me he suffers from a similar malaise: 'He always had difficulty with the word "tomorrow", even thirty years ago.'

Does spelling still matter? The arguments are well rehearsed. The antis point out that spelling was only standardised with the introduction of Samuel Johnson's *Dictionary* in 1755 and that some of the greatest writers couldn't spell – neither Shakespeare nor Hemingway could manage their own names, for God's sake. What does it matter if the sense is clear?

The traditionalists – a camp of which I am an uncomfortable member – point out that, rightly or wrongly, people draw inferences from bad spelling. The world didn't simply conclude that Dan Quayle couldn't spell 'potato'; they deduced that he was thick as two short ones.

Certainly, and perhaps ironically, *Guardian* readers care intensely about spelling. The readers' editor receives more mail complaining about spelling and grammar than any other subject. He says there are two schools of thought on the effects of the paper's patchy reputation for spelling: 'One is that it tends to undermine people's confidence in the facts as reported. The other is that it reminds people the *Guardian* is produced by human beings and gives the paper a human face.'

When it comes to Blair's 'toomorrow' gaffe, I subscribe firmly to the second view. Tony, you've got my voat.

29 March 2002

MADELEINE BUNTING

Getting rid of Good Friday

Good Friday. That means getting stuck in a traffic jam on the way to a country break, or getting stuck in an airport on the way to a spot of sun. Or it means a trip to the garden centre for grass seed and some compost. Or perhaps a bit of spring decorating – a fresh coat of paint for the bedroom. It feels like a time to be on the move and a time for renewal as finally the days lengthen and we can glimpse the summer's arrival after the winter.

These new spring rituals may feel good but they have absolutely nothing in common with Good Friday. On no other day in the year is secularisation quite so starkly evident as today; this is one part of 2,000 years of Christian tradition which has virtually disappeared from the public realm within a generation. Once the most sacred and sombre day of the calendar, Good Friday is hardly different from any other day.

Of all the bank holidays, it is the least observed. Millions of people go to work and go shopping as normal. For those who do take time off, the only rituals they observe are of the DIY, compost and traffic jam variety. Out of all the Christian feasts, Good Friday is the one that most people can quite happily do without. There is still a lot of sentimentality cheerfully indulged in at Christmas; school nativity plays to attend and carols with mince pies. On Easter Sunday, some might manage a church service before a good lunch and an orgy of chocolate. But Good Friday's Stations of the Cross is only for the seriously devout. The consensus is to skip Good Friday and get straight on to the celebratory renewal of Easter Sunday – which owes more to a pagan spring festival than to Christianity.

It's not difficult to see why we flinch from consideration of Good Friday. This is a day which marks three of our culture's biggest taboos: self-sacrifice, suffering and death. First, we've grown sceptical of self-sacrifice, and the kind of psychology which leads to self-denial, even to the point of undergoing a brutal death. That has added force this year after 11 September and the series of terrible suicide bombings in Israel. But our scepticism risks depriving us of the recognition that huge self-sacrifice has often been required of those who bear witness to truth and the transformation it can bring – whether it is Nelson Mandela's twenty-seven-year incarceration, or Dietrich Bonhoeffer, who was executed in a concentration camp for his opposition to Nazism.

Furthermore, our antipathy to self-sacrifice is fuelled by a culture of emotional entitlement fostered by decades of rapidly expanding consumer power. The satisfaction of needs and desires has become the primary focus of most people's lives. Want is quickly translated into 'need' and then into 'deserve' to justify our acquisitiveness. It was best summed up by L'Oréal's famous slogan: 'Because you're worth it.' Indeed, the discovery and expression of one's self is projected as the primary purpose of life. So 'I must find myself, I must be true to myself, I owe it to myself' becomes part of a bastardised version of duty. It runs into direct conflict with Christian ideas of self-sacrifice as service to others or as the path to liberation from the self.

Second, Good Friday is about the suffering of a good man. Even worse, Good Friday is asking a particularly difficult thing of us: to contemplate Christ's suffering inflicted by arbitrary cruelty – the whipping and malicious crowning with thorns of a man already condemned to death. That goes against the grain of a culture which deals with suffering in one of two ways: either avert the eyes or plunge into a frenzy of activity (the kind of 'it must not be allowed to happen ever again' campaigning energy which drives so many of the bereaved).

What gets forgotten is that the essence of compassion, according to its Latin root, is to 'suffer with'. But it's as if that is too painful an option. So suffering is tidied away in real life and glamorised on screen. The aim is to live the Good Life, to find a good 'quality of life', as if life is a product akin to a good cut of meat or a fine cheese. It's as if affluent, western cultures cannot accept that suffering is an inescapable fact of every human life. Out of that has come a hugely admirable drive to reduce human suffering, but it has also brought a blindness to reality which can cost dear when individuals are left to cope with suffering in their lives without recourse to any cultural understanding on how to do so.

Much the same can be said of the third taboo, death. No culture has so glamorised death and so compulsively hidden its reality. By the time our children reach sixteen, they have watched thousands of cartoon characters and actors meet their end; yet unlike previous generations, very few of them will have actually seen a dead body or attended a funeral. Even well into middle age, many adults find their experience of death is almost entirely mediated through film.

But the decline of Good Friday is not simply about its loss of traction with contemporary culture. It also reflects a degree of confusion about what exactly Christians believe the Crucifixion is about. Long before jeweller Theo Fennell was producing little diamond crosses for Cindy Crawford and Liz Hurley, the Cross had been degraded by Crusaders who turned it into a symbol of violence and religious intolerance.

So does the Crucifixion's significance lie in Christ as sacrifice to appease a wrathful God, the kind of God who demanded that Abraham sacrifice his son, Isaac? Or is it God's ultimate identification with his creation, the act of supreme compassion by which God revealed that there is no moment of human suffering from which s/he is absent? Over the course of the twentieth century, mainstream Christian belief shifted from the former to the latter; a process prompted by the terrible suffering of two world wars instigated by Christian Europe. As Wilfred Owen commented, he saw Christ dying all around him in the trenches. But enough of the image of a monster God is still written deep into the minds of many agnostics and atheists to horrify them.

For all these reasons, our culture is close to losing grasp of any meaning of the Cross. The symbol has been subverted, stripped of its religious content and recycled as a graphic shape with less meaning than a love heart or Chanel's linked 'C's. The only cross millions will see or hear about this week will have been the one around Naomi Campbell's neck in her interview with ITN on Wednesday or the £10,000 diamond crucifix which Liza Minnelli almost lost to a mugger in London last weekend. How did an instrument of torture become a fashion item? Would Naomi or Liza wear an electric chair around their necks? It's the cultural equivalent of the break up of the Larsen B ice shelf: the loss of a story which describes the darkest side of the human condition – betrayal, vindictive violence, doubt and faith – and its powerful message of consolation and inspiration.

13 April 2002

JOHN O'FARRELL

Goodbye, working class

This week a writ was submitted to the high court which stated: 'The words "working classes" are not now capable of any meaningful definition.' The judge looked up from his copy of the *Daily Star*, took a stubby pencil from behind his ear and said: 'Ooh dear, nah mate, a court case like that's gonna cost yer, innit? And we're booked up for ages – tell you what, I'll see if one of me mates can adjudicate for yer, I'll just get me mobile from the van.'

The assertion that the working classes no longer exist is being made by a property company which wants to develop a site in central London for luxury housing, despite a 1929 covenant which states that the land may only be used to provide housing for the working classes. The clause goes on to say that they must have stone cladding and a satellite dish on the front, a car stacked up on bricks in the front garden and a doorbell that plays an electric version of 'Maybe It's Because I'm a Londoner'.

You have to admire the brilliance of Dano Ltd to spot this particular gap in the market. I mean, luxury housing, what a brilliantly original idea! They must have sat around for ages in that board meeting till someone came up with that one.

'Another prime site has just come up in central London. Any ideas?'

'How about low-cost housing for public sector workers?'

'Not again; that's all we ever build!'

'Hey, here's a thought! What about some luxury housing?'

'Brilliant, why's nobody thought of that before?'

The original 1929 clause was clearly intended to safeguard housing for ordinary people doing low-paid jobs, and today this need is greater than ever. Obviously the working classes are not the same as they were in the twenties. They're not all wearing flat caps and saying to a wobbly black-and-white camera: 'Well I'm just a simple working man and don't know nuffink about no gold standard but if that Mr Churchill says we's ought go back on it, well that's good enuff for the likes of me.'

To hear some of the commentators on this story over the past couple of days you would think they'd never met a working class person in their lives. (Presumably their cleaners are from the Philippines, so that doesn't count.) It's like we're talking about some near-extinct species that could only be tracked down after days spent trekking through the urban jungle. You can almost imagine the next nature documentary from the BBC, featuring a memorable piece of footage in which David Attenborough encounters a surviving family group of the endangered species known as 'working-class people'. He whispers to camera that he is going to try to get closer.

At first they are wary of him; the dominant male grunts and furrows his eyebrows before returning to feed on his natural diet of crisps and Tango. The mother seems anxious about her new offspring – he's still not back from the shop with her fags – but the older cubs are more playful, and before long are climbing all over David Attenborough and nicking his mobile phone.

In the old days you could tell what social class people belonged to by the way that they voted. The middle classes voted SDP and the working classes all voted for Maggie. If you go further back in history it was even more confusing: the rich people were fat and the poor people were all thin. Apparently the poor didn't eat much and had to walk everywhere: in direct contrast to today, of course, where the Royle family lie around all day in front of the telly eating bacon butties while the high earners are starving themselves on a lettuce leaf and spending an hour a day on a Stairmaster treadmill.

But there are also all sorts of ways in which the classes overlap. I might decide to get myself a proletarian supper of fish and chips, but then I'll go and give myself away by asking if the vinegar is balsamic. (I hadn't had such a funny look since I asked if it was organic free-range chicken in the KFC bargain bucket.) Ultimately it still comes down to money. The working classes are embarrassed that they don't have more of it, and the middle classes are mortified that they have so much.

All of these determining factors will be gone over in the high court later this year. My prediction is that the court will rule in favour of Dano Ltd, thereby finally establishing in law that the British working class are indeed finally extinct. In other words, the law courts will have sided with the posh chaps from the property company in Surrey. And what more proof do you need that the English class system is alive and well and still screwing the working classes as much as ever? It makes my middle-class blood boil so much I want to tut and say 'Honestly!', but best not make a fuss, I suppose.

30 May 2002

TIMOTHY GARTON ASH

Travel by metal box

I am sitting in a large metal box. It is very hot inside this box. There are small, hinged windows, but a sign tells me not to open them. My right knee is wedged between the knees of the man sitting opposite. My back is twisted at a painful angle. Above a door at the end of the box, there is a liquid-screen display with space for seventeen letters. Words unscroll slowly along this screen, hang there for a few seconds, and then are slowly replaced by other words. IN THE INTEREST – it says – OF THE SECURITY – but already my attention is waning – OF PASSENGERS – I look down at my newspaper, and when I glance up again the screen says – SLOUGH.

For the next hour, these Dadaist messages continue to disrupt my consciousness, while the warm stench of beer, sweat and stale sandwiches seeps into the soul. This is the Thames Turbo train from London to Oxford, and every last detail of its interior is a miracle of bad design. The thing is a horror, a monsterpiece. The most antiquated, dilapidated Romanian rolling stock is, by comparison, a delight. Only with a giant effort of intellectual will can one imagine a train worse designed.

Actually, there are two kinds of window on the Thames Turbo: those you may not open (EXCEPT FOR EMERGENCY VENTILATION) and those you cannot shut. The latter are stuck open for the whole trip, though periodically passengers jump up to try to close them. The seats are plainly made for hobbits. Walking down the carriages, you see people either folded diagonally, in an attempt to avoid each other's knees, or defiantly thrusting towards the opposing crotch. CYCLES CANNOT BE – says the Dada screen, as you sway towards the lavatory, bouncing between protruding knees – BY TELEPHONE – a last lurch, and you are in. This lavatory has a water tap so feeble it takes ten minutes to make your hands wet, and a hand-dryer so emphysemic it takes another ten to get them dry. The mauve, plastic-studded floor is grungy and encrusted with . . . but delicacy forbids.

I am not talking here about safety or punctuality (the train is also mockingly called the Turbo Express). I am not talking about 'sheep on the line at Fenny Compton'. Nor am I talking about the hardened, heroic band of people – enjoying, in my eyes, something of the mystique of the Gurkhas or Tenzing Norgay – who negotiate this course twice every day. ('If you get close to the door,' they tell me, 'you can just cut across to the 10.13 from Reading.' The 10.13 being a proper, human-size InterCity train.) No, I am only talking about design.

Why is it – I wonder, as I lurch back to my crevice – that we are so bad at the design of public space? It's not just the Turbo trains. Arriving at Heathrow, you invariably find yourself walking through some variant of a Portakabin. Cheap 'n' cheerful adornments only emphasise the lack of thought-through industrial design beneath. It makes a painful contrast with almost any continental European airport – the wonderful, light and wooded spaces of Copenhagen, Warsaw's harmonious pastels, even the rather military but at least consistent black and grey aesthetic of Frankfurt. And why is it that we, alone among the nations of the developed world, are incapable of making a baggage trolley whose wheels run straight?

British public design was not always like this. The London Underground may now be a horror because of over-crowding and delays, but it still has the remains of a marvellously clean, modernist aesthetic imposed throughout the Tube system in the thirties by the benevolent design dictator Frank Pick. The flush-welded, well-proportional exterior lines of the carriages, for example, and the internal layout, at once functional and pleasing, combining bay seats for groups, individual seats arranged lengthwise and standing space. Nor do you need to be a young fogey to conclude that the old red telephone boxes designed by Giles Gilbert Scott were more beautiful and better made than the new metal and glass ones.

So what's gone wrong? As you move (if you do) from nightmarish public transport to swish designer offices you might think that the contrast between private elegance and public ugliness simply reflects that between private affluence and public indigence. Doubtless, that is often the case. Public under-investment shows. In the case of the Thames Turbo, the story is more complicated. The train was a product of the transition period of rail privatisation: largely designed in the last years of what used to be British Rail Engineering Ltd, but built in the first years of its newly privatised existence. It would appear that we got the worst of both worlds, public and private.

The design writer Stephen Bayley points to another reason. You cannot separate the weakness of our public industrial design, he argues, from the collapse of our manufacturing industry. Unlike, say, the Germans, we simply no longer have the skilled people, in well-equipped factories, to make the windows that open and shut properly, the non-emphysemic hand-dryers, the trolleys that run straight. In the areas of design where Britain is still strong, such as graphics, we do have the industries (media, advertising, publishing) to sustain them.

Then there's the low prestige that attaches in contemporary Britain – again, by contrast with Germany – to technical education and the skills of civil and mechanical engineers. Who would want to be a railway engineer when they could be a spin doctor in the Department for Transport? (You might lose your job, but the payoff will still be more than an engineer earns in years.)

When all this is said, I can't help feeling there is a deeper reason. The appearance of a country's public spaces tells you something about that country's character, just as someone's face tells you about his or hers. A country like Denmark has a public aesthetic which conveys a message about the kind of place it is, or at least, would like to be: modern, modest, egalitarian. These public aesthetics are often not a matter of conscious purpose. Poland's public spaces were dominated throughout the last years of communism by bold primary colours: the bright red and white of Solidarity against the communist red, with lots of black around them both. Suddenly, after the end of communism, there emerged a new aesthetic of pastel shades, pale lilac, light blue, many greys. It just happened but it said something, none the less.

Design is a story without words. A friend of mine once commented that Britain is a country 'that does not know what story it wants to tell'. Perhaps that is the deepest reason for the uncomfortable aesthetic confusion of so much of our public space.

Or perhaps my brain is just getting fuddled in this apology for a train. It is so hot. The air is stale. The mobile phones are going off all around. LONDON, WEEK-DAYS – says the Dada screen – BELONGINGS WHEN – someone has just put his elbow in my face – PLEASE BE ALERT – oh, SHUT UP AND GIVE US A PROPER TRAIN.

NORTH AND SOUTH

Clifford Harper

Larry Elliott's suggestion that the best way to bridge the gap between the under-populated north and the overheated south is for the government to move ('Use northern common sense to provide southern comfort', 4 March). I entirely agree, but why doesn't the *Guardian* set an example and move back to Manchester?

Letter from Laura Marcus, Leek, Staffordshire, 6 March 2002

JULIE BURCHILL

A taste of the cool north

With typical insouciance, I wasn't able to attend the first night of Tim Fountain's brilliant play *Julie Burchill Is Away*. Because, well, I was away – traipsing through the badlands of Manchester, Oldham, Rochdale, Washington, Sunderland and Newcastle in the course of making a BBC documentary about asbestos, going by the cheery working title of *Who Killed My Dad?* And finding those lands not bad at all.

Though the subject is depressing and the stories I heard sad beyond belief, I was in good humour during my three-day trip. I hadn't been to the north much, but like a lot of people born, raised and living in the south, you think it's either dark or daft satanic mills or *Coronation Street*. Geographically, the south is meant to be warm and the north cold, but not only were the people predictably warmer, we bathed in sunlight for the first time this month in Newcastle. You get superior down south. It must have something to do with being closer to the seat of government; prolonged exposure to politicians can't be good for anyone. Even allegedly socialist types show themselves up; I'll never forget 'Red' Robert Elms on some northern TV show in the eighties getting the camera to zoom in on his socks and yelling: 'This is how to dress, you northern scum!' Shamefully, we scummy southerners thought it a hoot. Now it looks like they're having the last laugh.

Pride is a tangible feeling up there when you go out of an evening, especially in Newcastle – and it's not just sad, brittle vanity as it is when Londoners take their cramped, hurried pleasures. A lot of it has to do with space up north, places look like they're the right size for the number of people in them. And the people are so smart, whether in flat cap or Fendi. I spent a day with a 76-year-old trades union organiser who wouldn't have dreamed of leaving the house bareheaded and an evening in a mid-price Newcastle pizza joint where all the blondes looked like Donna Air and all the brunettes like Catherine Z-J, all barelegged in a stiff breeze.

The north is so soulful, the south (south-east, that is) so insipid. You can see it in shallow miniature in the world of showbiz. Look at the Spice Girls: stuckup Posh, neurotic Geri and simpering Baby were southern – the only two with talent, the Mels, were northern, though their sparks dimmed after lengthy sojourns down south. The answer to the eternal Britpop choice between hard northern Oasis and soft southern Blur was always Pulp, anyway – and in Jarvis Cocker, the Man Of Sheffield Steel, we find the epitome of The Best A Man Can Get. The dry, self-mocking wit of a Morrissey or an Alan Bennett is far more impressive than the babyish rage of a Jagger or a Pinter.

In *Pop Stars*, it was the beautiful prole diva Kym Marsh (Wigan) who became sickened of the phoney southern set-up and jumped ship with the directness of

Bet Lynch leaping over the bar of The Rover's to sort out a love rat. In *Pop Idol*, it was the working-class, mixed-race sweetness of Gareth Gates (Bradford) and Zoe Birkett (Darlington) against the posh, wet whiteness of Will (Berkshire); losers, yet still champs. Saturday night TV is a better place since the smug slickness of Jim Davidson went down to Ant & Dec's motor-mouthed charm. Even their celebrity dollies are better. Read an interview with some barely sentient, educated southern It Girl, then read one with Donna Air. In one, she corrected the name of a suffragette who died almost 100 years ago: 'Sorry, but it was Emily *Wilding* Davison, not Emily Davidson.' Now that's class.

And there are big reasons why the north is more capable of inspiring affection than the south. Of course there are rich people up there and poor down here, but the overall tone of the north remains workerist. A few real jobs still exist; they haven't completely bought into the Thatcher-Blair lie that the only hope of employment for the bulldog breed is for the poor to wait on the rich in various combinations until the end of time; society as one big *Upstairs Downstairs*. Movement from south to north must be the most striking example of inverted economic migration. Time and again, I met Londoners, from pathologists to TV producers, who had strayed up north twenty years ago and never bothered going back. People move from north to south to get more money and/or careers in showbiz; they move south to north to get a better life.

It's gorgeous up north, and on such a wild, grand scale compared with the eternal gridlocked cock-up that is the capital. At our first sighting of the Angel Of The North, my friend and I were caught on camera screaming like a pair of thirteen-year-olds who'd just glimpsed Gareth. The Millennium Bridge in Newcastle, which I swooned over, has just been named Building of the Year. (Compare that with the tribulations of the look-but-don't-touch Millennium Bridge in London.) Don't feel at home in the Home Counties? Go north, young man, and find the real heart of England. Get me! I sound like some scummy ad man. Still, that's what living in the south will do to you in the end, you can't even fake sincerity.

18 April 2002

GERARD SEENAN

Rum notions

It is now a good deal easier to move to the island of Rum than it was in the days when its outrageously wealthy owner would fire guns to warn off any commoner who chanced to pass by in a boat. In those Edwardian times, only the aristocratic or similarly opulent could set foot on the Forbidden Island.

But today, hundreds of thousands of pounds are being spent on trying to attract new blood to revitalise the inner Hebridean island and its tiny population. Since 1997, the somewhat more progressive present-day owner of Rum, Scottish Natural Heritage (SNH), has been attempting to reverse a centuries-old trend – and bring back people to one of the most beautiful areas of Scotland. On paper, at least, it would not seem too difficult a task. Life on a stunning, crime-free island, a national nature reserve, where the teacher-pupil ratio is one to six and the greatest danger is from the sea has its obvious attractions. The reality, however, has been somewhat different.

Life on the isolated island has not been quite the rural idyll it would appear in theory. Marital bust-ups have caused huge tension; police from the mainland removed a rifle from one of the new residents following reports that he was a danger to himself; SNH was forced to send a welfare officer to Rum after the local doctor wrote to them voicing concern about the number of patients she was treating with stress-related illnesses.

At the start of SNH's ambitious ten-year plan to repopulate Rum, seventeen people lived on the 26,000-acre island. Today – though the island's population peaked at forty-two – there are only twenty-eight people who can call that part of the Hebrides home. As the halfway stage of the regeneration plan is reached, those left on the island, who now form a largely harmonious bunch, realise that if they are to get fifty people on Rum by 2007, things will have to change.

Yesterday, a radical rethink of SNH's plans for Rum was presented to the group's north areas board. Alongside proposals to open up land for new building and redevelopment of the island's archaic infrastructure, says the document, attracting new businesses and residents must be a priority. After the problems of the past, though, this comes with a caveat: 'Of . . . concern is the risk to community harmony resulting from the "wrong" people coming to live on and invest in the island.'

'There are a lot of challenges involved in bringing people to a small community like Rum,' said an SNH spokesman. 'It's fair to say that SNH had no experience of community development and it was uncharted land for the islanders too so there were inevitable hiccups. The relationships between the community are a lot better now and we have to work from that.'

Public cracks began to appear in Rum's community last year when the chairman of the residents' association, Peter Bird, left his wife and moved in with his friend, Derek Thomson, and his wife, Ann. Mrs Thomson, a warden for SNH, and Mr Bird embarked upon an affair, before eventually moving away and setting up home on South Uist.

For a while Mr Thomson, an unemployed deerstalker, stayed, but he was living in a cottage tied to SNH and he said he felt increasingly isolated after the police called from the mainland to take away his gun. '[The police] had been told I was a danger to myself, my family and the rest of the island, which was ludicrous,' he said.

Then, in May last year, Mr Bird's wife, Rachel, left Rum with her three young children. At the same time, islanders, many of whom were caught in the crossfire of the disintegrating relationships, were turning up at the visiting GP's surgery complaining of stress.

Although Rum has been inhabited for at least 8,500 years – it contains Scotland's oldest known stone-age settlement – it has never been the easiest place to set up home. The Vikings made difficult landlords for a time, and, as part of the Highland clearances, its 200 residents were thrown from their homes and shipped to Canada to make way for some sheep.

The Bullough family, who bought the island in the latter half of the nine-teenth century using money they made from engineering, were so wealthy that they eschewed the island's native granite and had sandstone shipped from the mainland to build their castle, Kinloch.

At the castle, when the family showed up in the autumn to stalk deer, they would throw lavish parties for the glitterati and aristocracy of the day. The methods used to guard privacy then were of a standard that today would make even Madonna blush: guns would routinely be fired at passing boats to discour-age the curious.

The Bulloughs eventually tired of Rum and Kinloch Castle and abandoned it – leaving instruments on the stands in the ballroom and wine in the cellar. Today, the parties come in the form of ceilidhs, and the guest list is nowhere near so exclusive.

'There's not many of us here, but we get tourists and contractors and the like coming along,' says Rhodri Evans, the nature reserve manager.

Winters on Rum are still tough; the ferry comes four times a week; there is no mains electricity or water and, recent history shows, personal problems can have drastically heightened consequences in a tiny island environment. For those who make it, though, it's worth the effort.

'I came here with no preconceptions, I knew about the troubles, but, frankly it's the best place in the world,' says Mr Evans. 'There are a lot of problems we have to tackle, and we have to tackle them in ways that don't spoil the island, but it's a great place to live and the community is tight now. Where else would you get one teacher to six pupils? Where else is it so safe for kids? Where else is so beautiful?'

6 April 2002

MARTIN WAINWRIGHT

Barnsley as Tuscan hill town

The news that Barnsley wants to reinvent itself as a Tuscan hill town broke on April Fool's Day, with predictable results. But it is not a spoof, and the chances of it happening are high. Strange people with long hair and arty hats are mak-ing sketches under the Mushroom, the public shelter in the open-air market, and no fewer than three international architectural practices are nosing round the south Yorkshire town.

The visitor with the wildest hair is the main promoter of the 'Tuscan alterna-tive': Stirling Prize-winner Will Alsop. But he is not out on some headline-win-ning but batty limb. His vision of slender towers rising from an encircling, inhabited town wall, a Santa Maria di Barnsli above the foaming river Dearnini, has chimed with his hosts.

'We wanted the wow factor and he's found it,' says the council's executive director David Kennedy.

You have only to travel the M1 to get the point. The motorway embankment sweeps up to a crest opposite the deer park of Wentworth Castle (home of Britain's best collection of rhododendrons) and the people of Barnsley sit on the top. Like their contemporaries in central Italy, the original settlers went for the high ground, where the air was healthier and there was less danger from hostile marauders. Merrie England endorsed their choice with a medieval street plan that survives, as crooked and higgledy-piggledy as any Fiorentino might wish.

Another six centuries have given the old stones of Monk Bretton Priory and Houndhill Manor the additional charm of tilting lintels and worn steps. The thirties at last brought the vital campanile – the Portland stone tower of the Civic Hall, which changes from pink to gold to mauve depending on the weather and the time of day. When they saw the place, Alsop and his collaborators – John Thompson (whose partnership created the Schlossplatz Square shared by reunited east and west Berlin) and Koetter Kim from Boston, Massachusetts – leaped out of their cars and demanded: 'Why haven't you told us about this place before?'

Local people promptly replied: 'Who is it wants to know and what on earth are you doing here anyway?' And that is another story which turns preconceptions on their head – in this case the notion that regional development agencies (RDAs) and the whole subject of regional government are yawn-making. Tuscan Barnsley was invented by the Yorkshire and Humber RDA, Yorkshire Forward, which has chosen six places (Barnsley, Doncaster, Halifax, Huddersfield, Grimsby and Scarborough) to be nothing less than 'Renaissance towns'.

The idea is Yorkshire Forward's unique interpretation of the government's 2000 Urban White Paper, which took the lead in regenerating small towns away from London and gave it to RDAs, along with stronger planning powers than local councils and a pot of money. Yorkshire is paying £1 million to have Alsop, Thompson, Koetter Kim and nine other international practices turn the Chosen Six, on paper, into Urbinos. Barnsley has £150 million from Europe to make the sketches real.

And that really is the plan, Alsop tells a meeting of local businessmen and women at the start of a vast consultation (Tuscany-on-Dearne has got to be agreed, not imposed). Big and burly, he can get away with his opening comment: 'We are looking for an idea for Barnsley based on beauty.' Especially when he follows it up with the more pragmatic slogan: 'Attractive places attract people. There are proven links between a vibrant economy and a good-looking town.'

Although constantly under siege by the 'spend our money on mending potholes' lobby, this is the simple philosophy that has transformed, in succession, the centre, national image and whole economy of nearby Leeds. The Italian idea was already in Alsop's head following his Vision on the Motorway, but is now more specific, after he and the other gurus trundled round Barnsley in March with camcorders, asking everyone they met: 'What would you do to the place with £150 million?'

The notion of the 'town wall', encircling the centre in a mile-and-a-half circumference, targets locally despised areas of dereliction or grotty, underused buildings. They would be replaced by small-scale housing developments, workshops and restaurants.

'Lots of greenery too, lots of inspirational "public realm",' Alsop promises, picking up on some of the strongest but often forgotten strands in Barnsley's past.

Both he and Thompson, who is also at consultation meetings, stress that 'the one thing we don't bring is a knowledge of Barnsley', but their wider experience and instincts have served them well. Greening central Barnsley, for example, promises to revive the exultation felt by the town's Victorian poet John Burland at the opening of Locke Park (still a splendid urban lung) in 1860: 'Dull fields no more! We now have grand Locke Park, / Where Barnsley's denizens may hear the lark.'

It also chimes with the views of contemporary Barnsley artist Mick Wilson, known locally as the Cudworth Pointillist, who got the courage to develop his Seurat-like style when a friend told him that his native town was 'really a little Paris because of its writers and painters, sculptors and actors – a sort of Left Bank of the Dearne'.

'Before that, it was always those flat caps and fish-and-chips that seemed to emerge as being typical Barnsley,' says Wilson. 'It made me feel very iconoclastic. After all, it was in Barnsley Library that I began my love affair with the Renaissance and Pre-Raphaelites.' He might have written Alsop's script.

A definite centre is a third part of remaking Barnsley: although the ancient street pattern survives, it is smudged in places with horrible results of the last great master-planning exercise in the sixties.

'That was different,' insists the Labour council's young leader, Steve Houghton. 'It was driven by commerce and it was imposed.'

It also has no friends. When John Thompson asks for suggestions from an audience of planners, one says: 'Blow up the Planning Department [one of the sixties eyesores] by Friday.'

'Why wait till Friday?' says a very Barnsley voice from the floor.

The 'old Barnsley' could still bite back; one of its greatest icons, the umpire Dickie Bird, is attending many of the consultations and issuing regular cautions about taking care with what he always calls 'the greatest little place in the world'. But Houghton is confident that cosy Barnsley and Tuscan Barnsley are not contradictory. Together, he says, they should foster tourism, the fastest-growing industry in the town.

Meanwhile, Yorkshire's other Renaissance consultants are preparing to astonish Grimsby. The Humber Amalfi, anyone?

21 November 2001

LEADER

The way we live now

Male *Guardian*-readers, as recent correspondence on this page confirmed, tend to have wispy beards and wear sandals. According to Kevin Hughes, the MP for Doncaster North, they are also a fraternity of yoghurt- and muesli-eaters who fret much about the human rights of terrorists.

We fear Mr Hughes may be living in a time warp where *Guardian* readers also wore kaftans, ate brown rice, drove Citroen 2CVs and marched to save the whale. The truth, as most people know, is that they now hang out in trendy Islington wine bars, where they eat sun-dried tomatoes drizzled in balsamic vinegar, being careful not to drop any on their unstructured £800 Armani suits. Mr Hughes is evidently out of the loop. Doubtless this is because – as a flat-capped, barmcake-eating, gravy-slurping, clog-wearing former miner living in a two-up, two-down in corrupt Doncaster – he spends too much time racing his whippets.

But, on closer examination, Mr Hughes appears to have a wispy beard himself, is an authority on social work and is an opera-loving Greenpeace campaigner. If he is not careful, we may have to make discreet inquiries as to his choice of daily newspaper.

11 March 2002

ROY HATTERSLEY

Built for eternity

I live an increasing part of my life in the land of viaducts – great celestial highways which look so solid against the skyline that it is easy to understand why the railway lines which they once carried were called the permanent way. In New Mills – ten miles away on Derbyshire's north-west frontier – there is the Victorian equivalent of spaghetti junction. The complex of massive arches carries both road and rail through the little town and above the river. It was financed by local subscription from burghers who believed that their solid society would last for ever. There is barely a stone or brick out of place in one of the mighty pillars. But they still look like the relic of a lost civilisation. Perhaps they are. Ye mighty look upon them and despair.

John Ruskin – busy in Sheffield creating a museum of geology for the education and enjoyment of working men – saw the viaducts of Derbyshire and despaired because he believed that nature had been disturbed and the countryside defiled.

'There was a rocky valley between Buxton and Bakewell,' he wrote. Until the railways came 'it was divine as the Vale of Tempe. You might have seen the gods there morning and evening.' But navvies 'blasted its rocks away'.

I travel along that valley every week. It always seems to me that the viaduct, built where the rocks once were, adds to its enchantment.

In nearby Monsal Dale the viaduct has become a thing of beauty in its own right – the subject of picture postcards and innumerable amateur watercolours. It has been sanctified by history as its stones mellowed by time. Whenever I see it, I am not quite sure if it leaves me breathless because of its intrinsic elegance, because of the ingenuity of its construction or because of what it says about the spirit of the age in which it was built. Men who were not sure of themselves and confident about the values and virtues of their society would never have embarked on such a massive enterprise. The viaducts were built at a time when England was certain that everything it stood for would last through eternity. Ruskin, in his didactic rather than destructive mood, illustrated that devout belief. 'When we build, let us think that we build for ever.'

It is easy to imagine how, in his destructive rather than didactic mode, he would have felt about a society that constructs some of its most notable buildings with the intention of knocking them down in fifty years' time. The Dome – beautiful beyond doubt and, I am told, a miracle of engineering – is a temporary construction, scheduled for early demolition at the time when it was built. All over our great cities, monumental piles of Portland stone – designed in the nineteenth century to house banks, shipping company offices and lawyers' chambers – are ripped down and replaced by office blocks that the architects assume will be replaced before the end of the century.

Engineers will argue that not building to last is as much a sign of certainty as the Victorian belief that their values were eternal. If the engineers are right, the confidence they claim is in different things – the discovery and development of building materials not yet invented, great leaps of imagination made by architects of a new age, and improved levels of education and prosperity that make society demand a different and better urban environment. The nineteenth century can claim that it had one or two inventions to its credit and that it certainly believed in what it called 'limitless improvability'. But it also had faith in the permanence of its solid values. There must have been immense comfort in seeing that certainty reflected in brick and stone.

The 'system-built', semi-prefabricated, part-plastic, easily demolished building is as much a reflection of our time as the great railway viaducts of the north were a mirror image of the society in which they were built. We live in a world in which we expect everything to change so fast that it can be properly described as temporary. Sometimes the change is improvement. Sometimes it is only change.

If there is such a thing as a golden age, it is in the future not the past. Life improves each year. But it would improve more quickly if the incessant drive for bigger and better was built on the confidence that comes from abiding values. 'All right for now' is not an ideal principle on which to develop an increasingly complicated civilisation. It is possible to be certain about virtues and values and still have ideas that change the world – as John Stuart Mill and Charles Darwin, in their different ways, demonstrate. The Victorians proved the importance of thinking about tomorrow as well as today. Their concern for posterity had a number of consequential benefits. One of them was the effect it had on their architecture. They regularly designed wonderful buildings. That is more than can be said about the age of uncertainty.

30 March 2002

LETTERS

King's Lynn

No one would argue with the gist of Jonathan Glancey's lament for our town centres – but a passeggiata in King's Lynn? Folk here have more sense than to bundle up against the wind and walk round their tiny town centre: if they're not tucked up at home, they're in decent little eating places and pubs, the cinema or theatre, a club or two, even line-dancing. Having lived for thirty years a spit from Oxford Circus, I know which is safer; and emerging with the crowd from the Corn Exchange on to a glowing Tuesday Market Place – still 'one of the most splendid open spaces in provincial England', as Pevsner called it – is more gently heart-lifting than battling through the passeggiata of Leicester Square – or, dare I say it, Piazza San Marco.

Stephanie Hamilton, King's Lynn

Jonathan Glancey asks why King's Lynn becomes 'so eerily bereft of life as soon as the shops shut' ('Dead-end streets', March 28). King's Lynn was recently voted by fans of the BBC TV comedy *The League of Gentlemen* the most 'local', and hence unfriendly, town in Britain. Its streets are as unwelcoming as any in south London. Having moved here by accident years ago, I can easily recall evenings spent in town centre pubs listening to the ill-informed waffle of locals and witnessing after-hours thuggery. King's Lynn's violent insularity and cultural poverty put it near the top of the league of dead-end rural towns. Maybe the way to refill its mean streets is to encourage tourists to come and marvel at this uniquely harrowing and often comical spectacle for themselves.

Chris Beanland, King's Lynn

23 February 2002

JONATHAN GLANCEY

The wobbly bridge has stopped wobbling

Short of a herd of wildebeest charging across, it was hard to know whether or not the Millennium Bridge in London would throw a wobbly when it reopened yesterday.

One newspaper – not this one, honest – invited a game young lady in a bikini to pose with a plate of jelly for its red-top snappers. This was a fishy thing to do, a little unfair too: yesterday was a particularly windy day.

A brisk westerly whipped along the Thames, setting the stressed-steel cables of the suspension bridge singing, while threatening umbrellas, wigs and jellies.

At nine o'clock sharp, a herd of big-wigs including Lord Foster of Thamesside,

Sir Anthony Caro and the engineers from Arup who designed the structure, together with at least one bishop, a town crier and the media, stepped foot on the bridge that had closed within three days of its first opening in May 2000. Hoi polloi waited patiently at either end, being allowed to cross an hour later.

Did the wobbly bridge live up to its name?

No. Over the past twenty months, £5 million has been spent installing thirty-seven viscous dampers and fifty-four tuned mass dampers (shock absorbers) beneath the four-metre wide walkway that was shaken and stirred by no fewer than 160,000 pedestrians in those infamous first three days. Jellies aside, the wobbling is now water under the bridge.

'This is the world's first lengthy lateral suspension bridge,' said Ken Shuttleworth, a partner of Lord Foster. 'It has never been dangerous, but it was a leap of faith. What happened was that the bridge 'lozenged', wobbled in a lozenge-like pattern, when so many people marched across it at once. It won't do that again.'

So what sort of heaving load will it take now?

'Elephants, horses, sure,' said Mr Shuttleworth as he looked along the cats-cradle of steel rods and braces that support the walkway finally linking Tate Modern to St Paul's Cathedral.

A lovely piece of lightweight engineering, the bridge's design appears uncompromised by the remedial work of the past twenty months. The shock-absorbing dampers are, for the most part, tucked away beneath the 320-metre (1,050-foot) long walkway.

The Foster-Caro-Arup 'blade of light' design beat more than 200 entries to build the bridge because it is elegant and discreet.

Its design interferes very little with the surrounding cityscape. By night it will be lit from below by a fine arc of fluorescence.

After all the problems, not even a spit of rain yesterday, much less a blustery wind and a wobbling jelly, could dampen the spirits of the tens of thousands of people who crossed the bridge formerly known as Wobbly.

7 August 2002

LEADER

Beautiful as a butterfly

As psychologists, psychoanalysts and psychotherapists scratch their learned heads today, they might ponder the fact that the name of their professions – and of everything to do with the mind – comes from that flutter of apparent inconsequentiality, the butterfly. Struck by the fragile beauty of the insect, which they called the psyche, the ancient Greeks transferred the term to describe the human spirit – the soul.

Today is a grand occasion to celebrate this, with the government's statement that farming diversity is helping the revival of Britain's butterfly species – sixty-six all told. This leaves no room for complacency, but the lesson for diversity –

that we must have mixed hedgerows, water meadows and the untidy straggle of urban buddleia and willow herb – is getting home.

It matters, because butterflies have a splendid place in the history of science to match their prestige in the classical world. Far up the Amazon in the 1850s, Henry Bates made discoveries about mimicry in butterfly wing patterns which set the course for modern genetics. His friend Alfred Russel Wallace was led to the sensational discovery of evolution by natural selection – contemporaneously but separately from Darwin – by studying butterflies (and other creatures) in Malaysia and Indonesia. Neither man was immune, however, from the simplest virtue of butterflies: their wonderful beauty, poignantly brief but encompassing every colour that an artist could imagine.

In one of his most famous passages, Wallace describes how just one set of 'glorious wings made my heart beat violently, the blood rush to my head and I felt more like fainting than I have done when in apprehension of imminent death'. His insect was the fabulously iridescent golden and green Croesus Birdwing butterfly; but children of all ages can experience the same sense of joy from the Commas, Red Admirals and Peacocks hatching and drying out their briefly perfect wings in our gardens now.

11 September 2002

VIRGINIA SPIERS

Country Diary, Cornwall

At the end of summer, glittery turquoise sea and green moors are temporarily overwhelmed with greyness. Mist and cloud blot out distant glimpses of the sea from Cheesewring on Bodmin Moor – Tintagel's streak of gold behind Browngelly; Looe Bay all hazy blue; and the Dodman bounding St Austell. West of Crowdy Reservoir, murky beneath shrouded Rough Tor, past slaty Delabole and the pale silhouette of St Endellion's hilltop church, a pall of fog encroaches on to Pentire Point. Across Doom Bar in Padstow Bay, Lelizzick dunes are gloomy in the fading evening light and offshore Gulland is a mere smudge of dark grey.

Above earthy rocks with lime green flowers of samphire and woody mallows, cliff-top montbretia and fleabane have faded to brownish orange and yellow. Below, off Polzeath, some forty surfers (perhaps one fifth of the numbers two weeks ago) ride in on the breaking waves. The most skilful practise cutbacks and top turns, trying to 'bash the lip' of modest two- to three-foot waves. Body-boarders have already returned up the darkening beach, heading towards cars and holiday houses. Around sunset, a hint of overhead pinkness momentarily reflects coppery on the grey sea, while turning waves become slightly green. Down at beach level, seaward of smooth sand, dusk is prolonged, shallow water before retreating surf still lit by pearly sky. Gradually surfers emerge, retreating up the long dark beach to shed wetsuits and pack up their precious boards. Bungalow lights punctuate the darkness and Trevose lighthouse flashes beyond Stepper Point.

COMING UP FOR AIR

Austin, 17 June 2002

It is unsettling to see a solicitor raping his wife, if only on the television screen, but there is the consolation of knowing that a modern-day Soames Forsyte would not be able to do so with legal immunity. The law now is that a husband can be found guilty of raping his wife. My guess is that Soames would have been sentenced to seven years' imprisonment.

Marcel Berlins' legal column, 23 April 2002

2 February 2002

NANCY BANKS-SMITH

Remember *Eldorado*!

I shall stand outside the *EastEnders* (BBC1) studio in beautiful, downtown Boreham Wood with a placard saying REMEMBER ELDORADO! Osbert Sitwell once founded the Remember Bomba League and was encouraged to discover how many people remembered Bomba. Sitwell was being perky. There was no Bomba but, by God, there was an *Eldorado* and you would think it would be carved on the hearts of the perpetrators.

Let me remind them. People hate soaps set in Spain. They think, with some justification, that the cast is having a better time than they are. Soaps are popular because they are about people who are having a worse time than we are. I live in the East End but, even so, the people in *EastEnders* have a far worse time than I do. As Peggy said to Frank, recalling their tear-soaked, marriage: 'I was your wife, but you cheated on me and you ran off with me money within eighteen months of me having a breast removed.' And he didn't say bye-bye to the budgie either.

This week's caper was a French farce set in Spain. Hearing that Frank had died there, Peggy went to his funeral with a large wardrobe of eye-catching mourning (I particularly liked the ruffled black bustier with sequined net bolero). Well, you could have knocked me down. The last we heard of Frank, he was in Manchester, a sort of siding where surplus characters are shunted. Now he is shacked up in Casa Butcher with Rula Lenska (flouncy red dress and flower behind ear), who is calling herself Krystal. I have never felt the same about leading ladies called Krystal since *Dynasty*, when I misheard it as Gristle.

Frank – still very much alive – is engaged in a land dealing scam so he can afford top and bottom dentures, Peggy's daughter – with a new head – is lap-dancing in a low joint and two blokes with overhanging eyebrows have kidnapped Peggy. Michael Jayson ('Vodka con tonico por favor!'), who is even now having words with his agent, urges a call to the police ('They have a unit that deals with this sort of thing'). That would be the dodgy corpses, head replacement and saucy hussy unit, would it? Now, there probably is a TV series in that.

Wogan's listeners, who remember *Dallas*, think Peggy will wake up and find it was all a dreadful dream.

20 November 2001

HOWARD JACOBSON

An accidental education

Televisually – by which I mean as a consumer of television – I go back a long way. Mine was the first family in the street to own a television. A six-inch set, scarcely bigger than a wristwatch, hand-built in a garden shed by a boffin friend of my father's. The screen was rounded and slightly bevelled and received pictures only in shades of green. For two years, until it blew up with over-use, we narrowed our eyes to make out the shapes of Sylvia Peters, Hopalong Cassidy, the train that did London to Brighton in four minutes, and never thought ourselves anything but blessed.

The next set we owned my mother won in a competition sponsored by the *Manchester Evening News*. She had to provide a second line to a poem in praise of television. I can't remember the first line, but my mother's contribution is burnt into my brain – 'A beam to enlighten our way'. That dates us.

'Enlighten'. The other thing burnt into my brain is the presentation ceremony – MacDonald Hobley kissing my mother and Mary Malcolm ruffling my hair. In the photograph, which my mother still has, I am in short pants and look in shock. Hardly surprising, since I was in love with Mary Malcolm and, what is more, expected her to be green.

So I do not need to be told that television is a medium which most naturally inclines towards the populist. In the early days, when there was hardly anything to watch, there was hardly anything I wouldn't. Others drew the line at *Double Your Money* or *What's My Line?*, but I was up for *Criss Cross Quiz* and *Take Your Pick*. I knew the difference. I knew that Bilko was a million times better than Dotto, but I saw no reason not to watch both. This preparedness to idle my life away on programmes that half the time I wasn't remotely entertained by – programmes which, frankly, made my head ache with their emptiness – has remained with me, keeping me riveted, that's how bad it is, even to *Celebrity Big Brother* and *World Darts*. And with it I must also confess to a sometime reluctance to watch more illustrious television, especially of the sort dispensing what Tim Gardam, director of programmes at Channel 4, sardonically labels the 'comfort of heritage'. I doubt I saw any of *Civilisation* the first time – around 1969, wasn't it? In which case, had it been a choice between that and *Monty Python's Flying Circus*, I'm pretty sure I'd have opted for Monty Python.

But that can't be my entire televisual history, because somehow, almost against my inclinations it would seem, television has acquainted me with the faces and the thoughts of philosophers, critics, sociologists, psychologists, controversialists or just plain good talkers. It familiarised me, far more than university did, with stimulating conversation. And it introduced me to more drama and music than I would ever have bothered watching in the theatre or listening to in a concert hall. It engaged me, in short, with doings in our society other than those inconsequential ones for which I, like much of the rest of the country, have always had a taste.

To revert to that prize-winning pun of my mother's, in the midst of all the darkness there was enlightenment. One needs no highfalutin arguments about responsibility to educate, no Reithian idealism, to justify this. It was simply an inclusive thing. Such people and such events were – as indeed they still are – and television, to everybody's advantage, represented them.

My father, who never read a book and couldn't be bothered with newspapers, knew from television who Kenneth Tynan was. He appeared inadvertently on the box one evening – not in any grand landmark heritage series, simply as a presence on some talk show – and my father became entranced with his waspish eloquence. The next time we found Tynan it was because we'd gone looking for him. My father, who had never been to an opera and certainly would not have been able to name one, fell into Verdi's *Falstaff* on television one Christmas and stayed with it, in rapt silence, until the end.

'Sheesh,' he sighed when it was finished, shrugging his shoulders, as though to say, 'That Verdi!' Except that he wouldn't have known who Verdi was.

The old serendipity argument. Television, for a while back then, made such accidents possible, by simple virtue of democratic inclusiveness. That perversion of democracy, by which the best is denied to the most, in order to spare them the embarrassment of not understanding, or because it is assumed that since they have a taste for the frivolous they can have a taste for nothing else, had not yet taken root. According to Jane Root, controller of BBC2, the 'centre of gravity' of her channel (by which she can only mean the equilibrium of lightness) is thirty-five. Leaving aside the question of whether those of us on either side of thirty-five ought therefore to be requesting a rebate on our licence fees, it isn't hard to figure out what such specific and limited targeting does to the idea of inclusiveness.

That it is most insulting of all to the 35-year-olds designated as being of the greatest mass or ponderability – insulting to the degree that it takes them to be culturally predictable – goes, of course, without saying.

As someone who managed to live without seeing a single episode of *Civilisation* the first time around, I can hardly pin my own colours to the mast of arts programming. Melvyn Bragg's bracing attack on BBC1 for giving up on the arts was triumphantly vindicated by the BBC's own suicidal response. Citing coming *Omnibus* specials on J. K. Rowling, the child star Jamie Bell, and Michael Bond, the creator of Paddington Bear, together with the Blue Peter Book Awards, the BBC claimed it was focusing on 'that crucial audience – families and children – who are the arts lovers of the future.' Which is rather like telling football fans they should be grateful for a diet of under-14 internationals. But it doesn't seem to me that we adequately address the dereliction of contemporary television if we concentrate only on the death of the arts programme, unanswerable though that is. What made it possible for my father to stumble on Kenneth Tynan and Verdi was that television was once permeated with seriousness. These things are relative. Let us say at least that television was once a lot more permeated by seriousness than it is today.

And when I say permeated by seriousness, I mean that people who were worth seeing and listening to – by virtue of their learnedness and humanity, the vitality of their conversation, the diversity of their interests – found their way into all manner of programmes, at all times of the day. So that not even a dedicated rubbish-watcher like myself could fail to pick up one or other of them – a Marghanita Laski here, a Bryan Magee there – most nights. They belonged to the schedules, this is my point. They were part of the fun. The division between entertainment and thoughtfulness, between the light and the weighty – often meaning that the latter, if you can find it at all, gets shunted off to somewhere after midnight – was not the stark thing it is today.

Postmodernism would have it that the mix I am referring to is in fact one of the glories of now, not of yesterday. That is Tim 'Two Brains' Gardam's position. 'We are going through a time of such fundamental change,' he has written recently, 'that the language in which we try to define what is socially and cul- turally significant borders on confusion.' To which the answer is: well and good – provided all sides to the confusion are presented. Vigorous as Tim Gardam is in his defence of the 'unselfconscious energy and hedonism of the new', he has less to say, as his channel has currently less to show, about all those activities of creativity and thought – our activities, the activities of our society – whose value is precisely their self- consciousness, their being in full possession of themselves. In the end, Tim Gardam's 'confusion', like that of many intelligent men and women who have embraced postmodernism, or hedonism in its cerebral form, is a smokescreen. And what it seeks to conceal is a distaste for educatedness, or if you like 'enlightenment', itself.

The Czech novelist Milan Kundera has coined a wonderful word – misomusist – to describe the sort of person who is at war with art and forces it to a 'purpose beyond the aesthetic'. Not to be confused with the person who is merely indif- ferent to art, the misomusist hates it and feels humiliated by it. I suspect we need another version of this word to describe a newer, post-ideological phe- nomenon: the automisomusist, the cultivated person who mistrusts and is embarrassed by his own feelings for art and for serious discourse in the way that spies are suspicious of their own class. Though he despises the puritanism of the elitist, the automisomusist is more puritanical still – a zealot in his distaste for the high-mindedness that made him, a false prophet of a vitalism to which he is by nature a stranger. This is not the place to examine postmodernism as a self- hating pathology, but that it is a child of idleness, a moth of peace, has been proved beyond all dispute in recent weeks. Only let something serious happen in the world and suddenly everybody knows what is culturally and socially sig- nificant and what isn't. The one bright spot in the gloom after the terrorising of New York was the absence from our screens of celebrities.

But it was only temporary. The new lightweight documentary in which no one tells us anything, because telling smacks of authoritarianism, is another offering on the altar of the postmodern, giving us less under the guise of giving us more. Out goes the authorial presence – the traveller, the adventurer of ideas, the controversialist – and in comes the line-up of celebrities. If you don't believe that commissioning editors would actually demand celebrity witnesses, even to events they didn't witness, and would insist, in the way that only commission- ing editors can, that they be good-looking, of a cheerful disposition and if at all possible not old, ask your nearest independent producer. An unspoken fascism of fame, of beauty and of youth prevails in this time of 'fundamental change'.

And an unspoken fascism of unintelligence as well.

'Make it so that the characters in *EastEnders* could watch it,' a producer of my acquaintance was recently told by a controller of television. The 'it' being not a make-over gardening programme or afternoon quiz show but an *Omnibus*, that orphaned BBC flagship of culture for the unborn. Again the issue isn't dumbing-down but talking-down, the assumption that we know the calibre of the characters in *EastEnders*, how incurious they are and how little, intellectually, they are capable of.

But westward look, the land is bright! We've got digital to look forward to. Looking back at Jane Root's dispatch of everything vaguely cultural on BBC2 first into an Arts Zone and then into oblivion, it's hard to avoid the conclusion that her appointment was always intended to be funereal – the Mrs Mopp of serious programming, paid to sweep the channel clean of whatever wasn't inconsequential. By their fatuities shall you know them. Engaging in a question and answer session for *Broadcast* a few months ago, Jane Root summoned up all her powers of intellect and social intuition – to say nothing of command of language – to tell us that 'we have become a well-educated country with sophisticated tastes in terms of things like DIY and shopping'. Followed by the assurance – to show she is no laggard when it comes to sophistication – that 'BBC2 is very much in tune with that social change'. In terms of things like DIY and shopping, then, BBC2 will do the business, and in terms of things like anything else, off we will have to go to the digitised arts channel. Which some of us, some of the time, no doubt will.

But where does that leave the serendipity of which I've spoken? The accidental discovery of C. E. M. Joad when you're actually looking for Eamonn Andrews? Joan Bakewell when the one you're after is Zoe Ball? My father would not willingly have tuned into an arts channel. Television for him was something you flopped down exhausted in front of, waiting to be done unto: entertained, educated, sent to sleep, whatever. His own fault if he missed Verdi, in that case? Maybe, but what then? To go on steering clear of enlightenment – of the principle of inclusiveness, of the very modest idea that television should represent the variety of what we think and do, allowing that we do not think and do compartmentally, and that we can never predict who's interested? How come, if our culture is so confusing that we cannot tell what matters from what doesn't – what's interesting from what isn't – how come that someone is suddenly able to distinguish after all, and knows not only what the serious is, but where he's going to shove it.

9 November 2001

JAMES WOOD

Jonathan Franzen

Jonathan Franzen is the slightly damaged child of Don DeLillo's peculiar relationship with American culture. DeLillo's *Underworld* has been the most influential American novel of the last fifteen years. *Underworld* might fairly have been called *The Connections*. It seeks to represent the interconnectedness of American society by picturing it as a web threaded on strings of paranoia and power – a kind of *Bleak House* of the digital age. It combined an old-fashioned solidity and social realism with the prospect of the American writer as a cool cultural theorist, writing riffs and knowing essaylets about the power of the image in American society, about TV, crowds, garbage, the military-industrial complex and so on.

But there was a problem with DeLillo's example. His novel was a Dickensian novel without any humans in it. DeLillo insisted on connections (the atom bomb is somehow connected to JFK's assassination and to paranoia) as Dickens's plots insist on connections (wills, lost relatives, distant benefactors). But in *Underworld* there are no connections at the human level at all, because there are no human beings in the novel, no one who really matters and whose consciousness matters to himself.

Franzen realised something like this when he read *Underworld*, and pledged to put the matter right by producing, in his novel *The Corrections*, a book of DeLillo-like breadth and intellectual critique which was centred on human beings. He proposed, in effect, a softened DeLilloism. So *The Corrections* is itself a correction, and as such it succeeds marvellously. At its centre is the Lambert family, dominated by Alfred, the difficult patriarch, and Enid, the yearning and frustrated matriarch. Three grown-up children, Gary, Chip and Denise, labour to live adult lives under the long shadow cast by their unhappy parents. Around this tale of family life, Franzen deploys a lot of social life: we learn about a sinister biotech company in Philadelphia, a big mid-western railroad company, a liberal arts college in Connecticut and the pharmaceutical culture.

Franzen's emphasis on the human is welcome, and doubtless explains the novel's enormous popularity in America (where it has been a bestseller since it appeared in September). Franzen is a very intelligent, very appealing writer, so much so that an essentially dark book stays in the memory as warm and comic. To call it Tolstoyan seems exaggerated, however. The novelist Michael Cunningham likens it to *Buddenbrooks*, but a comparison of those two novels shows *The Corrections* to be wide rather than deep, and smart rather than subtle. It has some of Mann's sweep and some of his gentle comedy (and even some of his Schopenhauer) but it lacks the luminous control of that great German book. Indeed, *The Corrections* suffers from a desire to put too much in. His novel is a kind of glass-bottomed boat through which one can glimpse most of the various currents of contemporary American fiction: domestic realism; postmodern cultural riffing; campus farce; 'smart young man's irony' of the kind familiar in Rick Moody and David Foster Wallace and, rather too often, an easy journalism of style.

But the book is frequently distinguished and challenging, and it was thus a surprise when Oprah Winfrey, not previously known for her taste in big postmodern novels, chose it for her televisual 'book club'. Franzen naturally accepted her invitation – such a decision commonly means royalties in the millions of dollars – and then complained to journalists that he felt he was being controlled and manipulated by Winfrey. Nervously, he explained that he felt that his book belonged to a 'high art' literary tradition, while many of the Winfrey choices were sentimental and trashy. Winfrey then rescinded her invitation to feature Franzen on her show.

Franzen was soon being pummelled all over America for his 'ingratitude'. He had committed perhaps the worst American sin, elitism and the second worst American sin, a lack of proper respect for the forces of commerce. He duly apologised for claiming his book as high art, and told newspapers that he and Winfrey were actually united in the great joint jihad of eliminating distinctions between high and low novels. The media beast, duly mollified, moved on to anthrax. But one sympathised with Franzen's dilemma. Indeed, the sight of a novelist acting in this rebellious, stubborn, difficult, old-fashioned manner was cheering. Franzen was right to identify commercial forces such as Winfrey for what they are – forces that may actually be antithetical to literature, for all that they come dressed as literature's helpmeet. Winfrey's 'book club', after all, has made a great contribution to American literacy, but has very little to do with American literature.

And one sympathised with Franzen's own literary status – anxiety; his novel may not be Tolstoy, but it does indeed belong to high literature. Franzen may himself be a little confused on this score. Five years ago, he wrote: 'I resist the notion of literature as a noble calling because elitism doesn't sit well with my American nature, and because . . . my belief in manners would make it difficult for me to explain to my brother, who is a fan of Michael Crichton, that the work I'm doing is simply better than Crichton's.' Eh? Franzen doesn't want to tell his brother that he is better than Crichton, for fear of offence, but he is sure he is better than Crichton anyway! Such is the modern, populist anxiety of a serious, talented, highbrow writer – an anxiety now made infinitely more acute by wild commercial success.

20 July 2002

SHASHI THAROOR

How the Woosters took Delhi

It was at the Hay-on-Wye Festival of Literature a few years ago that I realised with horror how low the fortunes of P. G. Wodehouse had sunk in his native land. I was on stage for a panel discussion on the works of the Master, when the moderator, a gifted and suave young literary impresario, began the proceedings by asking innocently: 'So how do you pronounce it – is it Woad-house or Wood-house?'

Woadhouse? You could have knocked me over with the proverbial feather, except that Wodehouse himself would have disdained the cliché, instead describing my expression as, perhaps, that of one who 'had swallowed an east wind' (*Carry On, Jeeves*, 1925). The fact was that a luminary at the premier book event in the British Isles had no idea how to pronounce the name of the man I regarded as the finest English writer since Shakespeare. I spent the rest of the panel discussion looking (to echo a description of Bertie Wooster's Uncle Tom) like a pterodactyl with a secret sorrow.

My dismay had Indian roots. Like many of my compatriots, I had discovered Wodehouse young and pursued my delight across the ninety-five volumes of the oeuvre, savouring book after book as if the pleasure would never end. When All India Radio announced, one sunny afternoon in February 1975, that Wodehouse had died, I felt a cloud of darkness settle over me. The newly (and belatedly) knighted Sir Pelham Grenville Wodehouse, creator of Jeeves and of the prize pig the Empress of Blandings, was in his ninety-fourth year, but his death still came as a shock. Every English-language newspaper in India carried it on their front pages; the articles and letters that were published in the following days about his life and work would have filled volumes.

Three decades earlier, Wodehouse had reacted to the passing of his step-daughter, Leonora, with the numbed words: 'I thought she was immortal.' I had thought Wodehouse was immortal too, and I felt like one who had 'drained the four-ale of life and found a dead mouse at the bottom of the pewter' (*Sam the Sudden*, also from that vintage year of 1925).

For months before his death, I had procrastinated over a letter to Wodehouse. It was a collegian's fan letter, made special by being written on the letterhead (complete with curly-tailed pig) of the Wodehouse Society of St Stephen's College, Delhi University. Ours was then the only Wodehouse Society in the world, and I was its president, a distinction I prized over all others in an active and eclectic extra-curricular life. The Wodehouse Society ran mimicry and comic speech contests and organised the annual Lord Ickenham Memorial Practical Joke Week, the bane of all at college who took themselves too seriously. The society's underground rag, *Spice*, edited by a wildly original classmate who was to go on to become a counsellor to the prime minister of India, was by far the most popular newspaper on campus; even its misprints were deliberate, and deliberately funny.

I had wanted to tell the Master all this, and to gladden his famously indulgent heart with the tribute being paid to him at this incongruous outpost of Wodehouseana, thousands of miles away from any place he had ever written about. But I had never been satisfied by the prose of any of my drafts of the letter. Writing to the man Evelyn Waugh had called 'the greatest living writer of the English language, the head of my profession', was like offering a soufflé to Bocuse. It had to be just right. Of course, it never was, and now I would never be able to reach out and establish this small connection to the writer who had given me more joy than anything else in my life.

The loss was personal, but it was also widely shared: P. G. Wodehouse is by far the most popular English-language writer in India, his readership exceeding that of Agatha Christie or John Grisham. His erudite butlers, absent-minded earls and silly-ass aristocrats, out to pinch policemen's helmets on Boat Race night or perform convoluted acts of petty larceny at the behest of tyrannical aunts, are familiar to, and beloved by, most educated Indians. I cannot think of an Indian family I know that does not have at least one Wodehouse book on its shelves, and most have several. In a country where most people's earning capacity has not kept up with inflation and book borrowing is part of the culture, libraries stock multiple copies of each Wodehouse title. At the British Council libraries in the major Indian cities, demand for Wodehouse reputedly outstrips that for any other author, so that each month's list of 'new arrivals' includes reissues of old Wodehouse favourites.

In the twenty-seven years since his death, much has changed in India, but Wodehouse still commands the heights. His works are sold on railway station platforms and airport bookstalls alongside the latest bestsellers. In 1988, the state-run television network Doordarshan broadcast a ten-part Hindi adaptation of his 1923 classic *Leave it to Psmith*, with the Shropshire castle of the Earl of Emsworth becoming the Rajasthani palace of an indolent Maharaja. (The series was a disaster: Wodehousean purists were appalled by the changes, and the TV audience discovered that English humour does not translate too well into Hindi.) Quiz contests, a popular activity in urban India, continue to feature questions about Wodehouse's books ('What is Jeeves's first name?', 'Which of Bertie Wooster's fiancées persisted in calling the stars "God's daisy chain"?') But, alas, reports from St Stephen's College tell me that the Wodehouse Society is now defunct, having fallen into disrepute when one of its practical joke weeks went awry (it appears to have involved women's underwear flying at half-mast from the flagpole).

Many are astonished at the extent of Wodehouse's popularity in India, particularly when, elsewhere in the English-speaking world, he is no longer much read. Americans know Wodehouse from re-runs of earlier TV versions of his short stories on programmes with names such as *Masterpiece Theatre*, but these have a limited audience, even though some of his funniest stories were set in Hollywood and he lived the last three decades of his life in Remsenberg, Long Island. The critic Michael Dirda noted in the *Washington Post* some years ago that Wodehouse 'seems to have lost his general audience and become mainly a cult author savoured by connoisseurs for his prose artistry'.

That is increasingly true in England and the rest of the Commonwealth, but not in India. While no English-language writer can truly be said to have a 'mass' following in India (where only 2 per cent of the population reads English), Wodehouse has maintained a general rather than a cult audience among this Anglophone minority: unlike others who have enjoyed fleeting success, he has never gone out of fashion. This bewilders those who think that nothing could be further removed from Indian life, with its poverty and political intensity, than the cheerfully silly escapades of Wodehouse's decadent Edwardian Young Men in Spats. Indians enjoying Wodehouse, they suggest, makes about as much sense as the cognoscenti of Chad lapping up Jay McInerney.

At one level, India's fascination with Wodehouse is indeed one of those enduring and endearing international mysteries, like why Pakistanis are good at squash but none of their neighbours is, or why the Americans, who can afford to do anything the right way, have never managed to understand that tea is made with boiling water, not boiled water. And yet many have convinced themselves that there is more to it than that. Some have seen in Wodehouse's popularity a lingering nostalgia for the Raj, the British Empire in India. Writing in 1988, the journalist Richard West thought India's Wodehouse devotees were those who hankered after the England of fifty years before (i.e. the thirties). That was the age when the English loved and treasured their own language, when schoolchildren learned Shakespeare, Wordsworth and even Rudyard Kipling . . . It was Malcolm Muggeridge who remarked that the Indians are now the last Englishmen. That may be why they love such a quintessentially English writer.

Those lines are, of course, somewhat more fatuous than anything Wodehouse himself ever wrote. Wodehouse is loved by Indians who loathe Kipling and detest the Raj and all its works. Indeed, despite a brief stint in a Hong Kong bank, Wodehouse had no colonial connection himself, and the Raj is largely absent from his books. (There is only one notable exception I can recall, in a 1935 short story: 'Why is there unrest in India? Because its inhabitants eat only an occasional handful of rice. The day when Mahatma Gandhi sits down to a good juicy steak and follows it up with roly-poly pudding and a spot of Stilton, you will see the end of all this nonsense of Civil Disobedience.')

But Indians saw that the comment was meant to elicit laughter, not agreement. If anything, Wodehouse is one British writer whom Indian nationalists could admire without fear of political incorrectness. My former mother-in-law, the daughter of a prominent Indian nationalist politician, remembers introducing Britain's last Viceroy, Lord Mountbatten, to the works of Wodehouse in 1942; it was typical that the symbol of the British Empire had not read the 'quintessentially English' Wodehouse but that the Indian freedom-fighter had.

Indeed, it is precisely the lack of politics in Wodehouse's writing, or indeed of any other social or philosophic content, that made what Waugh called his 'idyllic world' so free of the trappings of Englishness, quintessential or otherwise. Unlike almost any other writer, Wodehouse does not require his readers to identify with any of his characters: they are stock figures, almost theatrical archetypes whose carefully plotted exits and entrances one follows because they are amusing, not because one is actually meant to care about them. Whereas other English novelists burdened their readers with the specificities of their characters' lives and circumstances, Wodehouse's existed in a never-never land that was almost as unreal to his English readers as to his Indian ones. Indian readers were able to enjoy Wodehouse free of the anxiety of allegiance; for all its droll particularities, the world he created, from London's Drones Club to the village of Matcham Scratchings, was a world of the imagination, to which Indians required no visa.

But they did need a passport, and that was the English language. English was undoubtedly Britain's most valuable and abiding legacy to India, and educated Indians, a famously polyglot people, rapidly learned and delighted in it – both for itself, and as a means to various ends. These ends were both political (for Indians turned the language of the imperialists into the language of nationalism) and pleasurable (for the language granted access to a wider world of ideas and entertainments). It was only natural that Indians would enjoy a writer who used language as Wodehouse did – playing with its rich storehouse of classical precedents, mockingly subverting the very canons colonialism had taught Indians they were supposed to venerate.

'He groaned slightly and winced, like Prometheus watching his vulture dropping in for lunch.' Or: 'The butler was looking nervous, like Macbeth interviewing Lady Macbeth after one of her visits to the spare room.' And best of all, in a country ruled for the better part of two centuries by the dispensable siblings of the British nobility: 'Unlike the male codfish which, suddenly finding itself the parent of three million five hundred thousand little codfish, cheerfully resolves to love them all, the British aristocracy is apt to look with a somewhat jaundiced eye on its younger sons.'

That sentence captures much of the Wodehouse magic – what P. N. Furbank called his 'comic pretence of verbal precision, an exhibition of lexicology'. Wodehouse's writing embodied erudition, literary allusion, jocular slang and an uncanny sense of timing that owed much to the long-extinct art of music-hall comedy: 'She [resembled] one of those engravings of the mistresses of Bourbon kings which make one feel that the monarchs who selected them must have been men of iron, impervious to fear, or else short-sighted.' Furbank thought Wodehouse's 'whole style [was] a joke about literacy'. But it is a particularly literate joke. No authorial dedication will ever match Wodehouse's oft-plagiarised classic, for his 1925 collection of golfing stories, *The Heart of a Goof*: 'To my daughter Leonora, without whose never-failing sympathy and encouragement this book would have been finished in half the time.'

Part of Wodehouse's appeal to Indians certainly lies in the uniqueness of his style, which inveigled us into a sort of conspiracy of universalism: his humour was inclusive, for his mock-serious generalisations were, of course, as absurd to those he was ostensibly writing about as to us. 'Like so many substantial citizens of America, he had married young and kept on marrying, springing from blonde to blonde like the chamois of the Alps leaping from crag to crag.' The terrifying Honoria Glossop has 'a laugh like a squadron of cavalry charging over a tin bridge'. Aunts, who always loom large in Wodehouse's world, bellow to each other 'like mastodons across the primeval swamp'.

Jeeves, the gentleman's personal gentleman, coughs softly, like 'a very old sheep clearing its throat on a distant mountain-top'. Evelyn Waugh worshipped Wodehouse's penchant for tossing off original similes: 'a soul as grey as a stevedore's undervest'; 'her face was shining like the seat of a bus driver's trousers'; 'a slow, pleasant voice, like clotted cream made audible'; 'she looked like a tomato struggling for self-expression'.

My own favourites stretch the possibilities of the language in unexpected ways: 'She had more curves than a scenic railway'; 'I turned him down like a bedspread'; and the much-quoted 'if not actually disgruntled, he was far from being gruntled.'

This insidious but good-humoured subversion of the language, conducted with straight-faced aplomb, appeals most of all to a people who have acquired English, but rebel against its heritage. The colonial connection left strange patterns on the minds of the connected. Wodehouse's is a world we can share with the English on equal terms, because they are just as surprised by its enchantments. As we near the 100th anniversary of the publication of his first book, *The Pothunters*, in September 1902, perhaps that is as good an argument as any for a long-overdue Wodehouse revival in England.

Shashi Tharoor is Under Secretary-General for Communications at the United Nations.

5 August 2002

MICHAEL BILLINGTON

Stoppard's trilogy

As you might expect, Tom Stoppard's *The Coast of Utopia* in the Olivier is a bundle of contradictions. Comprising three three-hour plays, it is heroically ambitious and wildly uneven. It opens up the subject of revolution while being politically partial. And it contains passages of breathtaking beauty and surprising ordinariness. But I wouldn't have missed it for worlds and at its heart it contains a fascinating lesson about the nature of drama.

Each play in the trilogy, dealing with nineteenth-century Russian revolutionaries, has its own style. *Voyage*, the first and best, focuses on the anarchic Bakunin and the critic Belinsky and seems like a tonic combination of Gorky and Chekhov. *Shipwreck*, the least satisfying, deals with the impact of the 1848 French Revolution on a group of nomadic intellectuals, including the libertarian socialist Alexander Herzen and the westernised Turgenev. *Salvage*, the final play, is set mainly in London between 1853 and 1865 and offers a Dickensian portrait of the fractious émigré community.

Like Isaiah Berlin in *Russian Thinkers*, Stoppard leaves you in no doubt that Herzen is his hero. According to Berlin, Herzen believed that any dedication to an abstract ideal leads to victimisation and human sacrifice. So Stoppard presents Herzen as a man who rejects romantic anarchy in favour of practical reform and the emancipation of the serfs. Even when that turns out to be a disappointment, he retains his belief in achievable ends: 'The labourer's wage, the pleasure in the work done, the summer lightning of personal happiness.'

Stoppard loads the dice in favour of Herzen, beautifully played by Stephen Dillane, but the fact is that his rationalist moderation is dramatically unexciting. The great paradox is that Stoppard's trilogy comes most alive when dealing with characters he intellectually disowns, in particular Bakunin. Capriciously switching his allegiance from one German philosopher to another, cadging off all his friends and both defying and living off his estate-owning father, Bakunin is a rootless anarchist who believes in the 'abolition of the State by the liberated workers'. Stoppard condemns his ideas, but Bakunin, magnificently played by Douglas Henshall, takes over the trilogy as surely as Falstaff dominates Shakespeare's *Henry IV*.

The moral is that dramatic energy is more important than historical correctness, which makes me regret all the more that Stoppard marginalises the most visionary of all the revolutionary exiles, Karl Marx. But it seems harsh to criticise Stoppard for what he has left out when he has put so much in. In particular, he dramatises the capacity for change so that Will Keen's brilliantly feverish Belinsky begins by arguing in the 1830s that Russia has no literature and ends by claiming that it carries too many burdens. Stoppard also conveys the ambivalent role of women in revolutionary circles with Eve Best, who transforms herself from one of Bakunin's sexually innocent sisters to Herzen's free-loving wife and eventually the strict governess to his children.

Stoppard's vision is expertly realised in Trevor Nunn's production, apart from a descent into *Les Mis*-style flag-waving in 1848, and in William Dudley's projections. The stage is cleared for epic and intimate events, while in the background we see revolving vistas of everything from pine-filled Russian estates to an ice-covered Richmond Park. In the end Stoppard argues, with excessive hindsight, that Herzen was right and the romantic Utopians were wrong. But revolutionary fervour has its own unstoppable dramatic momentum, and it is their very wrongness that gives the trilogy its theatrical life.

9 September 2002

MICHAEL BILLINGTON

Scarborough fair

What links the three Alan Ayckbourn plays that make up *Damsels in Distress*? Partly the fact that they are all set in the same London Docklands flat. But essentially they are about the nature of acting. Written for a seven-strong ensemble, they celebrate theatrical virtuosity while exploring the social hazards of role-playing.

Each will have his or her favourite. Seeing the trio in a day, it is the concluding *RolePlay* that for me emerges as vintage Ayckbourn. A young couple called Justin and Julie-Ann, both in computers, are preparing to entertain their prospective in-laws: a nightmarish occasion made even worse by the unexpected arrival of a boxing promoter's moll and her minder from the flat upstairs. What Ayckbourn shows, brilliantly, is that the bourgeois guests are far more frightening than the interlopers. The heroine's dad, big in Yorkshire garden centres, is a model of bovine bigotry while Justin's mum is a rackety drunk who, as the dinner party crashes into disastrous pieces, suddenly asks: 'Anyone been to Glyndebourne this year?'

But the trilogy also proves that Ayckbourn, aside from being a matchless comic observer, is also a great director of actors. Two performers epitomise the mysterious duality of their craft. In the course of the three plays, Alison Pargeter undergoes an astonishing physical transformation. In *GamePlan* she plays, hilariously, a gawky, terrified schoolgirl acting as unwilling maid to a sixteen-year-old chum venturing into prostitution. In *FlatSpin* she becomes a sexually desperate actress caught up in some secret service mullarkey straight out of *North by Northwest*. And in *RolePlay* she turns herself dazzlingly into a good-hearted gangster's moll.

And Robert Austin, a rotund, balding Ayckbourn stalwart, looks virtually the same in each play yet subtly distils the essence of the contrasting characters. In *GamePlan* he conveys the loneliness of a widowed dry-cleaner resorting to call-girls. In *FlatSpin*, the slightest of the three, he endows the Leo G. Carroll role of the secret service boss with a roguish camp. And in *RolePlay* he nails the self-regarding fatuity of the Doncaster businessman. The French distinguish between the *comédien*, who has infinite variety, and the *acteur*, who imposes himself on the role; in that sense, Austin is the perfect *acteur*.

But the joy of this trilogy lies in seeing, for once, a Scarborough company take over London and each of the performers deserves tribute. I shall not quickly forget Jacqueline King as the sozzled mother-from-hell and Bill Champion as her horrified son in *RolePlay*, nor Saskia Butler as the tarted-up schoolgirl in *GamePlan* who can't wait to exit from her basque. This last is much the trickiest of the plays in that it deals with precocious adolescent sexuality. But Ayckbourn handles it with compassionate skill showing, as he does in the whole trilogy, the gnawing insecurity at the heart of all role-playing.

9 January 2002

DAVE SIMPSON

The immortal Ken Dodd

The recurring joke during Ken Dodd's marathon act is that he tends to go on a bit. Prior to the show, the venue advises people to book taxis. Meanwhile, Dodd himself warns us that his audiences 'go home in daylight'. However, after a mere two and a half hours, Doddy brings the curtain down. The audience is gripped by fascination and bemusement as the realisation dawns that this is only the half-time interval.

At seventy-four, nothing can stop Ken Dodd. Not his 1989 trial for tax evasion (Dodd won), not his asthma, which makes him cough and splutter through the show, and not the fact that his famously bedraggled hair now looks like a tumbleweed landed on his head in a storm. Almost the sole remaining performer of the post-war comic giants, he still pounds the road because of a pathological and touching love of what he does. If he dies on stage, like Tommy Cooper, his ghost will probably carry on the act.

Most of us, however young or old we are, have grown up with Doddy, his tickling sticks, his TV-era Diddymen and curiously innocent songs such as 'Happiness'. His rapport with the crowd is extraordinary. One woman explains she comes from Grenoside. 'Genocide?' quips Dodd, to roars.

His breathless delivery stems not just from his ailments but his determination to battle with the passage of time. He delivers every joke as if it were his last. He covers everything from stress to sex (naughty, but never blue), from being prime minister to the lottery, and that's just the first twenty minutes. Much of his humour is nostalgic, rooted in a mythical time of seaside postcards and front doors that were never locked. He plays the cuddly senior citizen, confused by the internet and mobile phones, with aplomb.

The 'remnants of the Knotty Ash Philharmonic' – two near-comatose old boys – provide occasional musical accompaniment. A female variety singer and a George Formby impersonator allow Doddy a chance to change suits and refresh his formidable quick-fire wit. Money features heavily and darkly: 'Self-assessment? I invented it.' Much of the show is spontaneous, although many jokes have remained sharp in his act for years. He brilliantly switches from comedy to poignancy, singing a Diddy puppet to sleep with heartbreaking significance. Five whole hours after his entrance, the audience is still urging him on. The world will lose a hero when Dodd waves his final 'Tatty bye'.

6 March 2002

MICHAEL SIMKINS

Playing the villain

Call me old-fashioned, but I don't think you can call yourself a proper actor until you've done a stage thriller. I don't know what's happened to them. Nowadays they're virtually unheard of, unless you live in Eastbourne, and when they are done they're invariably updated and camped about with in a knowing sort of way. But twenty years ago you couldn't move for thrillers in provincial theatres (alternating with what were called 'uproarious comedies'). They were always set in country houses or smart London flats, they always starred an actor off the television in a neckerchief and fawn slacks, and they always featured a drinks trolley, an attractive fiancée, a best friend and a stalwart detective who appeared after the interval. This, by the way, is a pivotal encounter; the detective must wander around for minutes on end picking up knick-knacks off the set and examining them in an absent-minded sort of way while grilling our star with endless questions. The dialogue has to include the line: 'Just what are you driving at, Inspector?' If it doesn't you should ask for your money back.

The first one I ever saw was called *The Shot in Question*, subtitled, just in case you were in any doubt, *Murder in a Doctor's Surgery*. When the detective ran onstage to arrest the TV star in the final moments, his slamming of the door behind him caused five separate items, including pictures, mirrors and coathooks, to crash simultaneously on to the floor. No matter – I still longed to be up there, to play that doctor, to wear that neckerchief and those fawn slacks. Over the following years I saw hundreds of these plays. *Deadlock*, *Deathgrip*, *Deadfire* – the titles changed but the evening was always much the same. The elderly ladies surrounding me in the stalls, who formed the bulk of the theatre-going public in my home town, loved them. After a while, so did I. For me, being an actor was synonymous with wandering round with a gin and tonic and plotting how to murder your wife by cutting the brake pipes on her car while offering to fix it for her ('You fools – anyone could have told you I wasn't a qualified mechanic'). But by the time I was out of drama school there were none to be had.

And then, just as I'd given up hope, my chance came. A theatre on the outskirts of London hired me to play the lead in *Dial M for Murder*. I was to play what was known as the Ray Milland part, after the Hollywood screen adaptation of the original – the evil tennis ace, Tony Wendice. The part had everything I could have wished for – the drinks trolley, the slacks, the London flat, the best friend and the dogged detective picking up knick-knacks. I was even allowed to hold a tennis racket. What's more, I had a fantastic moment on which to end the first half of the play. The best friend, poor unsuspecting fool that he is, stands with me for a moment to ponder who could possibly have wished to kill my wife with a pair of scissors. Then he turns and exits, leaving me alone, gin and tonic in hand, staring villainously into the middle distance. Slow descent of curtain.

And on the first night it was going fabulously. The audience of this Essex dormitory town were rapt as the interval approached. The best friend completed his musings on the identity of the assailant with the scissors, bade me goodnight, opened the door, and departed, leaving me alone with the audience and a knowing smirk – any moment now the curtain would slowly descend and the old ladies in the stalls would let out a long 'Ooooohhh' of appreciation.

Unfortunately the stage manager, in what she subsequently admitted to be a momentary brainstorm, pulled the lever to activate the fire sprinklers instead of the curtain. Instantly a torrential downpour began cascading into the London flat, staining my slacks and drowning the gin and tonic. Within seconds I was drenched. But there was worse to come. The actor playing the best friend, hearing the cacophony of water showering down from above and unable to resist the opportunities it afforded, waited a few moments, popped his head back in through the doorway and said laconically: 'By the way, I'd get that roof fixed if I were you.'

1 February 2002

PETER BRADSHAW

Gosford Park

If the late James Lees-Milne, diarist, pioneering country house secretary for the National Trust and indefatigable admirer of the pre-war leisured classes, ever directed a film, it would look like *Gosford Park*. This highly entertaining 1930s-set stately-home murder mystery is vigorously genial and anecdotal; it swoons over every just-so little detail of life above and below stairs, while briskly and approvingly establishing acquaintance with rank, title and precedence. No film could be more sublimely uncritical in its connoisseurship of these arcana and I suspect director Robert Altman used a medium to contact Lees-Milne for advice, or maybe got the Ouija board out for a conference call with Anthony and Lady Violet Powell.

But there's no need. Altman has had the services of a very startling new British screenwriting talent: former actor Julian Fellowes has composed for him a muscular, ambitious script, crammed with sparkling lines and terrific cameo turns for a star-studded cast. It may not have much in the way of individual depth and character development, but it takes Altman's aptitude for ensemble work and revitalises it with the structured discipline of a Priestleyesque well-made play.

When it comes to patrician culture, Fellowes knows his stuff and tackles it with gusto. This is never more obvious than when someone asks why a certain place-setting has forks on both sides. Because, comes the withering reply, it is a fish course. There will be no sending for the fish knives, Norman, in this movie.

What an incredible line-up of classy British acting talent Altman has marshalled. It is as if every single part, no matter how modest, has been filled by a big name. It reminded me not just of James Ivory's *The Remains of the Day* or Alan Bridges's *The Shooting Party*, but Sidney Lumet's 1974 version of *Murder on the Orient Express*: a stately period pageant of thespian big-hitters. In fact, it would almost be quicker to list the people who aren't in *Gosford Park*; the director keeps them all more or less in check, though, while keeping all the plates spinning, and something in the brassbound typecasting prevents anyone showing off too much.

Michael Gambon is the glowering master of Gosford Park who has invited distinguished company for a weekend shooting party. Kristin Scott Thomas is his elegant, disaffected wife: the languid chatelaine dying of ennui, and interested only in extra-marital excitement and horses – in her very first scene she is shown insouciantly taking a jump, but sadly only in long-shot. Below stairs, Clive Owen and Kelly Macdonald come close to a John Alderton/Pauline Collins double act. There is Tom Hollander, wincing over his money troubles, and Alan Bates, priceless as the tippling butler. Ryan Phillippe, as the mysterious Scottish manservant, joins the list of leading men whose heads are the wrong shape for a bowler hat: like Ralph Fiennes and Freddie 'Parrot Face' Davies. And many, many more.

It is such an embarrassment of riches that the actors can make a big impact with just the tiny moments they are allowed. Richard E. Grant has a delicious grimace of contempt, which got a very big laugh on its own. Charles Dance is the laconic, menacing Lord Stockbridge, asked how many times he was mentioned in despatches during the Great War.

'I forget,' he says with wintry self-satisfaction, and just that single line is imbued with a marvellous, steely force.

But there is one performer who blows everyone away with a deliciously unpleasant, scene-stealing performance: Maggie Smith as the vain, mean Countess of Trentham. Her exquisite snobbery and cruelty is too extensive to itemise here, but suffice it to say that if the company were to take a theatrical bow at the end of the film, Dame Maggie would be good-naturedly pushed forward for a solo flourish and the applause would treble in volume.

So everything purrs along nicely until someone is murdered, and an inspector calls, in the amusing shape of the bumbling Stephen Fry. Here the movie changes from a semi-serious anatomy of the class divide into a pretty broad *Cluedo* romp and, oddly, the murder victim's violent end does not cause any obvious grief or soul-searching in the breast of the one person who is supposed secretly to love the deceased. It is rather a flat, unsatisfactory ending. In *The Remains of the Day*, the point was that the toffs were an insidious bunch of Hitler-appeasers; in *The Shooting Party* it was that a lower-class poacher gets shot like the cannon-fodder in the forthcoming first world war. But here . . . well, there really is not much of a point. The class system is airily undisturbed, and psychological motivation is pretty cursory both for the rich man in his castle and the poor man at his gate.

That's all right for a whodunnit, but aren't we led to expect something more? When *Gosford Park* premiered at the London Film Festival last November, this jejune ending looked disappointing, but on a second viewing its compensatory pleasures are undeniable: lovely ensemble acting and exuberant, orchestral direction from Altman, back on course after the execrable *Dr T and the Women*. The whole thing might be quaint, like a highly polished old steam engine, with all its bells and whistles and pistons and levers. But like a steam engine, it can belt along the track at a heck of a rate.

11 March 2002

ANDREW CLEMENTS

Fidelio in the park

Birmingham Opera Company (BOC) evolved out of City of Birmingham Touring Opera two years ago. Graham Vick remained the company's artistic director, but the new name signalled an intent to concentrate on site-specific and community-based projects in the city. BOC's first production, of Berg's *Wozzeck*, was presented a year ago in a warehouse.

Now Vick has directed *Fidelio* in a gigantic circus tent pitched in the grounds of Aston Hall, within spitting distance of Villa Park stadium. It is a remarkable achievement that shows how community opera – a slippery, difficult concept at the best of times – can be an immensely powerful and intellectually challenging medium.

This *Fidelio* is as much an installation as a conventional staging of Beethoven's opera. The music (conducted by William Lacey) and drama (in David Pountney's English translation) are firmly at the heart of the show. Julian Grant's hugely imaginative arrangement for sixteen-piece orchestra never for a moment lacks the weight and incisiveness of the original scoring.

Around that core, though, Vick has created a vast and all-embracing evening of theatre, involving more than a hundred local amateurs, who provide the chorus and portray the myriad extra characters. Paul Brown has designed the environment, which aims to draw the audience into the exploration of the opera's themes of freedom and repression. They are moved around the performing space by 'security staff' as scenes develop around them.

To enter the main tent, everyone has to walk over a dungeon crammed with blindfolded prisoners. The first scene takes place at the end of a wedding reception: Jaquino (John Upperton) and Marzelline (Donna Bateman) have their tiff on a row of washing machines. Guests move through the audience carrying on their own dramas, and Rocco (Jonathan Best, superbly seedy and credible) strolls around to deliver his personal credo.

So the production continues, seamlessly and enthrallingly. Before the Prisoners' Chorus everyone is herded together in semi-darkness to hear Jane Leslie MacKenzie sing Leonore's great aria, and then asked to walk into the light just as the prisoners celebrate their taste of fresh air. The audience put black bags on their heads to simulate the sensory deprivation of Florestan (Ronald Samm), chained to a tree. It's hard to convey the power these ideas acquire in the context of this astonishingly committed and brilliantly choreographed performance, or the intriguing resonances created by the other arresting images of deprived people, who find the celebratory ending of the opera totally irrelevant to their lives. It is a complete and thoroughly exceptional achievement.

16 April 2002

ALEXIS PETRIDIS

When crusty critics conspire

One of the many troubling sentiments regularly expressed in the wake of the Queen Mother's death was that her funeral was redolent of a more innocent time, a better era than today. Imagining that the world was somehow nicer in the age of diphtheria and world wars is obviously sentimentality gone barmy, but it's not just *Daily Mail* columnists and flag-waving royalists who insist on viewing the past through glasses so rose-tinted as to completely obscure the vision. Recent weeks have seen a string of carping, dismissive articles from ageing music journalists, apparently startled by the fact that they don't enjoy rock and pop music as much in middle age as they did in their teens and early twenties.

Here they come, their bathchairs festooned with safety pins and *God Save Oz* stickers, their clothes still musty with the stench of the Roxy club and the Isle of Wight Festival. Their spiritual godfather is the early seventies *NME* editor Ian MacDonald. His 1995 book about the Beatles, *Revolution in the Head*, ends with a quite spectacularly disingenuous essay claiming pop music has been in 'catastrophic decline' since 1970 and that anyone who disagrees with him is 'soulless or tone-deaf'.

Last week in the *Independent*, the veteran rock hack Charles Shaar Murray was hymning the 'more innocent and ingenious era' of the sixties and early seventies and bemoaning the current charts. The month before, these pages played host to Colin Larkin, editor of the superb *Virgin Encyclopaedia of Popular Music*, throwing up his hands in horror at the state of pop. It can only be a matter of time before Tony Parsons chips in with his ha'pennyworth and we all have to endure his story about taking speed with the Clash for the umpteenth time.

I write this surrounded by teetering piles of CDs and records, all just released or out in the next few weeks. When I cast my eyes over them, do I see the graveyard of a once-vibrant culture? An irrevocably barren artistic wasteland? Curiously enough, I do not. I see a raft of fantastic, diverse new albums. There's the Streets' groundbreaking take on garage, a mix album from Soulwax that transforms old records into thrilling new shapes, Cornershop's dayglo eclecticism, Wilco, Doves and Badly Drawn Boy offering inspired, emotive songwriting, the Flaming Lips mapping out new psychedelic territories. I see exciting new bands: British Sea Power, the Yeah Yeah Yeahs, the Coral, the Polyphonic Spree. And I see a heap of wildly inventive and original singles by R'n'B artists like Brandy, Tweet and Aaliyah, proof that black music is in ruder health than it has been for years.

Ah, cry the doomsayers, but what of the singles chart, ruined by cynical, disposable teen pop? Charles Shaar Murray suggests we compare 2002 with the 'golden ages' of 1967 or 1977 to see firm evidence of a decline in standards, proof that 'the best stuff is now on the independent fringes'. In fact, examine the charts from twenty-five or thirty-five years ago, and you'll find nothing of the sort. In April 1967, the singles chart showed no evidence that the summer of love was beginning to bloom. Jimi Hendrix was being outsold by Engelbert Humperdinck. Harry Secombe was doing rather better than Pink Floyd. There were hits for Cliff Richard, Vince Hill, Val Doonican and someone called 'Whistling' Jack Smith, who I think we can safely assume was not one of the shock troops of the psychedelic revolution.

Punk was raging in April 1977, but you'd never have known it from tuning in to *Top of the Pops*. The big sellers were Starsky and Hutch's David Soul, manufactured disco act Boney M, swing nostalgists Manhattan Transfer, and Cliff Richard again.

No one in their right mind could claim that the current singles chart is a hotbed of originality, but it's not as if the charts of the past were filled with free jazz, dub reggae and *musique concrète*. The singles chart has meant manufactured fluff and unctuous easy listening for decades. The best stuff has always been on the fringes. What's the difference between Gareth Gates and Vince Hill, between Gates's karaoke 'Unchained Melody' and Manhattan Transfer's oily 'Chanson d'Amour'? Not much.

In fact, the only things that have changed over the years are the rock critics themselves. Rock and pop music has always been largely aimed at people twenty or thirty years younger than them. Complaining pop or rock doesn't move you in the way it once did is like complaining that you no longer find children's television riveting. You're somewhere between Homer Simpson – who famously announced 'everyone knows rock attained perfection in 1974, it's a scientific fact' – and a dad banging on the ceiling and telling his kids to turn that racket down.

The danger is not *Pop Idol* or sampling or charts filled with disposable rubbish. The danger is people listening to the moaning of disillusioned hacks and venerating a chocolate-box version of the past instead of seeking out new music. If that happens, rock and pop will end up as dead as some people are claiming it already is. Their personal grumble will become a self-fulfilling prophecy.

29 May 2002

NANCY BANKS-SMITH

Time travellers

The Edwardian Country House (Channel 4) has been the most moving and magnificent of all the time-travel documentaries. It was dipped in an Edwardian marinade for three months and came out rich and tender.

Last night it was all over. The family was the first to go. They were, understandably, far less eager to leave than the staff. At prayers, Sir John was so overcome he could not speak and his wife had to lean across and read 'For everything there is a season . . .' Their leave-taking of the staff was sincerely affectionate.

'I don't think their fondness is reciprocated,' said Edgar the butler drily.

'They don't know anything about us,' said Rebecca, the housemaid. 'We know infinite details about them. I know which side of the bed my lady and Sir John sleep on. Or even if Sir John hasn't slept with my lady. You have to question who is the most powerful in the house, who has the most knowledge.'

On the last day the hall boy and the scullery maid were caught, bare as babies, in Sir John and Lady Olliff-Cooper's bed by the butler and the housekeeper.

'What the hell do you think you're doing?' the housekeeper asked, bustling in, then, out of the corner of her eye, she saw something unexpected in the butler's expression. Astounded, she said 'You're smiling!'

The temperamental chef, Monsieur Dubiard, stuffed his white cap into the kitchen clock, the pendulum jammed and time stopped. As if by magic, Edwardians walked through the door and modern men and women came out. The scullery maid pinched the hall boy's bottom as they left together. The housekeeper ran towards her husband. The butler left alone.

Many of the great London stores and gentlemen's clubs were founded not by gentlemen but by servants. Fortnum's, for instance, by a footman. Servants knew how to run the show. I like to think that on his way home, Mr Edgar will encounter a kindred soul, Mr Swan.

The Edwardian Country House was set in the same period and transmitted at the same time as *Plain Jane* (ITV1). Swear to me you didn't choose the wrong one. I learned at my granny's bombazine knee that you were made for life if you joined the Gas, Light and Coke Company. People would always want coal gas.

Granny should have added that life would never be humdrum. I might have felt more tempted.

Take the career of Kevin Whately, a dedicated gasman, in *Plain Jane*. Arriving from Newcastle in an implausible beard, he manages to blow up west London, murder his wife, impregnate his pretty maid, get drunk, get fired, get found out and retire to Wimbledon to raise daisies in a decorative hat.

Meanwhile I was making hopeful bets about who in this family would be the first to put their head in the gas oven. Would it be the mistress, who was addicted to veronal? Or the master, who murdered her with carbon monoxide by blocking the flue of her gas fire? Or the young master, who dug up her grave and removed her heart for a wholly unofficial autopsy? Or Jane, the maid, pregnant with a child whose paternity was a matter of complete conjecture? Or, with increasing likelihood, me?

When Jane announced the arrival of a policeman, it was anyone's guess whether it was abortion, addiction, desecration or murder which had attracted the lackadaisical attention of the constabulary.

You will be glad to know that Jane marries the son, uses the father as unpaid help around the house and is finally observed entertaining the vicar to tea. A word in your ear, reverend, they're a funny family. Don't eat the scones.

In the last *Murder in Mind* (BBC1), Dennis Waterman, proving himself far better than he is usually allowed to be, is bankrupted by his bank, run by a new, hard-nosed chairman. His only contact at the branch, soon to be closed, is the adolescent Perry ('I am the assistant senior customer care adviser') whose voice rises at the end of each sentence as if his throat were being squeezed like a toothpaste tube. Which it should be.

He kidnaps the chairman of the bank. It is arguable that to make a chairman listen to his call centre endlessly repeating that he is held in a queue (when in fact he is held a few inches above a vat of acid) is excessive retribution. Oh, I don't know though. Simon Sharkey, who wrote it, will feel all the better now he's got that out of his system.

13 July 2002

NANCY BANKS-SMITH

Churchill

> 'Comfort me with apples'
> – *The Song of Solomon*

The pig, a large pied pig with floppy ears, was surrounded by a sea of rose and gold apples. It did not wait for grace but got stuck in straight away. The ciderous sound of scrunching filled the air. Like an old Roman senator exiled to the sticks, Winston Churchill sat watching it and said: 'Dogs look up to you, cats look down on you, but pigs treat you as equals.'

The pig and I had much in common, treated as we were to such a scrumptious windfall. *The Gathering Storm* (BBC2) credited Albert Finney, Ronnie Barker, Vanessa Redgrave, Jim Broadbent, Derek Jacobi, Linus Roache and Celia Imrie. Only the pig went unsung. American money, of course, went without saying. If I weren't so knee-deep in this apple thing, I'd say they had over-egged the pudding.

Hugh Whitemore's play was about Churchill the man, not the statesman. Derided and discounted in the House, he kept himself busy at home. Built a wall, constructed (after some chaos) an island, wrote 2,000 words a day, painted anodyne landscapes, found his children a trial, ate a hearty breakfast, rehearsed his speeches in the bath. It was a touching and often beautiful pastoral. You do feel, though, that Mrs Churchill, off catching dragons in Komodo, had a livelier time.

In dreams he saw Marlborough, his victorious ancestor, smiling at him through the smoke of battle. In reality, he felt his time had come and gone. Trudging through drifts of autumn leaves, as red as his once flaming hair, he roared: 'I've lived too long. I'm in the ruck. I've drunk too deeply of the cup. I cannot spend, I cannot fuck, I'm down and out. I'm buggered up.' Pushkin, apparently, and alone worth the price of admission.

The tour de force was Finney's Churchill. The rest had little to do and did it extraordinarily well. Notably, I thought, Jacobi playing Baldwin, or, as Churchill described him a fraction forcibly, an epileptic corpse. Jacobi could have just parted his hair in the middle and taken the money.

A closing caption told us that Churchill became prime minister and led his country through five years of war to victory. And you thought: my God, some people watching this don't know that. For nearly two years he rode out the storm alone. Tell 'em that.

10 June 2002

SIMON HATTENSTONE

Clive Dunn

Clive Dunn looks so much younger than he did thirty years ago. Back then, he was best known as Corporal Jones, or Jonesy to his mates, and he was ancient – though in reality he hadn't yet hit fifty when *Dad's Army* started in 1968. Today, he is eighty-two and there is a spring in his step. He is with his flame-haired wife Cilla, who is also in great nick. She says she is going to do a spot of shopping while we chat at the Chelsea Arts Club.

'Oh, you're not going to leave me to him are you?' Dunn says affecting camp frailty – unconvincingly.

He is over in Britain for a brief trip. Dunn lives in Portugal these days and has long since retired. There is absolutely nothing to promote but his good health, as he keeps reminding me.

Dunn was what they called a character actor, and his character was usually a few decades older than his true self. In *Dad's Army*, he played a bumbling relic. In the television series *Grandad* he played a bumbling relic. In most of his stage incarnations he played bumbling relics. Once he played Thora Hird's father – Hird is ten years older. In real life, he is surprisingly confident. Occasionally, he verges on the suave.

Today, he is wearing a big black Dolce & Gabbana coat. 'Second-hand,' he points out proudly.

Dunn was born into a family of performers – grandfather, mother, father, all of them on the stage. By fifteen he had made his debut in the Will Hay film *Boys Will Be Boys* – a guinea a day as an extra. He presumed he would follow in the family footsteps, but life was interrupted by Hitler and fascism.

He orders a Guinness and Cumberland sausages. We retire to a table. He places his brolly by his side. There is a torch woven into the brolly nose. 'It's great for when you're pissed,' he says.

In his memoirs, *Permission to Speak*, Dunn describes how he embraced fascism briefly at his public school. It was the thirties, Mosley was marching on the streets, and the British Union of Fascists was growing in popularity. Like many of his fellow pupils, he joined up.

'It seemed patriotic. I didn't know anything about it then. Then when I

The moment that did for Argentina: England captain David Beckham prepares to take the penalty which knocked England's most bitter rivals out of the World Cup, Sapporo, June. (Reuters/Ian Waldie)

We made it! Brazilian captain Cafu holds the trophy high at the end of the World Cup finals, Yokohama, June. (AP photo/Luca Bruno)

A smashing victory: new champion Lleyton Hewitt hits the ball into the crowd, Wimbledon, July. (Guardian/Tom Jenkins)

Alexandre Despatie of Canada dives during a practice session for the Commonwealth Games, Manchester, July. (Reuters/David Gray)

The end of a Manchester triumph: closing ceremony of the Commonwealth Games, August. (Guardian/Don McPhee)

realised they were beating up Jews I got out immediately.' He still keeps the card with the four-penny stamp on it as a reminder of his naivety.

After the flirtation with fascism, Dunn became a lifelong *Guardian*-reading socialist. At twenty he went to fight in Europe. He was captured by the Germans in Greece and was held as a prisoner for four years in Austria. He ended up as the medical orderly and, with his tiny bit of German, the prisoners' representative. He says the one thing the war taught him was that he was a coward.

'There were so many terrifying things happening . . . all those bullets and bombs.'

He stops and has a rethink. Actually, he says, the brave soldiers weren't those who ran head-on into the face of death, they were the ones who were terrified every second but faced up to that terror. When he talks about his experiences, he sounds anything but cowardly. He explains how every night he would tell fellow prisoners stories to keep the demons away. What were they about?

'Oh, anything that had a happy ending.'

He says they were kids really, just kids caught by foreign kids. Well, at least it wasn't like the first world war, I say, at least you knew what you were fighting for?

'No, that's not really true,' he says. 'We just knew that the Germans were marching across Austria and that we were there to fight them. But we didn't know anything about concentration camps.'

What emerges most strongly when Dunn talks about his wartime experience is his humanity. He doesn't really differentiate between the allied prisoners of war and the young German guards – all were victims.

'I felt sorry for them. They didn't really have much more than we had ourselves. They had nothing to eat – just pig potatoes. D'you know what pig potatoes are? Potatoes so rotten they were only good enough for the pigs. Some of the nicest chaps I met were German guards.'

Did war change him?

'Yes,' he says. 'I became more overheated about injustice and abuse of power by those in authority. I became more aware that those high in the establishment were given more opportunity than we were. In every sense. In situations where there was not a lot of food, for instance, certain people would get more food and water than we'd get. That's very basic isn't it?' He looks down at his food. 'Yes, one lot would get more Cumberland sausage than the rest of us.

'When I got home I just wanted to do the normal things – get a job, make love, get drunk.' He was still only twenty-five. And just as he had started putting his plans into action, he got a call from the army – despite all he had been through, the army wanted him back for another three years – this time in the north of England.

'I remember having a greatcoat on in August in Morpeth, and walking around doing nothing but picking up pieces of paper. Just as I thought I was free.'

After he was finally released from the army, he returned to his embryonic stage career – singing, dancing, acting, making people laugh, making out however he could.

'Until I was forty I'd been earning £6 a week and a free sandwich and coffee. If I did two performances a day I'd get £8 a week. I was working at a theatre and found out that the washer-up was getting £12 a week. It was Les Dawson. I could only deduce that his washing-up was funnier than my comedy act.'

But Dunn was a funny man. Still is. Between mouthfuls of sausage and mash and Guinness, and historical anecdote, he can't help breaking into a routine. It may be twenty years since he was on stage, but the jokes are slick, contemporary and surprisingly dirty.

'Woman goes into a shop and says her husband is having problems in the bedroom. Chemist says, "Give him some Viagra." She says, "Can you get it over the counter?" and the chemist says, "Only if I take six."'

He tells me about some of the great comics he has worked with. And the greatest: 'Spike Milligan made me laugh more than any comedian I worked with.' He is still upset at Milligan's death. 'People say he'd been ill a long time and he was old, but it's still too early to lose him. It was actually difficult working with him because he was so funny.'

Dunn and I are looking at portraits he drew of the *Dad's Army* cast in the seventies. 'Arthur Lowe: dead. John Le Mesurier: dead. Jimmy Beck – what an awfully good actor he was – dead. John Laurie: dead. Arnold Ridley: dead. There's only a couple left alive – Ian Lavender, Bill Pertwee . . . and me, of course.'

Thirty-four years on from its creation, sixty years on from the war, *Dad's Army* is still popular. Why?

'Well, it was very well written wasn't it,' Dunn says. 'You know, the story of these little old chaps deciding what they'll do if Hitler makes it over to Britain.'

Why do kids love it so much when the territory is so alien?

'Children love people in authority making idiots of themselves, don't they? You know, I'm so lucky. People come up to me and say thank you for all those years of enjoyment. How many people are thanked for doing their job? Bus conductors don't get told, thanks so much, that was beautifully collected.'

His autobiography, published way back when, was called *Permission to Speak* – a Jonesy catchphrase. On the back cover there is a picture of Dunn walking into the yonder, naked. I presumed it must have been a film still from one of his more bizarre projects.

'Oh, no, not at all,' Dunn says, 'it's just a photo that I liked. We were in Richmond Park one afternoon, and I thought it would make a good photograph. I suppose it's my ideal way of going to war. It's almost like Charlie Chaplin disappearing into the sunset. It's different isn't it?' He chews on his sausage and giggles. 'A friend looked at it and said, "It's good but it needs an ironing."'

In one of his last professional jobs, Dunn made his opera debut in *Die Fledermaus*. 'I was a Viennese prison guard, so I could play it rather well – had a lot of experience of guards.' It was by no means his first excursion into the world of music, though. At the tip end of the seventies he even had a Number One hit with 'Grandad', a song he is never allowed to forget. But then again, he wouldn't want to.

'It sold 90,000 in one day. I bought a house with it. D'you know what replaced me at Number One? "My Sweet Lord". See, George Harrison had to get in touch with heaven to knock me off the top.'

He takes out a picture of Alice and Daisy, his two grandchildren, and another picture of his Labrador puppy. 'So sweet,' he says. 'Shits everywhere, of course.'

Interview over, he just wants to sit and reminisce and swap jokes. 'Have you heard this one? A lord is lying on a lawn outside his mansion under a laburnum tree – white linen suit and panama hat, long cigarette holder. His wife, the lady, is lying in a chiffon frock smothered in Chanel No 5. He says, "The stock exchange is very dodgy at the moment darling, we're going to have to economise. If you could learn to cook we could sack the chef. And she says, "That's a good idea darling, and if you could learn to fuck we could sack the chauffeur" – Now don't put that in your bleedin' paper!'

But he knows I will. On the way out, a stranger walks up to him and thanks him for all the pleasure he's given her over the years.

'Gawd bless ya!' he says. And for a second, we're in the presence of Corporal Jones.

10 August 2002

JOE QUEENAN

All shook up

Elvis Presley's acting career breaks down into two distinct phases. In his early films – *Love Me Tender, Jailhouse Rock, King Creole, Flaming Star* – he honestly tried to make good movies. The public enjoyed the films, but not as much as Elvis would have liked. A desperately poor country boy, Elvis was always interested in making money, and after the massive success of the hokey, slapdash, just plain terrible *Blue Hawaii* in 1961, he decided to churn out an uninterrupted series of very bad, very corny motion pictures for the remainder of his career. For whatever the reason – most likely the sheer exhilaration of getting something for nothing – he threw in the towel.

The post-*Blue Hawaii* films were shot quickly and inexpensively, and had extravagantly absurd plots: Elvis as an actor trapped in a harem during a promotional tour for the State Department; Elvis as a beleaguered tuna boat captain; Elvis as a singing trapeze artist suffering from vertigo. In all of these films, he had to sing his way out of trouble and, almost without exception, the soundtracks were dreadful. Unlike *King Creole* and *Jailhouse Rock*, where he looked like a snarling thug, movies like *Tickle Me, Girls, Girls, Girls, Fun in Acapulco* and *Harum Scarum* displayed a domesticated, well-manicured Elvis. The films were mildly risqué – lots of skin-tight short-shorts and halter tops (on the girls, that is) – but generally wholesome. The defanged King was no longer a threat to middle America; Bob Dylan and the Rolling Stones were. The public had given its heart to Elvis, and Elvis gave the public *Viva Las Vegas!* in return. Thanks.

No pop star before or since ever achieved what Elvis did; the landscape is littered with the bones of his imitators. As I pointed out in a *Movieline* article eleven years ago, the one record in the motion picture industry that will never be broken is the King's string of thirty-one money-making films, almost all of them horrendous. None of us will ever witness a phenomenon like Elvis

Presley's movie career; he could literally get away with murder. Madonna tried and failed. Mick Jagger tried and failed. Sting, Prince and Dylan tried and failed, as will Puff Daddy and Eminem. The closest thing to Elvis's crossover success are the careers of Cher, Sting, Ice Cube, L L Cool J and Mark Wahlberg. Like I said: Elvis had no competition.

Unlike Frank Sinatra (a shorter, tougher man with a colossal ego), Elvis was probably not temperamentally suited to be an actor. He seemed nervous and embarrassed in his screen debut *Love Me Tender*, and did not show much more range in films like *King Creole* and *Flaming Star*, by far his best 'serious' pictures. His phrasing was mechanical; he tended to snarl and brood a lot. Of course, most people would snarl and brood a lot if they were trapped in a film where they had to play a hip-swivelling pharmacist's son who is being courted by a local gangster who wants him to come back and do his nightclub act in the lounge where he used to work as an underpaid busboy even though his father wants him to finish high school and enter a profession like, well, pharmacy. Elvis did his level best, working with the material given him, but the only time he seemed to relax was when he took centre stage to belt out one of his hits. Then, suddenly, magically, he stopped being a dour pharmacist's son and turned back into Elvis. The eyes lit up. The headlight smile returned. The hips swivelled. The King was back.

Someone, perhaps the rock critic Greil Marcus, once said that Elvis would have fared better in a TV action series like *The Six Million Dollar Man*. I agree. Elvis was never in a class with crossover artists like Sinatra and Dean Martin; they knew how to lighten up and enjoy themselves on the big screen. Elvis always seemed wound-up. Moreover, in his early films, he was often overshadowed by talented actors like Walter Matthau, John McIntire and Richard Egan, who could readily conjure up more than three facial expressions. Even the paunchy, middle-aged burnout clowning around as the bloodthirsty Kiowa chieftain Buffalo Horn, in *Flaming Star*, could act better than Elvis. In his later movies, this problem was corrected; now Elvis was generally cast opposite galoots and bimbos. And in his later movies, three facial expressions were two more than an actor needed.

To be fair, Elvis was never a terrible actor in the sense that Madonna and Mick Jagger are, and because he possessed great looks, his mere magnetic presence partially compensated for his lack of ability. Madonna, despite all her earnest huffing and puffing, is rather ordinary-looking and her attempts to 'emote' in films like *Body of Evidence*, *Shanghai Surprise* and *Dick Tracy* actually have been known to make grown men weep. Me, for instance. No matter how hard she tries, she still looks like the fat girl playing Eliza Doolittle in the school play. As for Jagger, he is a charismatic rock star who has the misfortune to look like a chimp. A chimp, I might add, who is no threat to John Gielgud, nor, for that matter, John Belushi. And let's not even talk about the puny Roger Daltry or the loveable but ineffective Ringo.

Oddly, because of their sheer ludicrousness, films like *Fun in Acapulco*, where Elvis dresses as a matador and sings songs about Pedro the Bull, are still entertaining, if only because they provide a glimpse into a society that obviously had a few screws loose. Contrasted with pathetic films like *The Next Best Thing*, where the facile but gifted Rupert Everett literally blows the frumpy, washed-out Madonna off the screen, Elvis's films are oddly charming, hypnotically absurd. The lamest Elvis song – for example, the shrimping tune from *Fun in Acapulco* – never makes your skin crawl the way Madonna's graveside rendition of 'American Pie' in *The Next Best Thing* does.

Nor did Elvis ever undertake anything as hopeless as Jagger's forlorn impersonation of a legendary Aussie highwayman in Ned Kelly. To this day, I am still trying to figure out how a man as physically unimposing as Mick Jagger could have possibly dominated the Outback. And where that accent came from. Elvis Presley's most amazing accomplishment is that he made dozens of unwatchable movies that are still fun to watch. Both of my children – eighteen and fifteen – are enthralled by these films, in large part because they cannot believe that anyone could get away with what Elvis did. When you see a film like *Harum Scarum*, where Elvis sets out to the Middle East on a State Department goodwill tour, crosses the Mountains of the Moon, is then abducted by bandits, gets gussied up in lime green pants and a golden cumberbund, dons a turban, and leads a peasant's revolution against the wicked oppressors, you can only shake your head in disbelief. Elvis Presley was a poor boy from Mississippi who grew up to be the biggest star in the world. He made twenty-six of the most mesmerisingly awful movies in the history of motion pictures. There's not a day that goes by that I don't miss him.

9 September 2002

ALAN RUSBRIDGER

Sir Simon storms Berlin

Our boy has made it. In charge of the best orchestra in the world at forty-eight. Every street corner in Berlin decorated with twice-lifesize welcome posters bearing the trademark curly grey locks and the dimpled smile. A city unified and resurgent (if broke). An orchestra and an audience eating out of the palm of his hand. Life does not get much better than this.

Exactly four years ago Simon Rattle said goodbye to Birmingham with Thomas Adès and Mahler. On Saturday night he said hello to Berlin with the same piece by Adès (*Asyla*) and Mahler (the fifth, rather than the second). Gallons of ink have been spent wondering about what signal Rattle was sending his new colleagues and public. Adès = change, Mahler = continuity; Adès = danger, Mahler = safety. And so on.

Well, possibly. In reality the Adès is not so very dangerous and, in Rattle's hands, Mahler is not so very safe. But plunging straight into the deep end with a vibrant and challenging piece of new British music was bold. And combining it with a masterly and fluid reading of an old favourite about to celebrate its century with the orchestra was astute. But then, that was why they hired him. The Philharmonic Hall was, predictably, packed and palpably buzzing with civic pride and a sense of anticipation for not just the next couple of hours but – in

Berliners' secret dreams – the next couple of decades. Saturday night was the beginning of a journey.

The journey began with the strange Balinese tones of the Adès work, said to be a play on the refuge/madhouse connotations of the word 'asylum'. In truth there is more madhouse than refuge in this four-movement minor masterpiece. Over the next twenty or so minutes we were subjected to the most graphic representation of madness: shrieks, wails, moans, bangs, mis-tunings, pain, sadness, alienation and the extremes of noise and quiet.

It is an unflinching and profound work – easy to see why Rattle is attached to it, and little wonder Adès is reported to have ended up hyperventilating in casualty the night he tried to finish off the frenetic third movement. Most of the audience was also hyperventilating as it furiously built on its own remorseless momentum. There was a telling moment when a bass player, startled by the furious drumming behind him, looked over his shoulder and then – there is no other word for it – began to jam.

There was no jamming in the Mahler, but there was plenty of spontaneity and impulsiveness. Rattle woos his players, cajoles them, alarms them. Sometimes he abandons the beat and describes the sound he's after with his left hand. There is no part of his body he won't use to implore or impose the effect he wants – eyes, mouth, left elbow, forehead, back muscles, hair, feet.

It all came together in an account of the Mahler that was, by some way, less rushed than some previous rattles through the work. There was a real sense of the overall architecture and drama – but plenty of whimsy, fun and mischief along the way. And if there is a more velvety string section anywhere in the world, it would be good to know of it.

At the final brass chorale Rattle simply stared at the brass section, raised his arms to the heavens and opened his mouth in glory. As the applause rolled around the hall the new Maestro was glimpsed between third and fourth trombone lapping it up. Our boy had well and truly arrived.

THIS SPORTING LIFE

Austin, 24 June 2002

Seaman scuppered as subs help Arsenal sink Grimsby.

Headline on match report
(Arsenal 2, Grimsby Town 0), 28 November 2001

2 February 2002

FRANK KEATING

Bill McLaren and I say goodbye to rugby union

Bill McLaren sets out today on his final international rugby union season. There's a coincidence: so do I. The BBC's mellifluous tartan sage, seventy-nine next birthday, will be acclaimed deservedly with garlands of gratitude at every step of his farewell procession. Fourteen years younger, bus-pass beckoning, I will softly hum a private swansong and, in solitary reverie, raise a surreptitious glass or two to conjure up some daydreams of remembrance. The championship is one of utter grandeur all right, both sporting and cultural. It has been ingrained in my consciousness for getting on for fifty winters now.

McLaren was first in his Murrayfield commentary eyrie – for radio then – on 7 February 1953, when Wales came up. The schoolteacher was so nervous he had given breakfast and lunch a miss.

'I managed to muddle through, I suppose,' he says. 'Wales won by twelve points to nothing, inspired by Cliff Morgan, crafty as a bag of weasels and with that scuttling pace like a kind of flying Charlie Chaplin.'

A broadcasting style was born. It is a surprise to realise that my own big-time debut came not many months later. Some twenty of us from school were croc-odiled into Twickenham to watch the All Blacks beat England. We were in the front row of the Eastern terrace, on the halfway line, and mittened and muf-flered against the freezing swirl of snowflakes.

Inside, however, the cockles were furnace-hot as we thrilled at a succession of rumbling charges by England's blond barn door winger Ted Woodward, the High Wycombe butcher who had opened up his shop that morning and served a few customers before catching the train for Twickenham. He would always, apparently, parcel up a packet of pork chops as a gift for his opposing winger, and he was my first international rugby pin-up.

By the time the school next bussed our first XV up for my Five Nations debut, Woodward had been dropped. I can remember no detail at all of that 1955 Calcutta Cup match (England won 9-6) except that we stood, sardine tight, on the Southern cinder terrace and the throng all around was alcohol tight.

After I left school with three O levels (enough to secure a trial on the *Stroud News*) the Celtic blood in my veins really kicked in when my uncle, John Kearney, a Cork man, began coming over with a treasured 'spare' for the Irish match. Along with all Ireland, north and south, uncle worshipped Jack Kyle and I still have, framed, the 1958 Twickenham programme (England by 6-0) when he played his final match there. They gave him a whole page in tribute: *Kyle's sportsmanship as well as his technical skill is unsurpassed and epitomises everything which is good in this great game of Rugby Football. We accord him today a tremendous welcome.*

Dead right, too, said Uncle John, pleased as punch, and then muttered: 'But I bet the bastards wouldn't have given Jack all that space if he hadn't been an Ulsterman.'

The Cork contingent's biennial pilgrimage to London had a strict routine. Friday night at the bar of the left-footers' Knights of St Columba club in Kensington; morning mass at the Oratory and much lighting of candles for good luck; a number of reviving hairs-from-the-dog en route to a general gathering of the clan at Waterloo, whence by boisterously jam-packed train south to rugby's suburb. The green chartreuse chasers ('green for luck, lads') and the offertory candles worked satisfactorily enough in the 1960 match, for, although Ireland lost by 8-5, all the tension was for the innocent-faced Cork boy with the button nose and crinkly fair hair from Presentation College, in his first international. He played a nerveless humdinger at full-back and the joy of my uncle's group was unconfined – and, of course, Tom Kiernan went on to be the world's most capped full-back, captain of the Lions, and Munster's coach when they beat the All Blacks in 1978. And I was to grow up and become a friend of his until we stupidly fell out – completely my fault.

By 1982 Tom was Ireland's coach when they won the Triple Crown for the first time since 1949 – and a good few years later, in these pages, I related how on the very eve of the crucial decider against Scotland a few of us, including Tom and his senior stalwarts on the team (Moss Keane, Willie Duggan, Phil Orr and the like), had been 'relaxing' into the witching hour in Sean Lynch's cosy bar down there opposite Dublin's Carmelite convent. 'Ah, that was the old-fashioned way for civilised coaches to behave,' I wrote. Tom read it and went ballistic. I had severely betrayed him. But it had been years ago; I pleaded I had kept mum when it mattered. And not only that, had Ireland not won later that afternoon by 21-12, precisely to prove my point? But he would not be placated.

I first joined the *Guardian* in March 1963 – 'We can offer £25 a week, increased by a guinea after six months' satisfactory service, pension scheme membership obligatory: Yrs W. Whittle, chief sub-editor.' Except for the free ticket from Cork every two years, the freemasonry of Twickenham was unbroachable for other internationals, but I somehow wangled entrance to the Calcutta Cup match on my very first Saturday off at the *Guardian*. England won 10-8 and I cannot recall any details (perhaps I was now grown up enough to join in with the all-day drinkers on that steep old Southern terrace). Not even, to be honest, Richard Sharp's mazy match-winning run to the far north stand in his final Five Nations game.

Later in the sixties I worked for half a dozen years for ITV Outside Broadcasts. My senior producer was the late Grahame Turner, not a rugby man but one who relished the craic all right (his son Martin is now, nicely, in charge of Sky's brilliant rugby output) and, pretending to examine the possibility of ITV dropping wrestling and outbidding BBC for its rugby contract, we took in no end of rugby weekend whoopees on full expenses. Mind you, the rugby itself was generally drear in the extreme – Scotland vs Wales in 1963 was a match of 111 lineouts and some whole seasons went past with fewer than ten tries scored.

By the time the extravagant resplendence of a new Welsh side blossomed to revolutionise the game at the beginning of the seventies I was back on the *Guardian* sports desk and soon began to carry the typewriter and tip the claret jug for our esteemed rugby correspondent, David Frost – more often than not in the company of that prince of coaches and regular *Guardian* contributor, Carwyn James. What luck. What larks.

And what men and what matches . . . the higgledy-piggledy memories tumble in of Dublin and Paris, days melting merrily into nights . . . Edinburgh in the whisky-warmed gloaming . . . old cabbage-green Twickers, strait-laced then and still last bastion of the upper-crust Forsytes . . . and, of course, Cardiff and its antique and then low-slung Arms Park, with its anthems and arias and maestros Gareth and Barry in concert, John Dawes conducting, JPR sounding defiance with the cymbals.

In that dragons' decade, even though Barry retired far too early, Wales won thirty-two and lost only seven championship matches (versus England's W31, L9 in the nineties). Looking it up more than a quarter of a century later, I see the Pontypool front row did not pack down together for Wales until 1975 – that was in Paris and also Ray Gravell's first cap. Ray sent a good-luck telegram to himself from his cat, Toodles, and afterwards the good fellow sought me out.

'How did I do, Frank, was I all right? Did I, you know, look the part?'

In those days the Welsh team would take in the Paris Opera the night before the match and, as often as not, the Folies Bergère the night after. That scarlet symphony came to an end in Dublin in 1978, a bloodbath of a match – I still wince at the memory of the hardest bone-on-bone collision of any I saw when JPR late-tackled the incomparable Mike Gibson. Afterwards Gareth came in, sat in shattered silence for ten minutes and announced that the French match in a fortnight would be his last.

The eighth Welsh grand slam was duly secured and the fabled Phil Bennett bowed out as well – end of an aura, end of an era, the most ravishing one of my time. Four or five winters I followed England cricket tours, and particular Saturdays in the tropics would have the rugby buff Ian Botham, Chris Old (brother of the England fly-half Alan) and me crowding round a crackly World Service radio for the commentary from Twickenham or wherever.

Alas for England, unable match after match to contrive a pass for David Duckham, the seventies had been pretty hopeless. Noble Bill Beaumont's side achieved the grand slam in 1980, after which the eighties were even more hopeless, Duckham's successor Rory Underwood receiving only two try-scoring passes in his first twenty games. The coach of the glorious 1980 aberration, Mike Davis, admitted: 'I've turned wine into water.'

In 1976 that carefree true amateur Andy Ripley smiled in a touchline interview and was heard, in soccer-speak, to explain away a Scottish try at Murrayfield: 'He just ran through me and next thing I knew it was in the back of the net, Brian.' Ripley never played for England again.

Seven years later another smiling chevalier, the captain Steve Smith, took his place on the skids when he came off after a 13-13 draw at Cardiff and cheerily told the microphone: 'A good away point, wouldn't you say, Brian?' Even in their upcoming seasons of Cooke, Carling and grand slams, Twickenham's 'old farts' continued to have difficulty in unbuttoning.

In many ways they still do. Meanwhile, as the Famous Five turned into a Sumptuous Six, the other nations' successive teams seemed unable, hard as they tried, to shake off their inborn national rugby characteristics . . . the Scots fast and fierce, over-committed and gloriously inconsistent; the French as hard as rock, but rock embellished with fantastical flying buttresses; the Welsh forever cresting the waves, braving the pressures of representing the national game; and Ireland, jaunty pessimism and jaunty optimism in turn – up and under, forwards, charge the line!

And here we go again. On with the motley and the merry dance . . . For some of us, poignantly, it is an emotional last waltz.

16 February 2002

LUKE HARDING

Football returns to Kabul

There is a moment when every nation becomes truly alive. For Afghanistan that moment finally arrived at 2.45 p.m. yesterday, when the striker Said Taher arced the ball over his head into what was, in effect, the England net. It was a goal of luminous, heart-stopping beauty, in the words of the former Southampton manager Lawrie McMenemy – who was watching wearing an Afghan woolly hat – a 'scissor-kick out of a fairytale'.

After twenty-three years of war and general mayhem, Afghanistan finally had something to cheer about. The 35,000-strong crowd went bonkers and surged briefly on to the pitch. It was not that football was coming home exactly, merely that the dark years of Taliban rule had been triumphantly dispatched by the beardless Taher's stunning masterpiece.

Yesterday's match between Kabul United and a team of mainly British soldiers from the 4,000-strong International Security Assistance Force (ISAF) took place at Kabul's national stadium. The grisly choice of venue was lost on no one. This was the place where the Taliban used to execute people or amputate their hands. Turbaned soldiers armed with Kalashnikovs would arrive with their prisoner in a pick-up truck before leading him towards the goal. They would open fire from a few feet away. British soldiers preparing the pitch discovered the remains of a heel and several other fragments of bone.

'We know that terrible things happened here. It made us more determined to come,' McMenemy said. 'My initial thoughts were trepidation and doubt. But I'm immensely happy now I'm here.'

Someone in government first came up with the idea for the match, but it soon acquired a surreal momentum of its own. McMenemy, together with the former England defender Gary Mabbutt, flew out to Afghanistan in a Hercules earlier this week to coach the ISAF. The Premiership trophy came too, together with four English referees. And so did the country's most famous Blackburn Rovers fan, Jack Straw.

The foreign secretary flew in to Kabul yesterday for talks with Afghanistan's new leader, Hamid Karzai, but failed to attend the game as planned for security reasons. Given what happened beforehand this was probably a wise decision.

News of the encounter swept the entertainment-starved city. It was inevitable that thousands of Afghan youths without tickets would turn up anyway. Well before kick-off they began clambering over the stadium's crumbling walls. When German soldiers repulsed them, they started lobbing bricks. Northern Alliance soldiers then fired into the air.

The riot never became too riotous; nobody produced a Kalashnikov, and by the time play eventually began at 2.30 p.m. everyone had settled down. It even began to rain – something of a miracle given the fact that Afghanistan has suffered four years of drought.

The Afghan team was made up of the best players from four local sides and they started well with Taher's spectacular opening goal. But the ISAF players were several inches taller than their Afghan counterparts and clearly better fed. They equalised during the first half, then managed to steal two late goals, finally overwhelming Kabul United 3-1.

The two sides then swapped shirts and posed for photos. Afghanistan had emerged from oblivion and was once more part of the world.

'It's been a great success. The highlight was their goal that nearly took the net off,' McMenemy said afterwards. 'The crowd roared. It was a terrific goal and the lad can dine out on it for ever.'

18 March 2002

MIKE SELVEY

Astle's match

It takes nothing away from England's 98-run victory in the first Test (a match, remember, which began with them losing two wickets in the first over and not a run scored) to say that in a truly memorable finale on Saturday the result paled into insignificance compared with the batting of Nathan Astle.

Like Dr Dolittle when confronted with a Pushme-Pullyou, the 3,000-odd people privileged to witness his staggering feat of hitting had never seen anything like it in their lives. Nor, for that matter – despite the sea change in approach that Test cricket seems to be undergoing thanks to the Australians – are they likely to do so again.

In a match that had already witnessed enough heroics from Nasser Hussain (who should have been Man of the Match, but was not), Graham Thorpe (who was), Matthew Hoggard and Andy Flintoff to satisfy anyone, Astle knocked them all into a cocked hat in 230 minutes of sustained savagery the like of which Test cricket has rarely experienced. While he was at the crease, and especially during a last-wicket stand of 118 in fifty-five blistering minutes with the injured Chris Cairns, even the impossible – 550 runs to win – seemed within his compass. As it was, the 451 New Zealand did make has been exceeded in the final innings of Test only by England's 654 for five in the timeless Test.

When Astle swept Ashley Giles for the single which took him to a double century even hardened cynics – those who watch the game for a living and have seen it and, in many cases, done it all – broke with habit, rose to their feet and applauded. This was the stuff of imagination – a vivid one at that – and mere figures, bewildering as they are, can scarcely do justice to what will be recorded, in a world where 'great' is often little more than average and 'awesome' is barely good, as genuinely great and awesome.

But the bare bones are still instructive: Astle made 222 from 167 balls and no batsman in Test history has scored more than that in a losing cause, never mind faster. His 200, from 153 deliveries, made him, by a hardly credible fifty-nine balls, the fastest, in those terms, to reach that landmark.

In South Africa the Australian Adam Gilchrist, who set the previous record only three weeks ago, could merely register his disbelief while Thorpe, whose own double century on Friday was the third fastest on record at the time, now seems pedestrian.

Had there not been delays while two lost balls were replaced, he would certainly have beaten the record of 214 minutes that Don Bradman required to reach 200 during his triple century against England at Leeds in 1930, and the Don would certainly have seen more bowling. Astle produced 28 fours and 11 sixes, the latter figure beaten only by the Pakistani Wasim Akram's dozen against Zimbabwe at Sheikhupura in 1996–97.

What comes close to matching it? In recent times, perhaps, only some of Gilchrist's own incendiary efforts, Viv Richards' 56-ball hundred against England in Antigua sixteen years ago and Roy Fredericks' 169 for West Indies in Perth in December 1975 had the potential to stand comparison.

Astle's first century, from 114 balls, took 13 deliveries fewer than the one he scored in the final one-day international in Dunedin less than three weeks ago. But it was a mere hors d'oeuvre for the assault that was to follow. The next 50 came from 22 balls only; the one following that from just 17, the same number Sanath Jayasuriya took when making the fastest one-day half-century.

A new ball has surely never been treated to such indignity. Taken with New Zealand on 315 for eight and still light years away from their objective, the first seven overs yielded 95 runs, including a maiden over in which Andy Caddick took the ninth wicket. Hoggard deployed his fielders in a revolutionary new-ball setting – to be known henceforth as 'The Hoggard' setting, with three slips and the rest on the fence – but still went for 18 runs off the first over and 23 off his next before being withdrawn.

At the other end, successive deliveries from Caddick were hit for 4, 6, 6, 4, 6, 6, 6, taking the gloss off his six-wicket haul. Astle, we know, has an eagle eye and wonderful co-ordination, and he pulled and he drove with 100 per cent commitment. But above all, and most memorably, he ran down the pitch and just belted the length ball back over the bowler's head.

Astle was, he said afterwards, 'in the zone', that state of nirvana when athletes believe that they can fly beyond the bounds of what is possible. Twice, during the assault on Caddick, the ball disappeared over the stands never to be seen again.

England appeared bewildered. Perhaps they were waiting for the inevitable, thinking it just could not last, though it so nearly did. Certainly, had it been a one-day match, the bowlers would have tried variations to break the rhythm.

Maybe it all happened so quickly they had no time to collect their thoughts. When he finally tried a slower ball, Hoggard, back on, claimed the final wicket and sanity was restored.

8 April 2002

MARTIN KELNER

The Grand National on the box

Although the BBC's coverage of the Grand National was, as always, pretty exhaustive, one extraordinary innovation we were promised failed to materialise.

'Over the next two hours', said Sue Barker on *Grandstand*, 'we will hear from the trainers, the jockeys, and the horses.'

Good, I thought. If we are going to have to listen to a lot of anthropomorphic guff about these horses' personalities, how such and such a horse is a game little battler and so on, it is only right that the animals themselves should be allowed a word or two. Why not get some really insensitive interviewer – Peter Sissons, possibly – to ask them if they are aware there is a possibility they might fall over and injure themselves, and then be shot dead?

'No, come on, you're joking. They wouldn't do that to us. They love us. They've been stroking my head all morning, and shining up my arse so I'll look nice in the paddock. They'd never shoot us.'

'No, really,' Peter might say. 'Bullet right through the head. "Go ahead, Dobbin, make my day," and the next thing you know you're Pritt stick.'

How would the equine interviewee reply?

'Ah well, in that case I might change my strategy. You know all that stuff about my never knowing when I'm beaten? Well, forget all that. What I might do is take it nice and steady, and then after a decent interval, say at the third or fourth fence, mysteriously refuse. Because, frankly, I am not ready yet to play my part in the adhesive industry.'

On which subject, why horses? Who first discovered they were sticky? As the comedian Jerry Seinfeld asks in his act: 'Was it some guy in a stationery store who saw a horse going past, and suddenly stopped in his tracks and thought, "Hey, wait a minute – you could be glue?"'

As it turned out, the horses obeyed tradition and disappointingly allowed their human keepers to speak on their behalf, so I can only assume that what Sue meant to say was that we would 'meet' some of the trainers, jockeys and horses, which indeed she did say later in her introduction.

If Sue was a little less sure-footed than usual at the start of *Grandstand* (although still more sure-footed than Wicked Crack, my unjustified belief in which animal some of the proceeds of this column will go towards financing), it was understandable after an opening sequence that seemed about as steady and rock solid as Garry Flitcroft's marriage.

There was a moody pre-credit sequence of horses being prepared for the big race, followed by a bit of a scripted intro from Sue, and Clare Balding, standing in front of the statue of three-time winner Red Rum, describing it as 'an image captured here for eternity to treasure and inspire'. All of which was perfectly fine. But then came the opening titles, which I think were meant to be a montage of golden Red Rum moments, but which for the first ten seconds, on my TV at least, were colour bars decorated with the slogan 'Aintree'. With the full-on vituperation Sue will have been privy to via her earpiece, it was hardly surprising she was thrown sufficiently to believe that talking horses might be next on the agenda.

This kind of live broadcasting is, of course, notoriously difficult to do, which is why Eamonn Holmes is worth however many millions he is to GMTV, despite presiding over possibly the dumbest show on television, and why ITV was so desperate to lure Des Lynam from the BBC. The good news is if you are not particularly good at it, nobody shoots you. You can just go back to writing your newspaper column, like Richard Littlejohn.

Des, I thought, was always at his best on Grand National day. Admittedly, it was easier for him. He just put on a suit, trimmed his tache, and knew that people like me were unlikely to comment too much on what he looked like. Sue and Clare have the added pressure of choosing the right outfit for the occasion. For the record, Clare went for a long black coat, rather like Clint Eastwood from his *Pale Rider* period, over a pair of black trousers, a selection that was both practical and in keeping with the *Daily Mail* dress code at this sad time. Sue was rather more daring, in a cream-belted jacket made out of some shiny material. She looked slightly futuristic, a little like Jenny Agutter in *Logan's Run*.

In as much as I am qualified to pronounce on such matters, they both looked lovely. My quibble is with the breathless, slightly frantic nature of their presentation. There is such drama in the race itself, it seems unnecessary for Clare to be always dashing about all over the place sticking microphones under the noses of trainers. I am sure Des just used to stand there and wait for people to come to him.

And what is it with Sue and the inappropriate laughter? I have mentioned before how on *A Question of Sport* she always seems to be cracking up over something that is not at all funny, and here she was at it again, punctuating her interviews with nervy laughter. She met her match, though, in the winning trainer Nigel Twiston-Davies. However much Sue chuckled, guffawed, and grinned, he remained as morose as someone who had just put a tenner on Wicked Crack. She really would have been better off interviewing the horse.

13 April 2002

MARK LAWSON

Beckham's foot

In 1738 the English seafarer Robert Jenkins publicly displayed the severed ear which he claimed had been cut off by Spanish coastguards. Such was the propaganda impact of the pickled body-part that the prime minister was forced to declare war on Spain.

Should any modern British politician wish to start a conflict against Spain or Argentina in the near future, they need simply wave in public places the x-ray of the England captain's metatarsal, cracked by a challenge from Deportiva La Coruna's Argentinian international Aldo Duscher. The Battle of Beckham's Foot would soon overshadow the War of Jenkins's Ear.

Any extraterrestrial filing a report on the English part of planet Earth this week might reflect on the odd relationship which this people seem to have with their bodies. Only twenty-four hours after huge crowds gathered in the capital to express grief that a heart had stopped beating after 101 years, newspapers were ringing up archbishops and asking them to pray that a small bone in a 26-year-old's foot might heal by 2 June.

Those who are not English or football fans must feel today much as republicans did last week. And, even to a lover of the game, these days in which everyone is suddenly a foot-doctor feel strange and medieval. Since television money made top footballers a new social grouping – boys earning millions as soon as they leave school – there's been much debate about what soccer heroes represent. Are they the new pop stars or an alternative aristocracy?

Since the Argentinian hacked at David Beckham's chances of making England's World Cup squad, the proper comparison for his status has seemed somewhere between saint and head of state. If the parallel with canonisation seems too much, who are the only other figures in history whose tiniest bones have been the subject of such reverent attention?

Just as Catholic worshippers pray to St Bridget's shinbone or St Anthony's ring-finger – preserved behind bullet-proof glass in some European cathedral – so now the dreams and hopes of English football supporters focus on a little chip of calcium. Indeed, Beckham's case is more remarkable because his bones have become sacred relics even while he is still using them. When he eventually comes to write a final testament, he will surely have to make arrangements for that left second metatarsal to go to the Football Association museum.

A saint, then, but also one who happens to be head of state. The tense analysis of statements from the hospital – members of the public sending in folk remedies or anecdotes about family members with the same complaint – recall the atmosphere in some frail and threatened nation as the news comes from the palace or the dacha that the State's best surgeons are gathering in frowning groups. These metaphors from monarchy and religion may seem mocking but – while Beckham's toe-fracture is a mere footnote against the news, for example, from the Middle East – the reverence and tension over his tootsies are not, in terms of English football, an over-reaction. Just as the peasants hearing of the king's illness fear that their leader is their nation, so Beckham has come to be the England football team: Henry V in shorts, and with a deal to endorse sunglasses.

Although, in medical terms, it's better to break a foot than a leg, this injury is especially vicious because it strikes directly at the point of all the money and the fuss. David Beckham has, in football parlance, 'lovely feet'. Television pictures are too flat to represent the true flight of the ball, but watching Beckham live you see his extraordinary caressing connection with the ball, a contact for which the words 'kicking' and even 'passing' are too tough. As the name of the game suggests, football is about the feet, but Beckham's are not just the ends of his legs – they're a legend.

The incident also reminds us of how literally fragile a top football career is. While the wages paid seem objectively ridiculous, football, like motor racing, is a profession in which talk of an 'annual' salary is crazily ambitious. A player on a million a year knows that his fitness may not last even through the first twelve months of banking those big cheques.

One of the greatest modern players, Ronaldo of Brazil, has scarcely played during what should have been the four peak years of his career because of successive injuries. Because the game entails kicking at a ball which is likely to be close to some of the most fragile bones in the human body, football is the cruellest part of the entertainment industry in this respect. Imagine Madonna developing terminal laryngitis after one Number One hit, or Julia Roberts being struck down with 100 per cent psoriasis after one movie. Every footballer knows that the equivalent could happen to their career in any match.

The kind of tackle which put Beckham in hospital is known as going over the top. To many, the subsequent coverage will have seemed the same. But, as with the death of the Queen Mother, for the people to whom it matters, it really matters. All our heroes have feet of clay, but our football heroes have feet of glass. When, as in Beckham's case, the glass is a work of art, there's real pain and poignancy in seeing it smashed. St Bridget's shinbone, pray for him.

10 June 2002

MATTHEW ENGEL

Nowhere to run, nowhere to hide for Tyson

If this marked the end of the road for boxing as a big-time global sport – and it just might – then the devilish old game went down in a blaze of something remarkably close to glory. As did its most devilish son. The morality tale took its course. Lennox Lewis – polite society's instrument of vengeance – savaged Mike Tyson in an awesome, breathtaking fight on Saturday night to retain the world heavyweight championship, as determined by pretty much anyone who cares or matters. For those who still lovingly maintain the annals, it will rank with the Thrilla in Manila and the Rumble in the Jungle: the Tempest in Memphis.

But it took two to make it awesome. Almost any other human on the planet would have crumpled in minutes against the ferocity of Lewis's assault, and it would have been remembered merely as a mismatch. Tyson stood there and took it. It was the eighth round before Lewis finally unleashed connecting punches Nos 191, 192 and 193 – according to the official stats – and the cumulative charges of dynamite did their work.

Tyson lay on the canvas, shielding his face with his glove while blood gushed from at least three openings, and his cornerman started to hug him like a baby.

And then, somehow, he rose. Suddenly he was no longer Tyson the Terrible. He was just a pantomime villain leaping out of character at the end of the show to reassure the children, beg their forgiveness and join in the closing singsong.

Until the fight began, Tyson and Lewis had to be kept separate by the preposterous sight of a dozen security men ranged diagonally across the ring, hands in front of their genitalia like a wall of defending footballers. Afterwards, there was no one between the two men except a little TV interviewer in a bow tie, and Tyson was stroking his conqueror's face and pleading: 'Thank you for the chance. Nobody wanted to give me a chance. I am thankful you gave me a chance. He knows I love him and his mother. I hope he gives me a fight one more time.'

What? Surely, even boxing isn't that desperate. This was an epic, but not as a contest. Compared with Lewis's 193 punches, Tyson landed 49. The shrewdies were proved right. The great boxer of the eighties died in jail a decade ago, if not before, a fact successfully concealed by the various hiatuses and horrors of his career.

Against an opponent as skilled and strong and relentless as Lewis, he had nothing to offer. And he knew it. Tyson did all his fighting at the press conference in New York six months ago. What he did on Saturday was take punch after punch without flinching: jab-jab-wallop, jab-jab-wallop. It was extraordinary. But the statue of Rameses II outside the Memphis Pyramid arena could have done the same.

He may still be a threat in taxis, hotel rooms and other confined spaces, but this marks the end of Tyson as a serious sportsman. From here there is only retirement or descent into some kind of novelty act: the World Wrestling Federation will probably be on the phone.

But even in Britain, with its loose attachment to Lewis, this was known as 'the Tyson fight'. People were still kidded by memories of his old grandeur, and also wanted to know what sexual, verbal or dental outrage might come next. And still the Pyramid was nowhere near sold out, something that routinely happens for college basketball.

That's why those who depend on boxing were desperate afterwards to talk up Lewis.

'I have never seen such a masterful performance,' said Jose Sulaiman, president of the World Boxing Council.

'There's never been a heavyweight this good,' insisted George Foreman. 'Never.'

Oh, come off it. The horrible truth is that this was a bonanza for everyone in the fight game, and nobody can envisage the next one. Lewis has never been much of a box-office name, but the rest of the heavyweight division would get few takers if the fights were broadcast even on we'll-pay-you-to-view. They need Lewis to stay on and star. Since he mentioned his 'legacy' afterwards more often than a morbid miser, it was unclear that he plans to be obliging.

And so boxing may have to turn away from the wider public and talk to itself for some time. But the memory of this night may be remarkably sustaining. Here was evidence that boxing does not have to be a sham or a farce. Here was the sight that has made it a compelling spectacle throughout history: two strong men, sweat glistening, urged on deafeningly by the crowd.

And Tyson's last stand went on seemingly for ever. By the third his face was bloodied. By the fourth there seemed no purpose in keeping the score. Lewis kept hitting him metronomically, like one of those nodding-donkey oil wells, each time drawing a barrel more of blood. Tyson would cover up, rather classically, looking as though it were the first minute and he was just contemplating his options.

By the seventh both Tyson's eyes were slits and he resembled some ancient statue of Buddha. Still he stood there, an improbable role model for non-violent resistance. When it finally ended, Lewis turned away to preen, not very graciously, and pound his chest repeatedly: Me, me, me, me, me, me, me, me, me!

This was Lewis's night and, as everyone can now see, it was always going to be. But in a curious way he was not the hero. The hero was that strange and ignoble man who has raged against the dying of the light longer and louder than anyone in sporting history.

8 June 2002

DAVID LACEY

England 1, Argentina 0

Once more England are a team of rising sons. For a moment last Sunday they gave a convincing impersonation of dropouts, but from now on no one will be fooled. Far from approaching a point of departure from the 2002 World Cup, Sven-Goran Eriksson's team now need only a point from Wednesday's final group game against Nigeria in Osaka to reach the second round. There they may face not France, as had been widely predicted, but Denmark or Senegal.

This singular turn of events is a result of a victory over Argentina in the Sapporo Dome last night, achieved by David Beckham's penalty late in the first half, which was as heartening as it was unexpected. The Argentinians went into the match with their status as one of the tournament favourites further strengthened by the imminent fall of France, the holders, and the likelihood of beating an England side which, in holding on for a 1-1 draw with Sweden, had made ineptitude a fine art. Now Argentina will almost certainly have to beat Sweden to avoid the premature exit so many were ready to reserve for England. Apparently there is no limit to the topsy-turvy antics of this World Cup.

Nevertheless England supporters would welcome nothing so much now as a period of pragmatic, predictable progress from their team. Just as it was wrongheaded to write off England so soon after yet another false start in a World Cup, so it would be rash now to declare them the new favourites on the evidence of one admittedly outstanding performance. Eriksson's side remain the strong outsiders they always were.

The important thing is that England, dear soppy old England, with their adherence to a foreign slayer of non-existent dragons, their enduring belief in a myth of football supremacy, their blindly loyal followers and their sceptical press, have faced down one of the world's best teams without blinking. The 5-1 victory over Germany in Munich was achieved with a ruthless display of attacking football which punished abysmal defending after Eriksson's own defence had looked flawed. For all-round quality last night's win was in a higher grade altogether.

It was born of the best defending seen yet from the centre-back partnership of Rio Ferdinand and Sol Campbell, backed once again by David Seaman's habit of making crucial saves at critical moments. More fundamental to the result, however, was the outstanding exhibition of defensive midfield play given by Nicky Butt, who with Paul Scholes managed to persuade Marcelo Bielsa to dispense with Juan Sebastian Veron for the second half and then prevented the replacement, Pablo Aimar, becoming the influence the Argentina coach was seeking.

From now on Butt is entitled to hear no more groans about Steven Gerrard and his groin. The pass from Butt which led to the shot Michael Owen poked through the legs of Walter Samuel midway through the second half, beating Pablo Cavallero only to see the ball hit a post, could not have been bettered by anyone. Butt and Scholes are now the springboard from which England can launch Owen at defences.

Mauricio Pochettino, all too aware of how the striker's speed and finishing power had torn Argentina apart in France four years earlier, was nervous of Owen all evening. Even as he was being sucked into giving away the penalty he was trying to withdraw the offending foot, which then took on a life of its own in the matter of Dr Strangelove's sieg-heiling right arm. When Eriksson took Owen off with eleven minutes to go so that Wayne Bridge could shore up the left flank against Aimar and the tireless Ariel Ortega, English hearts must have skipped a beat.

Tactically the change was vindicated because Argentina spent the remainder of the match entangled in a five-man midfield with Teddy Sheringham, who replaced Émile Heskey just before the hour, holding the ball up to offer England occasional relief. Yet Owen was still full of running, unlike Beckham who still looked short of match fitness.

Yet what a difference a win makes. England had come out of the draw against Sweden a team of disparate bits and pieces. Now the stray parts have fallen into place, most notably the much-travelled Trevor Sinclair, whose ability to run at opponents gave England natural width on the left for all but the first eighteen minutes.

Indeed, it could be argued that the biggest single contribution to England's success was the tackle that forced Owen Hargreaves, who had started brightly, out of the game at that point. The introduction of Sinclair enabled Scholes, who had started on the left, to be reunited with Butt in central midfield and from then on England's football swung easily between defence and attack.

If Argentina had more possession, England created more chances and Cavallero was the busier goalkeeper, making notable saves from Scholes and Sheringham. Argentina's forwards failed seriously to disturb England's defence and, when Ferdinand's one slip gave Pochettino a free header, Seaman blocked it on the line.

Ultimately Argentina's football looked one-dimensional. This was no accident because until relatively recently Eriksson, as a club coach in Italy, knew more about their players than he did about the squad he runs now. And it showed.

Argentina (3-5-2): Cavallero, Pochettino, Samuel, Placente, Zanetti, Simeone, Veron (Aimar, 46), Sorin, Gonzalez (Lopez, 63) Ortega, Batistuta (Crespo, 59). Bookings: Batistuta.

England (4-4-2): Seaman, Mills, Ferdinand, Campbell, A. Cole, Beckham, Hargreaves (Sinclair, 18), Butt, Scholes Owen (Bridge, 79), Heskey (Sheringham, 55). Bookings: A. Cole, Heskey.

Referee: P. Collina (Italy).

Man of the Match: Nicky Butt.

5 July 2002

EMMA BROCKES

In the land of Henmania

Nobody fancies Tim Henman. Even the teenage girls who have gathered in front of the screen on Henman Hill (the main hang-out for his Wimbledon fans) to scream their way through his quarter-final match against Andre Sa, are unmoved by his looks.

'His stomach's all right, but his nose scares me,' giggles Lara, fifteen, shaking her head. The bells on her red, white and blue jester's hat jingle.

'Don't be mean!' squeals her friend Claire. 'He looks like my brother.'

They have St George's flags painted on their faces, which are puckered with embarrassment. So why do they like him?

'We like him 'cos he's English!'

Henman, of course, is not just English, he is story-book English. He looks as if he has walked out of a poem by Rupert Brooke. Around the grounds of the All England club this week, mini versions of him could be seen swerving louchely about, hands in their pockets, proud graduates of the Home Counties tennis circuit. Their world – one of strictly enforced dress codes and intolerance of silliness – sits bizarrely alongside the excesses of the Henman fans.

'Is Henmania destroying Wimbledon?' sniffed Leo McKinstry in the *Daily Mail* this week, with reference to the fans' 'puerile yelling, cheering and jeering', when the more pressing question was surely: how does a man so seemingly devoid of passion inspire such buoyant responses in others?

Perhaps it's the primness of the setting, but the fanaticism of the Henman fans feels slightly forced, as if doing naughty things such as defying the no-banner-on-centre-court rule or shouting 'Go Tim!' in the library-like hush between points is as much of a thrill to them as watching the match. Some fans, even those who have queued all night to see him, filter their enthusiasm for Tim through a layer of sarcasm, the effortless irony of the middle-class teenager.

'Yeah right, I'm here 'cos I really love Tim's legs,' says Robert, sixteen, from north London. He is in the front row on centre court, and started queuing at 5 p.m. the previous night. He has written an alternative version to Kipling's 'If', which opens: 'If you can hold your serve when all about you / Are losing theirs and blaming the umpire . . .' He and his friends hold banners folded up like scrolls, which, when the steward isn't looking, they unfold and snap shut again before he turns around. The banners read: WE LOVE YOU TIM AND WE ALWAYS WILL.

Robert's friend Sam says, 'Tim is so arrogant,' to which Robert replies knowingly, 'He's not arrogant, he's quietly confident.'

Behind the boys sits Gillian, a childminder from Northamptonshire, and her daughter Louise. They also queued overnight for their £56 seats, even though Tim, admits Gillian, 'is a little bit boring'. Still, she's a big fan because 'he gives us something to be proud of'. Louise likes him because 'he's a solid British type, I like his net play'. They sometimes wish he would smile more, but, says Gillian, 'we've learned to love him'.

For many Henman fans, learning to love him means looking beyond his staring eyes, his US Marine's haircut and the humourless little punch in the air he does after scoring a point. When he retires from the tennis world he is guaranteed a lucrative second career on the motivational speaker circuit, lecturing executives on how to unleash the tiger within, or at least, how to channel it into a repertoire of tight-lipped gestures. The fans' love for him is based on a strange combination of admiration for his ability to win, and endearment at his one-of-us ability to lose.

'He shows a typical British vulnerability,' says Max, twenty-one, a philosophy student from Gloucestershire. 'He is a gallant loser.' How will Max celebrate if Tim wins today? 'I'll drive home in a slightly better mood than if he doesn't.'

'He's been playing like a complete pansy,' says Max's friend, Kate, fondly. A student on her summer break, she is employed at the tournament as a security guard.

While Anna Kournikova is mobbed every time she leaves the players' enclosure, Kate says Tim walks around more or less unmolested. His fans are not of the shirt-tugging, back-slapping, hands-on variety. While bearing all the trappings of crazy World Cup fans, 'Henmaniacs', like Henman himself, are essentially well mannered.

'We've had no grief,' says a policeman patrolling the grassy slope of Henman Hill like a park keeper. 'You don't get the lower grade of people in tennis, if I can say that. Tim is a good role model, although he might appeal more to young people if he changed his hairstyle and so forth.'

At lunchtime it starts to rain and over the seats on centre court rows of corporate umbrellas the size of satellites push open. The blazer brigade retreat to their enclosures. The fans on Henman Hill drape waterproof ponchos over their rucksacks and wander about like camels.

'This has been the year of the true fans, not all that lot in their hospitality tents,' says Jan, forty-three, a policewoman from Surrey.

Jennie, fifty-two, an accounts officer from Kings Langley, says, 'I think Tim's got less boring since he got married. Hopefully when the baby comes, he'll lighten up even more.' She is wrapped in a union flag left over from the jubilee. She doesn't support Greg Rusedski because 'he's not really British, is he?'

Some of Henman's fans found the World Cup too heady and think Wimbledon offers a more controlled environment for a nice bit of flag-waving.

'It's not so much about Tim Henman,' says Robert, thirty-eight, who got up at 4.45 a.m. to buy his tickets, 'it's about patriotism. But I like the fact he takes it seriously. It's his profession – why shouldn't he?'

At 4.30 there is a disturbance outside the players' enclosure. Kournikova is standing in the window, talking on her mobile phone and looking beadily down at the scrum of teenage boys screaming at her. A family of Henmaniacs dressed in red, white and blue look on disapprovingly. They have nets on their heads.

'We're called the Net Heads,' explains Janice. 'We do all the tournaments. We did the Davis Cup. We're from Atlanta, but we're supporting Tim today because he's the closest thing to an American we've got in the tournament. I think he's charming. You know, English.'

Sue, forty-four, runs a sports shop in Wiltshire. She is wearing a baseball cap decorated with Henman badges. She has posters of him in her home. She has flown her mother, Angela, all the way in from Gibraltar to see Tim play today.

'He's something for England,' she says. 'He pulled it off when he had that stomach bug.' What else does she like about him? She thinks for a while. 'He's very polite.'

Two elderly ladies are emerging from centre court, awkwardly eating slices of pizza. They stare, mouths agape, as the Net Heads walk by.

'Tim has a nice clean image,' says Marjorie, after recovering herself. 'He controls himself. He conducts himself very well under pressure. He's everyone's ideal son.'

Mary, her friend, thinks for a while and eventually says: 'I like Tim because in a funny way, he reminds me of Doris Day.'

25 March 2002

LETTER

Leg before wicket in Latvia

Stephen Moss recommends we should try explaining the l.b.w. law to a visiting Latvian ('What a turn-off', G2, 22 March). As possibly the only Latvian cricket-loving clergywoman, I have indeed spent many a happy fortnight explaining the intricacies of l.b.w., the reverse sweep, field positioning and googlies to visiting compatriots. Some of them have recovered quite quickly after only very short courses of anti-depressants. However, my proudest boast was the article on cricket that was refused by a reputable sports magazine in Latvia: they thought that I was simply making it all up and recommended that I resubmit it to a satirical journal.

Rev. Jana Jeruma-Grinberga, Enfield, Middlesex

LAST ORDERS

Austin, 26 July 2002

Notes & Queries: *On the M4 between London and Bristol there are several signs warning of deer. Has anyone ever seen one?*

Yes, I have seen at least one on that stretch of motorway. They are quite large, brown, reflective and have a picture of a deer on them.

Alex Boyle, Redland, Bristol

TIM RADFORD

Meet our ancestor

Three days ago, Toumai was a carefully guarded secret. Two days ago, Toumai became the world's most famous hominid. Toumai is the nickname given to the skull of *Sahelanthropus tchadensis*, a new candidate for the ancestry of humankind, who lived seven million years ago in what is now Chad, in the southern Sahara.

The steps that took a skull-shaped stone from an oblivion of wind-scoured sandstone to the global limelight are part of the greatest detective story ever told. They are also lessons in faith, human reason and blind luck.

First, the luck. That Toumai left behind even his head and jaw – researchers are sure he was male – as a calling card for posterity was a chance in a million. Wild things rarely die of old age. They tend to get eaten, then scavenged, and then decomposed by microbes. Every now and then a freak of burial means that as bone dissolves, the space occupied by the dissolving fragments of bone is slowly replaced by crystals of mineral, to leave a stone cast of what had once been living tissue embedded in rock far below the surface. That Toumai's fossilised skull was found was also a freak: millions of years of wind and water eroded and exposed the strata of fossils in which Toumai lay. A bit longer and the same process would have scoured Toumai and his mute companions to dust, and wiped away the evidence of their existence.

Then, faith. What brought a palaeoanthropologist to the scene of ancient death by sickness or misadventure began from a profound belief, dating only from the past 400 years, that some mysteries could be solved by systematically framing the right questions and then looking for the best answers. Isaac Newton was obsessed by the Bible, but he calculated the laws that keep the planets in motion around the Sun independently of God's will. The eighteenth-century biologists peered at the intricacies of creation, looking for God's signature, and instead began to see a web of interdependence from which life seemed to sustain itself. In the nineteenth century, natural historians and geologists began to accept that the Bible's version of history could not be literally true. They began to frame for themselves the great questions: where the universe came from, where life came from, where humans came from.

After Darwin, most churchmen accepted the evidence. Fossils were not sports of nature, bizarre patterns etched on the rocks by freak circumstances: they were the preserved remains of once living, but now long-vanished things. To accept this meant to accept change and renewal. The eruption of volcanoes, and the silts from floods, and the abrasion of wind and rain were enough to explain the rock formations. All it needed was time: epic quantities of time. The fossils in the rocks told a second story. During these aeons life also changed and renewed itself, long before humans appeared.

So, however special, humans were nevertheless animals, related in some way to other life that went before. Humans looked remarkably like the great apes, people reasoned: could there have been a common ancestor of man and the chimpanzees? And before that, a common ancestor of humans, chimps and gorillas? And long before that, a mammal forebear from which all the primates – including the Archbishop of Canterbury – are descended?

And then, the chain of reason. Darwin's theory of evolution by natural selection operating on random mutation was once provocative conjecture. Biologists have now confirmed the hypothesis again and again. But it left open the great problem of humanity: where did humans come from, why was *Homo sapiens* alone of its kind, and how did it get to be the only species known to be interested in its own evolution?

So began the ultimate manhunt: a search for creatures initially apelike, but increasingly human-looking, to install in a rogue's gallery of ancestors. But apes and ape ancestors lived in forests and forests mean moisture, and moisture means decay. Ape fossils are very rare. But at some point, the ape-human line walked on two feet, freeing hands for other things. The further its members walked from the tree cover, the better the chances of preservation.

And so, over the past seventy-seven years since the first discovery of an 'ape-man', the fragments have turned up: a skull here, a jaw there, a toe bone, a shin, a footprint, a collarbone, occasionally most of a skeleton. The evidence from the past two million years is quite good; the evidence from the five million years before that would fit into a set of Gucci luggage. That is why a complete skull from so long ago is such a dramatic find. Toumai's skull was found in the same bed as a distinctive set of mammal bones dating from seven million years ago: therefore, Toumai was part of the picture seven million years ago.

Toumai was one animal among scores of others living near a forested lake fringed by savannah and then desert. Toumai was not human, but there is enough about him that is human for humans to claim kinship. If he is an ancestor, then he is a remarkable one. Think about it: his descendants imagined him, then decided what he might look like, and then went looking for him. They identified his likely home in Africa, and found some of his younger, later, cousins – *Homo erectus*, Ardipithecus, the Australopithecines and so on – in the east of the continent. They knew there had to be an even older hominid, even more apelike, and yet still with human features. Some daring anthropologists began placing bets that if hominids existed in east and southern Africa, then they should have existed in west Africa too, and literally broke new ground. And on Thursday they announced they had struck gold, they had found something near the source, they had tracked the earliest hominid to his chance grave in a stony desert.

They used sophisticated physics to flash the news around the world in seconds. They used circling manmade satellites to bounce pictures of Toumai, and of his last resting place, into every home. Just think: Toumai could not have dreamed where his future lay, but his descendants all over the world – if humans are his descendants – have been able to look straight down the long tunnel of time, and catch a glimpse of him seven million years ago. They have done this using science, which has provided the greatest intellectual adventure of all time, precisely because it opens up all time itself to human inquiry.

That might be the most amazing thing about Toumai: that humans can peer into their own beginnings and see themselves emerging from the long dark night of the forest. The other amazing thing is that there are people in Britain – where the great achievements in physics and biology began – who are actually proud of not knowing anything about science at this level, and even a smaller number who choose not to believe in it at all.

29 April 2002

DAVID WARD

The Duke tells the ramblers: sorry

Rarely can so many rucksacks, cagoules, bobble hats and gaiters have been gathered in a gritstone quarry beneath a changeable Derbyshire sky. But suddenly the sea of Gore-Tex parted for a stooped and elderly figure wearing a long tweed coat and brown suede shoes. He leant heavily on a stick as he made his slow way to a marquee and settled into a plastic chair near the band. Andrew Robert Buxton Cavendish, the eleventh Duke of Devonshire and the biggest private landowner in the Peak District, had travelled from his stately home at Chatsworth to the village of Hayfield to make a public apology.

On 24 April 1932 his grandfather, the ninth duke, had set his gamekeepers on a bunch of trespassers who had dared to venture on to his grouse moors on Kinder Scout. Five of the trespassers were arrested and jailed for up to six months. At the weekend 1,000 ramblers gathered with their walking poles and map cases to celebrate in songs and speeches the seventieth anniversary of that mass trespass which led to the creation of Britain's eleven national parks and the recent Countryside and Rights of Way Act. They also wanted to hear what the 82-year-old aristocrat had to say.

He rose carefully to his feet and took the microphone. 'I am aware that I represent the villain of the piece,' he said with a smile that appeared to dissipate any lingering resentment against a toff. 'I am only too happy to take this opportunity to apologise for the conduct of my grandfather seventy years ago. The great trespass was a very shaming event for my family. But from that great evil and those appalling sentences has come great good.'

He said he loved to watch from his study window the ramblers who wandered across the park at Chatsworth, lovers of the countryside who caused no problems and left no litter. 'I like to think that I have tried to redeem that evil,' he added and then sat down to applause that was so long and so warm that you half expected him to take an acknowledging bow like a Branagh or a Rattle.

The writer Jim Perrin followed with a ringing eulogy to Benny Rothman – the five-foot rebellious motor mechanic who addressed the trespassers in this same quarry in 1932, led them up to Kinder, remained a passionate campaigner for access to the countryside and died aged ninety in January this year.

At one point Mr Perrin turned and shook the Duke of Devonshire heartily by the hand. It looked as if bygones were bygones.

But would the late Mr Benny Rothman, stomping across Elysium in his baggy khaki shorts, agree? Suddenly three geese crossed the quarry in a honking fly-past. Some took this as a sign of Mr Rothman's assent.

The ramblers joined writer and broadcaster Mike Harding to sing Ewan MacColl's 'Manchester Rambler' ('I may be a wage slave on Monday / But I am a free man on Sunday'), and then did the only thing they could on a day such as this: they went for a walk.

In a long crocodile of orange, blue, lovat and red, they wound past the reservoir and up towards the Kinder plateau, famous for its strange rocks, soggy peat and unpredictable weather. Many paused at William Clough, where the 1932 trespassers deviated from the official path and scuffled with the ninth duke's men.

And then the heavens opened. Over-trousers were pulled on and, after four weeks of a beautiful and untypical spring, life returned to normal in the Dark Peak.

26 June 2002

ROD LIDDLE

A symphony of silly signs

Look, I know there are some very grave things happening in the world, and that these are what should be concerning me today. But sometimes it is the little transgressions that niggle – and maybe in extreme cases, tip us over the edge. And in very extreme cases indeed find us, at the end, crouched nervously in Winchester town centre, dressed in combat gear and a balaclava, trembling slightly, with our fingers twitching on the trigger.

Let me explain. There is a large sign on the platform of Grateley railway station which says: WELCOME TO HAMPSHIRE WHERE PARTNERSHIP WORKS. What's that all about, then? What, exactly, does it mean? Is it implying that, three miles away in Wiltshire, partnership doesn't work and that consequently there are thousands of embittered people bemoaning the fact that their alliances foundered because they were forged under the jurisdiction of the wrong county council? And what sort of partnerships? Sexual? Financial?

And then travel west for eight miles and the sign at the next station says simply: SALISBURY. HOME OF JAMES HAY. Who the hell is James Hay – and how did he acquire such epic self-importance? I know now, after telephone calls, that 'he' is actually a pensions firm based in Salisbury – a city which is also, by the way, home to a glorious cathedral, the river Avon and at least one former prime minister.

What are your perceptions of Basingstoke? I don't want to prejudge, but you may well consider the town thoroughly forgettable, boring even. Will your appreciation of the place be altered by the sign there saying: WELCOME TO BASINGSTOKE. HOME OF WINTERTHUR LIFE INSURANCE? (This is a rhetorical question. You don't have to answer, really.)

We are assailed on all sides by gobbets of unnecessary, banal and self-aggrandising 'information'. I'm aware that the last two cases I've quoted are examples of advertising via corporate sponsorship, which is irritating. But it's not quite as simple as that. Everywhere, these days, seems to need some independent verification of its right to exist – as if it were insecure in its position as a place you might wish to visit for your own, private reasons. The assumption seems to be that the rest of us are too stupid to know why we're going somewhere and ignorant of what we might wish to see when we get there.

At Denmark Hill, south London, the station sign adds FOR KING'S COLLEGE HOSPITAL. Why? Is the suggestion that ill people should present themselves at Victoria and proceed to board Connex trains entirely randomly, in the hope that they might, at some point, chance upon a station with a sign advertising a hospital? Or is it for the merely curious – 'Hey, look . . . King's College Hospital. Shall we go have a mosey around?'

It is not the absurdities which annoy, but the subtext. Between entering Oxford Circus underground station and boarding a Central Line train I was submitted to a total of thirty-one written or spoken commands, injunctions or imprecations: in my inflamed, middle-aged psychosis, I counted them all. YOU MUST BUY A TICKET. STAND ON THE LEFT. DON'T LEAVE BAGS ON THE PLATFORM. MOVE FURTHER DOWN THE PLATFORM. MOVE RIGHT DOWN INSIDE THE CARRIAGE – and so on, and so on. Almost all of which are totally unnecessary unless you are a committed sociopath.

Some of it, I know, is down to a fear of litigation – 'They didn't tell me not to jump on the track. How was I to know my legs would be severed at the hip?' – but most is simply contempt for the public.

After purchasing my AK47 on the black market, I asked Hampshire county council in Winchester to explain the 'partnership' sign at Grateley. The council had apparently fitted some bike locks on the platform. Is that it, I asked?

'Well, it's in accordance with our local working practices,' said the press officer as I efficiently fitted a clip of ammo to the magazine.

4 May 2002

IAN JACK

On not throwing books away

'Books do furnish a room' – Anthony Powell, adapting an interior-design thought by William Morris. 'Books are a load of crap' – Philip Larkin, adapting nobody, so far as I can tell, other than the sour part of himself

Last weekend, 'sorting out my study' – as the excuse for my long absences from domestic life goes – I badly wanted to go along with Larkin. I have too many books. I have begun to hate their mess and reprimand ('You haven't read me in a long time,' or even, in the case of *Silas Marner*, 'You have never read me'). Many of them are crap. Don't even argue with the word. *Newman's Indian Bradshaw*, the issue of November 1976: how else could it be considered? Crap, crap, crap. Spine flaking, paper of the poorest, unbleached Indian stock: yellow, brittle, flecked with wood chips. Also an unquestionably utilitarian volume, soon surpassed by *Newman's Indian Bradshaw*, December 1976, and every monthly update of the Indian railway timetable in the twenty-six years since. Astonishing that it has been taking up shelf space in three different houses since the day it came back with me from Delhi, taking up valuable suitcase space (why?), in April 1977. Into the bin bag then; into the bin.

And yet, and yet. I opened it. A business card fell out: *H. M. Nandkeolyar, Factory Manager, Indian Linoleum Ltd, Budge Budge, nr Calcutta. Gram: Indoleum.* I must have met him, certainly at the linoleum factory (which I remember looking round) and perhaps initially on a train ('If you want to know about lino, I'm your man. A telegram will always find me. Please take my card').

I turned a few brittle pages. An interesting book, *Newman's Indian Bradshaw*. In 1976, they still had steam ferries across the Ganges at Patna; veg and non-veg catering rooms were available at Bandel Junction; the Upper Indian Express took an age to reach Upper India. I remembered being in one of its compartments a few days after the monsoon had broken, sticky with sweat and glad for the rain through the open window.

I put *Newman's* back on the shelf. Next, *Of Human Bondage* by W. Somerset Maugham, a nice hardback edition with William Heinemann's little windmill on the title page: first published 1915, this edition 1934. This was one of the first grown-up novels I ever read, but what could I remember of it? Young doctor with club foot has difficulties with girls – and even that memory may come from the film, with Kim Novak as the soiled and sullen flirt. I read a few sentences. 'He drew her into the darkness of the hedge.' Very good. The word 'sordid' appeared more than once. I could see the book's appeal to my fifteen- or sixteen-year-old self – a club foot in the head – and even its appeal to me now, though I shall never read it again. I have still to read all of Philip Roth. Then there is the vexing question of Proust.

Still, I put it back on the shelf. I remembered buying it from a second-hand shop called MacNaughton's in Leith Walk, Edinburgh. As a schoolboy I went there on many winter Saturday afternoons. You went down the stairs from the street to the basement, and there were all these books being warmed by a small electric fire. MacNaughton himself sat at the back and smoked, grimly. The silence was broken only when he announced the price – 'one and six' – and crackled the brown wrapping paper. Climbing back to the street again – corporation buses, men on their way to watch Hibernian FC – was like rising from the dead. *Of Human Bondage* was the key to that time, rather than the time it described.

The next pile was easier: Ed McBain, P. D. James, *The Year Book to Pakistan* (1978), all dumped in the culling bag. But then a strange book with green cardboard covers: *A Librarian Looks At Readers* by Ernest A. Savage, the Library Association, 1947. My name and a date, December 1962, was written inside. I had no memory of buying it, or of reading it. This might be because it belongs to an era of stultifying disappointment, when I left school and went to work in a library and thought, aged seventeen, that life had ended. How had I got this job? Because I didn't have (as the Peter Cook sketch has it) 'the Latin'. And why did that matter? Because in 1962 you needed Latin (higher Latin, in fact) to do honours English at Edinburgh University. So, couldn't I have done some other course? Probably, but as I told my encouraging English teacher, 'I want to be Kenneth Tynan.'

Instead I stamped books in the same town where I'd gone to school, often books borrowed by the people I'd gone to school with, who were now cheerfully kitted out in university scarves and possibly on the way to being Kenneth Tynan in my place. It was a fine old library in Dunfermline, where Andrew Carnegie was born and therefore generously endowed by him. The shelves were of carved wood, the halls and staircases of stone. Every morning we would get the fiction shelves back into A-to-Z order, each spine lined up with the shelf edge, and then move on to the more difficult non-fiction, arranged decimally by Dewey. Miss Roger, the librarian, would then make a brief tour of inspection, the janitor would lift the rope, and borrowers would be let in.

I brooded and tried to see my job as moral uplift. One day a maid came in from one of the big houses in the smart end of town (a maid – incredible!) and said that the lady she worked for wanted 'another of those novels about horse racing'. This was pre-Dick Francis; she probably meant Nat Gould. I gave her *Esther Waters* by George Moore, which I must have come across in MacNaughton's shop and persuaded myself was enjoyable and 'art', but it came back swiftly the next day.

Slowly, over the next year, books became . . . books, and not sacred objects. The janitor took me out for a drink and wondered if I wanted to join the Freemasons. At mealtimes we would smuggle in fish suppers and eat them at the far end of the reserved stock (books available only on request), where Havelock Ellis and *Ulysses* were kept and where there was a window that looked out on the graveyard of Dunfermline Abbey. But when I read somewhere that 'libraries breed meek young men' that was the beginning of the end of them for me, even though the statement was far from true and came, probably, from some Victorian Muscular Christian.

I still haven't decided what to do with *A Librarian Looks At Readers*. I should chuck it. On the other hand, surrounded by all these piles – books to be kept, books to be stored, books of uncertain destiny – I've come round entirely to the idea of libraries. Such sensible institutions. You borrow a book, you read it, which is what it exists for, and then you take it back. Otherwise, what are they? Memento vitae, furniture, ornament. This is the only spirit for the black bin bag.

© Ian Jack, 2002

22 July 2002

STEPHEN MOSS

The *Guardian* seizes a Spanish island

The invasion was planned for first light, but the Spaniards may have got wind of it. Our luggage – I am travelling with a courageous photographer – had mysteriously disappeared en route to Ibiza and was thought to be in Barcelona. It contained my inspirational Walter Raleigh outfit, a large union flag, a stout pair of boots and two boules. All we had left for the attack was the Walter Raleigh plumed hat, a megaphone, a tin of Harrods treacle biscuits, a stilton cheese, a die-cast model of a Grenadier guard and a pot of thick-cut marmalade. This was a sticky situation.

Our démarche had been hatched in response to Spanish hypocrisy: how can it go on harassing Gibraltar when it refuses even to discuss the status of Ceuta and Melilla, its enclaves in Morocco? Its storming of Parsley Island, a few hundred metres off the Moroccan coast, was the last straw. It was time to give the Spanish a taste of their own medicine.

Half a day's meticulous planning had gone into the attack. The *Guardian*'s fashion editor remembered seeing an uninhabited island about 400 metres off Playa d'en Bossa, a beach on the eastern coast of Ibiza. This was to be our target: Spanish for eight centuries, soon to be British. Raleigh, Drake, Moss – the names resonate, one golden Elizabethan age speaking unto another. My breast, even without the Walter Raleigh outfit, was swelling with pride.

We reach Ibiza airport (minus vital luggage) at midnight, and the woman on the information desk tells us about the island. Isla de las Ratas in Spanish, Illa de ses Rates in Catalan, Island of the Mice. She suspects nothing, despite the Walter Raleigh hat and the megaphone. The Island of the Mice will soon be ours.

But not that soon. At daybreak, there is still no sign of the luggage, which is now expected in the evening. The symbolic importance of the Raleigh outfit is such that we must delay. We recce the beach instead, which by eleven is already full of topless women turning lobster red.

The Island of the Mice is at the northern end of the beach. My heart leaps when I see it. But how do we reach it? There are children playing in the sea on inflatable alligators. Would they carry the weight of the boules, cameras and boots? It seems unlikely. There are several upturned rowing boats on the beach, but stealing one would be risky. We settle on a pedalo, available for €15 an hour.

The problem is that we want one for the duration of the mission. This is an occupation, not a visit. The man who looks after the pedaloes speaks no English, but a Frenchman called Renard translates for us. After half an hour of haggling, we have secured unlimited use of the pedalo for €250 plus my passport (recoverable, I hope). We tell them we want to stay on the island overnight to photograph the sunrise – Martin (hereafter called 'M.') is compiling a book called *Sunrises of the World*. They believe us.

M. goes back to see whether the Raleigh outfit has arrived from Barcelona. I face an arduous afternoon of swimming, sunbathing, pizza-eating and beer-drinking in ninety-degree heat. I buy shorts and flip-flops, have my hair cut short and get a scorpion tattooed on my shoulder to blend in with all the other British men on the beach. I also buy a butterfly net, so we can use the bamboo stick as a flagpole.

M. arrives with the luggage at 9 p.m. This has allowed too much time for San Miguel drinking for the security of the expedition. The security of the pedalo also gives cause for concern, since it is carrying two boules, a camera bag, a holdall, a shoulder bag, a megaphone, a case of San Miguel, a stilton cheese, a bottle of water, several pounds of tomatoes, a large packet of salami, a tin of treacle biscuits, a union flag (with flagpole) and a die-cast model of a Grenadier guard. We set off at 9.35 in fast-fading light and pedal furiously, ignoring the fact that the pedalo is listing badly to port (my side). This may be the first ever invasion undertaken by pedalo, though there is evidence that the Romans used a primitive version against Carthage in the second Punic War.

We have to follow a route mapped out by buoys; the distance to the island is about 1,000 metres. What begins as a gentle swell increases as we get further out, and the pedalo rocks back and forth alarmingly. But it is too late to turn back. The die is cast, and not just for the Grenadier guard.

We reach the island at 9.58 (I log the moment for future historians). It is dark by now and we have to steer round to the south of the island, avoiding rocks and dense seaweed, to find a place to land. We find a cove and guide the pedalo gently in, then pull it up on the beach and tie it to a rock. We stumble up a cliff, taking the baggage with us. I'm scared of heights, and so only carry the megaphone; M. carries everything else. I tell him he will get at least a CBE; I have my eye on a knighthood.

There is no one about, not even a mouse, and we hoist the flag and celebrate with beer, salami, tomatoes, cheese and treacle biscuits. The United Kingdom has a new chunk of territory; Spain has a bloody nose; and I have a headache caused by the beer and the furious rocking of the pedalo. It is time to sleep, secure on this fresh patch of British soil.

It is a clear night, though colder than we expected. There is a three-quarter moon, a richly starry sky and a lovely stillness, broken only by the charter flights coming in low over our heads every ten minutes and the pounding techno music from the Bora Bora club across the bay. By 4 a.m. all is quiet, but there is now a dampness in the air and every so often we have to walk around to prevent hypothermia.

We sleep fitfully until dawn breaks soon after six, waking to find large numbers of ants in the remnants of the salami. The lizards, which rise with the sun, prefer the treacle biscuits. Daylight gives us our first chance to explore the island in detail. It is bigger than we had thought – about 150 metres long and 90 metres wide. This is no mere crag in the sea, but a strategically significant land mass. Suddenly a peerage seems possible.

The island has one sheer cliff face, jutting out to sea, but the rest is gently sloping and covered in scree. There is some scrubby gorse and a few wild flowers. We had been wondering what to call the newly annexed island: Elizabeth (too many of those already); Blair (absolutely not); Rusbridger (it would be an honour, sir); Rosemary, Tarragon, Turmeric, Thyme (a nicely topical touch)? But then it hits us – actually, the smell hits us first. Stilton – the mice would be replaced by a quintessential British cheese.

I call the Foreign Office in London to tell them the joyous news – that Britain has a new dependency. It is 7.30 on a Saturday morning and the sleepy duty officer, far from being elated, sounds rather bemused. 'You couldn't call back on Monday, could you?' she says. Is this the stuff of which empires are made?

She puts me through to a press officer, who refuses to give me any guidance.

'I don't think there's a Foreign Office line on this,' he says, stifling what sounds suspiciously like a laugh. 'Look, it's a bit early – could you try after 10 a.m.?' This is all very depressing. Would Raleigh have captured Virginia, or Drake seen off the Armada and been British crown green bowls champion, if they had insisted on having a lie-in at weekends?

A couple of hours later I try again. This time the Foreign Office has its line worked out.

'I'm afraid you're about a hundred years too late,' says a jovial spokeswoman. 'We are more into sharing rocks these days than owning them. You're out of fashion.' (I'm not sure she would have said that if she could have seen me in my green pantaloons, doublet and plumed hat.)

'So if the Spanish were willing to share the island, would you be interested?' I ask.

'Quite possibly,' she says. 'It would be a matter for discussion between the foreign ministers. What's the island called?' she asks.

'Stilton,' I reply proudly. 'As in cheese. Any chance of assistance in defending the island?' I ask.

'Nothing to do with us,' she says. 'That's the MoD.'

'But you could have a word in their ear,' I suggest. 'What about that destroyer that was stuck on rocks? That must be free by now and the captain would welcome the chance to redeem himself.'

'Sorry, you'll have to speak to the MoD yourself,' she says. And she is gone, probably to a fawning ambassadorship.

I get through to a gruff-sounding official at the MoD, who has none of the charm of his Foreign Office counterparts.

'If you want to declare the island British sovereign territory, that's up to you,' he says.

'But we need your help to defend it,' I bleat. 'We've only got two boules, a half-eaten stilton cheese, a jar of marmalade and a die-cast model of a Grenadier guard. A couple of Tornados would make all the difference.'

'We can't do anything without Foreign Office say-so,' he explains. 'Sorry, it's a political decision.'

Annexation is a lonely business. It also crosses my mind that Raleigh was eventually executed. This may, though, have been a merciful release: sitting in the midday sun in a sweaty doublet and thick pantaloons is a nightmare. But I must press on: perhaps Spain will accept an accommodation, the diplomatic track suggested by the Foreign Office.

I call the office of diplomatic information, but no one there speaks English (how convenient!). I phone the civil guard in Ibiza to open talks, but no one there speaks English either. I can't even make it clear to them that Britain has established a strategically important base 400 metres off the coast of Ibiza, almost opposite the Cockney Rebel pub. The interior ministry, defence ministry and central police department all appear to have knocked off for the weekend. Spain is ripe for the taking: an Anglo-Moroccan expeditionary force could be in Madrid by tomorrow if the Foreign Office and MoD would buck their ideas up.

I am just pondering my next move when I hear a shriek. M., who has been collecting plant samples, has tripped and gashed his hand on a rock. An all too common casualty of war, I tell him. But I suppose the wound must be treated. We gather the equipment, ditch the stilton (which by now can be smelt over most of the eponymous island), and prepare to refloat the landing craft. But not before we leave behind our secret weapon: Gordon the Grenadier.

We encase Gordon in a small fortress built of stones, so that only the top of his bearskin is showing, and beside him, hidden beneath a rock, leave the following note: *Here stands Gordon the Grenadier, protecting Her Majesty Queen Elizabeth's sovereign territory of Stilton Island, taken from the Spanish by force of arms on 20 July 2002. God bless Queen Elizabeth.*

Gordon is unlikely ever to be disinterred and, as far as we are concerned, while he remains on Stilton Island it is rightfully British. We have a new territory in the Mediterranean, to set alongside Gib, and Spain has a new diplomatic headache. Your move, amigos. No doubt Peter Hain will be on the blower later today to discuss possible quid (or even euro) pro quos on joint sovereignty.

POSTSCRIPT

8 June 2002

ALAN RUSBRIDGER

Celebrating our yesterdays

Newspapers have a double life. On the one hand they date more quickly than milk and stale more quickly than bread. On the other hand – see the facsimile Coronation issues from 1953 that we published last week – they provide a fascinating dipstick into history.

Most journalists are too busy on the next edition to worry too much about preserving the past. As a result, many newspaper offices casually discard material that might in future be of huge interest, if not of historical importance.

The American novelist Nicolson Baker has recently written a book about his personal mission to save newspapers from being junked by libraries. He savaged the British Library for trying to ditch 60,000 volumes of old newspapers.

The *Guardian* is no exception. Over the years the paper has moved, grown and expanded. Along the way it never had the time, space or resources systematically to collect and catalogue its history. Much has been saved – in assorted libraries, warehouses and (thanks to the foresight of the company's transport manager, John Dowling) in a loft above a garage in Salford.

Next week all that changes when the *Guardian* opens The Newsroom, an archive and educational centre across the road from the newspaper office in Farringdon Road in London established by the Scott Trust, owners of the *Guardian*.

The *Guardian* is unique. Since its first edition in May 1821 (the day Napoleon died) it has been in the same family ownership – the Taylor and Scott families. Also housed in the new building – a bonded warehouse converted by Allies and Morrison – will be the archive of the *Observer*, the world's oldest Sunday newspaper.

There will be more than 58,000 editions of the two papers in bound volumes. Also stored in archival conditions will be a million photographs – including the fifty-year archive of the *Observer* photographer Jane Bown – as well as bound volumes, diaries, letters and notebooks.

We have arranged reciprocal lending rights with the John Rylands Library in Manchester, which has much material from the *Manchester Guardian* up to 1971. There is also an Epstein bust of the *Guardian*'s former editor, C. P. Scott, which has not been seen by the general public since it was cast in the twenties.

The intention is to use the collection not simply as an historical resource – though it will be that, with a small reading room for anyone wanting to consult back numbers or documents – but as a centre for schools and a resource for journalism and photography. A modest café will provide refreshment. In addition to a ninety-seat lecture theatre, there are two exhibition areas and a state of the art school room, wired up with the latest IT and white boards by Apple Macintosh and run on Adobe software. The centre will employ two teachers who will provide a range of curriculum-based programmes concentrating on issues such as citizenship.

Visiting school groups will get the opportunity to lay out their own front page using a mini-publishing system based on the one which produces the *Guardian*. Two archivists will begin the mammoth task of cataloguing the ever-increasing holdings and making them available for exhibition and research. The centre director is Luke Dodd, who, during the mid-nineties, designed and curated the Famine Museum in Ireland.

Seeking to preserve the newspapers' pasts is not to nurse great pretensions about the historical importance of the *Guardian*'s – or anyone else's – journalism. Nor is it to undervalue the role of the reporter, or a newspaper.

Courts of law and historians both know the value of contemporaneous evidence. It is no accident that Simon Winchester was asked to testify to the Bloody Sunday inquiry about what he saw that day in Derry while working for the *Guardian*. Or that Ed Vulliamy and Maggie O'Kane have been asked if they would testify at the international criminal court at The Hague as to what they saw in Bosnia and Kosovo. Or that Chris McGreal has been asked to give evidence at the Rwanda tribunal against a cabinet minister accused of genocide.

Regardless of the rights and wrongs of journalists testifying in courts, the very fact that their evidence is so often sought speaks to the role of the reporter, and the value of contemporary eyewitness testimony.

In a prescient introduction to the *Bedside Guardian* in 1959, Alistair Cooke acknowledged the role of the reporter in these terms: 'Let us honour . . . the writer who must say what is on his mind against the twilight's deadline, the professional scribbler who stands or falls by his ability to see clearly and write fast . . . There is less difference than the intelligentsia would have us believe between the daily grind of the "serious" novelist or biographer in his cloister and the reporter filing his daily dispatch, sometimes with the wind of the world in his face.'

He also went on to predict that future historians would indeed want to consult the works of his contemporaries on the paper. 'It may be that we should leave the excavation of the *Guardian*'s deposits to a later generation.'

The two papers have, between them, bred some of the greatest and rightly famous bylines in British journalism – Scott himself, Cardus, Arlott, Cooke, Tweedie, Frayn, Cameron, Ransome, Masefield, Philip Toynbee, A. J. P. Taylor, Koestler, Orwell, Clive James, Julian Barnes, J. L. Garvin, Anthony Sampson, Robert Harris, Ian Aitken, Philip Hope Wallace, Peter Jenkins, John Cole, R. H. Tawney, Muggeridge, Walter Lippman, Mary Stott and so on up to the present generation.

They are also papers which, as much as any, recognise that most journalists – indeed, some of the greatest journalists – are not great stars, or indeed known at all by the general public. The punctilious sub-editor, the layout genius, the anonymous desk editor, the web page producer, count as much as the writer with the picture byline. And they recognise that it is through their collective effort they produce papers which are today known throughout the world. That was what C. P. Scott celebrated in his famous essay on journalism in 1921, when he wrote about how the character of a newspaper was 'a slow deposit of past actions and ideals'.

It is that spirit which The Newsroom will honour and, we hope, pass on to future generations of journalists and readers.

For further information please visit guardian.co.uk/newsroom.

*The*Guardian

Also available from Guardian Books

To order any of the featured books please
call the credit card hotline **+44 1903 828 503**
or write to PO Box 4264, Durrington, Worthing BN13 3TG, UK

The Guardian Media Guide 2003

Lists the addresses, phone numbers, websites and key personnel for companies in every sector of the media.

'The most comprehensive in the business ... an essential on your desk'   Jon Snow, presenter of Channel 4 News

£17.99
1 84354 014 2

Playing to the Gallery

Parliamentary Sketches from Blair Year Zero

SIMON HOGGART

The hilarious new collection of sketches by the wittiest of all writers on parliament.

'The P. G. Wodehouse of Westminster'   P. J. O'Rourke

'No parliamentary sketch-writer has ever been funnier'
Clive James

£7.99
1 903809 66 5

Hoo-Hahs and Passing Frenzies

Collected Journalism 1991–2001

FRANCIS WHEEN

Brings together the best of Wheen's collected writings from the *Guardian*, *Observer* and magazines such as the *Modern Review*.

'I'll read anything by Francis Wheen'   Nick Hornby

'Witty, intelligent and possessed of much originality of thought'   *Daily Telegraph*

'An anthology of characteristically acerbic and razor sharp pieces on dizzyingly broad subjects from one of Britain's most highly rated commentators... Compulsively readable.'
Scotland on Sunday

£9.99
1 903809 42 8

Frontiers 01

Science and Technology 2001–02

Twenty-five original essays by leading science writers, including John Sulston and Martin Rees, covering all the major developments in science.

'In just 125 pages Frontiers 01 manages everything from cosmology to matriarchy'   *THES*

£10.99
1 903809 23 1

The Ultimate Book of Notes & Queries

The very best of the *Guardian*'s cult Notes & Queries column, offering informed and ingenious answers to brainteasers such as 'Has religion ever stopped a war?' or 'Has anyone ever died of boredom?'

£9.99
1 84354 008 8

Quick Crosswords
A Jumbo Selection

Includes 125 *Guardian* crosswords and 25 quiptics – the new puzzle that's halfway between the quick and the cryptic.

£5.99
1 84354 005 3

Monkey Puzzles
The Ultimate Cryptic Crossword Collection

The first ever collection of the *Guardian*'s best-loved cryptic crossword compiler – Araucaria – who has been delighting Guardian readers for over 40 years.

'How can anything so fiendish be so much fun?'
Simon Hoggart

£5.99
1 84354 004 5